DEEPENING DEMOCRACY IN GHANA
Politics of the 2000 Elections

Volume Two

CONSTITUENCY STUDIES

Edited by
JOSEPH R. A. AYEE

FREEDOM PUBLICATIONS
ACCRA
2001

Freedom Publications,
P. O. Box LG 313
University Post Office
Legon, Ghana

© Department of Political Science, University of Ghana, Legon 2001

ALL RIGHTS RESERVED

ISBN 9988-7716-4-9

First published in 2001

Overseas Distributor
African Books Collective Ltd
The Jam Factory
27 Park End Street
Oxford, OX1 1HU
England

PRODUCED IN GHANA

Printed by Livog Limited, Accra

Table of Contents

Preface   vii
Acronyms   xi
List of Contributors   xiii

1. Introduction (*Joseph R. A. Ayee*)   1

2. Institutions, Electoral Process, Value Preferences and Democratic Practice in Ghana (*Dan McKwartin*)   12

3. Survey of the 2000 General Elections and Presidential Run-off in Keta and Anlo Constituencies (*Joseph R. A. Ayee*)   34

4. Ayawaso West Wuogon and Kpone Katamanso Constituencies in the December 2000 Elections (*E. Gyimah-Boadi*)   67

5. Election 2000 in Ahanta West and Shama Constituencies and Democratic Consolidation in Ghana (*Kwesi Jonah*)   87

6. The 2000 Elections in Okaikoi North and South Constituencies (*F. K. Drah*)   108

7. Survey Patterns and Election Outcome in Mfantseman West and Cape Coast Constituencies (*Kwame Boafo-Arthur*)   146

8. Survey of the 2000 Elections in Berekum and Wenchi East Constituencies (*Kwasi Ansu-Kyeremeh*)   165

9. The 2000 Elections in Bawku Central and Nabdam Constituencies (*Daniel A. Smith*)   178

10. The 2000 Elections in Ellembelle and Jomoro Constituencies (*Beatrix Allah-Mensah*)   196

11. The 2000 Elections in Choggu-Tishigu, Tolon and Kumbungu Constituencies (*Dan McKwartin*) — 217

12. Determinants of Political Choice in Koforidua and New Juaben North Constituencies in the 2000 General Elections (*Gilbert K. Bluwey*) — 240

13. Election 2000 Politics in Komenda-Edina-Eguafo-Abirem and Agona West Constituencies (*A. Essuman-Johnson*) — 257

14. Explaining Voter Behaviour in Ho Central and Ho East Constituencies of the Volta Region in Ghana's 2000 Elections (*Stevens K. M. Ahiawordor*) — 273

15. Democratic Pluralism, Electoral Processes and Grassroot Participation in the Gukpegu/Sabongida and Savelugu Constituencies (*Togbiga Dzivenu*) — 293

16. The 2000 Elections and Politics in Manhyia and Obuasi Constituencies (*Kofi Baku*) — 311

17. Election 2000 and the Presidential Run-off in the Birim North and Yilo Krobo Constituencies (*Emmanuel Debrah*) — 325

18. Ghana's Election 2000: A Study of Political Behaviour in the Mampong and Effiduase-Asokore Constituencies (*Mike Oquaye*) — 338

19. A Comparative Analysis of Electoral Survey of Nkawkaw and Afram Plains South Constituencies in Ghana's Election 2000 (*A. Kaakyire Duku Frempong*) — 350

20. Ghana 2000 Elections: A Survey of Asunafo North and Tano North Constituencies (*Paul Agbedor*) — 378

21. A Survey of the 2000 Elections in the Asante Akim North and South Constituencies (*E. Ofori-Sarpong*) — 397

22. The 2000 Presidential and Parliamentary Elections in
    Ghana: Wa Central and Sissala Constituencies
    (*George Akanlig-Pare*)   417

23. The Future of Democratic Consolidation in Ghana
    (*Joseph R. A. Ayee*)   433

Appendix 1:   Pre-2000 Elections Survey Questionnaire   439

Appendix 2:   Post-2000 Elections Survey Questionnaire   456

Bibliography   471

Preface

Ghanaians went to the polls on 7 December 2000 to choose a president and Members of Parliament (MPs). A presidential run-off was held on 28 December 2000 because both of the two presidential candidates (John Kufuor of the New Patriotic Party and John Atta Mills of the National Democratic Congress) who scored the highest number of votes failed to get the 50 per cent of votes plus one required to win the presidential election. The December general elections and presidential run-off were arguably the most important since independence in 1957 because they marked not only the exit from Ghanaian politics of Flight Lieutenant Jerry Rawlings, who had served as the longest serving Head of State having been in power for over 19 years, but also the robustness of Ghana's nascent democracy by the smooth tranfer of the reins of government from a constitutionally elected government that served its two terms of office to another one, whose members belong to the largest opposition party, through the ballot box.

The importance of the 2000 elections to the democratic process in Ghana prompted the Department of Political Science, University of Ghana to write a proposal to the Royal Danish Embassy, Accra in 1999 to support a project on the 2000 elections. A similar venture with support from the Royal Danish Embassy had been conducted for the 1996 general elections.

Like the 1996 general elections project, the 2000 elections project has the following two components:

- Thematic studies written by lecturers from the Department of Political Science, University of Ghana, Legon that focus on selected problems and issues in Ghana's democratic politics such as factors that determined the outcome of the 2000 general elections and presidential run-off, the elections and democratic consolidation, indices of free and fair elections that were at play in the elections, gender, ethnicity, the role of local and international observers, post-Rawlings era politics and other related issues that promote or undermine democratic consolidation. These studies are contained in Volume One of this book;

- Constituency studies written by 20 lecturers from Departments of Political Science, Linguistics and History, School of Communication Studies and Legon Centre for International Affairs

(LECIA) that deal with surveys conducted in 40 of the 2000 constituencies. The aim of the surveys was to investigate citizens' voting behaviour at constituency level, the relationship between social groups and voting patterns and the factors (like key political and social issues at both national and local levels, ethnicity, symbolism, charisma, gender, chieftaincy) that influenced voter behaviour, perceptions and attitudes. The constituency studies form Volume Two of this book.

The surveys were conducted in two phases. Phase 1 (pre-2000 elections) was conducted 23 October–6 November 2000 while Phase 2 (post-elections) lasted 2 January–16 January 2001. The selection of the 40 constituencies was influenced by the following factors:

- equalization, that is, two constituencies were selected from each region as basic;
- remaining constituencies were selected on the basis of the number of constituencies in each region;
- urban-rural dichotomy;
- follow-up by some of the researchers in constituencies they had covered in the 1996 elections studies to identify the dynamics of electoral politics.

A rural-urban sampling was used to determine the electoral areas in the selected constituencies with a weighted balance of 35% urban and 65% rural electoral areas.

In all, 4000 respondents (who are all registered voters) were interviewed in the pre-elections survey while 3878 respondents (who are all registered voters) were interviewed during the post elections phase. A near fatal accident involving the research team in Wa Central constituency and the inability of the research team to conduct a survey in the Bawku Central constituency as a result of the post-general elections violence contributed to the shortfall in the number of persons interviewed for the post-election phase.

This book, which is in two volumes (One and Two), is the outcome of both thematic and constituency studies, which were presented by the researchers at a conference held on August 9–10, 2001 at the University of Ghana, Legon. It is the second by the Department on an election. The first publication was *The 1996 General Elections and Democratic Consolidation in Ghana*, published in 1998, which I understand became the "Bible" of most of the political parties in the run-up to the 2000 general elections. This book, *The 2000 General Elections and Presidential Run-off in Ghana* will further enhance the image of the Department of Political Science as one which has the competence to undertake election studies.

As earlier indicated, the 2000 elections project would not have been possible without support from the Royal Danish Embassy. Consequently, the Department wishes to express its deepest appreciation and gratitude to the Royal Danish Embassy for its continued support for the Department as a centre for elections studies. The Department is also grateful to Mr P. K. Mensah of MAP Consult and Mrs Florence Schmidt-Neilson of the Danish Embassy, who acted as consultants to the project, for their support and cooperation.

My sincerest thanks go to: Professor Ernest Dumor (Member, Electoral Commission), who gave the keynote address, and Professor Sam Woode, Professor Max Assimeng and Professor G. K. Nukunya for chairing the sessions and the inputs they made at the conference.

I am also grateful to the participants who attended the conference at which the papers were presented for their useful comments and interventions that made the papers richer. I must, however, be quick to add that any shortcomings or lapses in the book are the sole responsibility of the contributors and none of the people mentioned.

Finally, I wish to place on record the assistance and cooperation I had from the researchers, especially Professor K. Boafo-Arthur, Dr A. Essuman-Johnson and Dr Dan McKwartin as well as the administrative staff of the Department of Political Science, especially, Mr G. K. Mantey, Narku Noi and Redeemer Agbeti. I thank you all for making my work as project coordinator less frustrating and difficult in spite of my sometimes, irritating proddings for deadlines to be met.

In conclusion, I wish to say that the study of elections is a window of analysis, which enables the policy analyst to understand the workings of a democratic political system. It can be argued that the determination as to whether Ghana is democratic or not is ultimately, to a significant extent, settled by the country's electoral system. Put differently, the question depends on how and why those who govern are chosen by those whom they govern. The more democratic the electoral system, the more likely that those who govern will be sensitive to the wishes of the electorate in policy making in the spirit of the aphorism that "citizens have a right to be heard and officials have a duty to listen". This is the message that this book is sending to politicians and public officials.

JOSEPH R. A. AYEE
Editor

Acronyms

ACDRs	Association of the Committees for the Defence of the Revolution
AGE	Advocates for Age Equity
AN	Asunafo North
AWWC	Ayawaso West Wuogon Constituency
CCG	Christian Council of Ghana
CDD	Centre for Democratic Development
CI	Constitutional Instrument
CODEO	Coalition of Domestic Election Observers
COG	Commonwealth Observer Group
CPP	Convention People's Party
CSOs	Civil Society Organizations
DA	District Assembly
DACF	District Assembly Common Fund
DANIDA	Danish International Development Agency
DCE	District Chief Executive
DPP	Democratic People's Party
DWG	Donors Working Group
DWM	December Women's Movement
EC	Electoral Commission
EDGs	Election Day Guards
EGLE	Every Ghanaian Living Everywhere
ESTF	Election Security Task Force
EU	European Union
FES	Friedrich Ebert Stiftung
FM	Frequency Modulation
FIDA	Federation of International Women Lawyers
FORB	Forum of Religious Bodies
GA	Great Alliance
GBC	Ghana Broadcasting Corporation
GCPP	Great Consolidated Popular Party
GJA	Ghana Journalist Association
GLLRF	Ghana Legal Literacy and Resource Foundation
GPRTU	Ghana Private Road Transport Union
GTV	Ghana Television
HIPC	Highly Indebted Poor Countries
ID	Identity Card

IPAC	Inter-Party Advisory Committee
IPU	Inter-Parliamentary Union
JSS	Junior Secondary School
KEEA	Komenda-Edina-Eguafo-Abirem
KKC	Kpone Katamanso Constituency
KVIP	Kumasi Ventilated Improved Pit-latrine
MFJ	Movement for Freedom and Justice
MP	Member of Parliament
NAL	National Alliance of Liberals
NCCE	National Commission on Civic Education
NCWD	National Council on Women and Development
NCS	National Catholic Secretariat
NEDEO	Network of Domestic Election Observers
NDC	National Democratic Congress
NDI	National Democratic Institute
NLM	National Liberation Movement
NMC	National Media Commission
NRP	National Reform Party
NPP	New Patriotic Party
NPP	Northern People's Party
PA	Progressive Alliance
PNC	People's National Convention
PNDC	Provisional National Defence Council
PNDCL	Provisional National Defence Council Law
PP	Progress Party
SAP	Structural Adjustment Programme
SSS	Senior Secondary School
TEIN	Tertiary and Educational Institutions Network
TESCON	Tertiary Education Students Confederacy
TN	Tano North
UGM	United Ghana Movement
UNDP	United Nations Development Programme
UP	United Party
VR	Voters' Register

List of Contributors

Agbedor, Paul: Lecturer, Department of Linguistics, University of Ghana, Legon.

Ahiawordor, Stevens K. M.: Lecturer, Department of Political Science, University of Ghana, Legon and Barrister-at-Law.

Akanlig-Pare, George: Lecturer, Department of Linguistics, University of Ghana, Legon.

Allah-Mensah, Beatrix: Lecturer, Department of Political Science, University of Ghana, Legon.

Ansu-Kyeremeh, Kwasi: Associate Professor and Director, School of Communication Studies, University of Ghana, Legon.

Ayee, Joseph R. A.: Professor, Department of Political Science, University of Ghana, Legon and 2001 UNESCO/United Nations University Leadership Academy (UNULA) Chair in Leadership Studies.

Baku, Kofi: Lecturer, Department of History, University of Ghana, Legon and Barrister-at-Law.

Bluwey, Gilbert K.: Associate Professor, Legon Centre for International Affairs (LECIA) and immediate past Director of the Centre.

Boafo-Arthur, Kwame: Associate Professor, Department of Political Science, University of Ghana, Legon and Barrister-at-Law.

Debrah, Emmanuel: Lecturer, Department of Political Science, University of Ghana, Legon.

Drah, Francis K.:	Senior Lecturer, Department of Political Science, University of Ghana, Legon.
Dzivenu, Togbiga:	Lecturer, University of Development Studies, Tamale and Doctoral Candidate, Department of Political Science, University of Ghana, Legon.
Essuman-Johnson, Abeeku:	Senior Lecturer, Department of Political Science, University of Ghana, Legon.
Frempong, A. Kaakyire D.:	Lecturer, Department of Political Science, University of Ghana, Legon.
Gyimah-Boadi, Emmanuel:	Associate Professor, Department of Political Science, University of Ghana and Executive Director, Centre for Democratic Development (CDD).
Jonah, Kwesi:	Senior Lecturer, Department of Political Science, University of Ghana, Legon and Master, Legon Hall, University of Ghana.
McKwartin, Dan:	Lecturer, Department of Political Science, University of Ghana, Legon. Before joining the Department in 1999, he was Associate Professor of Political Science at Chicago State University, Chicago, U.S.A.
Ofori-Sarpong, Edward:	Professor, Department of Geography and Dean, Faculty of Social Studies, University of Ghana, Legon.
Oquaye, Mike:	Associate Professor and Head, Department of Political Science, University of Ghana, Legon; Ambassador Designate.
Smith, Daniel A.:	2000 Senior Fulbright Fellow, Department of Political Science, University of Ghana, Legon.

CHAPTER 1

Introduction

JOSEPH R. A. AYEE

This volume contains 23 chapters. It is devoted to the analyses of surveys of 40 constituencies out of the 200 constituencies during the pre-2000 and post-2000 elections periods (see Table 1.1 for list of constituencies). The chapters examine citizens' voting behaviour at constituency level, the relationship between social groups and voting patterns and factors (like key political and social issues at both national and local levels, ethnicity, symbolism, charisma, gender, chieftaincy) that have influenced voter behaviour, perceptions and attitudes, all of which in one way or the other had a bearing on the outcome of the elections. Specifically, they examine the major developments within the campaign, including the government's record in office, party fortunes in the run-up to the elections, the impact of specific events, the popularity of candidates, strategies and tactics, media coverage, election issues and profile of constituencies.

The chapters have mainly been structured in the following format:

- Profile of the constituencies;
- Demographic data of respondents;
- Political participation;
- Voter perception of, and involvement with, political parties;
- Voter perception of the economy;
- Evaluation of the democratic process;
- Evaluation of the electoral process;
- Evaluation of the party system;
- Election issues — national and constituency issues;
- Evaluation of running mates;
- The media;
- Identities and social capital; and
- Presidential run-off

The volume has interesting findings from the fieldwork conducted in the 40 constituencies. In Chapter 2, "Institutions, Electoral Process,

Table 1.1: List of 20 Researchers and 40 Constituencies Covered in the 2000 Elections Survey

Researcher	A	B
	Ashanti	
Prof. A. M. Oquaye	Mampong	Effiduasi-Asokore
Prof. E. Ofori Sarpong	Asante Akim North	Asante Akim South
Dr Kofi Baku	Manhyia	Obuasi
	Eastern	
Mr E. Debrah	Birim North	Yilo Krobo
Mr A. K. D. Frempong	Nkwakaw	Afram Plains South
Prof. Gilbert K. Bluwey	New Juaben North	Koforidua
	Central	
Dr Kwame Boafo-Arthur	Mfantseman West	Cape Coast
Dr A. Essuman-Johnson	Agona West	Komenda-Edina-Eguafo-Abirem (KEEA)
	Western	
Ms Beatrix Allah-Mensah	Ellembele	Jomoro
Mr Kwesi Jonah	Ahanta West	Shama
	Northern	
Mr Togbiga Dzivenu	Gukpegu/Sabongida	Savelugu
Dr Dan McKwartin	Choggo Tishigu	Tolon, Kumbungu
	Volta	
Prof. Joseph R. A. Ayee	Keta	Anlo
Mr Stevens K. M. Ahiawordor	Ho East	Ho Central
	Greater Accra	
Prof. E. Gyimah-Boadi	Kpone Kantamanso	Ayawaso West Wuogon
Mr F. K. Drah	Okaikoi South	Okaikoi North
	Brong Ahafo	
Prof. Kwasi Ansu-Kyeremeh	Berekum	Wenchi East
Dr P. K. Agbedor	Asunafo North	Tano North
	Upper East	
Dr Daniel A. Smith	Bawku Central	Nabdam
	Upper West	
Mr. G. Akanlig-Pare	Wa Central	Sissala

Value Preferences and Democratic Practice in Ghana" McKwartin, using an analysis of the national survey data, focuses on the extent to which liberal democracy is being consolidated in Ghana through the institutionalization of voting. He discusses the nexus between institutions, issues and social forces as determinants of voting. Based on the data, he assertes that political parties, media, the electoral process and personal values in Ghana reveal that the act of voting as a condition of consolidating democracy is multi-dimensional. In addition, the ability to provide or distribute political benefits does not necessarily maximize the chances of the re-election of the incumbent candidate or government. Furthermore, a clear articulation of the issues by candidates and voters' identification with these issues enhances voter participation.

In Chapter 3, "Survey of the 2000 General Elections and Presidential Run-off in the Keta and Anlo Constituencies" Ayee aims to measure public opinion in the two constituencies on key political and economic issues such as voter attitude and perceptions of key national and constituency level political and economic developments, evaluation of the democratic process, participation in the election process and also identities and social capital. From indicators of participation such as financial contribution to party activities, attendance at party campaign rallies and congress and interest in leadership positions, the degree of political participation of voters in the activities of political parties in the two constituencies is not only discouraging but also limited. There was a disparity of voters' perception of political parties in the two constituencies. This may be due to the scepticism the people of Keta hold about politicians who, in spite of the numerous promises, were unable to complete a sea defence wall for the town. The majority of respondents questioned the lack of internal democracy within the parties, especially the NDC. Indeed, the majority of respondents did not even know how candidates were selected to contest parliamentary seats. Respondents' perception of the state of the economy, unlike that in 1996 which was positive, was negative this time round. The majority of respondents indicated that the economy was very bad while the household standard of living since the 1996 election was much worse. Unemployment constituted the greatest economic problem followed by inflation. The responses on the economy reinforce the view that Ghanaians generally adopt an instrumentalist approach to politics. Governments are held responsible for the provision of practically everything and it was the inability to adequately fulfil this that caused the downfall of the NDC government.

Responses showed a general satisfaction with democracy and the political system, which is good for democratic consolidation. In addition, the majority of respondents thought the 1996 and 2000 elections had been generally free and fair. However, they were unaware of the activities of the EC and therefore were unable to comment on the question of its independence.

Even though the majority of respondents acknowledged that political parties lack the resources to pursue their goals and programmes, they nevertheless were not in favour of the idea of state funding of political parties because according to them such funds could be used to develop the rural areas for the benefit of all rather than being given to political parties to pursue parochial interests.

On social identities and social capital, the majority of respondents valued their religious and ethnic backgrounds more than their affinity to region or membership of CSOs which is not surprising given the rural background of the two constituencies.

Ayee identifies two types of claim: claims for personal help and claims for more political (albeit local) action. Under claims for personal help, the three important means of help are family members, neighbours and trade unions while recourse to government institutions for assistance was negligible. On claims for more political (albeit local) action, respondents indicated that even though they had problems concerning issues like water, KVIP, electricity and water, they did not contact the District Assemblies (DAs) because they thought that the DAs were not in a position to solve their problems either because of their shoestring budgets or their ineffectiveness. This confirms earlier studies of the irrelevance of DAs in the development of the rural areas.

Ayee found that irrespective of prevailing political, social and economic condition, some voters would cast their ballots not on issues but on traditional lines. Even though respondents in the two constituencies were not happy with the economy they still voted for the NDC.

Chapter 4, "Ayawaso West Wuogon and Kpone Katamanso Constituencies in the December 2000 Elections" by Gyimah-Boadi has some useful findings. The elections in the two constituencies not only reflected national trends and patterns but also were a race between the NDC and NPP. He found that even though ethnicity may be a muted factor in the elections, the emphasis on "nativism" and the type of music selected to advertise the presence of the candidates in the various electoral areas of the two constituencies showed the saliency of ethnic undertones. In addition, Gyimah-Boadi found that respondents had mixed perceptions of party politics and mixed evaluations of the electoral process. This discrepancy is due to the differences between the socio-economic profiles of the two constituencies. Kpone Katamanso is a generally rural and poor constituency while Ayawaso Wuogon is rated as a "super first class constituency . . . inhabited by some of the most affluent Ghanaians". There is, however, unanimity in responses from the two constituencies concerning negative voter perception of the economy, general positive evaluation of the electoral process and low political participation in registration. Another finding is that the elections in the constituencies confirm the progress made in the democratic process and confidence in the electoral system.

In Chapter 5, "Election 2000 in Ahanta West and Shama Constituencies" Jonah asserts that Ghana's democratic experiment is gradually being consolidated for a number of reasons. They include the generally peaceful atmosphere within which the elections were conducted in the two constituencies, the increasing rationality of the voter, the very high and growing "challenger quality" progressive growth and development of a democratic political culture, which enhances the capacity of citizens to evaluate the institutions of the political system and economy. Jonah, like Ayee, also found that even though respondents eagerly registered and voted, their participation in activities such as contributing to party financing or seeking office in political parties or aspiring to become MPs was low. This notwithstanding, he commends the high evaluative orientation of respondents with regards to the rating of democracy. However, respondents' rating of the state of the economy was very bad. There was also dissatisfaction with the quality of representation they received from MPs. Evaluation of political parties by respondents was mixed. Although majority were happy with the way parties elect candidates to contest elections, the parties were perceived as financially weak and tending to project personalities rather than policies.

Chapter 6, "The 2000 Elections in the Okaikoi North and South Constituencies" by Drah has some equally interesting findings. Even though all respondents were registered voters who voted in the 2000 elections, the turnout in the two constituencies was low. This, Drah, attributed to either a bloated voters' register or voters who refused to vote. His chapter confirms the point made by the two earlier ones that most of the respondents were not registered members of political parties, and thus political participation is low. It is also heartwarming to learn that party politics was accepted as a necessary element of democratic governance, in spite of the cynical views of a few respondents.

Drah found that even though respondents were aware that political parties lack adequate funding and logistics and ruling parties have an undue advantage they rejected state funding of political parties, ostensibly because they thought that the economy was not strong enough to support such a programme, especially when most of them lamented the poor state of the economy and their dwindling standard of living since the elections of 1996.

Another important finding is that the media were heavily relied on for political information while the majority of respondents considered private radio as the most trustworthy media source for telling the truth. This is understandable because of the numerous private FM stations operating within the city of Accra.

The link between the economy and voting behaviour pattern is reinforced in Boafo-Arthur's, "Survey Patterns and Outcomes in Mfantseman West and Cape Coast Constituencies" in Chapter 7. To him, the responses on the state of the economy in the pre-election survey showed that the NDC would lose the elections. Consequently, a government which aims to retain power must tackle nagging economic problems. As usual respondents listed unemployment, high inflation and the rapid depreciation of the Cedi as the three most important problems facing the country. At local level, the key development issue was unemployment.

On the evaluation of democratic institutions, Boafo-Arthur found that there is continued mistrust of the EC because of the perception or suspicion of it not being independent of the ruling government. Respondents also saw improvement in democratic practice since the last elections and appreciated the role of political parties in democracy. They also supported the idea of state funding of political parties because of the inadequate financial resources and logistics of political parties.

Chapter 8, "Survey of the 2000 Elections in the Berekum and Wenchi East Constituencies" by Ansu-Kyeremeh extends the arguments of the earlier chapters regarding the low political participation of respondents, the bad state of the economy, the unemployment problem, the positive perception of Ghana's democracy, the lack of independence of the EC and the little progress made in improvement in standard of living of the respondents since the 1996 elections. Apart from this, Ansu-Kyeremeh gives us insights into local politics. He notes the extent of violence in Berekum before the elections that led to the closure of a local FM station, CHRIS FM, on which voters depended for information about the elections. To him, respondents believed that the NPP candidates better articulated the most important national issues and local development needs of the constituencies. This resulted in more votes for the NPP flag bearer.

As a continuation of Ansu-Kyeremeh's insights into local politics, Chapter 9, "The Politics of Bawku Central and Nabdam Constituencies and the 2000 Ghanaian Elections" by Smith sheds light on the political complexities in the two constituencies within the context of the 2000 elections. Smith notes the ethnically homogenous nature of Nabdam as compared to the ethnically heterogenous state of Bawku Central Constituency (it has 14 mother tongue languages such as Kusaal, Bisa, Hausa, Mampruli and Mosi) and opines that that difference largely explains the rather peaceful post-election atmosphere that prevailed in Nabdam as against the eruption of ethnic violence in Bawku Central that led to the deaths of 50 people. In this connection, the main cause of the violence in Bawku Central was ethnic misunderstanding attributable to the political machinations of partisan elites rather than "innate hatred among the ethnic groups". He contends that the NDC played an ethnic card which engendered fear among the Kusasi that an NPP government would revert control of the Bawku skin back to the Mamprusi. He however concedes that even though the violence had a tangible ethnic dimension, it was far "too simplistic to view it as just a chieftaincy turf battle between the Kusasi and Mamprusi". Consequently, he asserts that the ethnic landscape has been shaped by what he referred to as the "contours of national politic, chronic poverty and a pervasive feeling of exclusion and marginalization."

Allah-Mensah in Chapter 10, "Political Decision-making in Ghana's Election 2000 in the Ellembelle and Jomoro Constituencies" emphasizes that the need for a change of government to ensure "positive change" not only in governance for its own sake but as a means to achieving social and economic development which would improve the quality of living was the main determining factor that influenced political decision making in the two constituencies. Consequently, as the previous studies have shown, the main election issue was the economy. However in Ellembelle, KVIP was the main development issue while for Jomoro it was unemployment. The majority of respondents deplored the bad state of the economy which led to a drop in the standard of living of respondents and their families.

Respondents indicated that high inflation aggravated the unemployment problem in the two constituencies. Consequently, most respondents adopted "survival strategies" to enable them to live.

In spite of the poor state of the economy, most respondents thought that democracy had taken root. There was the perception that political parties had tended to project personalities more than policies. A slight majority of respondents recommended state funding of political parties.

To address gender imbalance in the two constituencies, Allah-Mensah recommended that "gender fashionable" should give way to "gender functional".

In Chapter 11, "Constituency-National Linkages: Explaining the Outcome of Ghana's 2000 Elections in the Choggu-Tishigu, Tolon and Kumbungu Constituencies" McKwartin explains the influence, if any, between responses in the three constituencies and national ones with the aim of building linkages between constituency electorate decisions and national electorate ones. This is done using the impact of the campaign theme, the advantages and disadvantages of incumbency, saliency of election issues, candidates' image and relevance of partisanship. To him, political expressions in the three constituencies are a microcosm rather than an aberration of macro-political dynamics in Ghana.

Bluwey's Chapter 12, "Determinants of Political Choice in Koforidua and New Juaben North Constituencies in the 2000 General Elections" is an attempt to explain electoral success from a local politics perspective. He postulates that voter choice in the two constituencies was based on rational decisions rather than on "habit" or "bandwagon voting". A number of factors were identified as those which have contributed to the defeat of the NDC candidates, who were ministers, in the two constituencies. They were the strong anti-NDC feelings in the two constituencies occasioned by the neglect of Koforidua in terms of development infrastructure, the personal standing of the NPP candidates who, even though did not belong to the incumbent government, provided amenities out of the MPs' Common Fund, the bad state of the economy and the cash-and-carry system of health care delivery. For once, respondents rated cheap and accessible health care as a top priority, followed by water and good roads.

In Chapter 13, "Election Politics in Komenda-Edina-Eguafo-Abirem and Agona West Constituencies" Essuman-Johnson uses voter choice, voter turnout and political participation to explain electoral politics in the two constituencies. As in the previous chapters, he notes that the general economic situation in the two constituencies prior to the elections was very poor with unemployment being the single major important problem. The two key development issues were education and unemployment. Respondents thought that democracy had improved in the county while the majority replied that Ghana could be described as a democracy. There was the perception that the electoral process had been free and fair, in spite of a few scattered incidents of intimidation. Respondents however, were opposed to state funding of political parties.

On identities and social capital issues, the majority of respondents indicated that they did not approach the District Assemblies about issues of development in their area. On the other hand, most respondents were strongly attached to their families while household incomes were inadequate and the standard of living was much worse.

Ahiawordor's Chapter 14, "Explaining Voter Behaviour in the Ho Central and Ho East Constituencies", apart from focusing on what previous chapters have said relating to voter perception of the economy and democratic institutions, emphasizes the general extent of illiteracy in both constituencies that affected respondents' understanding of the democratic process. As a result of the extent of illiteracy, some respondents were unaware of the existence of other political parties apart from the NDC. Consequently, the gullibility of the voters is not in question. For instance, some voters were told not to vote for the NPP because in the event of the NPP winning, they would be expelled to Togo. He asserts that ethnicity in voting patterns cannot be ignored. There was evidence of aliens (in this case Togolese) voting because of the closeness of the borders and the long tradition of friendship. The strength of the NDC in the two constituencies is not in doubt.

In Chapter 15, "Democratic Pluralism, Electoral Process and Grassroots Participation in the Gukpegu/Sabongida and Savelugu Constituencies" Dzivenu examines the role of grassroots institutions in enhancing political participation and free and fair elections as well as their influence on voter behaviour. He points out that the principal limitations of grassroots institutions such as the district office of the EC and National Commission for Civic Education (NCCE) are inadequate staffing and poor allocation of resources and logistics.

Most respondents did not register with political parties for fear of political victimization, ignorance of membership registration procedures and apathy.

The success of the elections was the outcome of facilitative roles played by CSOs such as the Ghana Private Road Transport Union (GPRTU), which, for instance, supplied and distributed logistics to the various polling stations.

In Chapter 16, "The 2000 Elections and Politics in Manhyia and Obuasi Constituencies" Baku bases his paper on five questions: who are the competitors?; what are the issues?; how are the elections conducted?; who won and who did not win?; and what is the effect of the election on the general direction of politics at the time? As in previous chapters, he notes that the foremost issue that agitated respondents was the national economy. Most respondents indicated that "life was difficult" and blamed the NDC government for their plight. In addition, respondents exhibited a high degree of awareness, in spite of their mistrust of the electoral process. The anti-NDC feelings in the constituencies influenced the respondents to point to the longevity of the then NDC incumbent government and the need for it to give way to another party because of its failure to improve living standards.

Debrah's Chapter 17, "Election 2000 and the Presidential Run-off in the Birim North and Yilo Krobo Constituencies" shows that most respondents had knowledge about the candidates and election issues. Party campaigns were rigorous and intensive while they were free from violence and intimidation. Campaign messages focused on policy issues such as a strong economy, job creation, domestic tranquility, quality education and wealth creation. To Debrah, the NPP won the elections in Birim North because it articulated local issues while the NDC won in Yilo Krobo because of the people's "love" for Jerry Rawlings.

He also identifies new strategies for mobilizing voters in the two constituencies such as a brass band procession, keep fit and *jama*, which involves the singing and chanting of war songs in a route march.

Like the previous chapters, Oquaye's Chapter 18, "Ghana's Election 2000: Study of Political Behaviour in the Mampong and Effiduase-Asokore Constituencies" reinforces respondents' views on key political and economic issues. The majority of respondents did not support state funding of political parties. They were, however, satisfied with the progress of democracy. The economy was the biggest issue that influenced the voting pattern in the two constituencies, which are traditionally NPP strongholds. Most respondents felt the economy was very bad while their standard of living had become worse since the 1996 elections.

In Chapter 19, "A Comparative Analysis of Electoral Survey of

Nkawkaw and Afram Plains South Constituencies in Ghana's Election 2000" Frempong points to the generally free and fair elections in the two constituencies. The selection of candidates by the political parties was not transparent enough for the majority of respondents. A number of local issues influenced the outcome of the elections. For instance, in Afram Plains South, the fear of settler chiefs losing the land they occupied should the NPP win the elections influenced the electorate to vote for the NDC.

Chapter 20, "The 2000 Elections in the Asunafo North and Tano North Constituencies" by Agbedor rated as high the political awareness among respondents while their participation in the affairs of the political parties was low. To him, the high awareness may have been the result of improvements in the dissemination of information through the proliferation of the private media. Most respondents were not happy with the poor state of the economy, which had deepened their poverty. As usual, in spite of a few hiccups, democratic institutions such as political parties and the EC were highly rated by respondents for doing a good job.

Ofori-Sarpong's Chapter 21, "A Survey of the 2000 Elections in the Asante Akim North and South Constituencies", catalogues a number of cases of political violence and intimidation in the two constituencies, notwithstanding the views by the majority of respondents that the elections were free and fair. The chapter stresses that Ghanaians are more politically awake than before because the electorate are prepared to change a government, which failed to deliver goods as far as parties' manifestos and campaign promises were concerned. It recommends that electoral violence could be minimized if political parties and other stakeholders intensified education on the need for tolerance of each other's views.

In a similar vein, Chapter 22, "A Survey of the 2000 Presidential and Parliamentary Elections in the Wa Central and Sissala Constituencies" by Akanlig-Pare dilated on similar themes earlier on covered. The incumbent government was voted out of power because of its failure to effectively manage the economy. Reactions of most respondents also show that democratic institutions and security services played a crucial role in ensuring democracy. The progressive sophistication of the Ghanaian voter in terms of his ability to make choices based on issues is underscored.

In Chapter 23, "Conclusions: The Future of Democratic Consolidation in Ghana" Ayee summarizes the main findings from the chapters and their implications for democratic consolidation. He also offers some useful lessons that should engage the attention of the incumbent government, political parties, EC and the general public.

CHAPTER 2

Institutions, Electoral Process, Value Preferences and Democratic Practice in Ghana

DAN MCKWARTIN

Introduction

The most heralded elections in Ghana's political history took place on 7 and 28 December 2000. These elections were highly heralded because they served as a litmus test of Ghana's experimentation with liberal democracy. The extent of sustainability and resilience of the country's infant liberal philosophy occupied the centre stage in the election exercises.

The 2000 elections were the third time since 1992 that Ghanaians freely chose their president and parliamentary representatives under the Fourth Republican Constitution. The previous 1992 and 1996 elections may be viewed as institutional attempts to move Ghana from authoritarianism to popular participation and public contestation spurred in part by the world-wide democratic revolution which Samuel Huntington (1991) has described as "third wave of democratization". Huntington explains:

> A wave of democratization is a group of transitions from non-democratic to democratic regimes that occur within a specified period of time and that significantly outnumber transitions in the opposite direction during that period of time. A wave usually involves liberalization in political systems that do not become fully democratic. Three waves (first wave, second wave, and now third wave) of democratization have occurred in the modern world (Huntington, 1991: 15).

Ghana which embarked on the democratic path (second wave) in 1957, became an effective authoritarian state in the 1980s. Authoritarianism which characterized Ghanaian politics in the 1980s encountered the Huntingtonian democratic wave when the Fourth Republican Constitution was adopted in 1992 and popular elections were conducted in the same year.

It is assumed in this chapter that Ghana has made a successful transition from authoritarianism to liberal democracy, that is, popular participation, competitive free and fair elections, and free flow of information, after going through two peaceful elections in 1992 and 1996 (Sandbrook & Oelbaum, 1999; Anebo, 1998; Ayee, 1998; Linz & Stepan, 1987). The focus will rather be on the extent to which liberal democracy has been or is being consolidated in Ghana through the institutionalization of voting. The nexus between institutions, issues, and social factors as determinants of voting decisions will be discussed.

Some General Theories of Voting

The right to choose freely the representatives of the people through voting is the most fundamental right endowed to the people or citizens in a liberal democratic state. William Riker (1988) writes: "Democrats of all persuasions would probably agree that participation built on the act of voting is the focus of democracy" (p.8). In his summary of James Madison, a major proponent and paragon of liberalism, Riker further writes:

> In the liberal view, the function of voting is to control officials, *and no more*. Madison, who is the original American spokesman for liberal democracy (or republicanism, as he called it) defined a republic as 'a government that derives all its powers directly or indirectly from the great body of the people, and is administered by people holding their offices during pleasure, for a limited period, as during good behaviour.' The first [requirement of liberal democracy is] popularness; the second [is]election and limited tenure.... Popularness... ensures participation and equality.... [E]lection and limited tenure... ensure liberty... [T]he liberal remedy [against tyrannical officials] is the next elections... [T]he defense of liberty lies in the discipline of elections (1988: 9).

These two conditional requirements of liberalism are aggressively being pursued in Ghana. For example, Article 42 of the Constitution of the Fourth Republic of Ghana, 1992 states:

> Every citizen of Ghana of eighteen years of age or above and of sound mind has the right to vote and is entitled to be registered as voter for the purposes of public elections and referenda.

How do the people or citizens decide whom to vote for in a liberal democracy? What actors shape their calculus of voting decisions?

The literature on voting/electorate behavior is very extensive. However, three popular themes — party identification, issues, and social factors —

pervade most of the studies on voting behavior. For example, Angus Campbell *et al.* (1960) argue that voters vote for the candidate of their political party and that opinions and perceptions about issues are not good indicators of electoral outcome. Others privilege social factors. According to Donald Stokes (1966), it is the candidate's image rather than issues that affect electoral outcome in the short term. On the other hand, V. O. Key (1966) points out that it is the issues of the period that decide voters' choice of party and candidate. Gerald Kramer (1971) concludes that voters punish incumbent candidates when the economy is bad. The relationship between saliency of issues and voting choices has been demonstrated by David RePass (1971).

These conclusions about the efficacy of party identification, issues and social factors in voting were obtained from empirical studies of developed countries, particularly the United States of America, with a strong civic culture. The applicability of the findings of these studies to developing countries is subject to empirical verification. For example, Lewis-Beck and Rice (1992) have provided us with a simple but robust model for forecasting elections in the United States of America. The extent to which their model is applicable to a developing and emerging democracy such as Ghana is not fully known at the moment.

The literature on elections in Africa in general and Ghana in particular is also growing (Apter, 1963; Austin, 1964; Austin & Luckham, 1975; Dunn & Robertson, 1973; Chazan & Le Vine, 1979; Jeffries, 1980; Cohen, 1983; Chazan, 1983; Chazan, 1987; Hayward, 1987; Jeffries & Clare, 1993; Ninsin & Drah, 1993; Herbst,1993; Oquaye, 1995; Nugent, 1995; Badu & Larvie, 1996; Badu & Lavie, 1997; Lyons, 1997; Gyimah-Boadi, 1997; Sandbrook & Oelbaum, 1997; Ayee, 1997a, 1997b; McCarty, 1997). As much as these studies have added to the scholarship of African and Ghanaian elections, one observer asserts that "(a)ll . . . [these] useful studies leave unanswered several questions about the social, institutional and normative basis of Ghanaian politics and how these could shape democratic practice as well as stabilize institutions" (Ayee, 1998: 3). The scope of these earlier studies has been limited in terms of coverage of the multi-dimensionality of the democratic process, that is the entire electoral politics, institutions and processes.

What has happened in Ghana during the last eight years of democratic rule from 1992 to 2000? How do our observations of certain events and processes help us to explain and perhaps predict the outcome of elections in particular and electorate behavior in general in Ghana?

In answering these questions, we look at how institutions/structures, electoral processes, and normative considerations influence individual voting choices. Our analytical model may be functionally represented as follows:

> Voting decision — politico-social institutions, electoral rules and procedures, individual preferences]

According to Samuel Huntington (1968), for orderly political participation to take place, there must be requisite institutions or structures – organizations and procedures — installed to effect the participation. This study is also informed by the democratic theory that electoral success is a function of satisfaction of electorate demands or their expected utility (Mueller, 1979). Without doubt, state-society relations have been redefined and reordered in Ghana since the adoption of the 1992 Constitution, and a new political culture with its corresponding values and norms is emerging in the country. Hence, we are proposing a nexus between these social and institutional reconstructions and democratic practice.

The propositions made in this chapter are derived from pre-election and post-election national surveys of 8,000 randomly selected registered Ghanaian voters — 4,000 in each survey —, conducted by the Department of Political Science of the University of Ghana in December 2000 and January 2001.

Institutions/structure and Voters' Choice

In our examination of the institutional or structural antecedents of voting decisions, we specifically look at three institutions — political parties, mass media, legislative (parliamentary) representation — and how they interact with the institution of voting.

In his comparative study of Ghana's 1992 and 1996 elections, Kwesi Jonah (1998) noted:

> ... that structural variables constitute the most basic reference points deeply embedded in the consciousness of the voter on the basis of which other considerations are weighed. Structures set the ultimate parameters within which voters exercise their free choice. One cannot therefore analyse voters' (sic) choices and the reasons behind those choices without careful reference to their structural parameters. One cannot be divorced from the other (p.234).

In short, the voter is a free agent who decides whether to vote for Candidate A or Candidate B subject to the constraints imposed or the inducements created by the institution or structure in which he/she finds himself/herself. Again, Jonah (1998) remarks:

> The Ghanaian voter does not only participate in politics and exercise his vote; he believes his or her vote counts, it has political weight and can make a great difference in his or her life. He or she is in addition quite capable of evaluating his or her political institutions, political leaders and his or her own political efficacy. Indeed, the Ghanaian voter has a firm faith in his or her own political efficacy (pp. 251–252).

Operationalizing structure by region/ethnicity, industrial, and urban-rural setting of the voter, Jonah (1998) concluded that "[t]he overall influence of ethnicity, industrial, rural and urban structure of Ghana on the 1996 elections could . . . be expressed in the way individual voters exercised their voting power and the reasons for voting the way they did" (p.255). Structure thus both constrains and enables agents (voters) to make certain choices.

This study tests the institution/structure-voting hypothesis by examining the dynamics of the party system, political representation, and the mass media.

Political Party and Voting Outcome

Article 55, Section 3 of the Constitution of Ghana, 1992 states:

> Subject to the provisions of this article, a political party is free to participate in shaping the political will of the people, to disseminate information on political ideas, social and economic programmes of a national character, and sponsor candidates for elections to any public office other than to District Assemblies or lower local government units.

It is assumed that political parties and voters behave in response to one another based on rational theories of political behaviour (Downs, 1957). Since it is the goal of every political party to win elections and control the government, we hypothesize that:

> *Hypothesis 1:* Voters vote for candidates who belong to the same political party as the voters or the political party whose platform is close to the preferences of the voters.

Were the political parties in Ghana able to shape the political will of the people by inducing the people to vote for their party's candidate? We answer this question and test the party-voter hypothesis by evaluating the electoral gains (votes obtained and seats won) of the seven political parties — National Patriotic Party (NPP), National Democratic Congress (NDC), Peoples National Convention (PNC), Convention Peoples Party (CPP), National Reform Party (NRP), United Ghana Movement (UGM), Great Consolidated Popular Party (GCPP) — in the 7 December 2000 Parliamentary and Presidential elections.

In the 1997 Parliament, the incumbent NDC controlled 133 (67%) out of the 200 seats; The NPP had 61 (31%) of the seats; People's Convention Party (PCP) had 5 (1.5%) seats; and the PNC had 1 seat (0.5%). Thus, the NDC had complete numerical/majority control of Parliament: almost two-thirds of the total seats (See Table 2.1).

Table 2.1: Composition of Parliament by Political Party, 1997 and 2000

Political Party	1997 Number of seats	2000 Number of seats
NDC	133 (67%)	92 (46%)
NPP	61 (31%)	100 (50%)
PNC	1 (0.5%)	3 (1.5%)
PCP*	5 (1.5%)	–
CPP	–	1 (0.5%)
UGM**	–	0
NRP**	–	0
GCPP**	–	0
Independent	–	4 (2%)
TOTAL	200 (100%)	200 (100%)

*Did not run in 2000   **Did not run in 1996
Source: Electoral Commission of Ghana

The 2000 elections resulted in dramatic changes in the political party composition of Parliament in favour of the opposition parties especially the NPP. The NDC won 92 seats compared with 133 seats that it won in 1996, constituting a net loss of 41 seats. On the other hand, the NPP, which won only 61 seats in 1996, grabbed 100 seats in 2000, constituting a net gain of 39 seats. The PNC increased its seat of 1 in 1996 to 3 in 2000, and the CPP won 1 seat.

In the 2001 national legislature, the NDC fully controls four regions (all the 7 seats in Upper West; 8 of the 12 seats in Upper East; 18 of the 23 seats in Northern; all the 19 seats —17 plus 2 independents who support NDC — in Volta) and has a marginal control of two regions (10 of the 19 seats in Western; 9 of the 17 seats in Central).

On the other hand, the NPP now fully controls four regions (16 of the 22 seats in Greater Accra; 31 of the 33 seats in Ashanti; 14 of the 21 seats in Brong Ahafo; 18 of the 26 seats in Eastern) and has a weak presence in Northern (3 of the 23 seats) and Upper East (2 of the 12 seats).

The CPP managed to win 1 seat in Western whereas the PNC won 1 seat each in Northern, Upper East, and Upper West (see Table 2.2).

Asked which of the parties they voted for in the 2000 Parliamentary elections, 55% of respondents (4,000) nation-wide voted for NPP candidates; 27% voted for NDC candidates; 18% voted for the remaining parties. These statistics explain the dramatic changes in parliamentary seats between the NDC and NPP. When asked why they voted for this particular party: 21% said that the party had good and honest candidates; 35% said that the party had good policies to ensure development of the country; and 21% said that there was the need for change of national leadership.

Mass Media and Voting Outcome

Article 162, Section 1 of the Constitution of Ghana, 1992 states "Freedom and independence of the media are hereby guaranteed" and Article 163 states "All state-owned media shall afford fair opportunities and facilities for the presentation of divergent views and dissenting opinions".

The media, indeed, have the responsibility of informing the public. Citizens in a democratic state, especially in a representative democracy, need information to make rational choices such as electing their representatives. In elections, the citizens should know what the issues are, the candidates contesting and the position of the candidates on the issues. In which case, the state-owned media particularly have the constitutional duty to present the divergent views in terms of parties/candidates' platforms

Table 2.2: Regional Parliamentary Seats Distribution by Political Party, 2001

Region	Independent	NDC	NPP	CPP	PNC
Western	–	10	8	1	–
Central	–	9	8	–	–
Greater Accra	–	6	16	–	–
Volta	2	17	–	–	–
Eastern	–	8	18	–	–
Ashanti	–	2	31	–	–
Brong Ahafo	–	7	14	–	–
Northern	1	18	3	–	1
Upper East	1	8	2	–	1
Upper West	–	7	–	–	1
TOTAL	4	92	100	1	3

Source: Electoral Commission of Ghana.

and policy pronouncements as demanded by the Constitution.

We are interested in knowing how the state-owned media — print, electronic, radio — contributed to the shaping of electorate choices through the dissemination of political information.

Hypothesis 2: *The mass media provided the requisite information to the electorate to make informed choices about the elections.*

Table 2.3 and Table 2.4 depict the interaction of the mass media institution and voting.

An overwhelming 85% of respondents indicated that the mass media disseminated the requisite information about the elections to the electorate compared to a tiny 5% who indicated otherwise. Not only did the respondents indicate the adequacy of media coverage of the elections but

Table 2.3: Was the coverage of the elections by the state print and electronic media adequate?

Response	Frequency	Percentage %
Yes	3,301	85.1
No	178	4.6
Don't know	352	9.1
No response	47	1.2
TOTAL	3,878	100.0

Source: Survey data

Table 2.4: Was the Coverage of the Elections Fair to all the Parties and Candidates?

Response	Frequency	Percentage %
Yes	2,957	76.3
No	479	12.4
Don't know	352	10.3
No response	43	1.0
TOTAL	3,878	100.0

Source: Survey data

76% of respondents also pointed out that the mass media fairly covered all the political parties and candidates as depicted in Table 2.4.

Electoral Process Voting

Here, we examine how electoral rules and procedures encourage or discourage voting. How are elections managed in Ghana? The importance of the electoral process in maximizing democratic practice has been succinctly summarized by Francis K. Drah (1998):

That the kind of electoral process a democratizing state establishes for selecting individuals to its government is of the greatest significance cannot be denied. That is the more reason why it needs stressing that the mere holding of elections involving more than one party at regular intervals irrespective of malpractices is not enough; this is "electoralism.' Instead, a cardinal requirement of democratization is that the electoral process must be developed in such a manner as to make free, honest and fair elections (p.524).

The Electoral Commission is charged with developing and managing the electoral process pursuant to Articles 43–54 of the Constitution of Ghana, 1992. Specifically, Article 45 stipulates:

The Electoral Commission shall have the following functions—
(a) to compile the register of voters and revise it at such periods as may be determined by law;
(b) to demarcate the electoral boundaries for both national and local government elections;
(c) to conduct and supervise all public elections and referenda;
(d) to educate the people on the electoral process and its purpose;
(e) to undertake programmes for the expansion of the registration of voters; and
(f) to perform such other functions as may be prescribed by law.

In light of this constitutional mandate, we hypothesize that:

Hypothesis 3: *Citizens will vote when a conducive or an enabling environment exists for them to exercise their right to vote; and also the citizens will be inclined to vote if their vote is perceived as a legitimate determinant of a political outcome.*

In short, the electoral process should be perceived as legitimate and voter-friendly. Thus, the way that election is conducted and supervised forms part of the voter's decision matrix. In testing the hypothesis above, the following questions were asked of the electorate during the pre-election survey:

- Do you think conditions exist in Ghana for free and fair elections for the 7 December 2000 elections?

- Do you think the Electoral Commission is independent of government control?

Table 2.5 and Table 2.6 summarize the responses.

Table 2.5: Do you think Conditions Exist in Ghana for Free and Fair Elections for December 7, 2000 Elections?

Response	Frequency	Percentage %
Yes	2,497	62.4
No	599	15.0
Don't know	853	21.3
No response	55	1.4
TOTAL	4,004	100.0

Source: Survey data

Table 2.6: Do you think the Electoral Commission is Independent of Government Control?

Response	Frequency	Percentage %
Yes	1,303	32.5
No	1,367	34.1
Don't know	1,254	31.3
No response	80	2.0
TOTAL	4,004	100.0

Source: Survey data

More than 62% of respondents stated that prevailing conditions were favourable to free and fair elections compared with 15% who did not think so and 21% who were ambivalent. In the eyes of the electorate, the independence of the Electoral Commission was still suspect. An almost equal number of respondents — 33% and 34% — perceived the Commission as independent and not independent respectively. This dichotomous perception is disturbing for democratic consolidation. Implied in the Commission's function of conduct and supervising elections, is identifying and setting up voter-friendly polling stations. The Commission scored high on this aspect as depicted in Table 2.7.

Table 2.7: When you went to Vote, did you Face any problems at the Polling Station?

Response	Frequency	Percentage %
Yes	205	5.3
No	3,584	92.4
No response	89	2.3
TOTAL	3,878	100.0

Source: Survey data

An overwhelming 92% stated that they had not encountered any problem such as not finding their name, not being allowed to vote due to improper identification or shortage of ballot papers at the polling stations during the elections. This positive evaluation is a feather in the cap of the Electoral Commission. Tables 2.8, 2.9, and 2.10 shed more light on the electoral process. More than 90% of respondents stated that the election officials were helpful when they went to vote; 92% stated that they had not encountered or observed any kind of intimidation at the polling station; and another 90% described the polling stations as orderly during voting.

Issues, Value Preferences and Voting

The saliency of issues in voting has been well documented as pointed out earlier in this chapter. The issues may relate to the national economy, social demands, national security or sovereignty. Normative considerations (value judgements) such as personality and ethics may also enter into the calculus of decision of the voter.

Table 2.8: Were Election Officials Helpful When you went to Vote?

Response	Frequency	Percentage %
Yes	3,500	90.3
No	179	4.6
No response	199	5.1
TOTAL	3,878	100.0

Source: Survey data

Table 2.9: Did anybody try to Intimidate you at the Polling Station?

Response	Frequency	Percentage %
Yes	116	3.0
No	3,571	92.1
No response	191	4.9
TOTAL	3,878	100.0

Source: Survey data

The most important national issues identified by the respondents in the 2000 pre-election survey were: the economy (31%); change and development (24%); improving democracy (15%); Ghana's future in the 21st century (15%) and continuity and stability (13%).

The centrality of the national economy in the electoral decisions of voters has been the focus of political studies (Alt & Chrystal, 1983; Tufte, 1980). For example, Lewis Beck and Rice write:

> Before an election people supposedly assess the national economy. If they conclude that times are good they vote for the incumbent president (or the candidate of the president's party). If they think times are bad they vote against the incumbent president (or the candidate of the president's party) (1992: 30).

Table 2.10: How would you Describe the Voting at the Place you Voted?

Response	Frequency	Percentage %
Orderly	3,479	89.7
Not orderly	8	0.2
Chaotic	200	5.2
Don't know	35	0.9
No response	156	4.0
TOTAL	3,878	100.0

Source: Survey data

Thus we hypothesize that:

Hypothesis 4a: The electoral success of the incumbent national candidate and his party depends upon the good performance of the economy.

Conversely,

Hypothesis 4b: Poor performance of the economy increases the electoral success of the challenging national candidate and his party.

Not only did the challenging NPP score a decisive victory over the incumbent NDC in the 2000 Parliamentary elections (100 vs. 92 seats) as discussed earlier, but NPP also won the presidency against the candidate of the incumbent president's party, NDC, in the Presidential Run-off elections held on 28 December 2000 (57% vs. 43%) (see Table 2.11).

High interest rates, the depreciating value of the national currency (cedi) and unemployment were cited as major concerns. Did the national economy issue determine the outcome of the 2000 Presidential elections in favour of the challenging party? We test the economy-voting outcome hypothesis by examining the post-election survey responses elicited from respondents in Table 2.12 and Table 2.13.

Table 2.11: Presidential Elections Results by Candidate and Political Party, 1996 and 2000

Candidate/Political Party	1996 Votes received	2000 Votes received 1st Election 7 December	Run-off 28 December
Rawlings* (NDC)	4,099,760 (57.4%)	–	–
Kufuor (NPP)	2,834,878 (39.6%)	3,131,739 (48.2%)	3,631,263 (56.9%)
Mahama (PNC)	211,136 (3.0%)	189,659 (2.9%)	–
Mills** (NDC)	–	2,895,575 (44.5%)	2,750,124 (43.1%)
Larrey** (GCPP)	–	67,504 (1%)	–
Hagan** (CPP)	–	115,641 (1.8%)	–
Brobby** (UGM)	–	22,123 (0.3%)	–
Tanoh** (NRP)	–	78,629 (1.2%)	–
TOTAL	7,225,161 (100%)	6,500,870 (100%)	6,381,387 (100%)

* Completed two-term limit in 2000   ** Not candidate in 1996

Source: Electoral Commission of Ghana

Table 2.12: In your view, which of the Political Parties best Articulated the most Important National Development Issues?

Party	Frequency	Percentage %
NPP	2,417	62.3
NDC	1,077	27.8
PNC	129	3.3
CPP	72	1.9
NRP	68	1.8
GCPP	25	0.6
UGM	15	0.4
No response	75	1.9
TOTAL	3,878	100

Source: Survey data

Table 2.13: If you Voted for Mr Kufour (NPP), Give Reasons for your Answer

Reason	Frequency	Percentage %
I like him	83	2.1
Leader of my party/Member of my party	115	3.0
He represented a change/want change	1,576	40.6
Better candidate/right person for the job	381	9.8
His policies are good	250	6.4
We want to try him	51	1.3
I was cheated	15	0.4
Humility & tolerance	48	1.2
He became popular	1	0.0
Because of the alliance	11	0.3
Followed the majority	7	0.2
From my tribe	—	—
No response	1,340	34.6
TOTAL	3,878	100

Source: Survey data

Normatively, Mr J. A. Kufour and his NPP were preferred by the respondents to the other candidates and their parties. More than 62% of respondents stated that the NPP was the political party which best articulated the most important issues facing the country compared to the combined 38% for the other six competing parties. Over 40% stated that they wanted a change of government and policies, and that Kufour and NPP represented the change that they were seeking. On the personality dimension, Kufour was perceived as humble, tolerant, likeable and the right person for the job. All of this dovetailed with NPP's promises of good governance, honest and sincere leadership, rule of law and better management of government finances. And, indeed, these positive value evaluations of NPP and challenger Kufour were reflected in the actual outcome of the elections. The campaign slogan of the NPP was "Positive Change", and that of the NDC was "Stability and Continuity." And in this confrontation, positive change won!

Did Ghanaians vote sincerely or strategically in the 2000 elections? Ghanaian voters rejected the incumbent NDC party even though the NDC pointed out that it had brought development — water, rural electrification, roads, political stability — to them as was constantly shown in the party's pre-election political advertisements.

In the first elections held on 7 December 2000, the two top presidential candidates, J. A. Kufuor and J. E. Atta-Mills, received 3,131,739 (48.2%) and 2,895,575 (44.5%) votes respectively. The other five candidates combined received 473,556 (7.2%) votes.

In the Run-off election of 28 December 2000, Kufuor, the final winner, received 3,631,263 (56.9%) votes, an increase of 17% over his first round votes; and Mills, the loser, received 2,750,124 (43.1%) votes, a decrease of 14% in his first round votes.

Clearly, the 7% of the voters who voted for the other candidates in the first round and conceivably some supporters of the NDC shifted their votes to Kufuor in the second round, looking at his margin of victory of 14% (57% vs. 43%) over Mills. What explains this shift?

Political party affiliation or loyalty cannot be a plausible explanation of this voting shift since the shifters presumably came from the other competing parties. In which case, it appears that the voters in the Presidential Run-off election voted strategically (in accord with some generally held value) rather than sincerely (a sense of civic responsibility or strict adherence to party).

The voters wanted a change and Kufuor symbolized that change. The outcome of the elections may thus be looked in terms of a social welfare function (aggregated individual preferences) derived from normative public choice. Citing A. K. Sen, Mueller (1979) writes:

> ... [T]here are certain personal matters in which each person should be free to decide what should happen, and in choices over these things whatever he or she thinks is better must be taken to be better for the society as a whole, no matter what others think (p.201).

Table 2.14 tells us that 11% of respondents did not vote for the same presidential candidate as they did in the first round. Indeed, it is this 11% that accounted for Kufuor's victory. Regardless of whatever political benefits the incumbent NDC party claimed to have brought to Ghanaians, majority of the voters chose not to continue with the policies and government of the NDC.

Table 2.14: Did you Vote for the same Presidential Candidate in the First Round?

Response	Frequency	Percentage %
Yes	3,256	84.0
No	410	10.6
No response	212	5.5
TOTAL	3,878	100

Source: Survey data

Without doubt, the assertion in Ghana that, irrespective of whoever is in power, there is no difference to what happens at national level is disproved on the basis of the broad cross-party support given to Kufuor and the NPP. Presumably, the nearly twenty years of Provisional National Defence Council (PNDC)/NDC rule was enough for the majority of Ghanaians.

Conclusions

This study examined how institutions, issues, and value judgements cojointly influence political choices in a democratic polity. The study was informed by liberal polyarchic notion of democracy a la Robert Dahl (1971), which emphasizes popular participation and public contestation. Liberal democratic practice is a dynamic inter-play of institutional characteristics and performance, the individual's value orientation and rules and procedures that maximize political participation. An examination of political parties, the mass media, the electoral process and personal values in Ghana revealed that the act of voting as one of the conditions of consolidating democracy is multi-dimensional.

It is not always the case that "... the voters choose a representative, legislature, or government expecting that this individual or body would mediate between them and the state in the distribution or allocation of goods and services" (Ninsin, 1993: 182). The instrumentalist meaning that is attached to voting has little relevance in the present Ghanaian case because NDC's claim of having provided water, electricity, roads, etc. did not translate into an electoral victory for the party. Other factors, indeed, account for the re-election of incumbent candidates and the electoral success of the challengers.

In summary, our empirical study of the 2000 elections leads to the following conclusions:

1. More voters identified with NPP in 2000 than they did in 1996;
2. The voters' support for NDC declined in 2000;
3. The cross-party voting in the Presidential Run-off indicates that voters vote for the party whose platform is close to their value preferences;
4. Institutions such as the mass media and the legislature (parliament) impact on electoral choices through the dissemination of political information and effective representation respectively;
5. Perceived favourable electoral rules and procedures enhance political participation;
6. Clear articulation of the issues by candidates and voters' identification with these issues enhance voter participation;
7. Ability to provide or distribute political benefits does not

necessarily maximize the re-election chances of the incumbent candidate or government; additionally

8. Individual value judgements about the efficacy of the candidate may positively or negatively affect the candidate's electoral chances.

In this chapter, we delineated some of the variables that contribute to the sustenance of liberal democratic practice. Other variables such as elite consensus, cordial state-society relations, buoyant civil society, rule of law and a free market system are also important in sustaining liberal democracy.

REFERENCES

Alt, J. E. and K. A. Chrystal (1983) *Political Economics* (Berkeley and Los Angeles: University of California Press).
Anebo, F. K. G. (1998) "The December 1996 Elections and its Aftermath: Ghana on the Path to Democratic Consolidation?" in Joseph R. A. Ayee (ed.), *The 1996 General Elections and Democratic Consolidation in Ghana* (Accra: Department of Political Science).
Apter, D. (1963) *Ghana in Transition* (New York: Atheneum).
Austin, D. (1964) *Politics in Ghana, 1946–1960* (London: Oxford University Press).
Austin, D. and R. Luckham (eds) (1975) *Politicians and Soldiers in Ghana, 1966–72*. (London: Frank Cass).
Ayee, J. R. A. (ed.) (1998) *The 1996 General Elections and Democratic Consolidation in Ghana* (Accra: Department of Political Science).
Ayee, J. R. A. (1997a) "Ghana's 1996 General Elections: A Post-Mortem," *African Association of Political Science Occasional Paper Series*, Volume 1, Number 1: 1–27.
Ayee, J. R. A. (1997b) "The December 1996 General Elections in Ghana," *Election Studies*, Volume 16, Number 3 (September): 416–427.
Badu, K. A. and J. Larvie (1996) *Elections 96 in Ghana*, Part 1 (Accra: Gold Type).
Badu, K. A. and J. Larvie (1997) *Elections 96 in Ghana*, Part 11 (Accra: Gold Type).
Campbell, A. P. E. Converse, W. E. Miller, and D. E. Stokes (1960) *The American Voter* (New York: Wiley).
Chazan, Naomi (1983) *An Anatomy of Ghanaian Politics: Managing Political Recession, 1969–1982* (Boulder, CO: Westview Press).
Chazan, Naomi and V. LeVine (1979) "Politics in a 'Non-Political' System: the March 30, 1978 Referendum", *African Studies Review*, Volume XXII, Number 1: 177–208.
Cohen, D. L. (1983) "Elections and Election Studies in Africa", in Barabgo, Y. (ed.), *Political Science in Africa: A Critical Review* (London: Zed Press).
Constitution of the Republic of Ghana, 1992.
Dahl, R. A. (1971) *Polyarchy: Participation and Opposition* (New Haven, CT: Yale University Press).

Drah, F. K. (1998) "The 1996 Elections and Democratization: A Case Study of Okaikoi", in Joseph R. A. Ayee (ed.), *The 1996 General Elections and Democratic Consolidation in Ghana* (Accra: Department of Political Science).

Downs, A. (1957) *An Economic Theory of Democracy* (New York: Harper & Row).

Dunn, J. F. and A. F. Robertson (1973) *Dependence and Opportunity: Political Change in Ahafo* (London: Cambridge University Press).

Gyimah-Boadi, E. (1997) "Ghana: The Challenges Ahead", *Journal of Democracy*. Vol. 8, No. 3 (April): 78–91.

Hayward, F. (ed.) (1987) *Elections in Independent Africa* (Boulder, CO: Westview Press).

Herbst, J. (1993) *The Politics of Reform in Ghana, 1982–1991* (Berkeley and Los Angeles: University of California Press).

Huntington, S. P. (1991) *The Third Wave: Democratization in the Late Twentieth Century* (Norman, OK: University of Oklahoma Press).

Huntington, S. P. (1968) *Political Order in Changing Societies* (New Haven, CT: Yale University Press).

Jeffries, R. and Thomas Clare (1993) "The Ghanaian Elections of 1992", in *African Affairs*, Vol. 92 (July): 331–366.

Jonah, K. (1998) "Agency and Structure in Ghana's 1992 and 1996 Presidential Elections", in Joseph R. A. Ayee (ed.), *The 1996 General Elections and Democratic Consolidation in Ghana* (Accra: Department of Political Science).

Key, Jr. V. O. (1966) *The Responsible Electorate* (Cambridge, MA: Harvard University Press).

Kramer, G. H. (1971) "Short-Term Fluctuations in U.S. Voting Behavior, 1896–1964", *American Political Science Review*. Volume 65 (March): 131–143.

Lewis-Beck, M. S. and T. W. Rice (1992) *Forecasting Elections* (Washington, DC: Congressional Quarterly Inc.).

Linz, J. J. and A. Stepan (1987) "Toward Consolidated Democracies", *Journal of Democracy*, Vol. 8, No. 2 (April): 14–33.

Lyons, T. (1997) "Ghana's Encouraging Elections: A Major Step Forward", *Journal of Democracy*. Vol. 8, No. 2 (April).

McCarty, C. (1997) *Public Opinion in Ghana, 1997* (Washington, DC: IFES).

Mueller, D. C. (1979) *Public Choice* (New York: Cambridge University Press).

Ninsin, K. A. and F. K. Drah (eds.) (1993) *Political Parties and Democracy in Ghana's Fourth Republic* (Accra: Woeli).

Ninsin, K. A., (1993) "The Electoral System, Elections and Democracy in Ghana," in Ninsin, K. A. and F. K. Drah (eds.), *Political Parties and Democracy in Ghana's Fourth Republic* (Accra: Woeli).

Nungent, P. (1995) *Big Men, Small Boys and Politics in Ghana: Power, Ideology and the Burden of History, 1982–1994* (London and New York: Pinter).

Oquaye, M. (1995) "The Ghanaian Elections of 1992: A Dissenting View", in *African Affairs*, Vol. 94 : 259–275.

RePass, D. E. (1971) "Issue Salience and Party Choice", in *American Political Science Review*, Vol. 65 (June): 389–400.

Riker, W. H. (1988) *Liberalism Against Populism: A Confrontation Between the Theory of Democracy and the Theory of Social Choice* (Prospect Heights, Illinois: Waveland Press, Inc.).

Sandbrook, R. and J. Oelbaum (1997) "Reforming Dysfunctional Institutions Through Democratisation? Reflections on Ghana", in *The Journal of Modern African Studies*, Vol. 35, No. 4: 603–646.

Sandbrook, R. and J. Oelbaum (1999) *Reforming the Political Kingdom: Governance and Development in Ghana's Fourth Republic* (Accra: Centre for Democracy and Development).

Stokes, D. E. (1966) "Some Dynamic Elements of Contests for the Presidency", *American Political Science Review*, Vol. 60 (March): 19–28.

Tufte, E. R., (1980) *Political Control of the Economy* (Princeton, NJ: Princeton University Press).

Verba, S. and N. H. Nie (1972) *Participation in America: Political Democracy and Social Equality* (New York: Harper & Row).

CHAPTER 3

Survey of the 2000 General Elections and Presidential Run-Off in Keta and Anlo Constituencies

JOSEPH R. A. AYEE

Introduction

This paper is the result of pre- and post- 2000 elections and presidential run-off surveys conducted in the Keta and Anlo constituencies in the Volta Region. The pre-elections survey was conducted 23 October–6 November 2000 while that of the post-election was done 2 January 2001–16 January 2001. The aim of the survey was to measure public opinion in the two constituencies on key political and economic issues that emerged before, during and after the general elections and presidential run-off. These key political and economic issues include voters' attitudes and perceptions of key national and constituency level political and economic developments, evaluation of the democratic and electoral process, participation in the election process as well as identities and social capital.

A Brief Profile of the Keta and Anlo Constituencies

The Keta and Anlo constituencies are the two constituencies of the coastal district of Keta, which has a population of 137,751 (Male 64,302 — 46%; Female 73,448 —53.3%) according to the 2000 Population and Housing Census. Keta district is a "deprived" and rural one. This classification is based on the 1989 Ministry of Local Government and Rural Development categorization of districts into "developed", "moderately developed", "deprived" and "most deprived".

Keta and Anlo constituencies have a registered voter population of 42,081 and 45,429 respectively. While Keta has 20 electoral areas, Anlo has 28. Keta is the home town of the mother of former President Rawlings while Anloga is the seat of the Anlo Traditional Council headed by the "Awoamefia" (paramount chief) of Anlo.

The choice of the two constituencies was influenced by a number of factors. First, they are constituencies in the Volta Region, popularly referred to as the "World Bank" of the National Democratic Congress (NDC). In the 1996 elections, the Volta Region gave the NDC the highest total number of votes of 690,421 while the opposition New Patriotic Party (NPP) had 34,538. In addition, Anlo and Keta constituencies gave former President Rawlings 99.3% and 98.7% of the votes respectively in the 1996 elections to occupy the first and second positions out of the 200 constituencies. Second, even though the two constituencies are considered "safe seats" of the NDC, they were keenly contested by the parties and candidates. For instance, Anlo constituency had as many as 8 candidates including three independent candidates (Victor Gbeho, Esther Nyamalor and Goyimwole Kpodo (who withdrew) — who all belong to the NDC), and the incumbent NDC MP Squadron Leader Clend Sowu, while Keta fielded 5 candidates belonging to the five major parties, the NDC, NPP, PNC, CPP and NRP. Third, the writer wanted to do a follow-up of the dynamics of electoral politics in the two constituencies since they were the ones in which the writer conducted the 1996 elections survey.

In the 2000 general elections and presidential run-off the two constituencies produced interesting results worth noting. First, in the presidential elections, Anlo constituency recorded 26,960 (94.6%) votes for the NDC candidate, John Mills, while Keta constituency gave him 25,327 (94.2%). These figures show a decrease of more than 5% in the figures obtained by former President Rawlings of the NDC in 1996 elections in the two constituencies. On the other hand, the NPP candidate, John Kufuor had 541 (1.9%) and 776 (2.9%) votes for Anlo and Keta constituencies respectively. These figures show a slight rise of about 1.5% if compared with the 1996 elections results of 221 (0.6%) and 335 (1.0%) for Anlo and Keta constituencies respectively. In other words, while the NDC lost some percentage of votes in the two constituencies, the NPP on the other hand, gained some votes in the 2000 elections. Similarly, in the presidential run-off, the NPP candidate increased his votes as against those of the NDC candidate (see Table 3.1). The constituencies' results confirm a general trend of the decrease of NDC votes in the 2000 elections in the Volta Region vis-à-vis those of the 1996 elections (see Table 3.2).

The proportional change in the voting pattern in the two constituencies and the Volta Region is due to the following factors:

Table 3.1: 2000 Presidential Run-off Results in the Anlo and Keta Constituencies

Constituencies	Mills %	Kufuor %	Valid Votes	Rejected Votes	Total Cast	Reg. Voters	Turnout %
Anlo	33,381 96.7	1,149 3.3	34,530	538	35,068	45,429	77.2
Keta	34,737 96.0	1,435 4.0	36,172	396	36,568	42,081	86.9

Source: Ghana Gazette, Friday, 12 January 2001.

Table 3.2: Comparative Analysis of the Trend of Voting in 1996 and 2000 Presidential Elections and Presidential Run-off in the Volta Region for NDC and NPP

NATIONAL DEMOCRATIC CONGRESS (NDC)			NEW PATRIOTIC PARTY (NPP)		
1996 Votes	2000 Votes	Presidential Run-off	1996 Votes	2000 Votes	Presidential Run-off
690,421 94.5%	505,614 86.18%	589,719 88.47%	34,538 4.7%	49,768 8.48%	76,839 11.53%

Source: Electoral Commission, Accra and Ghana Gazette, Friday, 12 January 2001.

- the absence of Rawlings, who is considered as the "son of the soil" in the election;
- the poor state of the economy;
- the NPP's campaign strategy of "Positive Change" appealed to the voters;
- the imposition of an unpopular candidate on the constituencies by the National Executive of the NDC. A classic example is in the Anlo constituency where the NDC candidate, Clend Sowu was not popular because most of the electorate regarded him as "arrogant, uncooperative and abrasive"; and
- the increase in the number of candidates who contested the elec-

tions in the two constituencies. The National Reform Party, whose members broke away from the NDC, contested the two constituencies in addition to the NDC, NPP, CPP, PNC (totalling 5). Furthermore, three independent candidates all from the NDC (totalling 8) also contested the Anlo constituency. This is far more than the candidates who contested the 1996 elections, which was more or less a contest between the NDC and the NPP. Anlo had four candidates including two independent ones while Keta had two.

Second, even though the NDC won the Keta parliamentary seat, it lost the Anlo one to an independent candidate, Victor Gbeho, who had been the foreign minister in the NDC government. The decision by Gbeho to contest the parliamentary election in the Anlo constituency resulted in a bitter struggle between him and Sowu. According Gbeho he decided to contest the elections to enhance the development of the Anlo constituency, to prevent the NDC from losing the seat and to heed the call by chiefs, opinion leaders and supporters to represent them. He also accused the NDC of lack of transparency in the nomination process regarding the selection of a parliamentary candidate for the constituency, which he claimed had prejudiced the choice in the eyes of those on whose behalf the party had sought to act. For his part, Sowu indicated that the decision by Gbeho to contest the elections as an independent candidate was contrary to the letter and spirit of the constitution of the NDC. To him, Gbeho's decision to flout the NDC's decision with regard to his retention as a candidate for the parliamentary elections was contrary to Article 35 of the NDC constitution, which regulates the conduct of members of the party and in addition set a bad precedent, which would be exploited by other party members in the future. He also drew the attention of those who filed the nomination of Gbeho to Article 36 of the party's constitution, which also defines the procedure for such an exercise.

Efforts were made by the NDC party executive to resolve the feud between Sowu and Gbeho. In the midst of the reconciliation exercise, which Mr Sowu never attended, the NDC issued a stern warning to its members who were contravening its policies by presenting themselves as independent candidates to refrain from such unilateral actions forthwith or face disciplinary action. The warning stressed that party members were bound by decisions taken by its "competent organs" including the National

Executive Committee, which acted on the issue of parliamentary candidates. Even though the NDC conceded that there was room for dissent in the party as in any other democratic organization, it found it unacceptable for any member to "hide behind the façade of expressing contrary opinions to indulge in and propagate acts that have the potential of creating indiscipline and undermining the unity and cohesion of the party" (*Daily Graphic*, 15 September 2000: 1). The NDC further pointed out that it would not allow individuals who had gained public recognition and enhanced their images and reputations on the back of the NDC to turn round and undermine the party's political fortunes in the 2000 elections.

To the NDC "no one who is not officially designated as our candidate for the impending elections would be permitted to profit from the image and good standing of our party in the eyes of the electorate" (*Daily Graphic*, 15 September 2000). Consequently, those party members who were known to have defied the official party position and filed as independent candidates had their names compiled and submitted to the disciplinary committee of the party. This seems a timid threat as nothing came out from the disciplinary committee on the members of the party who contested as independent candidates. Meanwhile Gbeho, who won the Anlo seat as an independent candidate, has not been officially expelled from the party. In parliament, he is more or less an NDC MP because of his sympathies towards the NDC on all major issues.

Profile of Respondents

One hundred respondents were interviewed in each of the two constituencies in both the pre-election and post-election survey, making a total of 400. For the pre-election, 55% males and 45% females were interviewed in the Keta constituency as against 57% males and 43% females in the Anlo district. This is in contrast to the post-election survey in which 64% males and 37% females (for Keta) and 62% males and 38% females (for Anlo) were interviewed. Even though it was the intention of the survey to interview both sexes equally, it was not possible because of well-known cultural barriers that account for the low participation of women in local politics.

On educational qualifications of respondents, 8% and 17% reported that they never attended school in the Keta and Anlo constituencies respectively. Of those respondents who reported that they attended school, the majority had primary education: 37% in Keta and 46% in Anlo. Three per cent of respondents had university education. As in the 1996 elections survey, female respondents had lower levels of education than the male ones.

The occupational range of the respondents varied. However, traders constituted the highest number of respondents interviewed (52%) in the two constituencies while teachers ranked second with 29%. Because 23% of respondents were unemployed, employment became one of the three most important development needs in the two constituencies.

Even though some respondents were not willing to disclose their personal/individual income for apparent fear of being asked to pay income tax on their earnings by the Internal Revenue Service, over 76% of those who disclosed their income indicated that they earned less than one million per annum. It is possible to interpret this to mean that either respondents had concealed their real income or they did not know what they earned or their income was low, given the fact that the two constituencies are located in the rural area.

Political Participation

Political participation of the voters in some of the key aspects of the electoral process is a very important aspect of the democratic process. Even though all the respondents were registered voters and had voted in the 1996 general elections and the 1998 district assembly elections, only 40% claimed they were registered members of the NDC.

Participation may be measured by the financial contributions that members can make towards the activities of their parties. Asked whether they paid dues or financially contribute towards the activities of the party as members of the NDC, over 80% of respondents replied in the negative saying that they were too poor to be saddled with dues or make any financial contribution. This is true for the other parties. Strangely enough, 20% had NDC party cards while the rest did not. Those who had party cards indicated that they had their card from the party's headquarters through the party executive in the district. This may not be the true picture since it is possible that the respondents did not know how the card was acquired. The remaining 60% did not register with the party because they were unaware of how to register as members of the party, were not encouraged by the party or did not like party politics.

A few respondents (about 6%) belonged to other parties such as NPP and CPP. This is not surprising given that the two constituencies are NDC strongholds. Like their NDC counterparts, a few respondents (39%) had party cards while they rest did not. This notwithstanding, some of the respondents openly talked about the need for change. Furthermore, in contrast with the 1996 elections, the NPP, CPP and PNC mounted campaigns as well as erecting scattered billboards in the two constituencies.

Another way of measuring participation is based on whether members patronize activities of their parties such as campaign rallies or a national/regional congress. Even though 50% of respondents attended political rallies and meetings of the parties of their own volition, they were quick to point out that they were sometimes mobilized by their parties with promises of incentives if they did attend such rallies and meetings. Furthermore, only 5% (Keta) and 8% (Anlo) of respondents ever attended either a regional or national congress of the parties.

Participation in party activities could also be measured on the basis of members' interest in holding the leadership position or contesting party positions. Consequently, respondents were asked whether they were interested in holding the leadership position in the party or contested a party position. Only 21% replied that they were interested in holding the leadership position because they wanted to contribute to national development and the progress of Ghana. The remaining 79% of respondents were either not personally interested or thought they were not qualified for the leadership position. This is reflected in the number of respondents who hold party executive positions. Of the 100 respondents interviewed in each of the two constituencies, 6% and 4% of respondents in the Keta and Anlo constituencies respectively held party executive positions such as chairman and secretary at constituency, ward or village/town level. These positions were contested and they won on merit.

From indicators of participation such as financial contribution to party activities, attendance at party campaign rallies and congress and interest in leadership party positions, one is tempted to believe that the extent of political participation of voters in the activities of political parties is not only discouraging but also limited. This may be due to the perception, whether rightly or wrongly that party politics is "dirty" and active involvement or participation in party activities depends on one's financial standing.

Voters' Perception of Political Parties

Respondents' views on political parties were sought to confirm or reject the somewhat negative image of parties. First, respondents' views were sought on what they thought of party politics in Ghana today. While 10% of respondents in the Keta and 33% in the Anlo constituencies replied that politics had improved the quality of living of Ghanaians, 59% in Keta and 24% in Anlo felt that politics had enriched a few people, while 10% in Keta and 8% in Anlo were of the view that politics had brought division among Ghanaians.

The disparity between the responses in the two constituencies about politics may be due to the scepticism the people of Keta hold about politicians who, in spite of numerous promises, were not able to complete a sea defence wall for the town. Even though the Rawlings government started the sea defence wall before it left office, the people of Keta had the feeling that the Rawlings government dragged its feet on the issue for far too long. Thus when the sea defence wall started, the euphoria which should have accompanied the project subsided because of the long wait for unfulfilled promise.

The disparity in responses on politics has also influenced the responses given when respondents were asked to comment on the performance of political parties. While 55% of respondents in the Keta constituency responded that parties were doing neither a good nor a bad job, 47% of respondents in the Anlo constituency indicated that the parties were doing a good job. However, when respondents were asked whether, irrespective of the party in power, there was not going to be any difference in what happens at the national level, 61% of respondents in the two constituencies felt that, irrespective of the party in power, there was going to be a difference in what happens at national level while 39% replied that there was not going to be any difference. This may be interpreted to mean that in spite of the general cynicism about political parties, Ghanaians still believe that political parties hold the key to efforts being made to promote development.

Party organization and the resources at its disposal are important in building a winning party for elections. Respondents were therefore asked what was lacking in their party's organization at constituency, regional and national level and whether they had adequate logistics to contest the 2000 elections. While inadequate finance and inadequate logistics such as cars and loudspeakers featured as the prominent problems confronting political parties in the two constituencies, 76% and 71% of respondents in the Keta and Anlo constituencies respectively were quick to add that they would not favour state funding of the parties because that money should be used to finance development projects in their areas (see Table 3.3).

Table 3.3: State Financing of Political Parties

Response	Keta Constituency Frequency	Percentage %	Anlo Constituency Frequency	Percentage %
Yes	6	6	5	5
No	76	76	71	71
Don't know	18	18	24	24
TOTAL	100	100	100	100

Source: Survey data

On whether the parties had adequate logistics for their campaign in the 2000 elections, 68% of respondents in the Keta constituency felt that there were inadequate logistics since, according to them, the NDC had far more cars and loudspeakers than the other parties. This is in sharp contrast to the responses from Anlo were 74% respondents replied that all the parties had adequate logistics (see Table 3.4). The disparity in the responses

Table 3.4: Adequacy of Parties' Logistics for Campaign in the 2000 Election

Response	Keta Constituency Frequency	Percentage %	Anlo Constituency Frequency	Percentage %
Yes	28	28	74	74
No	68	68	7	7
Don't know	4	4	19	19
TOTAL	100	100	100	100

Source: Survey data

may be due to the fact that respondents in Keta constituency saw the campaign as that between an incumbent NDC with extensive resources such as the vehicles of the District Chief Executive and Information Services Department and an opposition NPP, while those in Anlo saw it as one between Gbeho and Sowu, both of whom had access to logistics.

In spite of the disparity in responses concerning adequacy of logistics, over 92% of respondents responded that all the parties had been given a chance to campaign freely in the 2000 elections. There were however, a few cases of removal of campaign posters of opposing parties, particularly by NDC agents. A classic example is the removal of the PNC posters on the walls of Keta Secondary School, facing the Residency by people suspected of having been sent by the District Chief Executive, who had earlier at a meeting called on the PNC candidate to remove his posters.

The lack of internal democracy within the parties, especially the NDC, was questioned by a majority of respondents in the two constituencies. For instance, when respondents were asked what they thought of the process for selection of the parliamentary candidate of the constituency, 23% of respondents in Keta and 34% of respondents in Anlo felt that the it had been "undemocratic" while 25% and 12% respectively thought it had been "democratic". The high percentage of "undemocratic" response in the Anlo constituency is due to the perceived imposition of the incumbent MP, Sowu on the constituency. Over half the respondents, 52% (Keta) and 54% (Anlo) replied that they did not know anything about the process of selection of candidates (see Table 3.5). The "don't

Table 3.5: Opinion on the Selection Process of the Parliamentary Candidates

Response	Keta Constituency Frequency	Keta Constituency Percentage %	Anlo Constituency Frequency	Anlo Constituency Percentage %
Democratic	25	25	12	12
Not Democratic	23	23	34	34
Don't know	52	52	54	54
TOTAL	100	100	100	100

Source: Survey data

know" response may be indicative of the fact that most voters were unaware of what happens in their parties. Is it because of apathy or lack of information and therefore lack of transparency? Ones speculation is that it could be both reasons. As a follow-up on the issue of the lack of internal democracy in the parties, respondents were asked whether parties projected personalities more than their policies. Forty per cent of respondents replied "Yes" while 37% (Keta) and 34% (Anlo) said "No" (see Table 3.6). This confirms the view that most political parties in Ghana revolve around personalities and, because of the emphasis placed on them rather than policies, it has affected even the voters. Consequently, rather than the electorate voting on policies and issues they tend to vote for personalities.

Table 3.6: Opinion on Parties Projecting Personalities more than the Policies

Response	Keta Constituency Frequency	Keta Constituency Percentage %	Anlo Constituency Frequency	Anlo Constituency Percentage %
Yes	40	40	40	40
No	37	37	34	34
Don't know	23	23	26	26
TOTAL	100	100	100	100

Source: Survey data

Voters' Awareness

The awareness of the voters is dependent on how they follow the campaigns of the candidates and the issues through the media. In this connection, respondents were asked to indicate the sources from which they had received most information about the issues and the candidates in the election. Radio and TV were the main sources from which the respondents received information (see Table 3.7). In addition, informal inter-personal communications from friends and family was also an important source because of the absence of electricity in most electoral areas and the inability of the uneducated to read the print media. Newspapers attracted a low response because few people had access to them in the urban areas while they remain poorly circulated in the rural areas.

Table 3.7: Most Useful Media Source in Influencing Electorate to Vote for the 2000 Election

Response	Keta Constituency Frequency	Keta Constituency Percentage %	Anlo Constituency Frequency	Anlo Constituency Percentage %
Television	10	10	8	8
Newspaper	7	7	3	3
Friends and family (word of mouth)	13	13	13	13
Campaign rallies	16	16	19	19
Radio	38	38	38	38
Posters/fliers	9	9	11	11
Don't know	7	7	1	1
Other	–	–	7	7
TOTAL	100	100	100	100

Source: Survey data.

Of all the sources, radio was found by 38% of respondents in the two constituencies as the most useful in deciding whom to vote for in the elections (see Table 3.7). Rallies of the candidates and the political parties rank as the second most useful means of influence. Through the rallies, some voters were able to see the candidates campaign in person and were therefore able to understand most of the issues they put across.

The credibility of media sources was also explored in the light of the proliferation of media houses and their political biases since 1992. Asked about the medium of information they trusted most to tell the truth, state-owned radio (31% for Keta and 39% for Anlo) was listed as the most credible and trusted. This is understandable because the respondents were used to state-owned radio, which until 1992 was the only radio station in the country. On the other hand, 17% (Keta) and 12% (Anlo) trusted private radio while 20% (Keta) and 21% (Anlo) replied that they did not know (see Table 3.8). The showing of private radio is commendable given the fact that most of them started operation in 1992 and have tried to build their credibility in the face of stiff competition in the arena.

Table 3.8: The most Trusted Media Source to Tell the Truth to Voters

Response	Keta Constituency Frequency	Percentage %	Anlo Constituency Frequency	Percentage %
State-owned TV	6	6	6	6
Foreign TV	-	-	1	1
Foreign radio	8	8	2	2
State-owned newspapers	9	9	10	10
Don't know	20	20	21	21
Private TV	3	3	-	-
State-owned radio	31	31	39	39
Private radio	17	17	12	12
Other	6	6	9	9
TOTAL	100	100	100	100

Source: Survey data.

Table 3.9: State of the Ghanaian Economy Today

Rating	Keta Constituency Frequency	Percentage %	Anlo Constituency Frequency	Percentage %
Very good	7	7	5	5
Good	6	6	16	16
Bad	26	26	20	20
Very bad	50	50	46	46
Neither good nor bad	3	3	2	2
Don't know	8	8	11	11
TOTAL	100	100	100	100

Source: Survey data.

Voters' Attitude and Perception of the Economy

There is a nexus between satisfaction with economic conditions and satisfaction with the political environment. Indeed, the electorate point accusing fingers towards politicians if the economy is not doing well. Consequently, an electorate that is satisfied with the economy is a morale booster for the politicians. With this in mind, respondents were asked to reflect on the state of the Ghanaian economy as at the time of the elections. In contrast with the 1996 survey when perceptions of respondents on the economy in general were positive in the two constituencies, the 2000 survey shows a contradictory picture, which point to the fact that Ghanaians are far from content with economic conditions. Fifty per cent and 46% of the respondents in the Keta and Anlo constituencies respectively felt that the state of the economy was "very bad" while 26% (Keta) and 20% (Anlo) thought that it was "bad". It was only 7% (Keta) and 5% (Anlo) respondents who replied that the economy was "very good" (see Table 3.9). On the other hand, when they were asked whether over the past four years the Ghanaian economy had improved or become worse, 34% (Keta) and 26% (Anlo) of respondents felt that the economy had "sharply deteriorated" while 33% (Keta) and 39% (Anlo) indicated that

Table 3.10: Improvement or otherwise of the Economy Over the Past Four Years

Response	Keta Constituency Frequency	Keta Constituency Percentage %	Anlo Constituency Frequency	Anlo Constituency Percentage %
Considered improved	3	3	4	4
Just improved	24	24	18	18
Become worse	33	33	39	39
Sharply deteriorated	34	34	26	26
Don't know	6	6	13	13
TOTAL	100	100	100	100

Source: Survey data

the economy was "worse" (see Table 3.10). Furthermore, when respondents were asked whether their household's standard of living had improved since the 1996 elections 44% (Keta) and 51% (Anlo) respondents responded that it was "much worse". On the other hand, 27% (Keta) and 17% (Anlo) of respondents felt that their household's standard of living was "a little better" (see Table 3.11).

Table 3.11: Improvement of Household's Standard of Living Since the 1996 Elections

Response	Keta Constituency Frequency	Keta Constituency Percentage %	Anlo Constituency Frequency	Anlo Constituency Percentage %
Much better	–	–	3	3
A little better	27	27	17	17
A little worse	29	29	25	25
Much worse	44	44	51	51
Don't know	–	–	4	4
TOTAL	100	100	100	100

Source: Survey data

A number of major problems facing the Ghanaian economy were identified. When respondents were asked to identify the major economic problem in Ghana today, fifty one per cent of respondents in the Keta constituency responded "unemployment" while 43% of respondents in the Anlo constituency replied "inflation".

The responses of respondents on the economy reinforce the view that Ghanaians generally adopt an instrumentalist approach to politics. Governments are held responsible for the provision of practically everything: food, consumer goods, roads, schools, hospitals, etc. A government, to many Ghanaians, is legitimate if it is able to direct the economy so as to provide instrumental goods for individuals, communities and groups (Owusu, 1970; Chazan, 1983; Rothchild, 1991). The notion of instrumental goods is a complex package that includes macro-economic development, but concentrates upon certain micro-economic goods and commodities. It also incorporates non-quantifiable variables such as elite-satisfying access to positions of power. But even in the latter category, Ghanaians are materialist. Positions of power are desired not primarily for status but for the access they ultimately bring to material benefits via mechanisms such as government regulatory licensing. Consequently, Maxwell Owusu's finding in his study of Agona-Swedru (1970: 3) that "power relations are considered extensions or primary dimensions of economic relations" is valid for the whole Ghana. Because the Ghanaian economy has been in crisis since the early 1980s, the ability to satisfy the instrumental demands placed on governments has been very low. It is this that caused the downfall of the NDC government.

The Election Issues

The pessimism expressed about the economy is also reflected in the election issues at both national and constituency levels. When respondents were asked to mention the three most important development issues at national level employment, education and agriculture were mentioned. Similarly, the three most important development needs of the two constituencies are employment, a good road network and education. It is not surprising that unemployment featured as both a national and constituency issue. As in other constituencies, there is extensive unemployment. The people of the two constituencies are mostly fishermen but because the sea and lagoon on which their livelihood depends have become less productive most of them are jobless. Indeed, the unemployment situation has led some unscrupulous people to engage in petty stealing, a situation rare in the two constituencies. In addition, traders cannot sell their wares because the majority of the people are unemployed.

There seems to be no correlation between the real economic situation on the ground and the way the electorate in the two constituencies voted. Not surprisingly, 59% (Keta) and 92% (Anlo) of respondents indicated that both national and constituency issues influenced the way they voted. One is therefore at a loss as to why the two constituencies voted for the NDC. The explanation may be that the people voted for personalities rather than the issues in the elections.

Evaluation of Democratic Institutions and Processes

The robustness of democracy depends not only on institutions and processes but also on the perceptions of the citizens of democracy and their confidence in the political system. Overall, respondents were satisfied with democracy and the political system, which is good for democratic consolidation. Respondents were asked to indicate whether Ghana could be described as a democratic country. The responses were overwhelming and positive (see Table 3.12). Similarly, when respondents were asked whether democracy had improved over the past four years, responses were also extremely positive (see Table 3.13).

The political parties and media are key players in the democratic consolidation process. Indeed, they perform multifarious roles, which cannot be easily ignored. Thus in assessing democracy, there is the need to examine

Table 3.12: Ghana Could be Described as a Democratic Country

Response	Keta Constituency Frequency	Percentage %	Anlo Constituency Frequency	Percentage %
Yes	93	93	89	89
No	3	3	4	4
Don't know	4	4	7	7
TOTAL	100	100	100	100

Source: Survey data.

Table 3.13: Democracy Has Improved in Ghana Over the Past Four Years

Response	Keta Constituency Frequency	Percentage %	Anlo Constituency Frequency	Percentage %
Yes	90	90	86	86
No	10	10	–	–
Don't know	–	–	14	14
TOTAL	100	100	100	100

Source: Survey data

the electorate's perceptions of them. Respondents were therefore asked whether the media had more freedom now than four years ago. Seventy two per cent and 63% of respondents in the Keta and Anlo constituencies respectively responded that the media had more freedom now than four years ago (see Table 3.14). In the same vein, respondents expressed similar positive sentiments on the freedom of political parties and other associations (see Table 3.15).

Table 3.14: The Media Have More Freedom Now Than Four Years Ago

Response	Keta Constituency Frequency	Percentage %	Anlo Constituency Frequency	Percentage %
Yes	72	72	63	63
No	–	–	1	1
Don't know	28	28	36	36
TOTAL	100	100	100	100

Source: Survey data.

Table 3.15: Political Parties and Other Associations Have More Freedom now than Four Years Ago

Response	Keta Constituency Frequency	Percentage %	Anlo Constituency Frequency	Percentage %
Yes	76	76	66	66
No	–	–	2	2
Don't know	24	24	32	32
TOTAL	100	100	100	100

Source: Survey data.

Evaluation of the Electoral Process

Did respondents think the general elections and the presidential run-off had been generally free and fair on 7 December 2000 and 28 December 2000? Overall, 96% (Keta) and 81% (Anlo) of respondents felt that the elections had been free and fair while 4% (Keta) and 19% (Anlo) reported that some of the parties or candidates had an unfair advantage (see Table 3.16). This is an appreciable increase in the percentage of respondents who responded positively when they were asked to give an opinion on the freedom and fairness of the 1996 presidential and parliamentary elections: 80% (Keta) and 72% (Anlo).

Table 3.16: The Freedom and Fairness of the 2000 Elections

	Keta Constituency		Anlo Constituency	
Response	Frequency	Percentage %	Frequency	Percentage %
Yes	96	96	81	81
No	3	3	12	12
Don't know	1	1	7	7
TOTAL	100	100	100	100

Source: Survey data.

When asked to assess the fairness of the media's coverage of the parties, candidates and issues during the campaign period, 94% (Keta) and 78% (Anlo) of respondents said that the coverage had been adequate, while a negligible percentage said it had been inadequate (see Table 3.17). Again, when asked whether the coverage had been fair to all the parties and candidates, 92% (Keta) and 68% (Anlo) said "yes", while a small percentage of respondents replied "no" (see Table 3.18). Most respondents spoke approvingly of the allocation of slots equally by GBC radio and television to the various political parties to make political broadcasts in the immediate run-up to the elections, in spite of the perceived bias towards the NDC.

Table 3.17: Adequacy of Media Coverage of the 2000 Elections

	Keta Constituency		Anlo Constituency	
Response	Frequency	Percentage %	Frequency	Percentage %
Yes	94	94	78	78
No	1	1	7	7
Don't know	5	5	15	15
TOTAL	100	100	100	100

Source: Survey data.

Table 3.18: Fairness of the Coverage of 2000 Election to all Parties and Candidates

	Keta Constituency		Anlo Constituency	
Response	Frequency	Percentage %	Frequency	Percentage %
Yes	92	92	68	68
No	3	3	7	7
Don't know	5	5	25	25
TOTAL	100	100	100	100

Source: Survey data.

The freedom and the fairness of the elections depend on the performance of the Electoral Commission (EC), which is constitutionally mandated to conduct and supervise all public elections and referenda in Ghana. Appropriately, questions were asked to elicit responses from respondents on the performance of the EC. A question was asked on the independence of the EC. The perception was that the independence of the EC has been compromised because its members were appointed by the ruling government. The responses, however, show that majority of respondents were unaware of the operations and therefore the independence of the EC (see Table 3.19). This is strange because the two constituencies have a district branch of the EC. However, most respondents did not even know anything about the activities of the district office of the EC when they were asked to comment on the fairness of the EC to all the parties (see Table 3.20). More public relations work therefore, needs to be done by the EC headquarters and its district branch to enable the electorate to understand their activities.

The fairness of an electoral process also depends on the creation of a level playing field through a de-linking of government resources and

Table 3.19: The Independence of the Electoral Commission of Government Control

Response	Keta Constituency Frequency	Keta Constituency Percentage %	Anlo Constituency Frequency	Anlo Constituency Percentage %
Yes	37	37	22	22
No	7	7	3	3
Don't know	56	56	75	75
TOTAL	100	100	100	100

Source: Survey data.

Table 3.20: Fairness of the District Office of the Electoral Commission to all the Parties

Response	Keta Constituency Frequency	Keta Constituency Percentage %	Anlo Constituency Frequency	Anlo Constituency Percentage %
Yes	28	28	29	29
No	3	3	–	–7
Don't know	59	59	71	71
TOTAL	100	100	100	100

Source: Survey data.

personnel from those of the ruling party. In this connection, respondents were asked to comment on whether the NDC got undue advantage over opposition parties. As with the responses on the independence of the EC and its district branch, the majority of respondents were unaware of the over-exploitation of incumbency advantages (see Table 3.21). In addition, a significant percentage of respondents were also unaware of any other ways to influence the elections (see Table 3.22). These responses show the trust and faith most of the electorate have in the electoral process.

Table 3.21: Undue Advantage of the Ruling Party Over Oppositon Parties in the Elections

Response	Keta Constituency Frequency	Keta Constituency Percentage %	Anlo Constituency Frequency	Anlo Constituency Percentage %
Yes	33	33	18	18
No	11	11	14	14
Don't know	56	56	68	68
TOTAL	100	100	100	100

Source: Survey data.

Table 3.22: Any Other Ways to Influence the Elections Apart from the Electoral Commission

Response	Keta Constituency Frequency	Keta Constituency Percentage %	Anlo Constituency Frequency	Anlo Constituency Percentage %
Yes	9	9	18	18
No	25	25	14	14
Don't know	66	66	68	68
TOTAL	100	100	100	100

Source: Survey data.

A final indicator for determining the freedom and fairness of the electoral process is to identify the improprieties (such as intimidation, minors voting, orderliness of the elections) sometimes associated with elections. Over 92% of respondents in the two constituencies replied that they did not face any problems at the polling stations in which they voted. They commended elections officials whom they described as very helpful. They also described the process as clear and easy while the voting was orderly. On the other hand, 1% (Keta) and 4% (Anlo) of respondents said that they did not find their names in the voters' register. There were few incidents of intimidation as only 3% (Keta) and 11% (Anlo) indicated that they had been intimidated at their polling stations. The Anlo constituency figure of intimidation is higher than the Keta one because of the intense rivalry between Gbeho and Sowu.

The issue of voting with a photo identity card became a big issue before the elections. The Supreme Court ruled that both photo identity cards and thumb-printed identity cards should be used to vote as the earlier directive by the Electoral Commission for the use of only photo ID was said to disenfranchise a lot of people. Respondents were therefore asked whether they voted with a photo ID card. The responses show that 99% (Keta) and 92% (Anlo) of respondents voted with photo identity cards while the rest voted with thumb-printed cards (see Table 3.23). This finding somehow vindicates the Electoral Commission's stance that the majority of voters had acquired photo identity cards and hence its use only for voting in the 2000 elections.

On the efficiency of the electoral process, over 95% respondents

Table 3.23: Vote with a Photo ID Card

Response	Keta Constituency Frequency	Percentage %	Anlo Constituency Frequency	Percentage %
Yes	99	99	92	92
No	1	1	8	8
TOTAL	100	100	100	100

Source: Survey data.

responded that the following five indicators were present on the day of polling:

- There was enough information about the voting process;
- The ballot paper was not confusing;
- Election officials were helpful;
- The polling station was not difficult to get to:
- The polling station did have enough supplies

Evaluation of Presidential Running Mate

The issue of the selection of running mates for the presidential candidates by all the parties took some time to be settled because of the perception of a north-south balance as the leading criterion that would determine the choice. In what is considered the politics of the selection of running mates, most parties selected running mates based on the north-south divide to attract votes from both areas. Respondents were therefore asked what they considered to be the most important factor in the choice of a presidential running mate. The majority of respondents (63% from Keta and 62% from Anlo) replied that experience was the most important factor. Only 25% (Keta) and 19% (Anlo) felt that the selection must be based on regional balance (see Table 3.24). However, when respondents were asked

Table 3.24: Most Important Factor in the choice of a Presidential Running Mate

Response	Keta Constituency Frequency	Percentage %	Anlo Constituency Frequency	Percentage %
Ethnic balance	–	–	–	–
Regional balance	25	25	19	19
Gender balance	–	–	2	2
Experience	63	63	62	62
Party loyalty	4	4	9	9
Other	8	8	8	8
TOTAL	100	100	100	100

Source: Survey data.

whether it was important to have a regional balance on the presidential ticket, 67% (Keta) and 54% (Anlo) of respondents replied "yes' while 18% (Keta) and 33% (Anlo) replied that it "does not matter" (see Table 3.25). Even though these responses may seem contradictory, the majority of respondents were only trying to emphasize that the choice of presidential running mate would not have affected the party they wanted to vote for since most of them made up their minds to vote for the NDC (see Table 3.26).

Table 3.25: Importance of Regional Balance on the Presidential Ticket

	Keta Constituency		Anlo Constituency	
Response	Frequency	Percentage %	Frequency	Percentage %
Yes	67	67	54	54
Doesn't matter	18	18	33	33
No	11	11	6	6
Don't know	4	4	7	7
TOTAL	100	100	100	100

Source: Survey data.

Table 3.26: Effect of Choice of Presidential Candidate Affecting the Party Respondents will Vote For

	Keta Constituency		Anlo Constituency	
Response	Frequency	Percentage %	Frequency	Percentage %
Yes	16	16	8	8
No	84	84	92	92
TOTAL	100	100	100	100

Source: Survey data

Presidential Run-off

The presidential run-off was conducted on 28 December 2000 because neither of the two candidates (John Mills and John Kufuor), who had the highest number of votes, had the fifty per cent of votes plus one required by the 1992 Constitution to win the seat of president. As expected, 91% (Keta) and 80% (Anlo) of respondents voted for the NDC candidate Mills. They voted for him for two main reasons. First, they claimed that Mills was the better candidate, honourable and honest. Second, they voted for him for the sake of continuity. On the other hand, the few who voted for Kufuor said he represented change while his policies were good. As in the general elections, over 90% of respondents did not experience any problems at the polling stations. There were also no intimidations.

Identities and Claim-making Issues

The groups based on identities can be classified by gender, occupation, religion and language, ethnic background, urban versus rural/internal and region. Respondents were therefore asked how strongly or otherwise they felt towards region, religion, ethnic group and association. Responses indicate that the majority of respondents in the two constituencies did not have any strong attachment to or feeling for the region in which they lived as only 8% felt they were "strongly attached" to region. From the responses, one can deduce that although region is a criterion for classifying group identities, respondents did not regard region as important. However, 37% and 36% (Keta) and 36% and 40% (Anlo) of respondents replied that they were "strongly attached" to religion and ethnic group respectively. This means that people in the two constituencies valued their religion and ethnicity more than the affinity to region and membership of civil society organizations, which is not surprising given the rural background of the two constituencies.

The adequacy of respondents' household income was also explored. Reflecting the general poor economic situation in the country, which was a contributory factor to poor showing of Rawlings's National Democratic Congress in the December 2000 elections, as many as 75% (Keta) and 83% (Anlo) of respondents replied that their household income was not really enough to survive on while only 6%% (Keta) and 1% indicated that their income was enough for a fair standard of living (see Table 3.27).

Similarly, when respondents were asked whether their household's standards of living had improved over the last five years, 51% (Keta) and 55% (Anlo) of respondents indicated that it was much worse while 6% (Keta) and 7% (Anlo) replied that it was much better (see Table 3.28). These

Table 3.27: Adequacy of Household Income

Response	Keta Constituency Frequency	Keta Constituency Percentage %	Anlo Constituency Frequency	Anlo Constituency Percentage %
Not really enough to survive on	75	75	83	83
Only just enough to survive	17	17	14	14
Enough for a fair standard of living	6	6	1	1
Don't know	2	2	2	2
TOTAL	100	100	100	100

Source: Survey data.

Table 3.28: Household's Standard of Living Over the last Five Years

Response	Keta Constituency Frequency	Keta Constituency Percentage %	Anlo Constituency Frequency	Anlo Constituency Percentage %
Much better	6	6	7	7
A little worse	12	12	18	18
A little better	24	24	14	14
Much worse	51	51	55	55
Don't know	7	7	6	6
TOTAL	100	100	100	100

Source: Survey data

responses show that Ghanaians are strikingly more pessimistic about their current economic situation now than they were five years ago. Consequently, respondents had a low perception of state institutions since they felt that they would not be able to assist them when they were in difficulty. The majority of respondents had limited expectations that government would advance their welfare and confidently declared their intention of relying on their own initiative.

As with their current situation, the majority of respondents were also pessimistic, if not fatalistic, about the future. For instance, when respondents were asked to look ahead to the next five years and say whether their household's standard of living would improve or not, 44% (Keta) and 50% (Anlo) of respondents replied that they "don't know", 21% (Keta) and 21% (Anlo) "much worse, 19% (Keta) and 17% (Anlo) "much better", while 16% (Keta) and 12% (Anlo) responses showed that their household's standard of living would get a "little better (see Table 3.29). The responses seem to contradict the so-called Ghanaian optimism of everything being okay when the going is tough. The optimism may have waned because Ghanaians expected their lot to improve, which it never did, since independence.

Under conditions of economic hardship, one wonders what sorts of strategy Ghanaians use to meet their basic needs. When formal channels

Table 3.29: Household's Standard of Living Looking Ahead to the Next Five Years

Response	Keta Constituency Frequency	Keta Constituency Percentage %	Anlo Constituency Frequency	Anlo Constituency Percentage %
Much better	19	19	17	17
A little better	16	16	12	12
Much worse	21	21	21	21
Don't know	44	44	50	50
TOTAL	100	100	100	100

Source: Survey data

are insufficient to provide for necessities, people must search for alternative options; they may look to family members, other social contacts, seek help from the local community or civic organizations, petition, government officials or District Assembly. The relative use and availability of these different channels are important indicators of the extent of claim-making and the quality of institutional forms of intermediation.

The survey identified two types of claims, namely:

(a) claims for very personal help; and
(b) claims or more political (albeit local) action.

Claims for Very Personal Help

Those people who responded that they could not survive on their own household income were asked to list the three most important sources where they thought they might get help from. The three most important sources mentioned were family members 61% (Keta) and 60% (Anlo), neighbours 27% (Keta) and 24% (Anlo) and trade union 4% (Keta) and 7% (Anlo). Furthermore, when respondents were asked of all the alternative options of intermediation, which one would likely provide the most help, 71% (Keta) and 73% (Anlo) responded that family members were the most likely source of help. The survey thus confirms that family networks are important in Ghana, providing the most recourse in time of need. When family networks were unavailable or depleted, the next most common alternatives were trade union and friends.

In general, recourse to governmental institutions for assistance is low; for instance, a scant 4% of respondents looked to officials in some government office for help while only 2% indicated that they turned to Members of Parliament. The low recourse to Members of Parliament (MPs) by respondents for help seems to contradict the impression created by MPs that they had been inundated by demands from their constituents who sought help (mainly in the form of financial assistance) from them. In addition, the low response to state institutions shows the lack of confidence that respondents had in them since they believed that the institutions would not be able to advance their welfare.

In a nutshell, the responses have reinforced the view that Ghana is a kin-based society that in time of need relies principally on emergency assistance from relatives. Beyond this line of defence against need, Ghanaians seem somewhat more likely to rely on friends, neighbours and church members rather than on government or civil society organizations.

Claims for more Political (albeit local) Action

The survey probed citizen participation in political activities. Most political activity at local level, where the District Assemblies are the political and administrative authorities, takes place mostly on a face-to-face basis through oral communication and in parochial settings. When respondents were asked to list the three most effective ways of getting the District Assembly to take the necessary action if they were concerned with a problem that could be solved by the District Assembly, 51% (Keta) and 55% (Anlo) of respondents indicated contacting officials of the District Assembly itself, 38% (Keta) and 38% (Anlo) contacting representatives of the District Assembly while 9% of Keta respondents replied that they would write to the newspapers about the problem and 4% of Anlo respondents responded that they would contact friends about the problem (see Box 1).

The performance of the District Assemblies (DAs) since their inception in 1988 has been the subject of debate and controversy. While

Box 1: The most Effective way of getting the District Assembly to take the Necessary Action on a Problem in Order of Importance

1. Contacting officials of the District Assembly
2. Contacting representatives of the District Assembly
3. Contacting friends and neighbours about the problem
4. Writing to newspapers
5. Going through Member of Parliament
6. Joining together with others who were specially concerned
7. Through your church/religious organization
8. Going through a political party or political organization
9. Contacting other members of your ethnic group
10. Going through your trade union
11. Signing a petition
12. Taking part in a protest

Source: Survey data

officials of the erstwhile National Democratic Congress (NDC) had applauded the contributions of the DAs in the development of their communities, scholars like Ayee (1996, 1999; 2000a;b) and Crook and Manor (1998) have found their performance to be poor, particularly in the formulation and implementation of locally-oriented development policies.

As a follow-up to the existing studies, the survey asked respondents whether during the last five years they had had problems that could have been solved by the District Assemblies. Eighty nine percent (Keta) and 71% (Anlo) of respondents replied in the affirmative that they had had problems concerning issues like water, toilet, electricity, road network and credit facilities which they thought could be solved by the District Assemblies (DAs) while 11% (Keta) and 29% (Anlo) did not contact the DAs even though they had problems (such as water, toilet, electricity), which they thought could not be solved because of either the shoestring budgets of the DAs or their ineffectiveness.

Respondents who indicated that they had had problems that could be solved by the District Assembly (DA) were asked what result they got when they tried getting the District Assembly to take action on any problem. As many as 63% of respondents in the Anlo constituency responded that they did not try, while 62% in the Keta constituency said they were unsuccessful (see Table 3.30). Among the reasons identified by respondents as contributing to the low success of the DA are:

- Lack of concern about problems by the DA due to apathy on the part of officials;
- Lack of financial resources of the DA;
- Partisanship of the DA; and
- Lack of vision on the part of the DA members

The survey has, therefore, confirmed that most Ghanaians do not see the importance and relevance of the District Assemblies — a finding consistent with earlier studies on the performance of the District Assemblies — and yet inconsistent with the National Commission for Civic Education survey on the performance of District Assemblies undertaken in March 1997 which shows that "more than half the total number of respondents acknowledged the credible performance of the district assemblies" (NCCE, 1997: xv).

Table 3.30: Result from Efforts to get District Assembly to take Action on a Problem

Response	Keta Constituency Frequency	Percentage %	Anlo Constituency Frequency	Percentage %
Successful	7	7	9	9
Unsuccessful	62	62	23	23
Did not try	28	28	63	63
Don't know	3	3	5	5
TOTAL	100	100	100	100

Source: Survey data

Conclusion

This survey of the 2000 elections and presidential run-off in the Keta and Anlo constituencies is an effort to investigate citizens' voting behaviour, the relationship between social groups and voting patterns and factors (like ethnicity, symbolism, gender, religion, chieftaincy, local and national issues) that have influenced voter behaviour, perceptions and attitudes. Consequently, the survey was primarily oriented toward finding opinions on the following key issues:

- Did respondents in the two constituencies think that the 2000 elections and presidential run-off and indeed, those of 1996 were free and fair;
- Did the respondents have faith and trust in the democratic institutions and electoral process; and
- Were the respondents satisfied with the direction of the Ghanaian economy?

This survey has demonstrated a number of issues related to voter behaviour, attitude and perceptions as well as democratic consolidation. First, irrespective of prevailing political, social and economic conditions, some voters will cast their ballots not on issues but on traditional lines.

Even though voters in the two constituencies were not happy with the NDC government's handling of the economy, they voted overwhelmingly for the party. Second, the lack of internal democracy within the parties, particularly the NDC, had the tendency of springing up Independent Candidates, which can pose a serious threat to party stability and unity. Third, citizens' evaluation of the democratic institutions and practices as good is an important building block towards democratic consolidation. The perception of the majority of respondents that Ghana can be regarded as a democratic state is a healthy sign that Ghanaians are determined to hold on to democratic rule in spite of its imperfections and problems. This should be an eye-opener for future coup makers to think twice before they intervene in politics again.

REFERENCES

Ayee, J. R. A. (1996) "The Measurement of Decentralization: the Ghanaian Experience", *African Affairs*, Vol. 95, No. 378 (January): 31–50.

Ayee, J. R. A. (1999) "Decentralization and the Provision of Local Public Services in Ghana" in Karl Wohlmuth et. al. (eds.) *Good Governance and Economic Development*, African Development Perspective Yearbook 1997/98, Vol. 6: 459–478.

Ayee, J. R. A. (2000a) "Decentralization and Civil Society in Ghana: Lessons for the African Continent" in Thomas Scheidtweiler (ed.) *Human and Economic Development: The Importance of Civil Society and Subsidiarity*. Africa Publications Vol. III (KAAD, Bonn): 27–45.

Ayee, J. R. A. (2000b) "The State of Decentralization in Ghana", Consultancy report to the Canadian International Development Agency for its Governance Strategy Programme in Ghana, August–October 2000.

Crook, R. C. and Manor, J. (1998) *Democracy and Decentralization in South Asia and West Africa: Participation, Accountability and Performance* (Cambridge: Cambridge University Press).

Daily Graphic September 2000.

National Commission for Civic Education (NCCE) (1997) *An Assessment of the Performance of District Assemblies*, A study conducted by the Research Department of the National Commission for Civic Education (October).

Owusu, M. (1970) *Uses and Abuses of Political Power: A Case Study of Continuity and Change in the Politics of Ghana* (Chicago: Chicago University Press).

CHAPTER 4

Ayawaso West Wuogon and Kpone Katamanso Constituencies in the December 2000 Elections

E. GYIMAH-BOADI

Introduction

The Ayawaso West Wuogon Constituency (AWWC) and Kpone Katamanso Constituency (KKC) share some important similarities. They are both located in indigenous Ga areas and in the Greater Accra Region — administrative and commercial capital of Ghana. The parliamentary seats in both constituencies at the time of the December 2000 polls were held by the National Democratic Congress (NDC), the then ruling party. But they also have interesting differences: AWWC is urban and largely affluent; KKC is largely rural and poor. In addition, KKC was a relatively safe seat for the incumbent NDC (with a two-term lady MP as the incumbent), whereas the seat in AWW was controversially held by the NDC and the site of protracted but unresolved court litigation over the results of the 1996 legislative polls. While the NDC was able to retain its parliamentary seat in the December parliamentary elections in KK, it lost the AWWC seat to the to the NPP.

What do the elections and electioneering in the two constituencies tell us about the December 2000 elections and the factors that shaped its outcomes? What do we learn about Ghanaian politics and democratization process from an examination of election politics in the two constituencies?

Methodology

The analysis is largely based on primary and secondary data. The primary data include surveys conducted in the pre-election period (October 2000) and post election (January 2001) involving about 100 people in each of the two constituencies, and informal personal interviews with party candidates, party executives and selected residents.

In KKC, questionnaires were administered to 57 males and 47 females with a rural urban distribution of 60 and 40 respondents respectively in Pinkwai (16), Hebron (6), Tunmai (6), Appolonia (6), Bossah (7), Dengla (10), Akweitse-Gon (6), Onukpai-Abu (3), Katasonanka (24), Afieye (9), and Laaloi (11).

In AWWC, questionnaires were administered to 51 males and 50 females with a rural-urban distribution of 79 and 22 respondents respectively in Legon (21), Okponglo (20), Dzworwulu (20), Abelemkpe (20), and Airport Residential Area (20).

Profiles of the two Constituencies

AWWC is located in part of the Accra Metropolitan Assembly (AMA) area. It shares boundaries with the Ayawaso Central, Ga North, and Ledzokuku constituencies. KKC is located in the Tema Metropolitan Assembly area and is bordered by the constituencies of Tema West, Tema East, Ashaiman and a constituency in the Dangbe-East District. AWWC has 5 electoral areas — Okponglo, Legon, Roman Ridge, Dzorwulu and Abelemkpe electoral areas. KKC has as many as 12 electoral areas with almost 16,000 registered voters.

The Ayawaso West Wuogon constituency is also an indigenous Ga area, at least nominally. This is true in particular of Shaishie, Bawaleshie, Abotsiman, Mempeasem etc. There is however a typical Ewe settlement area at Abelemkpe where the Ewe population is believed to be around 80%. There is also a small group of Northerners at Abelemkpe and the presence of a large mosque in the community reflects this. The more developed parts of the constituency are inhabited by people of diverse ethnic backgrounds, though Akans seem to dominate.

The people of Kpone-Katamanso constituency are mainly Ga (mainly from Nungua) and Dangbe-speaking indigenes. People of other ethnic backgrounds are few and far between.

There are major differences between the socio-economic profiles of the two constituencies. Survey respondents in Ayawaso Wuogon clearly tended to be more educated than participants from Kpone Katamanso — 23.5% of respondents from Ayawaso Wuogon had University education compared to only 2.9% of people from Kpone Katamanso, while 21.4% of participants from Kpone Katamanso had no schooling, as opposed to only 4.9% from Ayawaso Wuogon. This disparity in education is also reflected in the occupations of survey participants, as those from Kpone Katamanso tended to hold occupations generally requiring less education. For example, 39.8% of respondents from Kpone Katamanso said they were farmers and another 18.4% identified themselves as traders, compared to 2.9% and 8.8% of respondents who identified themselves as such, respectively, from Ayawaso Wuogon. Meanwhile, 36.6% of respondents from Ayawaso Wuogon identified themselves as holding "other" occupations (those not listed in the pre-selected set of options) and another 17.6% said that they were professionals.

Ayawaso West Wuogon is classified by the Accra Metropolitan Assembly (AMA), as a super first class constituency. The Ayawaso West Wuogon has some of the plushest suburbs of Ghana (Dzorwulu and Abelemkpe, Airport Residential Area, Roman Ridge and East Legon.). AWWC is inhabited by some of the most affluent Ghanaians, though there also poor people living in the constituency. The occupational categories range from top notch professionals, technocrats, politicians and large traders to white-collar and construction workers as well as artisans.

The constituency boasts the nation's premier university, and some of the cream of the nation's secondary schools and primary schools. There is a long stretch of first and second-class roads and streets. It generally well endowed with public utilities. However, AWWC has a few pockets of slums, and the drainage network is poor, combining with other factors to make the constituency flood-prone. Moreover, there is a dearth of street lights, some of its roads are bad and it lacks public places of convenience and an open market.

By contrast, Kpone-Katamanso is generally rural and poor. It has no great educational institutions sited there. Its subdivisions are generally rural and peri-urban, though Kakasonka and Michel Camp Barracks are relatively urban and somewhat well-endowed with infrastructure. There are semi-urban houses in the electoral areas of Dengla, Laaloi and Afieye. There are no landmark infrastructures here.

The main economic activities commonly engaged in by the people of Kpone-Katamanso constituency are fishing, farming (tomato, pepper and tuber) and petty trading. During the dry season, the inhabitants here augment fishing and farming yields by breaking stones for construction workers and selling wood for fuel.

As in AWWC, most inhabitants of KKC describe themselves as Christians, but reverence for African Traditional Religion is relatively prominent in KKC. It was somewhat common to find especially the elderly clad in white apparel and decorated with traditional beads and designs on their bodies. The indigenous Ga areas of Ayawaso West Wuogon have local Ga Chiefs, but the presence of Chiefs is hardly felt in the cosmopolitan parts of the constituency. By contrast, given its relative homogeneity and rural socio-economic setting, the presence of traditional authorities is a lot more pronounced in Kpone-Katamanso. KKC also maintains strong cultural ties with the 12 royal clans of Nungua Traditional Area.

The Electoral Contest in AWWC and KKC

In 1992 and 1996, the elections in both constituencies had been won by the NDC. In 1992, the NDC won the presidential elections and parliamentary elections with the NPP boycotting the latter. In 1996 Rebecca Adotey was declared winner of the Ayawaso West Wuogon parliamentary election, to be unsuccessfully challenged in court for the next four years. The Katamanso parliamentary seat was held by a two-term NDC MP, Naa Afieye Ashong.

The elections in both constituencies were a two-way race between the ruling NDC and main opposition NPP. When respondents were asked: "which of the parties do you have an inclination towards?" Ayawaso Wuogon proved to be predominantly NPP supporters, as 30.4% of respondents favoured the party as compared to 15.7% who chose the NDC. But the opposite trend was observed in Kpone Katamanso: as 35% of respondents said that they had an inclination towards the NDC while only 16.5% claimed an inclination towards the NPP. The CPP registered only mild support the in two constituencies, as 7.8% of respondents from Kpone Katamanso claimed an inclination towards the party, as did 6.9% from Ayawaso Wuogon.

Similarly, when asked which party they would vote for, there was relative parity between the NDC and NPP: in Kpone Katamanso 37.9% of respondents said they would vote for the NDC and 30.1% chose the NPP, while in Ayawaso Wuogon 24.5% identified the NPP as their party of choice, compared to 16.7% who selected the NDC.

It did matter very much which party ticket a candidate was standing on. Ashong (NDC) is believed to have won because Kpone-Katamanso would vote for the NDC irrespective of who stood for or against the party. The recent death of her son earned her some voter sympathy, notwithstanding her lacklustre performance as an MP. But with the NDC and NPP enjoying some sort of parity in AWWC, other factors appeared to have been important. Amoo's struggles against the incumbent NDC appeared to have earned him considerable voter sympathy nationally and in AWWC.

Personalities appeared to have played key roles in the constituency elections. Indeed, analysts believe that Amoo (NPP) won the Ayawaso West Wuogon electoral because of the influence of J. A. Kufuor as well as the belief by some that he had been cheated in 1996.

Ayawaso West Wuogon is the home of many high-profile personalities such as J. A. Kufuor, presidential candidate of the NPP in 1996 and 2000, and NPP stalwarts such as Hon Nana Akuffo Addo-Shadow Attorney General, Hon. Kofi Apraku — Shadow Minister of Finance, Hon. Hackman Owusu Agyeman — Shadow Minister of Foreign Affairs, Dr Wayo Seini, first vice president of the party and B. A. Mensah, business tycoon. NDC strongmen in the constituency included ministers of state and NDC party leaders Mrs Cecilia Johnson and Mr Totobi Kwakye (chief of national security), as well as Eddy Palmer (Deputy Regional Chairman), Sheilk Ali Yemoh — executive member of Committee of Progressive Voluntary Organization and Nii Arma — chairman of the Legon branch of the Tertiary and Educational Institutions Network of the NDC.

The pro-NDC power brokers at Kpone-Katamanso included Nii Ama Ashietey — District Chief Executive for Tema Metropolitan Assembly (TMA), Alhaji E. A. Tetteh — Greater Accra Chairman of Ghana Private Road and Transport Union, traditional rulers such as the Chiefs of Gbetsile, Sebrepor, Mr Afari (a Greater Accra Region Best Farmer), Nii Adumuah II presiding member of Tema Municipal Assembly and an avowed NDC propagandist

Pro-NPP power brokers in KKC include Alhaji Tetteh Kwao (businessman and a royal, who built a mosque to assert his influence and was said to oppose the NDC because he contested for and lost the royal stool to an NDC supporting relative), traditional rulers such as the chief of Kpone and Appolonian, Solomon Appiah (businessman), W. N. Josiah (Secondary School teacher), D. Q. Annan (an agricultural economist, NPP parliamentary candidate in 1992 parliamentary election and presumed financier of the NPP campaign in the constituency) and George Noi (a respected local "rich man."

The main power broker for the CPP was its parliamentary candidate, Godfried Allan Lomotey whose popularity stemmed partly from the reputation he gained for assisting the youth in the constituency to gain employment when he was an employee of the multinational Lever Brothers in Tema. And the PNC's parliamentary candidate, Theophilus Tei Okunor was the party's biggest card (though many thought he was unlikely to fare better than the 138 votes he got in the whole constituency in 1996).

However, survey findings present mixed evidence on the dominance of personalities and power brokers in the electoral politics at constituency level. Respondents held divergent views on the question whether the "parties in Ghana projected personalities more than their policies." In Ayawaso Wuogon 46.1% of respondents said that they did, but only 18.4% from Kpone Katamanso agreed. An equal 46.1% of respondents from Ayawaso Wuogon said that the parties did not project personalities more than policies, and 33% of people from Kpone Katamanso held the same opinion.

Issues in Election 2000

Naturally local issues were important in the constituencies. But given the heterogeneous social and economic complexion of Ayawaso West Wuogon, different parts of the constituency espoused different concerns.

Inhabitants of Shiashie and Bawaleshie in particular, seemed most concerned about how they could make ends meet on a daily basis. In the undeveloped parts of Abelemkpe (a typical Ewe settlement area), residents complained that the area had not seen any developmental projects since 1992.

For residents of East Legon, the erratic supply of water was a major issue. Another issue was the frequent power outrages they experience. Some of them complained about the absence of street lights, a development, which they believe, creates fertile grounds for untoward activities.

A striking difference between the undeveloped and developed areas of the constituency was that the former saw food, jobs and better accommodation as the issues at stake in the elections, but the latter considered good governance, interest rates, currency depreciation etc. to be the most important issues.

Many in the constituency were critical of the NDC and spoke of neglect by the previous and incumbent MPs — Hon. Ken Dzirasah and

Hon. Rebecca Adotey, describing them as "self-seeking people" who had failed to use the District Common Fund to bring improvements. Supporters of the NDC, especially those resident in disadvantaged areas were also likely to believe that the NDC's choice of a new parliamentary candidate (a man who had lived among them for some time) was a clear indication that the NDC was concerned about their welfare. They were also likely to express the hope that things would get better and they would have easy access to healthcare and education if the NDC was given another chance.

The people of Kpone-Katamanso were mainly concerned with basic bread and butter issues: the rising cost of fertilizers, fishing gear, jobs, food and accommodation. However, a small group, especially in Kakasonanka and Michel Camp Barracks, considered the value of the cedi, the cost of building materials etc. to be the most important issues.

Many also complained about the bad state of the roads, many of which were impassable during the rainy season. They also found it worrying that a health post built by the Rotary Club of Tema and commissioned by the then President, J. J. Rawlings, was performing well below capacity (largely because of lack of accommodation facilities for health workers unwilling to live in Kpone).

Lack of electricity was also considered a major problem. With the exception of Kpone Township, Michel Camp, Sebrepor, Bethlehem, Mlitsakpo, Ataa Saki (all in the Kakasonanka electoral area) and Apollonia, which have power, largely generated with biogas, no other area of the constituency has electricity. Oyibi, which was connected to the national grid, fell into darkness after its transformer blew up eight months before the elections. In addition, the constituency lacked public places of convenience and sewerage systems, and about 80% of the constituency had no potable water.

And in some villages chieftaincy was a major issue. For instance, for some months before the election, the village of Mmnanman had been without a chief.

Nonetheless, people in both constituencies, especially Ayawaso Wuogon, appeared dissatisfied with the performance of their parliamentary representatives. When asked "Do you think your MP has represented you the way you expected him/her to over the past four years?" 50% from Kpone Katamanso said that their MP had lived up to their expectations but 34% admitted that he or she had not. In Ayawaso Wuogon the evaluation was much worse, as only 10% said that their MP had met expectations and a full 63% felt that he/she had not.

Negative Voter Perception of the Economy

Notwithstanding the different socio-economic profiles of the two constituencies, their ratings of economic conditions in the country were similar. Respondents from both constituencies gave the current state of the economy a negative rating. In Kpone Katamanso, 74.8% of respondents described the economy as "very bad" and another 14.6% called it "bad," while people in Ayawaso Wuogon were only slightly more generous: 55.9% categorized the economy as "very bad," 17.6% called it "bad" and, somewhat surprisingly, 16.7% categorized the economy as "good." Similarly, people from both constituencies generally seemed to believe that the economy had become worse in the past four years. In Kpone Katamanso, 61.2% of respondents said that the economy had "become worse" and 21.4% said that it had "sharply deteriorated." In Ayawaso Wuogon the evaluation was more scathing, as 16.7% of respondents said that the economy had "become worse" and a large percentage, 67.7%, claimed that it had "sharply deteriorated." However, in this constituency 13.7% of respondents claimed that the economy had "just improved" over the past four years.

When asked what they consider to be the major economic problem in Ghana today, the two constituencies showed both similarities and differences. In Kpone Katamanso, 41.7% of respondents cited inflation, which was named by only 14.7% of respondents from Ayawaso Wuogon. A significant portion of people from both constituencies saw unemployment as a major problem, as it was named by 36.9% of respondents from Kpone Katamanso and 35.3% of respondents from Ayawaso Wuogon. A large percentage of people from Ayawaso Wuogon (28.4%) also cited the depreciation of the cedi as the major economic problem, but not as many respondents from Kpone Katamanso (15.5%) saw this as the problem.

However, people seemed to be cautiously optimistic about their economic prospects. In Kpone Katamanso 55.3% of respondents said that they expect their household's standard of living to get "a little better" over the next five years, as did 35.5% from Ayawaso Wuogon. Also of note though, is that 20.4% of people from Kpone Katamanso said that they expected their standard of living to get "much worse," while nobody from Ayawaso Wuogon shared this expectation.

Candidate Profiles

The profiles of the candidates of the five political parties who contested the parliamentary elections in both constituencies were:

The NDC candidate for AWW — Elvis Afriyie Ankrah (resident in East Legon and working as a salesman) was born in Accra on 1 October 1967. He holds a BA degree from Legon, where he had been active in student politics as president of the Student Representative Council; George Isaac Amoo, the NPP candidate (a resident of Dzorwulu) was born in Accra on 21 April 1962. A contestant in the 1996 parliamentary election (which he lost to Rebecca Adotey of the NDC, and has been embroiled in court battles to claim that seat since 1996) he holds a certificate in agricultural extension from Legon and has been working as an agricultural development consultant; The NRP fielded Mary Elsie Yirenkyi (born in Kukurantumi in the Eastern Region on 26 October 1938) holder of a post-graduate degree and lecturer at the University of Ghana; while the CPP fielded Jane Chinebuah, an educationist born on 17 February 1950 who holds a university degree. The PNC put forward the youngest candidate and the one with the fewest credentials — Samuel Addy. He was born 22 May 1976 and is self-employed as a refrigeration mechanic.

The contestants in the KKC race were Naa Afienye Ashong, (NDC), native of Kpone, but born in Koforidua on 1 March 1940, and trained elementary school teacher (Cert A); Godfried Allan Lomotey (CPP), born in Koforidua, 2 January 1940, secondary school education, and private school operator; Tetteh Issac Akueteh (NRP), native of Kpong born 22 May 1953, secondary school education and a storekeeper in a food company; E. Amporng Agbozo (NPP), native of Kpone, but born (13 December 1936) in Dodowa, a graduate of the University of Ghana and a retired educationst.

The candidate profiles reveal some important aspects of recent Ghanaian elections; the average level of educational attainment of candidates was higher than the national average. Most candidates in the two constituencies had post secondary education.

The Media

The media appeared to have played a leading role in the December 2000 polls. A large majority of respondents from each constituency said they were inclined to follow the activities of the political parties in the news media. In Kpone Katamanso 73.8% of respondents said that they did so, as did a very substantial 92.2% of people from Ayawaso Wuogon. Only 5.9% of respondents from Ayawaso Wuogon said that they did not follow the parties' activities in the media, as did 26.2% from Kpone Katamanso.

People from both constituencies strongly relied on radio for political information. When asked "Which source have you found to be the most useful in deciding who to vote for in your constituency?" radio was cited by 70.9% of respondents from Kpone Katamanso and 49% from Ayawaso Wuogon. In the latter constituency 10.8% of respondents cited television and another 9.8% cited "friends and family (word of mouth)" as their most useful source, as did 6.8% from Kpone Katamanso. In terms of trust in the media, responses to the question "which source of media information do you trust most to tell the truth?" were mixed. In Kpone Katamanso 31.1% of respondents cited private radio, 21.4% named state-owned radio and 6.8% named state-owned newspapers. Meanwhile, in Ayawaso Wuogon a majority of respondents (52.9%) cited private radio as their most trusted source, while 12.4% cited state-owned television and 10.8% named private television.

Campaign Sponsorship

It was extremely difficult to get information on how the constituency election campaign was financed. Self-sponsorship appeared to have been important. Ankrah who apparently ran a well-heeled campaign claimed to have provided 35% of his campaign funds and received 40% from friends and sympathizers; Amoo claims to have provided 40% of his funds from his own resources and 55% from friends; and Mary Yirenkyi claims to have funded 90% of her campaign. However, the NDC candidates appeared to have received comparatively more logistical assistance from the party. Both Mr Ankrah and Mr Ashong admitted to receiving vehicles, "T" shirts and drinks from the party for campaign rallies. Ankrah reported receiving about 25% of his total sponsorship from the party, compared to 5% for Amoo.

At the same time, the NDC and NPP candidates appeared to have received considerable moral and political support from the national levels of their parties. At Ayawaso West Wuogon, the national NDC selected the leader for all NDC campaign activities, aided by party activists such as Ali

Yemo and Lee Ocran. In Ayawaso West Wuogon, the national NPP organized rallies and floats to shore up the image of their candidate.

Campaign Strategies and Messages

Candidates adopted a similar mixture of campaign strategies. Rallies were central to the campaign of some candidates. The NDC candidate remembers at least six of them. The NPP candidate in AWWC used mini-rallies, targetted particularly at the youth, to convey his message. In addition candidates held closed-door meetings with key organizations (women's groups, youth clubs, churches) in the constituency to canvass votes. Other campaign strategies included door-to-door visits, posting of posters displaying a portrait of the candidate and party colours and symbols.

Media coverage was also crucial. Enjoyment of airtime and space in some newspapers provided invaluable exposure for candidates. A Vibe FM radio programme for all the candidates of Ayawaso West Wuogon constituency provided a forum for them to present their plans of action to the electorate. Candidates in the Kpone-Katamanso constituency engaged in hot discussions on election 2000 by courtesy of Adom FM in Tema and other media.

Campaign messages were somehow similar with strong emphasis on making glowing, often baseless promises. Elvis Ankrah of the NDC promised the electorate hard work, consultation at all levels, consensus building and teamwork. He also promised to help provide toilet facilities, a market place, improve on the drainage system and provide street lights. The NPP's Amoo promised youth mobilization and mobilization of funding and resources from the government, AMA and other sources to develop the constituency. And Mary Yirenkyi of National Reform Party (Ayawaso West Wuogon) promised to bring development to the constituency.

But in heterogeneous AWWC, campaign message and tone were often modified to suit the pocket of the constituency being addressed. For instance, Ankrah promised jobs in deprived areas, promised to facilitate the publication of policy papers on national issues at the University of Ghana and promised to help the youth procure funds for economic ventures. And in a bid to excite the youth in the constituency, Amoo challenged them to aspire to reach to the top — citing his own success in rising out of ashes to become the owner of cars and a house and to have good business standing.

Constituency Party Organization

The degree of organization of the NDC and NPP in AWWC was roughly equal. Neither party maintained permanent offices in the constituency. Meetings were held in the house either of the parliamentary candidate or of one of the local party executives. Both the NDC and NPP maintained offices at Kpone (but not in the other areas of the constituency).

The NDC appeared to be much better organized in KKC where it appointed an executive held quite regular mini-rallies and had more logistics. NDC affiliated organizations such as the 31st December Women's Movement (DWM) were active in Ayawaso West Wuogon, semblances of the June 4 Movement and the DWM could also be found at Kpone-Katamanso.

The percentage of people making financial contributions to the parties was generally low: nobody in Kpone Katamanso said that they made such a contribution, and only 16% from Ayawaso Wuogon claimed to have done so.

Internal Party Democracy

The candidate selection process for the parliamentary seats in the two constituencies gives a good indication of the practice of internal democracy in the various parties. Four of the five candidates contesting in AWWC were nominated "unopposed" and the NDC candidate was only indirectly "elected."

The NPP candidate selection process was widely perceived to be democratic. The candidates were chosen after primaries involving an electoral college (comprising one representative per polling station within the constituency and eight executives). But the AWWC experience also underscored major shortcomings in the process. Both Alhaji Isaka Inusah and George Isaac Amoo had paid their fees to contest the primaries for the candidate to stand on the NPP ticket, but the party leadership pressured the former to stand down in favor of Amoo. The National Executive Council (made up of National Executive Committee, Council of Elders, all the ten Regional Chairmen, four other selected prominent members, all minority spokespersons, in parliament, ex-national executive members and ex-presidential candidates) played a central role in this decision. In recognition of Amoo's nationally famous legal battles to claim the parliamentary seat for the constituency occupied by Hon. Rebecca Adotey, he was treated as something of a sitting MP, giving him preference over other contestants. But that also underscored the limited influence the constituency exercised in the selection of candidates. It is also instructive to note that this nomination process triggered the dramatic and last minute resignation of Alhaji Inusah (a former campaign manager of the NPP flag bearer) from the party and his defection to the NDC — citing lack of internal democracy.

The candidate nomination process for running on National Democratic Congress ticket was even less democratic. The NDC candidates in the two constituencies were selected after a basketful of names had been collected in both constituencies. The party hierarchy appeared to have decided that there would be no primaries at constituency level where there was a sitting MP. And where there was no sitting MP or the incumbent voluntarily relinquished the seat (as Mrs Adotey decided to do), a committee was set up by the National Executive of the Party, was instructed to review nominations from Regional Executives (ostensibly after consultation at various levels, including the chiefs and elders of the area and the opinion leaders as well as the Tertiary Educational Institutions Network (TEIN) of the NDC). Elvis Ankrah was eventually selected to represent the party in the constituency after he and Desmond Baiden emerged successful from the screening by the National Executive,

Democratic selection of candidates was something of a moot issue for some of the smaller parties. They tended to have a thin membership base hence very few candidates to elect or select for the contest. The case of the NRP candidate is instructive. NRP executives simply persuaded Ms Yirenkyi to move from the Okaikoi North Constituency where she was contesting the primaries against two others to AWWC where she was selected unopposed.

There seems also to have been a strong "nativist" element in the candidate selection within the NDC and NPP in AWWC (and KKC). Not withstanding the cosmopolitan nature of AWWC, the two candidates claimed Ga ethnic origins.

Political Participation

Residents of both constituencies seem to be very politically active. Of those surveyed in Ayawaso Wuogon 92.2% claimed to have been attending political rallies in connection with the 2000 elections, while a smaller, but still substantial, percentage of people from Kpone Katamanso (57.3%) said they did so. When asked if they had voted in the 1996 Presidential and Parliamentary elections, 81.4% of respondents from Ayawaso Wuogon said "yes" and only 13.7% said they had not, while 93.2% of respondents from Kpone Katamanso said that they voted in 1996, and only 6.8% said that they had not. But voter participation was significantly lower in the 1998 District Assembly elections: 64.7% of respondents from Ayawaso Wuogon claimed *not* to have voted then, compared to 33.3% who had, while 84.5% of respondents from Kpone Katamanso said they voted, compared to only 15.5% who had not.

Indeed, no respondent in the two constituencies responded "no" to the question as to whether they were registered to vote. When asked if they would vote, only 89.3% of respondents from Kpone Katamanso said that they would and 79.4% from Ayawaso Wuogon said they planned to do so. Only 10.8% of respondents from the latter constituency said that they would not vote.

However, political party registration was not especially high. Only 36.9% of respondents in Kpone Katamanso and 11.8% in Ayawaso Wuogon said that they were registered with a particular party. In Kpone Katamanso 19.4% of respondents were registered with the NDC, 11.7% with the NPP and 5.8% with the NRP, while in Ayawaso Wuogon 7.8% were registered with the NDC and only 2% with the NPP.

Weak Party Development

There were significant distinctions in terms of what respondents felt was lacking from their party's organization in their constituency. People in Kpone Katamanso seemed rather disillusioned with their party: when asked "What do you think is lacking in your party's organization in your constituency?" 34% said that the party lacked "loyal and committed members," and 22% cited the absence of "active honest and dedicated leadership." In was a different story in Ayawaso Wuogon, as the 22% of respondents said that "adequate finance" was lacking, while only 8% cited "loyal and committed members" and another 8% chose "active honest and dedicates leadership." The exact same pattern was evident in both constituencies when respondents were asked what was lacking from their party's organization at the national level. This time 38% of respondents from Kpone Katamanso lamented the lack of "loyal and committed members" and 23% cited "active honest and dedicated leadership," while in Ayawaso Wuogon 27% cited the lack of "adequate finance."

Respondents evinced fairly strong support for state funding of political parties. A majority of respondents from Ayawaso Wuogon (57.8%) said that political parties should be funded by the state, as did 37.9% from Kpone Katamanso. Roughly the same percentage (35%) of people from Kpone Katamanso said that the parties should not be financed by the state, as did 33.3% from Ayawaso Wuogon.

Mixed Reviews of the Party System

People from both constituencies seemed to have mixed perceptions of party politics in Ghana. In Kpone Katamanso 32% of respondents said that party politics "has improved the quality of living of Ghanaians." More cynically, though, 28% said it "has enriched a few people" and another 15% chose the option "it is a dirty game." Meanwhile, though 21% of respondents from Ayawaso Wuogon said that party politics had "improved the quality of living of Ghanaians," 20% said that: "it had enriched a few people," another 20% said "it has brought division among Ghanaians" and 16% said "it is a dirty game."

However, they were moderately positive in their rating of the performance of political parties. A majority of respondents from each constituency, 51% from Kpone Katamanso and 58% from Ayawaso Wuogon, said that the parties "are doing a good job," and a further 22% from Kpone Katamanso and 19% from Ayawaso Wuogon said "they are doing a very good job." Nobody from Kpone Katamanso rated the parties negatively, and only 4% of respondents from Ayawaso Wuogon said "they are doing a bad job." Furthermore, people seemed optimistic that the party elected could make a difference at national level. When asked "Do you agree with the view that irrespective of the party in power, there is no difference to what happens at the national level?" 59% of respondents from Kpone Katamanso and 77% from Ayawaso Wuogon said "no," and only 8% and 12%, respectively, agreed with the statement.

Mixed Evaluation of the Electoral Process

In terms of evaluating the electoral process, there were significant discrepancies between the two constituencies. While 42.7% of respondents from

Kpone Katamanso and 45.1% from Ayawaso Wuogon responded in the affirmative when asked "Do you think conditions exist in Ghana for free and fair elections for the December 7, 2000 elections?" 42.2% of respondents from Ayawaso Wuogon said "no," but only 17.5% from Kpone Katamanso answered in the negative. A similar pattern was evident in responses to the question whether the 1996 elections had been free and fair: 39.8% of respondents from Kpone Katamanso and 40.2% from Ayawaso Wuogon said "yes," but a substantial 48% of respondents from Ayawaso Wuogon said "no," compared to only 17.5% of respondents from Kpone Katamanso.

People in Ayawaso Wuogon seemed to have a similarly pessimistic view of the activities of the Electoral Commission (EC). Almost half of respondents from the constituency (45.1%) said that the EC was not independent of government control, and only 32.4% of respondents said that it was. Both percentages were lower in Kpone Katamanso, as 11.7% of respondents said that the EC was independent of government control and 16.6% said that it was not.

However, respondents rated the degree of fairness of the election highly. In Kpone Katamanso 89% of respondents said that all parties had the chance to campaign freely, and 83% from Ayawaso Wuogon agreed. But more respondents felt that the parties did not have adequate logistics for campaigning. From Kpone Katamanso 32% said that the parties lacked adequate logistics, as did a majority of respondents from Ayawaso Wuogon (68%). There was a mixed verdict on whether there had been intimidation of party members and supporters during the campaign, as only 5% of respondents from Kpone Katamanso said that there was but 42% from Ayawaso Wuogon felt that intimidation had taken place. When asked which parties were responsible for intimidation, 36% of respondents from Ayawaso cited the NDC and only 4% named the NPP.

Mixed confidence in the electoral system is also reflected in the fact that respondents from both constituencies seemed altogether optimistic about the chances of an opposition party winning the presidential election: 45.6% of respondents from Kpone Katamanso rated the opposition parties' chances as "good" and another 13.6% said they were "very good," while 32.4% of respondents from Ayawaso Wuogon said their chances were "good," and 23.5% rated them as excellent. However, the same people also rated the chances of the Progressive Alliance winning the presidency highly, as 30.1% of respondents from Kpone Katamanso rated their chances as "very good" and 30.1% called them "good," while 26.5% of people from Ayawaso Wuogon called their chances "very good" and another 26.5% rated them as "good."

Somewhat surprisingly, most people from both constituencies failed to predict the presidential run-off that was necessitated by the inconclusive first round of voting. When asked "Do you think a second round presidential run-off is more likely in the 2000 elections than in the 1996 one?" only 10.7% of respondents from Kpone Katamanso and 28.4% from Ayawaso Wuogon said is was more likely, while 50.5% from Kpone Katamanso and 58.8% from Ayawaso Wuogon said that it was not.

Generally Positive Evaluation of the Democratic Process

Evidence from the pre-election survey gives a positive indication of growing public satisfaction with the actual performance of democracy in Ghana. Respondents in both constituencies had a largely negative take on their standard of living. In Kpone Katamanso 65% of respondents said that their household income was "not really enough to survive on," and 41.2% of respondents from Ayawaso Wuogon chose the same description. In that constituency an additional 31.4% of respondents said that their income was "only just enough to survive on," as did 25.2% from Kpone Katamanso. Only 4.9% of people from Kpone Katamanso said that their income was "enough for a fair standard of living," but 23.5% from Ayawaso Wuogon chose this description.

Nonetheless, people from both constituencies seemed to be relatively optimistic about the state of democracy in Ghana, though respondents in Ayawaso voiced greater satisfaction with the performance of Ghana's democratic institutions. When asked "Do you think Ghana today could be described as a democratic country?" 63.1% of respondents from Kpone Katamanso and 52.9% from Ayawaso Wuogon said "yes." Perhaps surprisingly, though, 41.2% of respondents from Ayawaso Wuogon said that Ghana today was not democratic, as opposed to only 27.2% from Kpone Katamanso. The responses to a closely related question, "Over the past four years has democracy improved in Ghana?" yielded the opposite trend, though, as 57.3% of respondents from Kpone Katamanso responded in the affirmative (31.1% said "no") and 72.5% of people from Ayawaso Wuogon said "yes" (while 23.5% said "no.")

Respondents from Ayawaso Wuogon also had a more positive take on the freedom enjoyed by political parties. When asked: "Do you think political parties and other associations have more freedom now than four years ago?" 81.4% of respondents from Ayawaso Wuogon said "yes," as did 68.9% of respondents from Kpone Katamanso. A greater percentage of people from Ayawaso Wuogon responded in the negative, as 14.7% answered "no," compared to only 5.8% from Kpone Katamanso.

However, residents of Ayawaso Wuogon also showed pessimism when asked "Do you think the party in power gets undue advantage over the parties in opposition when it comes to elections?" A full 73.5% of them said that the incumbent party did take undue advantage, and only 7.8% said that it did not. In Kpone Katamanso, though, only 40.8% of respondents said that the party in power took undue advantage, and 13.6% of respondents said that it did not.

Conclusions

The elections in the two constituencies significantly mirrored national trends and patterns. For instance, the smallness of the percentages of people who said that they voted on 7 December without a photo ID card (4% of respondents in Kpone Katamanso and 2% from Ayawaso Wuogon) was close to the national average of about 1%.

The election was a two-way race between the NDC and NPP. This is reflected in the findings of the post-election survey: 55% of respondents from Kpone Katamanso said that they voted for the NDC and 30% said they chose the NPP, while in Ayawaso Wuogon 60% said they voted for the NPP and 30% for the NDC in the presidential elections of 7 December. The parliamentary voting patterns broke down along the same lines, as 66% of respondents from Kpone Katamanso voted for the NDC candidate and only 26% chose the NPP competitor, while in Ayawaso Wuogon 56% chose the NPP candidate and 34% opted for the NDC candidate. And in the 28 December run-off, the same patterns were evident: 48% of respondents from Kpone Katamanso said that they voted for Mills and 30% opted for Kufuor, while in Ayawaso Wuogon 63% selected Kufuor compared to only 27% for Mills. The same findings also confirm the growing electoral strength of the NPP, especially in the urban areas.

Ethnicity may have been silent in this election, but it was salient. The emphasis on "nativism" in the selection of the NDC and NPP parliamentary candidates is but one indication. Another indicator is the type of music selected to advertise the presence of the candidate in the different subdivisions: Akan highlife songs for the cosmopolitan areas of AWWC, Ga or Ewe music in the Ga or Ewe enclaves of the same constituency. The NDC's popularity in the Ewe enclaves in AWWC seemed to have transcended the record of performance of the party or the incumbent NDC MP in the constituency. On the whole, linkage between support for party and performance/policies on one hand was weak, slogans, styles and personalities and avid tapping of ethnicity/ethnic mobilization of votes dominated the election and influenced voter preferences.

The elections also confirmed the growing competitiveness of elections in Ghana. The NPP and the NDC were quite evenly matched in this contest, at least in the AWWC. The NDC parliamentary candidate was highly articulate and personable. His campaign appeared to be well endowed as reflected in the prominence and ubiquity of his posters, as well as the lavishness of his campaign rallies. Amoo was less articulate, but was much better known because he had contested in 1996. Most importantly, he enjoyed widespread sympathy for what many regarded as ruling party manipulation of the legal system to keep the parliamentary seat. Moreover, candidates were able to campaign freely in all areas of the constituency and minor acts of electoral vandalism such as ripping off the posters of opponents in the two constituencies did not seem to enjoy official backing.

Finally, the elections in the two constituencies also confirm the democratic progress of Ghana. Voter turnout in the two constituencies was quite high. In the first round of elections, according to survey respondents, it was extremely high. A full 96% of respondents from Kpone Katamanso claimed to have voted on 7 December. Not far behind, 95% from Ayawaso Wuogon said that they voted. Turnout among respondents was lower in the 28 December run-off, though, as only 81% of respondents from Kpone Katamanso and 92% from Ayawaso Wuogon said that they had voted.

Confidence in the electoral system is also confirmed by post-election survey. It found that there seemed to be relatively few problems at the polling stations in either round of elections. Only 4% of respondents from Kpone Katamanso said that they had a problem on 7 December, as did 6% from Ayawaso Wuogon. No respondents from Kpone Katamanso reported problems at the polling stations on 28 December and only 5% from Ayawaso Wuogon had difficulties.

Furthermore, a large majority of respondents — 96% from Kpone Katamanso and 92% from Ayawaso Wuogon — characterized the 7 December vote as "orderly." A vast majority of survey participants thought that the elections had been "generally free and fair" — 96% of respondents from Kpone Katamanso and 94% from Ayawaso Wuogon. They also seemed to agree that election coverage by the state-owned print and electronic media had been adequate, as 92% of respondents from Kpone Katamanso said that it was, as did 75% from Ayawaso Wuogon. Furthermore, when asked: "was the coverage of the elections free and fair to all the parties and candidates?" 84% from Kpone Katamanso said "yes" and 75% from Ayawaso Wuogon also answered in the affirmative.

It is significant to note that the results of the national and constituency elections in December 2000 were readily accepted. Against the background of the disputes over the results of the 1992[1] and 1996[2] elections, this augurs well for Ghana's political progress[3].

REFERENCES

1. For details of the disputes surrounding the 1992 transition election, see, Richard Joseph and Clare Thomas, "The Ghanaian Elections of 1992", *African Affairs*, (92) 1993: 335–37; Mike Oquaye, "The Ghanaian Elections of 1992: A Dissenting View", *African Affairs* (92) 1995; E. Gyimah-Boadi, "Ghana's Uncertain Political Opening", *Journal of Democracy* (5) 1994: 75-86.
2. See E. Gyimah-Boadi, Ghana, the Challenges of Consolidating Democracy" in Richard Joseph (ed.) *State, Conflict, and Democracy in Africa* (Boulder: Lynne Rienner, 1999) 409–427; Joseph Ayee (ed.), *The 1996 General Elections and Democratic Consolidation in Ghana* (Accra: Department of Political Science, 1998).
3. For an analysis of the December 2000 elections, see Daniel Smith, *The Structural Underpinnings of Ghana's December 2000 Elections* (Accra: CDD Critical Perspectives, No. 6, February 2001) also E. Gyimah-Boadi, "A Peaceful Political Turnover in Ghana", *Journal of Democracy* (April) 2001 (12, 2): 103–117.

CHAPTER 5

Election 2000 in Ahanta West and Shama Constituencies and Democratic Consolidation in Ghana

KWESI JONAH

Introduction

This is a study of Ghana's election 2000 in Ahanta West and Shama Constituencies in Ghana's western region. The election is studied not as an independent or isolated political event or phenomenon but as an integral part of the process of democratic consolidation in Ghana. Rather than attempting bold broad strokes on the national political canvass, we have opted for a more limited surface of two rural constituencies for greater detail and attention.

Since 1992, when Ghana held its first democratic elections in nearly a quarter of a century, the country's democratization process has been making steady progress. In 1996, the country recorded a major political success when an incumbent president was democratically returned to power without violence. Then in December 2000, the country again added another colourful feather to its political cap when it staged an unprecedented transfer of power from a ruling to an opposition party peacefully smoothly and transparently. A bird's eye view of Ghana's contemporary political landscape points to the political success story of a country that is gradually taking slow but firm, confident steps towards democracy.

Main Argument

The main argument of this paper therefore, is that Ghana's nascent experiment in democratic politics is slowly but surely becoming consolidated because of the peaceful conditions in which the elections were conducted, increasing voter rationality, a very high and growing challenger quality and the progressive growth and development of a democratic political culture which enhances the capacity of the citizens to evaluate the institutions of Ghana's political system and economy.

Thrust of Recent Studies

The study of democratization in general and democratic consolidation in particular (consolidology) has in recent years engaged the full-scale attention of scholars to the extent of ignoring many aspects of election studies. To begin with, there is the general survey of the progress and problems of democracy in various regions of the world. In some regions, such as East Asia, studies have captured a "democracy boom" which is most welcome news.[1] In other regions, such as the Arab world, titles such as "illusions of change"[2] a "record of failure"[3] are sufficiently indicative of the story of doom and gloom that the contemporary wave of democratization faces in those parts of the world. In Russia, Shevtsova[4] has perceptively observed the blatant institutionalization of "electoral autocracy" rather than democracy. Mcfaul[5] sounds even more pessimistic. For him, democracy in Russia is something of a political waltz. For every forward step taken, two are taken backwards.

Viewed against a general global trend of democratic pessimism, the frustrations expressed about Africa's democratization process is not surprising.[6] The critical issue then is the extent to which African countries have gone in their quest to consolidate democracy and how they are getting there.

This survey represents a modest attempt to examine this but only at the level of two small rural constituencies.

Democratic Consolidation

The consolidation of democracy refers to how stable and deeply rooted democracy in a particular country has become. When democracy is so firmly planted in the political soil of a country that a return to the past authoritarian politics is rendered politically unfeasible, then democracy can be said to be consolidated. Diamond[7] has reckoned that the stage of democratic consolidation is considered to have been reached when major sections of the political public, the political elites, parties and organizations as well as the vast majority of the masses are firmly committed to the democratic constitutional system and regularly comply with its rules and constraints.

Diamond[8] has gone further to draw a useful distinction between electoral democracy and liberal democracy. Electoral democracy successfully institutionalizes electoral competition for power while liberal democracy goes the extra mile by bringing to the citizenry basic civil liberties, the rule of law under which citizens enjoy equal treatment before the law, an independent judiciary and other institutions of horizontal accountability that check the abuse of power, an open and pluralistic society and civilian control of the military.

Democratic consolidation in this sense would imply not only abandoning the authoritarian political system in favour of electoral democracy, but also moving on to liberal democracy and preventing authoritarian regression.

Schedler[9] makes a positive contribution by separating negative notions of democratization from the positive. Negative motions refer to those studies whose primary focus is on how to stabilize democracy by avoiding regression to non-democratic or semi-democratic regimes. Positive notions concern themselves with the business of moving on to some higher quality democracy.

Central to Schedler's two notions of democratic consolidation is a four-stage democratic progression from authoritarianism through electoral democracy to liberal democracy before terminating at advanced democracy where the majority of western developed countries today find themselves.

Most African countries, whether they are striving to move their democracy forward or struggling to avoid the fate of democratic breakdown or erosion, have not gone beyond the very first but important step of electoral democracy. Liberal democracy is still a long distance away and advanced democracy but a dream.

Conceptual Basis

Critical to the process of democratic consolidation is the commitment of the citizenry to the values of democracy and to the democratic institutions of their society. Without the capacity to undertake a rational evaluation of democratic institutions such a commitment will be hard to achieve. Accordingly importance is attached to the concept of voter rationality. In election studies in the Western countries the rational voter hypothesis is one of the fundamental theories of public choice. According to Darren

Grant[10] the rational voter hypothesis states that citizens weigh the costs and benefits when deciding whether or not to vote and whom to vote for.

In western social science, the rational voter hypothesis which sometimes, appears in the guise of tactical voting[11] has several implications, including voter turnout. The implication is that the voter calculates the possibility of electing the preferred candidate and probability of being the deciding vote. As used in this context however it refers to the capacity of the voters to undertake a full evaluation of democratic institutions, candidate policies and their economy before casting their votes. To the concept of rational voter there is a corresponding rational tactical party which is extremely calculating in its campaign and campaign spending in order to achieve the best results possible.

Closely related to the concept of voter rationality is the evaluative orientation by the citizens of a democracy. Democratic political culture presupposes a citizenry that is highly capable of evaluating democratic institutions leaders and policies. Borrowed from the old studies of political culture, the evaluative orientation, if developed, gives rise to a participant political culture, which is highly conducive to the growth and institutionalization of democracy. In a participant political culture citizens have both a very high evaluative orientation and the confidence that they can influence their leaders institutions and policies.

Finally, of vital importance to the election 2000 is the concept of challenger quality, according to which, election outcomes, to a large extent, hinge on the performance of the challenger.[12] The concept states that challengers who raise adequate funds and run good campaigns do much better against incumbents than their less organized and under-funded counterparts. Challenger quality is the function of two variables, challenger profile or prominence of the challenger in the eyes of the voter and campaign skills. The humiliating defeat which NDC incumbent MPs outside the Volta Region suffered in the last election argues for an examination of challenger quality even if on a tentative and rudimentary basis.

Survey Method and Sampling Technique

The central tool in this survey was the structured questionnaire which was administered in October 2000 and after the presidential run-off on 28 December 2000. The structured questionnaire was supplemented with free-flowing interviews in which detailed notes were taken. Interviewees were selected on the basis óf a simple random sample in which every fifth household on principal street or streets was selected with an eye to gender balance. Subject to the objective of achieving some gender balance the first adult encountered in a household was selected for interview. Towns and villages in the constituencies however, were selected not randomly, but in such a way as to achieve a good balance between urban and rural representation.

What is "New" in this Study?

A similar study of the 1996 elections in the same constituencies produced interesting findings.[13] It turned out in that study that:

(i) the politics of Ahanta West and Shama is basically the politics of the farmer-teacher-trader-businessman, with a low educational level and income.
(ii) In the perception of respondents people voted for Jerry John Rawlings because of the quality of his leadership rather than the benefits from his economic and social policies.
(iii) the degree of political interest among the voters of Ahanta West and Shama was high and the degree of political participation quite widespread.
(iv) People had a very high sense of their own political efficacy, in that their vote could make a difference.
(v) The two constituencies were split between the NDC and NPP. The NDC won in Shama and the NPP in Ahanta West.

This study is "new" for a number of reasons. First, while the voters of Ahanta West remain virtually unchanged in terms of their nature or character and political behaviour there is a new dimension. They stand out in this study as predominantly a non-wage, self-employed population of farmers/fishermen artisans and traders with a low educational attainment and income.

Second, and more important, is the position and role of Jerry John Rawlings whose long duration in Ghana's recent politics combined with his charismatic and controversial personality made him a central factor in the explanation of electoral outcomes. In the 2000 elections Rawlings was not a candidate in the elections and his influence on its outcomes doubtful. He therefore does not feature in this study.

Third, an interesting finding in the study of the 2000 elections is that the political interest and participation of voters is still high as in 1996. However these are uneven and skewed in favour of some political activities such as voting rather than attending political rallies, registering as members of political parties or financing political parties. Even more important they are not manifest in any strong desire to seek party office or election to Parliament.

Fourth, the voters have become very rational in the sense of an increasing capacity to undertake a critical evaluation of their political institutions, the economy and policies. In some cases, however, this evaluation is characterized by uncertainty and even wide differences between respondents in Ahanta West and Shama.

Fifth, in the specific context of Shama there has been a remarkable improvement in challenger quality. This is evident in the fact that Angelina Baiden-Amissah, the NPP candidate was able to improve upon her campaign and beat her old rival, Dornu-Nartey of the NDC. In addition to this a new challenge emerged in the person of Miss Emelia Arthur (NRP) a charming and charismatic politician who made the parliamentary elections a very close fight.

Sixth, in the 2000 elections Shama an NDC stronghold fell to the NPP bringing both Ahanta West and Shama into the fold of Western region constituencies controlled by the NPP.

Voter Profile and Political Participation

It was considered important in a survey of this nature to determine the socio-economic profile of the voters who constituted the principal subject of the study. An analysis of the data turned up by both the pre-and post-election surveys revealed that the voters in these two rural constituencies along the coast of Ghana's Western Region are:

(a) relatively young and predominantly male Christians who are
(b) a primarily non-wage earning self-employed population of farmers/fishermen traders and artisans, of
(c) low educational level (mostly primary school) and consequently of:
(d) lower income, 62% of whom receive not more the ¢200,000 per month while 18.5% have no income whatsoever.[14]

A critical look at the political characteristics of these respondents gives grounds to believe that there exists in Ahanta West and Shama a body of voters capable of providing the appropriate human resource base for the process of democratic consolidation in Ghana. The data suggest a voting population with a very high degree of political participation, though there is room for improvement. Political participation was very high in some political activities and not so high and even low in others.

The survey results show that in these two constituencies political participation was highly uneven and even skewed into particular political activities. Primarily it takes the form of a very high propensity to exercise one's franchise in district, parliamentary and presidential elections. It does not take the form of mass registration for party membership or affiliation or high attendance at political rallies and financial contribution to political parties. Participants did not demonstrate a very high political propensity to join political parties or to attend rallies or party congresses.

It should not be surprising that only a few people reported taking party executive positions or even vying for the parliamentary tickets of their parties. At any one time only a few people can undertake this kind of political activity. It is therefore not a good index of popular participation in politics.

Evaluative Orientation

Equally important for the process of democratic consolidation is the evaluative orientation of the citizen. The citizen's evaluative orientation is the capacity to evaluate the performance of political institutions and their policies. It is different from affective orientation which is the citizen's emotional attachment to the political system and its institutions. It is also different from cognitive orientation, which is the recognition of the existence and role of political institutions. A sharpened evaluative orientation is good for democratic consolidation and citizens of a democratic state should be capable of a critical assessment of the performance of political institutions and their policies.

The capacity of the Ghanaian voter to subject to critical evaluation the political and economic institutions and policies of the state was put to the test in a number of survey questions. The questions related to the state of the economy, the growth of democracy in general and of the freedom of the press and association in particular. The responses strongly indicate the Ghanaian voter's ability to evaluate the state of the economy, which affects the daily lives of the people as well as the growth of democracy and basic freedoms of the press and association.

Citizens' judgment like citizens' political participation is skewed and uneven. On the state of the economy citizens' evaluation is fairly accurate and supported by reported indicators and there is a reasonable degree of agreement between the two constituencies. On political issues however there is disagreement between constituencies and an element of uncertainty as more people tended to tick an "I don't know" answer.

On the state of the economy around the time of election 2000, 76% of respondents in Ahanta West and 100% in Shama rated the economy as bad or very bad. About 64% in Ahanta West and 90% in Shama stated that over the past four years the Ghanaian economy had become worse. Even more revealing 81% of respondents in Ahanta West indicated that their household standard of living had become worse since last election. In the Shama Constituency 82% said their standard of living had become much worse within the same period.

On the growth of democracy in Ghana there was no disagreement or uncertainty as the majority of respondents in both constituencies admitted that Ghana could be called a democratic state. There was also no disagreement and uncertainty about the growth of freedom of association as the majority in the two constituencies agreed that freedom of association had improved over the past four-year period.

On the question whether democracy had improved during the last four-year term of the Rawlings government there was disagreement and uncertainty. About 58% of respondents in Ahanta West said there had been improvement but 33% said they did not know. In the Shama Constituency 45% said there had been improvement but 49% said they did not know.

The same disagreement was noticeable in responses to the question on press freedom. While 71% of respondents in Ahanta West said press freedom had improved since last election only 37% in Shama thought so.

Evaluation of Political Parties

Questions were posed in the pre-election survey to test the chances of the political parties in the December 2000 elections. More often the respondents of Ahanta West were proved correct by the election results. They gave the opposition parties 48% chance of coming to power and the NDC and its allies only 40%. Surprisingly, however, they could not predict the run-off. Most Ahanta respondents stated that there would be no run-off. Shama respondents gave the opposition parties 28% and the NDC and its allies 72% chance of winning the elections. A run-off was obviously out of the question.

One or two questions were posed about some of the strengths and weaknesses of political parties. The first was about whether political parties projected personalities rather than policies. Whereas the majority in Ahanta West said they did not know, the majority in Shama affirmed that political parties project personalities rather than policies. Further, only 42% of respondents in Ahanta West and 23% in Shama said parties were financially sound, but 48% of Ahanta West voters and 85% in Shama would not agree to state funding for parties.

Two further questions were designed to test respondents evaluation of internal democracy of political parties. Voters were asked whether they liked the candidates selected by their parties to stand election in their constituency. The overwhelming majority in both constituencies answered in the affirmative. In addition 53% in Ahanta West and 70% in Shama were convinced that the process of selection of parliamentary candidates to stand for the parties was democratic.

Evaluation of the Legislature

Very few people in the two constituencies thought highly of their legislative representatives. Between 13% and 35% of those interviewed thought that their M.Ps had represented them the way they expected. This however should not be construed to be a general reflection on legislators in Ghana. The M.P for Ahanta West Mr Samuel King Kwofie is a man of frail health who spent much of his Parliamentary term seeking medical treatment rather than representing his people. Mr Richard Dornu-Nortey on the other hand was caught between his heavy schedule as Deputy Minister for Lands and Natural Resources and his commitments as his people's representative. Naturally therefore contact between the M.P,s and their constituents was low and usually through meetings and rallies in Shama and personal contact in Ahanta West.

The Election

The results of the Parliamentary Presidential and Presidential run-off elections in both Ahanta West and Shama indicated that the NPP handed the NDC a humiliating defeat. In Ahanta West, John Agyekum Kufuor the NPP candidate obtained 17,172 votes against the 7,749 obtained by John Atta Mills the NDC candidate. In the Presidential run-off however the results were John Agyekum Kufuor 19,485 votes and Atta Mills 5,655 votes. In Ahanta West therefore the NPP candidate did not need the votes of the minor opposition parties to win the run-off. The 2313 votes Kufuor gained in the run-off was roughly equivalent to the 2,094 votes lost by Atta Mills in the run-off.

In the parliamentary elections Samuel Johnfia the NPP candidate of Ahanta West collected 16,478 votes, more than double the votes of Sylvester Cudjoe the NDC candidate who obtained 8107. The NPP candidate obtained approximately 60% of the 27,038 valid votes counted. This is not surprising since Ahanta West together with Sekondi, Takoradi and Effia-Kwesimintsim constituencies have always constituted the NPP strongholds of the Western Region. The surprise was in Shama constituency where the NDC had always won. Ahanta West also retained an important feature of elections there in that the winning Presidential candidate polled more votes than the parliamentary candidate.

In Shama, a traditional NDC stronghold things turned out differently in 2000. The NDC presidential candidate Atta Mills could poll only 8,304 votes, approximately two-thirds of the 12,184 obtained by John Agyekum Kufuor the NPP candidate. In the run-off almost all the votes gained by John Kufuor came from the minor opposition parties. Atta Mills lost only 881 votes but Kufuor gained more than 2,140 votes in the run-off. This is in sharp contrast to the situation in Ahanta West where Kufuor drew almost all the additional votes he gained in the run-off from the NDC candidate, Atta-Mills.

In the parliamentary elections the NPP for the first time since the 1992 elections captured the seat. Angelina Baiden-Amissah, the NPP candidate obtained 8,284 votes as against 6,998 by the NDC candidate, R. Dornu-Nartey and 6,498 by Emelia Arthur the National Reform Party candidate. Contrary to the popular belief that the NRP candidate Emelia Arthur was the principal cause of the NDC's defeat, the NRP candidate was more of a threat to the NPP than to the NDC. The difference between the votes polled by R. D. Nartey, NDC parliamentary candidate and those of Atta Mills, NDC Presidential candidate was less than 1,500. On the other hand the gap between Angelina Baiden Amissah (NPP) and her Presidential candidate was nearly 4,000 votes. The trouble is Angelina Baiden Amissah (NPP) and Emelia Arthur (NRP) had more or less the same appeal for the electorate and the election was perceived as more of a contest between them. Both were articulate female university graduates with equal physical attractions, though age and youthfulness were more on the side of Emelia Arthur, while political experience favoured Mrs Baiden-Amissah.

Table 5.1: Parliamentary Election Results in Ahanta West and Shama Constituencies – December 2000

Ahanta West		Shama	
S. Johnfia NPP	16,478	Angelina B. Amissah	8,284
S. K. Cudjoe NDC	8,107	R.D. Nartey NDC	6,998
J. K. A. Mensah CPP	1,358	Emelia Arthur NPP	6,498
J. K. Arthur PNC	509	S. Atta Panyin Anaman CPP	576
Eva Parker NRP	416		
J. J. Amoah UGM	170	TOTAL	22,356
TOTAL	27,038		

Source: EC. 2001, Accra

Profile of Parliamentary Candidates

Most candidates in the 2000 parliamentary elections in Ahanata West were very respected people in their communities. In Ahanta West the NPP candidate Mr Samuel Johnfia, a graduate of the University of Ghana has been working with the Ahanta Rural Bank for many years. The perception in Ahanta is that he had been very instrumental in getting a lot of people small loans for their businesses. Mr Sylvester Cudjoe the NDC candidate who died soon after the elections was also quite a respectable gentleman known in the Ahanta area as an accountant at the Headquarters

Table 5.2: Presidential Election Results in Ahanta West and Shama Constituencies — December 2000

	Ahanta West	Shama
J. A. Kufuor NPP	17,172	12,189
J. E. A. Mills NDC	7,749	8,304
G. P. Hagan CPP	1,107	271
G. Tandoh NRP	261	783
D. Lartey GCPP	249	187
É. N. Mahama PNC	191	94
G. W. Brobey UGM	96	48
TOTAL	26,818	21,876

Source: EC, 2001 Accra

Table 5.3: Result of Run-Off Presidential Elections — December 2000

	Ahanta West	Shama
J.A. Kufuor NPP	19,485	14,324
J. E. A Mills NDC	5,655	7,432
TOTAL	25,506	22,136

Source: EC. 2001, Accra

of the Ghana Private Road Transport Union (PRTU) in the Hall of Trades Union, Accra.

Mr John Argo Mensah, the CPP candidate is well known as the proprietor of Kimball Preparatory School at Agona Junction, the District Capital. Many parents who have lost confidence in the public school system have enrolled their children at Kimball. Mr Joseph Arthur is one of the very few Ahanta graduates and since his graduation from Cape Coast University in the mid 1970's has been teaching in Secondary Schools in or around the Ahanta District. He is currently teaching Economics at St. Mary's Secondary Schools, Apowa. He has the other advantage of being a royal from the Upper Dixcove Royal Family. Miss Eva Parker NRP candidate is a retired educationist who until five years ago worked in the District Education Office at Agona Junction, the district capital.

Parliamentary candidates of Shama had an equally high profile. Angelina Baiden Amissah a graduate of the University College of Education, Winneba is the assistant head of Kinbu Secondary Technical School in Accra. Mr Richard Dornu-Nartey the (NDC incumbent MP) a graduate of the University of Ghana was a civil servant until he entered politics and became the Deputy Minister of Lands and Natural Resources.

Miss Emelia Arthur a graduate of the Kwame Nkrumah University of Science and Technology (KNUST) studied Estate Management and currently works with the Volunteer Services Organization, (VSO) a British NGO. She worked with the Centre for Development of People (CEDEP) in Kumasi as a Consultant for a while.

Mr Samuel Atta Panyin Anaman who was educated at Asuansi Technical Institute, and Accra Polytechnic is currently a JSS teacher at Konfueku in the Shama constituency.

Organization of the Election

The study of the organization of the election focused on two key aspects. The first relates to peaceful conditions for the campaign period, which were investigated with police assistance. The second is voter perception of the organization of the election. In the Ahanta West constituency the two main police stations at Dixcove and Agona Junction were visited for investigations about the degree of peace that prevailed during the campaign period but specifically in October 2000 and January 2001.

All police officers interviewed confirmed that the election campaign on the whole had been peaceful in the constituency. The peaceful election campaign in the constituency was the product of effective collaboration between stakeholders especially the parties and voters and the security agencies. To ensure peace the political parties in collaboration with the District Police command organized a march for peaceful elections during the second week of October 2000.

The joint effort for a peaceful election was so successful that very few violent incidents were recorded. The first incident involved some suspected West African aliens, mainly from Mali and Niger who attempted to obtain photo IDs for voting. They were violently stopped by several Ghanaian citizens. According to the police, though the incident was widely reported on GTV no formal complaint was lodged at the police station.

The second incident occurred at Akentenchie an Ahanta village where a man who saw an NDC poster on his window promptly tore it off. Though the constituency executives of the NDC reported the case to the police the two parties opted for an amicable settlement before police investigations began.

The Shama constituency election campaign 2000 was equally calm and peaceful. Police Officers interviewed at Shama, Inchaban and Beposo, however, attributed the peace to the late start of campaigns. By October 2000 election campaign was still low key.

The views of constituents were solicited to reinforce information provided by the police. In both Ahanta West and Shama people perceived the election 2000 as free, fair transparent and orderly. The election, according to respondents was also well endowed with police security. Respondents gave the Electoral Commission a pat on the back for issuing photo ID to voters and awarded the media high marks for their excellent coverage. As a consequence of the vigilance and commitment of all stakeholders violation of electoral rules was kept to the minimum.

A large number of voters, between 84% and 94% in both constituencies, believed that all parties had the chance to campaign freely in the election 2000. There was however disagreement over the presence of intimidation in the election and equality of access of all parties to logistical support in the form of campaign vans and loudspeakers. In Ahanta West respondents were divided about the equality of access of parties to logistics while in Shama the majority stated that access was highly unequal.

Issues in the Elections

Respondents were asked to indicate what they considered to be the crucial national development issues and the most pressing development needs in their constituency. The responses revealed sharp differences in the perception of people in the two constituencies.

Respondents in Ahanta West pin-pointed employment, the high cost of education and the refund of poverty alleviation fund as the three key national issues. In Shama respondents chose education, poor salaries and high hospital fees. The top priority constituency needs that came up were electricity, employment and KVIP toilet for Ahanta West and public toilet facilities and education for Shama. There is an overwhelming consensus among respondents that electoral choices are influenced by a combination of both national and local issues rather than of either of them separately.

Why the NPP Defeated the NDC

In Ahanta West and Shama five sets of factors combined to help the NPP defeat the NDC in the parliamentary and Presidential elections of December 2000. There were:

- Personal Factors
- Local Factors
- Effective campaign financing
- National economic conditions
- General cry for Political change

Personal Factors

In the Ahanta West Constituency one personal factor that worked to the advantage of the NPP but undermined NDC efforts was the change from the incumbent NPP M.P, the ailing S. K. Kwofie, a mathematics teacher to a relatively young rural Banker of robust health. Johnfia was perceived as someone who had assisted a lot of people in the constituency to gain access to credit facilities at Ahantaman Rural Bank at Agona Junction, the district capital.

The second personal factor was the active personal involvement of the widely respected lawyer and M.P for Sekondi, Paapa Owusu Ankomah in the NPP campaigns in the Ahanta West constituency. Paapa Owusu Ankomah is very highly respected in the Ghana Parliament, Sekondi, his home town Dixcove and Ahantaland as a whole as a "very nice gentleman". Though he was contesting again in Sekondi constituency, his victory there was a foregone conclusion. He therefore placed his personal reputation and resources at the service of his party in Ahanta West where he comes from. In the end the political dividends were good.

In their search for a suitable parliamentary candidate for Ahanta, the NDC unfortunately jumped from the frying pan into the fire. For the 2000 parliamentary elections the NDC selected Sylvester Cudjoe instead of Fynn (NDC MP for 1993–96) who flopped hopelessly in the 1996 elections for lack of rapport and goodwill among even his own NDC members and supporters. Cudjoe, a trade union accountant, was kind and generous but inarticulate and suffered from incurable stage fright which affected his campaign negatively.

Whereas the NPP candidate had a positive push from a popular politician the MP for Sekondi, the NDC candidate drew support from the District Chief Executive (DCE) whose contribution to his campaign was doubtful and ineffective. After serving two terms the DCE was widely blamed for lack of development in the district. The main critics of the DCE were NDC members and supporters.

In the Shama constituency personal factors were equally important in the NPP victory and NDC defeat. The key player in the election was Mr Richard Dornu-Nartey the NDC MP and very busy as Deputy Minister for Lands and Natural Resources. With their MP in such a high profile position the constituents had a high expectation of seeing visible signs of development in their towns and villages. To their disappointment they saw little or nothing. Even worse, NDC members and executives complained that it became increasingly difficult to see their MP. In their frustration they decided to vote for Emelia Arthur, the parliamentary candidate of the National Reform Party that split from NDC and the NDC presidential candidate Atta Mills.

Above all, the NDC candidate was perceived by many Shama voters as a politician with a very low personal identification with the constituency. Many complained that he had not been known in the constituency before he contested elections in 1992. Therefore, serving them two terms in Parliament was more than enough for him and the time for change had come.

Angelina Baiden-Amissah, the NPP candidate for Shama who won, was the exact opposite of Dornu Nortey. A graduate teacher and assistant head of Kinbu Secondary Technical School in Accra, she had more time especially during vacation to visit her constituency and supporters regularly and identify with them. She maintained her membership of the Catholic Church Choir at Shama. Though born of an immigrant family she was perceived as more indigenous than the indigenes.

The personal factors at play in Shama's election 2000 became even more complicated when a charming and charismatic young woman, Emelia Arthur, registered as a candidate for NRP. With a unique electoral strategy she split the potential NDC vote down the middle and shared the political marks for feminine charm equally with the NPP candidate.

Local Factors

Ahanta West and Shama are coastal constituencies with fishing as their major occupations. The difficulties of the fishing industry therefore became a local factor influencing electoral outcomes. The biggest problem facing the industry was the high cost of fishing inputs and acute shortage in the election year of pre-mix fuel for the outboard motors used for fishing. The price of fishing nets twine, cork, lead and outboard motors had skyrocketed because of the depreciation of the cedis against the dollar. Fuel prices were high and the commodity unavailable. To make matters worse political disturbances in the neighbouring Ivory Coast resulted in a huge influx of Ghanaian immigrant fishermen a few months before Ghana's election 2000. A major political problem had appeared: too many fishermen but little or no fuel for fishing. The fishermen knew too well whom to blame; the NDC government that was seeking their mandate and they thought it did not deserve this mandate, because of the many difficulties they were facing in their occupation.

Effective Campaign Financing

In terms of campaign financing the NDC MPs of Ahanta West and Shama started off from a big disadvantage. Richard Dornu-Nartey was perceived in the Shama constituency as a rich Deputy Minister of Lands and Natural Resources with access to unlimited campaign funds. In the Ahanta constituency Sylvester Cudjoe actually won the NDC ticket on the basis of his reputation for financial generosity. Their supporters, therefore expected them to bear all by themselves virtually the entire cost of the campaign. Mr Dornu-Nartey could not bear this burden and became alienated from some of his supporters members and executives of his party. Sylvester Cudjoe borrowed heavily and overstretched himself financially. The result was a huge debt burden and suspected suicide three months after the election. Apparently he had dissipated his financial resources on huge handouts to local influential elites such as chiefs rather than on effective campaigning. The chiefs could not deliver the votes of their people to the NDC.

The two NPP Parliamentary candidates in Ahanta West and Shama started their campaigns with a greater understanding and sympathy for their limited financial means on the part of their supporters. Angelina Baiden Amissah a Secondary School teacher and Samuel Johnfia a rural banker did not need to convince their supporters of their limited means. The supporters knew that too well. The NPP candidates in Ahanta West and Shama were therefore in tune with their supporters on the state of their financial constraints.

With popular sympathy and understanding on their side the NPP candidates then devised strategies for local fund-raising. Samuel Johnfia prepared a detailed costing of his campaign activities and used it to raise funds from wealthier constituents, supporters and sympathizers. Angelina reached out to friends and supporters in adjoining constituencies, in particular the more industrialized Takoradi constituency for financial assistance and support. In the end they both earned a well-deserved electoral victory.

National Economic Conditions

The national economic condition in election year 2000 was an extremely difficult one. Gross macro-economic instability primarily fuelled by unbridled fiscal indiscipline was exacerbated by plummeting export prices and the rising cost of imports especially petroleum. End of year inflation was in excess of 40%, the national currency had plunged into an uncontrollable depreciation against all major currencies, unemployment was high and the cost of child education unbearable. The people of these two rural constituencies strongly believed that something had to be done to alleviate the plight of the people. The very first step and one which was within their power to do in an election year was to change the government. This is what they did in December 2000.

General Cry for Change

Apart from the general economic difficulties there was also a certain strong feeling among the populations of the two constituencies that they were fed up with the Rawlings/NDC government and needed a change. This feeling was easily discernible among the generality of the population. Though President Rawlings and his NDC led a constitutional government for only two 4-year terms, to the people of Ahanta West and Shama this looked like eternity, largely because Rawlings had headed a ten year military government just before a return to constitutional rule. In post-colonial Ghana no other leader had ruled the country for so long. Therefore the mass of Ghanaians in Shama and Ahanta West yearned to see what another government could do differently.

A pre-election interview with a 40 year old educated storekeeper at Dixcove neatly summed up the general yearning of the people for a political change. He said:

> Generally in this town the decision people have taken is that the country needs a change of government. Therefore the majority of the people have decided to vote NPP regardless of what the NDC says it will or will not do. The political message in this town is clear. We need a change of government. Therefore in both the presidential and parliamentary elections people will vote massively for the NPP.

Conclusion

The survey of Ghana's election 2000 in the Ahanta West and Shama constituencies permits us to come to a number of vital conclusions.

First, primarily the politics of Ahanta West and Shama is the politics of a predominantly non-wage population of farmers/fishermen artisans and traders of low education and income.

Second, though political participation of the voters in Ahanta West and Shama is high it is also uneven and skewed into a limited number of political activities. Participation is high when it comes to registering to vote and actually voting in district, parliamentary and presidential elections. Participation is low in other activities such as joining political parties, attending political rallies, contributing to party financing and seeking office in political parties or aspiring to be a member of Parliament.

Third, the evaluative orientation of the voters of Ahanta West and Shama is very high. They rate some institutions and policies very high and others very low. Their evaluation of yet another set of institutions and policies is mixed.

In their evaluation respondents sounded quite positive about the state of Ghana's democracy in particular the presence of the freedom of association and to a limited extent of the press. Respondents were also quite happy with the Electoral Commission and the efficient manner in which it organized the 2000 Parliamentary and Presidential elections.

On the other hand respondents were quite negative about the state of the Ghanaian economy, which they rated as bad or very bad. They were also dissatisfied with the quality of representation they had received from their MPs.

Respondents' evaluation of political parties was very mixed. On the whole they were happy with the way political parties elected candidates to contest elections in the constituencies. The parties were however perceived as financially weak and tended to project personalities rather than policies.

NOTES

1. Peter Eng "The Democracy Boom", *Development Dialogue*, 1998, pp. 23–36.
2. Emmanuel Sivan, "Arabs and Democracy: Illusions of Change", *Journal of Democracy* Vol. 11, No. 3, 2000, pp. 69–82.
3. Mohamed Talbi, "Arabs and Democracy: A record of Failure", *Journal of Democracy* Vol. II No. 3, 2000 pp. 58–67.
4. Lilia Shevtsova, "Can Electoral Autocracy Survive?" *Journal of Democracy*, Vol. 11 No. 3 2000, p.36.
5. Michael Mcfaul, "One Step Forward Two Steps Back", *Journal of Democracy*, Vol. II No. 3, 2000, pp. 9–32. Similar reviews of Iran have been performed by Haleh Estandiari, "Is Iran Democratizing?: Observations on Election Day", *Journal of Democracy*, Vol. II No. 4 (October) 2000, pp. 108–113; and Ladan Borroumand with Roya Borroumand, "Once Again Reformist Victory has been Followed by Political Setback", *Journal of Democracy*, Vol. II No. 4 (October) 2000, pp. 114–128.
6. Said Adejumobi, "Elections in Africa: A Fading Shadow of Democracy", *Africa Development*, Vol. 23, No. 1 1998, p.41.
7. Larry Diamond, "Is Pakistan the (Reverse) Wave of the Future?" *Journal of Democracy* Vol. 11, No. 3, 2000, pp. 91–120.
8. *Ibid.*
9. Andreas Schedler, "What is Democratic Consolidation?", *Journal of Democracy*, Vol. 9 No. 2, 1998.
10. Darren Grant, "Searching for the Downsian as Simple Structural Model", *Economics And Politics*, Vol. 10 No. 2 (July) 1998.
11. E. A Fieldhouse, C. J. Pattie R. J. J. Johnston, "Tactical Voting and Party Constituency Campaigning at the 1992 General Election in England", *British Journal of Political Science* Vol. 26 Part 3 (July) 1996, pp. 403–439.
12. Peverill Squire and Eric R. A. N. Smith, "A Further Examination of Challenger Quality in Senate Elections", *Legislative Studies Quarterly*, Vol. XXI No. 2 (May) 1996, pp. 235–248.
13. Kwesi Jonah, "The 1996 Elections and Politics in the Ahanta West and Shama Constituencies" in J. R. A. Ayee (ed.) *The 1996 General Elections and Democratic Consolidation in Ghana* (Department of Political Science University of Ghana, Legon, 1998).

14. The principal sources of data for this chapter are:

    (i) Pre-Election Survey 2000 Elections (Ahanta West and Shama) February 2001
    (ii) Post-Election survey 2000 Elections Ahanta West and Shama March 2001.

    Note: Both documents are available in the Databank of the Department of Political Science University of Ghana, Legon.

CHAPTER 6

The 2000 Elections in Okaikoi North and South Constituencies

F. K. DRAH

Introduction

The enormous sigh of relief the majority of Ghanaians heaved and the concomitant unbounded joy they expressed in respect of the outcomes of the 2000 presidential and parliamentary elections were captured in the front-page, bold banner headlines of practically all the private sector "opposition" newspapers. One such headline read: "FREE AT LAST! GREAT GOD ALMIGHTY, WE ARE FREE AT LAST" (*The Ghanaian Chronicle*, 3–4 January 2001). In the considered estimation of *The Independent* (11 January 2001): "After almost 20 years of living under the rule of Jerry John Rawlings [and his so-called 'men and women of integrity'], Ghanaians of all walks of life are experiencing *a new air of freedom* reminiscent of the mood in the country when Kwame Nkrumah declared Ghana's independence on 6 March 1957" (my emphasis).

Indeed, an event of historic proportions occurred on 7 and 28 December 2000. For the first time in post-independence Ghana what appeared to most observers as an impregnable ruling party, the National Democratic Congress (NDC), was "thumb-printed" out of office and replaced with the opposition New Patriotic Party (NPP) in elections which have been generally adjudged free and fair as well as relatively peaceful; again, for the first time an incumbent president could complete his constitutionally mandated terms of office.

It is, of course, an exaggeration to conclude that this feat is unique in post-1991 Africa, as not a few observers have done. For a change of a civilian government through the ballot box ("thumb power") had occurred earlier in Benin (when Kerekou defeated Soglo) and in Senegal (when Wade defeated Diouf). Yet, for a great many Ghanaians, that achievement is unprecedented. It needs stressing, though, that such a feat has its flip side as well. For there were credible reports in the news media of irregularities, malpractices, intimidation of, and sporadic violence against, political opponents, regrettable attempts by the NDC particularly to "play the ethnic card" against its major rival, the NPP etc. during the elections.

This chapter is based on data gathered in pre-elections and post-elections surveys (Survey I and II respectively, for short), which this writer and two research assistants undertook in the North and South constituencies (the North and South respectively, for short) of the Okaikoi metropolitan sub-district in the Accra metropolis. The purpose of the chapter is to discuss the attitudes to, and the opinions on various issues of selected respondents in the twin constituencies with specific reference to voter participation, party politics, the electoral and democratic processes, as well as the presidential second round (run-off) election. For the sake of clarity and convenience the two surveys are analyzed separately.

Analysis of the Pre-elections Survey

Introduction

The Okaikoi North and South constituencies were chosen for a couple of reasons. First, since the resumption of electoral politics at national level in 1992, the Okaikoi constituencies have been two of the key constituencies in Accra which the NPP has consistently carried in all national elections except the 1992 parliamentary election which, together with the other opposition parties, it boycotted; hence the two constituencies have so far become NPP strongholds. Thus, they constitute an interesting case for study. Secondly, this writer is fairly acquainted with their political and social landscapes and has previously used them as a case for the study of the 1996 elections (Drah, 1998: 487–534).

Demographic Data

The Okaikoi constituencies are situated in northern Accra. Each constituency comprises six electoral areas. Those in the North are Achimota, Akweteman, Nii Boiman, Wuoyeman, Blema Gor and Gbemomo; while those in the South are Awudome, Bubuashi, Bubii, Gonten, Mukose and Kaatseian. Like other metropolitan sub-districts of Accra, Okaikoi is dotted with slums interspersed with modern commercial and dwelling houses. There are still mud houses, while containers and kiosks have been converted into homes for not an inconsiderable number of residents as, for example, in Akweteman, Fadama and Alogboshie, and many households lack flush toilets. Besides, many areas are flood-prone because of the poor drainage system.

Sample Sizes

One hundred and ten respondents from the North and 100 from the South were chosen for interview. The researchers made every effort to obtain a fairly balanced spatial distribution.

Gender Distribution

In Okaikoi North (the North) the sample comprised 69 (92.7%) males and 41 (37.3%) females, with the corresponding figures in Okaikoi South (the South) being 59 (59%) and 41 (41%). Clearly, the gender distribution was more balanced in the South than in the North. Even so it was found in the field, on the whole, that the females were much more willing to be interviewed than they had been during the 1996 election survey.

Of 110 respondents in the North 61 (55.5%) were in the 18–40 age bracket; while in the South 75 (75%) of 100 respondents fell into the same age range. In percentage terms respondents in the South were more youthful than their counterparts in the North, and in both constituencies respondents in the 18–40 age range were more prominent than those in the 41–71 and above age bracket. Interestingly, there was only one respondent in the 71 and above age range in the North but none in the South. These findings which compare favourably to those of the Political Science Department (2001:28) confirm the point made in the study of the 1996 elections in Okaikoi that the "Ghanaian population is becoming younger" (Drah 1998: 491).

Educational Background

The educational backgrounds of respondents as a whole were fairly impressive Remarkably, only 11 (10%) in the North and 7 (7%) in the South did not benefit from primary school education; while 4 (3.6%) and 5 (5%) respectively were university graduates. Thirty (27.3%) in the North and 46 (46%) in the South were secondary school leavers; while 10 (9.1%)

and 6 (6%) respectively attended Teacher Training or Technical College. It is unnecessary to belabour the point here that all this is the result of the concentration of educational facilities in the urban areas, especially Accra.

Occupation

On the whole the majority of respondents were gainfully employed in one way or the other. Only 14 (12.7%) out of 110 in the North and 19 (19%) out of 100 in the South were unemployed. This hardly implies that unemployment was not an issue for respondents as a whole, as will be seen later. Artisans and traders predominated in both constituencies followed by public servants. However, in specific respects the occupational distribution varied between the twin constituencies. For instance, while there were 13 (11.8%) professionals among respondents in the North, the South could boast only 1 (1%). Similarly the North had only 4 (3.6%) teachers compared with 13 (13%) in the South. There were no farmers in either constituency.

Christianity was the religion espoused by a large majority of respondents: 95(86.4%) in the North and 87 (87%) in the South. Muslims numbered 10 (9.1%) in the North and 5 (5%) in the South, with the adherents of the African traditional religion accounting for 6 (6%) in the South and only 1 (0.9%) in the North.

Income (P.A.)

Of those who were willing to disclose their annual incomes 39 (35.5%) in North and 5 (5%) in the South earned less than 5 million cedis; 5 (4.5%) and 1 (0.9%) in the North earned 5 to 10 million and above 10 million respectively but none in the South earned the same amounts. A whopping 95 (95%) in the South and a sizeable 63 (59.1%) in the North did not offer any answers. The failure to disclose income is, of course, not peculiar to the majority of Okaikoi respondents. It is a common habit with Ghanaians as a whole, but much more so with business persons and professionals, for obvious reasons.

Region of Birth

In the North 29 (26.4%) out of 110 and in the South 37 (37%) out of

100 were born in the Greater Accra region while the rest were born in the other regions. The figures for those born in the Akan-speaking regions are: *North* — Eastern 30 (27.3%); Ashanti 24 (21.8%); Central 6 (5.5%); Brong Ahafo 4 (3.6%); and Western 1 (0.9%) — all adding up to 65 (59.1%). *South* — Central 22 (22%); Ashanti 14 (14%); Eastern 11 (11%) and Western 2 (2%) – all totalling 49 (49%).

For the remaining regions the distribution is as follows: *North* — Upper East 2 (1.8%); Upper West 1 (0.9%); and Volta 11 (10%). *South*-Northern region 1 (1%); Upper West 2 (2%) and Volta 11 (10%). On the issue of region of birth a cautionary note is apposite: the fact that one was born in a particular region does not necessarily mean that one was a native of that region. When Survey I was conducted, 100 (90.9%) and 100 (100%) respondents were domiciled in the North and South respectively. But in respect of the North 1 (0.9%) respondent was living in the Ashanti, Volta and Northern region apiece while 4 (4.5%) were living in the Eastern region.

Political Participation

Voter Registration

Of all the 210 respondents in the two constituencies only a tiny fraction, 1 (0.9%) in the North and 7 (7%) in the South, were not registered voters. The major reasons offered by the latter were that, first, voting benefitted only the politicians and not the voters and, secondly, since such respondents considered their personal affairs/commitments more crucial, they could not find the time to register as voters. The first view, however cynical it is, may pass muster but the second view is anti-civic in the extreme. Obviously, the National Commission on Civic Education (NCCE), the Electoral Commission (EC) and so on will have to step up the *political education* of Ghanaians who hold such views.

Registration as Party Members

When respondents were asked whether or not they were registered members of any political party, 31 (28.2%) in the North and 56 (56%) in the South responded positively. But a great number, 76 (69.1%) and a sizeable proportion, 43 (43%), respectively answered in the negative.

Of the registered party members in the North 12 (10.9%) belonged to the National Democratic Congress (NDC), 15 (13.6%) to the New Patriotic Party (NPP) 2 (1.8%) to the People's National Convention (PNC) and 1 (0.9%) to the National Reform Party (NRP). In the South 41 (41%) belonged to the NPP, 4 (4%) to the NDC and 2 (2%) to the Convention People's Party (CPP). On the other hand, the Great Consolidation Popular Party (GCPP), United Ghana Movement (UGM) and the Democratic People's Party (DPP) were hardly mentioned at all. Despite the disappointing figures on registered party membership, especially in the North, the NPP clearly stood head and shoulders above its major rival, the NDC. Twenty-four (21.8%) respondents from the South variously explained their failure to register as members of any political party. Eighteen respondents in each constituency (16.4 and 18% from the North and South respectively) expressed their distate for party politics; 2 (1.8%) in the North and 10 (10%) in the South explained that none of the existing parties was sufficiently good for them; 9 (9%) in the South and 1 (1.8%) in the North believed that the parties were more concerned with personalities than with policies; and 3 (2.7%) in only the North opined that party politics in Ghana had lost its purpose and had become commercialized.

Party Inclination

Even though not many respondents were registered members of any political party, they indicated their inclination towards some of the parties. Here again, the NPP was the most preferred party. It attracted the sympathy of 34 (30.9%) respondents as against 21 (19.1%) for the NDC in the North and 43 (43%) contrasted with 5 (5%) for the NDC in the South.

Following Party Activities

As the Table below portrays a great many respondents (100 or 90.9% in the North and 84 or 84% in the South) in contrast with a tiny minority (9 or 8.2% and 13 or 13% respectively) observed the activities of the parties in the news media, thereby underscoring how significant the news media in Ghana have become as the major means for garnering information of many kinds.

Attendance at Party Rallies

In view of the above finding, it is not surprising that the number of respondents in each constituency (41 or 37.3% as against 69 or 62.7% in the North and 40 or 40% as against 60 or 60% in the South) who attended party rallies in connection with the 2000 elections was not as considerable as that of those who followed the activities of the parties in the news media. As is happening worldwide, the news media, particularly radio and television, are increasingly becoming alternatives to political party rallies.

The 2000 Elections

Voter Intention

A vast number of respondents in either constituency, 103 (93.6%) in the North and 81 (81%) in the South, indicated their intention to vote in the 2000 elections, with a mere 3 (2.7%) and 9 (9%) respectively indicating otherwise. Three (2.7%) in the North and 10 (10%) in the South were undecided while 1 (0.9%) in the North did not respond.

Presidential and Parliamentary Elections

The distribution of the responses of respondents to the question of which party they would vote for in the presidential poll reads thus:

North — NPP: 47 (42.7%); NDC: 26 (23.6%); PNC: 3 (2.7%); GCPP and NRP: 1 (0.9%) each. Twenty-two (20%) could not decide and 5 (4.5%) did not answer.

South — NPP: 49 (49%); Independent: 11 (11%); and NDC: 5 (5%); while 14 (14%) did not know and 18 (18%) could not respond. Incidentally, no Independent candidates featured in the 2000 elections in the twin constituencies.

Regarding the party preferred in the parliamentary election the pattern of responses was nearly the same in both constituencies. In the North 49 (44.5%) and in the South 49 (49%) opted for the NPP; 24 (21.8%) and 6 (6%) respectively for the NDC; 3 (2.7%) and 1 (0.9%) respectively for the PNC; and 1 (0.9%) for the NRP in the North only. Evidently, the majority of respondents in both constituencies, though not too large, intended to vote for the NPP.

The various reasons given by the few who did not intend to vote in the presidential poll were that they did not believe in party politics (South 3%) and whoever came to power would not make any difference in their lives (North 1.8% and South 3%).

Voter Perception of the Economy

To a large number of respondents in either constituency, the state of the economy prior to the 7 December elections was very dismal. According to 84 (76.4%) in the North and 86 (86%) in the South the economy was "bad" to "very bad". Only 5 (5%) in the South considered it "very good" and 6 (6%) "good". But revealingly all the 110 (100%) did not think that the economy was "very good", although 11 (10%) felt it was "good".

Table 6.1: Voter Perception of the Economy

	NORTH Frequency	NORTH Percentage %	SOUTH Frequency	SOUTH Percentage %
Very good	–	–	5	5
Good	11	10.0	6	6
Bad	23	20.9	32	32
Very bad	61	55.5	54	54
Neither good nor bad	11	10.0	3	3
No opinion	3	2.7	–	–
No response	1	0.9	–	–
TOTAL	110	100	100	100

Improvement or Deterioration of the Economy

On whether over the past four years the economy had improved or deteriorated, the responses were equally most unfavourable.

Table 6.2: Whether the Economy had Improved or Deteriorated Over the Previous Four Years

	NORTH Frequency	NORTH Percentage %	SOUTH Frequency	SOUTH Percentage %
Considerably improved	6	5.5	11	11
Just improved	9	8.2	8	8
Become worse	62	56.4	67	67
Sharply deteriorated	26	23.6	9	9
No opinion	6	5.5	5	5
No response	1	0.9	-	-
TOTAL	110	100	100	100

Household Standard of Living

Given the highly poor opinion the majority of respondents held about the economy's performance, it is not strange that an equally very large proportion, notably in the North, opined that their household living standard had slumped from "a little worse" to "much worse" since the 1996 elections as the Table below unambiguously spells out. Significantly, only 5 (4.5%) in the North and 5 (5%) in the South considered their household living standard to have become "much better" while 15 (13.6%) and 17 (17%) respectively thought it had become "a little better".

Major Economic Problem

The views of respondents on what they considered the major economic problem in contemporary Ghana were split between both constituencies. The foremost economic problem for those in the South was unemployment (40%) followed by the depreciation of the cedi (32%), high interest rates (14%), lack of private investments (6%) and, interestingly lastly, inflation. In the North, on the other hand, the leading economic problem was the depreciation of the cedi (33 or 30%) followed by unemployment (30 or 27.3%), inflation (18 or 16.4%) and competition from cheap imports (9 or 8.2%).

Table 6.3: Household Standard of Living

	NORTH Frequency	NORTH Percentage %	SOUTH Frequency	SOUTH Percentage %
Much better	5	4.5	5	5
A little better	15	13.6	17	17
A litter worse	29	26.4	18	18
Much worse	55	50.0	56	56
No opinion	5	4.5	4	4
No response	1	0.9	–	–
TOTAL	110	100	100	100

That unemployment featured prominently in the ranking belies the very low level unemployment in the two constituencies as indicated earlier in the section on "Occupation". The prominence given to unemployment is officially confirmed in a Report on core welfare indicators by the Statistical Service (1997) which was launched recently. According to the Report "at 7.8%, overall unemployment in the Greater Accra Region is the highest in the country. Urban poor households have the highest unemployment and underemployment rates (15.9% and 3.4% respectively). . . ."

Assessment of the Electoral Process

Independence of the Electoral Commission

In view of the constant criticisms of the Electoral Commission by certain sections in the country that it was a pliable tool of the NDC government (an issue to be discussed later), it is, perhaps, not coincidental that the responses of Okaikoi respondents as a whole to the question whether or not the EC was independent of government control were not emphatic either way, even though those in the North were a little more charitable than those in the South. Here, again, one must not gloss over the number of those who did not know.

Table 6.4: Independence of the Electoral Commission

	NORTH Frequency	NORTH Percentage %	SOUTH Frequency	SOUTH Percentage %
Positive	47	42.7	33	33
Negative	36	32.7	39	39
No opinion	23	20.9	28	28
No response	4	3.6	–	–
TOTAL	110	100	100	100

Other Sources of Iinfluence on the Elections

The same number of respondents (39) in each constituency (35.5% in the North and 39% in the South) believed that besides the EC there were other ways of influencing the 2000 elections. But 27 (24.5%) in the North and 43 (43%) in the South believed otherwise.

In the North the variety of ways cited by some of the respondents included: international institutions who were expected to supervise the elections (5 or 4.5%); government control of state institutions; the capacity of the government in power to influence the EC; and the possibility of the NDC declaring the results void (3 or 2.7% apiece); the government's possible control of the EC; intimidation of voters; and the likely bribing of party agents (2 or 1.8% each). In the South some respondents mentioned such other ways as religious bodies/NGOs/foreign observers who should supervise the elections (6 or 6%); the likelihood of party agents being bribed (3 or 3%); the influence of the government in power on the EC as well as the printing of extra ballot papers for rigging purposes (2 or 2% each). On the whole, although the numbers involved are not large in either constituency (22 in the North and 13 in the South), it is significant that some respondents could identify at all certain possible benign and malevolent sources of influence on the 2000 elections. A few respondents even went further to suggest that the Association of the Committees for the Defence of the Revolution (ACDRs), for instance, could be used as an inimical election rigging tool.

Incumbency and Elections

The precise impact of incumbency on elections is a matter of heated debate among political analysts. However difficult it is to measure such an impact, it is now acknowledged worldwide that governments do in varying degrees exploit their incumbency during elections (Commonwealth Secretariat, 1997: 15 and 28).

In the North as many as 71 (64.5%) respondents as against 27 (24.5%) and in the South a fairly sizeable 31 (31%) as against 47 (47%) felt that the ruling party had undue advantage over the opposition parties during elections. The national averages are 55% (positive) and 22.5% (negative). Thus on the issue of undue exploitation of incumbency the North was more emphatic than the South; and the scores for the North compare favourably to the corresponding national averages (Political Science Department, 2001: 15).

Environment for Free and Fair Elections

Be that as it may, the majority of respondents in each constituency (67 or 60.9% in the North and 69 or 69% in the South) were convinced that conditions existed for free and fair elections for the 7 December, 2000 polls. A fairly sizeable number (25 or 22.7% in the North and only 8 or 8% in the South) were not so convinced; and 15 (13.6%) and 21 (21%) respectively had no opinion.

The opposition parties spearheaded by the NPP could not have agreed less with the majority opinion in Okaikoi. They persistently pointed to certain seemingly intractable flaws in the electoral process including the bloated voters register of 10.7 million registered voters which was hardly on all fours with the provisional population total of 18.4 million released after the 2000 population census. Even though the ruling party was too pleased with the anomaly, the EC's chairman graciously acknowledged, and promised to rectify it. But the rectification exercise was not thoroughly done partly because of the time constraint. No wonder at election time on 7 December the number of eligible registered voters still stood at 10,698,652! (For further details, see *Daily Graphic*, 21 September 2000, and Centre for Democracy and Development — CDD, 2000: 1–4).

Evaluation of the Party System

Prospects of Opposition Ruling Parties in Presidential Poll

When respondents were invited to assess the prospects of an opposition party winning the presidential election of 7 December, 2000, 65 (59.1%) in the North and 59 (59%) in the South rated its chances from "good" to "very good" as against 23 (20.9%) and 20 (20%) respectively who thought that its prospects were not "so good". By contrast 42 (38.2%) in the North and 27 (27%) in the South considered the chances of the Progressive Alliance (PA) to be "good" to "very good"; while 46 (41.8%) and 38 (38%) respectively did not think they were "so good". Thus, Okaikoi respondents as a whole were more optimistic about an opposition party's victory in the presidential election than that of the PA.

Presidential Run-off

No wonder 52 (47.3%) as against 40 (36.4%) in the North and 49 (49%) as against 38 (38%) opined that a presidential run-off was more unlikely in the 7 December, 2000 presidential poll than that of 1996. This was in sharp contrast to the prediction of a possible presidential second round election by a number of political analysts (see e.g. the *Weekend Statesman*, 24–30 November 2000; *Public Agenda*, 20-26 November 2000).

The reasons advanced by those respondents who expected a run-off were the following: (i) there was an increase in the number of parties: *North* — 20 (18.2%) and *South* — 18 (18%); (ii) there was a lack of charismatic presidential candidates: *South* — 11 (11%) and *North* 3 (2.7%); and (iii) the party manifestoes were similar in content: *South* — 5 (4.%) and *North* — 5 (5%).

Parties, Personalities and Ppolicies

Respondents were asked certain specific questions in order to elicit their views on the party system in Ghana. One such question was whether the parties projected personalities more than policies. As between the two constituencies opinions were rather sharply divided. Twenty-six (23.6%) from the North and 49 (49%) from the South thought so; while 76 (69.1%) and 24 (24%%) respectively thought otherwise. For the South, therefore, Ghanaian parties considered personalities as more significant than policies.

Financial Soundness of Parties

On the worrisome issue of how financially healthy most of Ghanaian parties were, the majority of respondents were agreed that they were not. In that case their operations must have been seriously hamstrung.

Table 6.5: Financial Soundness of Parties

	NORTH Frequency	NORTH Percentage %	SOUTH Frequency	SOUTH Percentage %
Positive	27	24.5	18	18
Negative	62	56.4	56	56
No opinion	17	15.5	23	23
No response	4	3.6	3	3
TOTAL	110	100	100	100

State Funding of Parties

The question of the imperative necessity of state funding of political parties in Ghana has been in the public domain since 1992 especially. Many political analysts and practitioners in Ghana have advocated it. In 1995 a group of political analysts meeting in Accra considered the subject in all its ramifications and made concrete proposals for adoption throughout West Africa in particular (Kumado, 1995: 1–23; Drah, 1995: 240–252). Another sizeable majority (68 or 68%) in that constituency rejected state funding of such parties. In the North, however, 50 (45.5%) compared with 41 (37.3%) supported it.

Constituency Candidate Nomination Process

Respondents were asked if they liked the candidates nominated by their parties to stand for election to parliament in their constituencies and if they thought the nomination process was democratic. Although a respectable majority of 58 (58%) as against just 9 (9%) in the South liked the candidate, 49 (49%) as against 40 (40%) thought the selection process was democratic. In the North 60 (54.5%) compared with a bare 8 (7.3%) liked the candidate and 52 (47.3%) compared with 10 (9.1%) considered the process democratic.

Despite the favourable majority opinion regarding the selection process, some respondents insisted that it was not without its difficulties even in the NPP, the internal democratic processes of which are widely claimed to be much stronger than those of its major rival, the NDC.

Admittedly, the NPP retained the mode of selecting parliamentary candidates through the constituency primaries "where there is more than one parliamentary candidate" as demanded by Article 14 of the party's Constitution. However, as is common knowledge, in 2000 the national leadership was determined to retain the party's incumbent MPs who numbered 61 for strategic reasons.

In the view of some respondents and other observers the constituencies involved could be described as untouchable "bishoprics". This policy may have in no small way fuelled a measure of discontent among the aspiring parliamentary candidates ("the outsiders") and their band of supporters in many such constituencies. The NPP incumbent in the North Okaikoi constituency, for instance, was reportedly not retained without some barbed grumblings by certain constituency influentials (*Free Press*, 26 April 2000; *Ghana Palaver*, 27 September and 13–14 November 2000; Advertiser's Announcement in *Daily Graphic*, 20 November, 2000).

In 1996 the NDC tried to experiment with a mode of choosing its parliamentary candidates which involved some grassroots participation akin to constituency primaries implied by Article 14(4)(b) of the party's Constitution. The national leadership abandoned this type of selection process in 2000 for what the party's general secretary dubbed "the consultative, assessment and consensus reaching method".

According to him, the constituency primaries not only brought confusion; they were also undemocratic because of "the probability of rich contestants influencing delegates with money". By contrast, "the new selection method" encompassed "a wider spectrum of opinion than primaries" where a tiny minority of delegates "decided for the majority" (see Ken Noonoo in *The Evening News*, 13 July 2000). The "new method" was, in practice, nothing short of the further entrenchment of *diktat* from above.

As is well known, this selection process brought even more confusion, disunity, acrimony and betrayal to the constituencies including the twin Okaikoi constituencies. In the South for one, the DPP unsuccessfully vied with its senior partner in the PA, the NDC for the parliamentary seat; while in the North the less popular contestant was preferred to the more popular one (*The Evening News*, 12 May, 2000).

Evaluation of the Democratic Process

Ghana as a Democracy

It is a contentious issue whether Ghana today could be described as a democracy. To 69 (62.7%) respondents in the North and 52 (52%) in the South Ghana could be described as such; while a fairly sizeable 30 (27.3%) and 25 (25%) respectively were of a contrary view. Sixty-four (58.2%) contrasted with 33 (33%) in the North and 39 (39%) contrasted with 41 (41%) in the South were positive that democracy in Ghana had improved since 1996. It is evident that on both counts the South was rather less certain.

More Media Freedom since 1996

Respondents in the South who were evenly split, 42 (42%), were more sceptical than their counterparts in the North 72 (65.5%) as against 28 (25.5%), that the media have experienced more freedom than they did four years ago. It is not as if a great many respondents, notably in the North, were not aware that not a few journalists suffered harassment, intimidation, heavy fines for civil libel and even imprisonment at the hands of several NDC government officials and party functionaries.

More Associational Freedom

With respect to the issue whether political parties and other associations including civil society organizations (CSO) have had more freedom than they did four years ago, respondents in the South 54 (54%) compared with 27 (27%), were once again less emphatic than those in the North, 80 (72.7%) compared with 24 (21.8%), as the Table below indicates.

There is ample evidence to suggest that the ruling NDC made attempts, not all successful, to use certain affiliate organizations to crowd out several CSOs which are very essential to the continuing democratization of Ghana (Sandbrook and Oelbaum, 1999; Hart and Gyimah-Boadi, 2000; Drah, 1996).

Evaluation of Presidential Running Mates

In response to what respondents considered as the most crucial factor in the choice of a presidential running mate, an overwhelming majority in the North (85 or 77.3%) and a sizeable majority in the South (60 or 60%) singled out experience rather than ethnic background the scores for which are: 10 (9.1%) in the North and 1 (1%) in the South. The regional balance factor did not fare well either in the South 11 (11%) and in the North a negligible 4 (3.6%) felt it was the most important factor. The national average scores are: experience — 56.1%; regional balance — 14.7%; and ethnic balance — 3.5% (Political Science Department, 2001:19). Nor did an even more overwhelming majority (95 or 86.4% in the North and 89 or 89% in the South) think that the presidential running mate chosen would impact on the party they would vote for. Only 12 (10.9%) and 11 (11%) respectively thought so.

As to whether it was important for the parties to ensure regional balance in the choice of the presidential running mate, 12 (10.9%) in the North and 12 (12%) in the South agreed, 59 (53.6%) and 33 (33%) respectively disagreed, while 32 (29.1%) and 44 (44%), respectively, were indifferent. The pattern of responses to the question whether it was important for the presidential tickets to be ethnically balanced was similar: 9 (8.2%) in the North and 11 (11%) in the South thought so, 62 (56.4%) and 31 (31%) respectively thought otherwise, while 35 (31.8%) and 47 (47%), respectively, were indifferent.

All this indicates that respondents in both constituencies combined put a very low premium on ethnic or regional balance in party presidential tickets. Such a position would seem to run counter to the strategically motivated policy of some parties, notably the NDC and NPP, to present regionally and/or ethnically balanced presidential tickets, presumably in response to the frenetic demands by some influential segments of public opinion to move in that direction.

Election Issues

Respondents were invited to identify what they considered as the three major issues in the 2000 elections at national level and the three most significant development issues in the constituency.

To respondents in the South the main national issues were the economy (47 or 47%), change and development (19 or 19%) as well as continuity and stability (16 or 16%). But Ghana's future in the twenty-first century and improving democracy were of concern to 12 (12%) and a mere 2 (2%) in the South respectively.

In striking contrast a whopping majority 99 (90%) in the North identified the economy as the major issue, while continuity and stability as well as change and development were identified by a scant 3 (2.7%) apiece. Only 1 (.9%) picked Ghana's future in the twenty-first century while improving democracy was hardly mentioned.

The kind of emphasis the majority of Okaikoi respondents put on the economy, change and development is not surprising. For these were the very issues that were most often emphasized by the opposition parties, notably the NPP with its captivating slogan of "Positive Change" — that is, change of the existing economic, political and social malaise for the good of all.

At constituency level respondents in the North chose as the most crucial development issues KVIP toilets 31 (28.2%), a good road network 16 (14.5%) and water 11 (10%). Those in the South picked a good road network 13 (13%), employment 12 (12%) and sanitation 10 (10%). Considering the feelings of horror and fear evoked by the serial killings of women in Accra particularly, it is rather strange that of the whole lot only 1 (1.8%) respondent in the North identified crime control or the provision of more police posts as a priority development issue.

Voting for Party, Candidate or Both

Respondents were asked whether in the 7 December, 2000, presidential and parliamentary elections they would vote for the party or the candidate, or both. This raises the fundamental issue of where one's loyalty lies. The responses of the interviewees are indicated in Tables 6.6 and 6.7.

It must be tolerably clear from the above two Tables that the majority of respondents in the North attached the greatest importance to the

Table 6.6: Presidential and Parliamentary Election: South

	South Frequency	Percentage %	National Average Frequency	Percentage %
The Party	66	60	5	18.3
Both Party and candidate	31	28	46	61.8
The candidate	7	6.4	35	13.8
No opinion	2	1.8	14	3.7
No response	4	3.6	–	24
TOTAL	110	100	100	100

Table 6.7: Presidential and Parliamentary Election: North

	North Frequency	Percentage %	National Average Frequency	Percentage %
The Party	67	60.9	12	13.9
Both Party and candidate	30	27.3	40	60.1
The candidate	7	6.4	35	20.3
No opinion	2	1.8	13	4.0
No response	4	3.6	–	1.6
TOTAL	110	100	100	100

party, implying that they would vote for the party irrespective of the candidate fielded. In a significant sense such a stance, of which party hierarchies are enamoured, strengthens the party. The danger here is that it allows the party leadership to impose all sorts of candidates of their choice on the party.

In the South and in the country at large however, the majority, though not as sizeable as in the North, preferred to vote for both the party and candidate, meaning presumably that the party must present the candidate they would not hesitate to vote for. Those who would vote for the candidate only may be non-party floating voters whom the parties must zealously court.

Sources Most Useful to Voter

Some of the sources which respondents found most useful in deciding whom to vote for in their constituencies included the following: *radio*: North — 72 (65.5%), South — 39 (39%); *posters/fliers:* North — 7 (6.4%); *Television*: North — 18 (16.4%), South — 6 (6%); *newspapers:* South — 12 (12%), Norty — 6 (6%). Only a negligible 2 (1.8%) in the North cited friends and family, implying that the largest number of respondents were presumably not dependent on this source.

Most Trustworthy Source of Media Information

Respondents were invited to identify the source of media information which they most trusted to tell the truth. *Radio* was cited as the most trustworthy by 52 (47.3%) from the North and 29 (29%) from the South, followed by *private newspapers* which were cited by 22 (20%) from the North and 13 (13%) from the South. That the scores for each of the state-owned print and electronic media are in single digits is a measure of public distrust of them. For instance, the state-owned radio attracted a bare 3 (2.7%) and 8 (8%) respondents in the North and South respectively; while the corresponding scores for state-owned newspapers were 4 (3.6%) and 9 (9%).

Analysis of the Post-elections Survey

Introduction

For the post-elections survey (Survey II) the sample covered 100 respondents in either constituency; and every effort was made to target a fresh crop of respondents. The interviews were conducted without any major hitches, and not a few of the interviewees were even expansive on some of the issues raised. However, the possibility that the victory of the NPP could have affected the mood of some respondents, depending on whether they belonged to the winners or losers, was not discounted.

Demographic Profile

There were 54 males and 46 females in the South and 64 males and 36 females in the North. Once more, just as in Survey I, the gender distribution is more unbalanced in the North than in the South. In not a few of the interviews married women did not hesitate to do most of the talking

Age Distribution

Fifty-eight (50) percent of respondents in the North and 60% in the South were in the 18–40 age range, with the corresponding national average being 65% (Political Science Department, 2001:28); while there were a paltry 2% in the North and none at all in the South in the 71 and above age group; the national average is 1.7% (*ibid.*). The representation of the 18–40 age bracket was about equal in both constituencies. Once again the figures indicate a youthful crop of respondents in Okaikoi as a whole as was found in Survey I.

Educational Background

Respondents with secondary school education predominated in the South, 40, as against 32 in the North; the score for primary school education was higher in the North with 36 than in the South with 16; sixteen in the South had polytechnic education as against 5 in the North; the scores for university education were about evenly split between the North (7) and the South (8); and just 1 in the North and 2 in the South had no primary school education. Thus the Okaikoi respondents like those in Survey I had good educational backgrounds.

Occupation

The number of the unemployed among respondents was greater in the South (30) than in the North (12). As in Survey I artisans (8 in either constituency) and traders (19 in the South and 18 in the North) constituted the major occupational groups. Teachers accounted for 10 in the North ad 6 in the South; business people 9 and 8; professionals 3 and 6; and public servants 5 and 8, all respectively. There were no farmers.

Monthly Income

To begin with, as many as 78 respondents in the South and 14 in the North did not respond on this matter. Twelve in the North and 1 in the South earned nothing at all; while respectively 22 and 5 earned between 1 and 100,000 cedis and 4 and 23 earned between 101,000 and 200,000. Only 1 in each constituency had a monthly income of 601,000–700,000 and 701,000–800,000; while just 1 and 4 (and only in the North) fell into the income ranges of 801,000-900,000 and over 1 million cedis respectively. Obviously, the majority of those who disclosed their monthly income levels were very low income earners, which reflected the poor state of the Ghanaian economy.

Religion

As in Survey I the overwhelming majority of respondents were Christians in both constituencies (95 in the North and 73 in the South). Muslims numbered 21 in the South and the African traditionalists 3 (two in the South and one in the North).

Region of Birth

About an even proportion of respondents in both constituencies were born in the Akan-speaking regions (61 in the North and 58 in the South). In the North, of the Akan-speaking regions, the score for the Eastern region was the highest (36), followed by Ashanti (15); while in the South the score for the Eastern region was again the highest (20) followed by Ashanti (17), Central (12) and Western (2). The distribution for the other regions was as follows: *Northern* — 10 in the South only; *Volta* — 7 in the South and 1 in the North; Upper East and West — 2 apiece in the South only; and *Greater Accra* — 19 and 34 in the South and North respectively.

When the interviews were conducted almost all respondents lived in Greater Accra (95 in the South with one apiece living in Ashanti, Central and Upper East and 99 in the North with one living in Volta). The reader is reminded of the comment made earlier on that there is no necessary connection between the region of birth and the ethnic origin of a respondent; it must be repeated, though, that in reality Okaikoi is multi-ethnic.

Participation in the 2000 Elections

Just as was found in Survey I all respondents, with the exception of three in the South only, were registered voters. Equally remarkably, they voted in their large numbers in the 7 December 2000 presidential and parliamentary elections. Barely 4 in either constituency did not vote, while 3 in the South only did not respond.

Voter Evaluation of Party Politics

Registered Party Members

A relatively low number of respondents in the North (22) and in the South (27) were registered party members. Hence the extent of political party affiliation of respondents was relatively lower than that of those interviewed before the elections.

In any case the NPP claimed the highest number of respondents who were registered party members with 16 in the North and 23 in the South, followed by the NDC with a paltry 5 and 4 respectively. Just one in either constituency belonged to the CPP; and the PNC and the GCPP had one each in the North only.

It is a serious indictment of all the parties that two of the reasons given by the non-registered party members were their ignorance of party registration procedures (17 and 21 in the North and South respectively) and the failure of the parties to encourage them to register (10 and 7 respectively).

Party Inclination

Of respondents who were non-registered party members, 53 in the North and 49 in the South inclined towards the NPP, followed by the NDC with 14 and 6, the PNC with 4 and 6 and the CPP with 2 and 7 respectively. A mere 4 and 1 in the North only inclined towards the NRP and GCPP respectively; the UGM was hardly mentioned. If the above findings are anything to go by, then it would seem that all the parties have so far been largely dependent on sympathizers and supporters for their continued existence, which is not healthy for any serious party, as has been repeatedly emphasized by many political analysts (see for example, Hess, 1994).

Media and Party Rallies

Just as in Survey I the vast majority in either constituency followed the activities of the parties in the news media (91 in the South and 94 in the North). But not as many (37 and 46 respectively) attended political rallies during the run-up to the 7 December elections for the major reason already noted in the analysis of Survey I.

Perception of Party Politics

Respondents had varied perceptions of party politics. In the view of 37 in the North and 30 in the South party politics "has enriched" a tiny minority of people — what some people call the "commercialization of politics"; to 8 (North) and 10 (South) "it is a dirty game"; and to 20 in the North and 7 in the South "it has brought division among Ghanaians". These are, of course, some of the usual indictments of party politics mostly emphasized by actual or potential megalomaniacs who do not have it in them to tolerate political pluralism. But it is, perhaps refreshing to hear from such apparent idealists as 28 respondents (26 from the North and 2 from the South) that party politics "has improved the quality of living of Ghanaians"!

Party Performance

Despite the jaundiced views of party politics noted above, a good many other respondents had a favourable opinion of its performance in Ghana so far. According to 30 respondents in the North and 5 in the South, the parties "are doing a very good job". Fifty-two (52) in the North and 32 in the South felt "they are doing a good job". Thirty (30) in the South and 5 in the North were undecided in that they could not tell whether the parties "are doing a god job or a bad job". At the other end of the spectrum were 6 respondents in the North and 2 in the South who opined that the parties "are doing a bad job" besides 3 in the North only who believed that "they are doing a very bad job".

The "Cynicism Syndrome"

As is well known Ghana like other countries has its fair share of people who believe that irrespective of whichever party is in power there is no assurance of a significant, positive change to the status quo. All this translates into Akan as "obiaa ba saa". Those who share such a view may be said to have been bitten by the bug of what may be crudely termed the "cynicism syndrome".

When respondents were asked if they agreed to such a view, an overwhelming 84 in the North and a sizeable 40 in the South encouragingly disagreed. The reasons for their disagreement ranged from "every leader has his own vision or new team" through "everybody should be given a chance" to "we want change", implying that change was inevitable. Ten respondents in the South and 5 in the North agreed. They reasoned variously that "nothing has changed since the beginning of time", "the trend says it all", or "change must come from the people" themselves.

Activities Relating to the Elections

Party Campaigns

The vast majority of respondents (89 in the North and 84 in the South) were emphatic that all the parties had the opportunity to campaign freely for the elections. On the issue of whether all the parties had sufficient logistics for their campaigns, 22 respondents as against the large number of 62 in the North and 46 as against 33 in the South were positive.

Fifty-six respondents in the North and 27 in the South were of the view that some party members were intimidated by their counterparts in opposing parties, but 41 and 34 respectively said that there was no intimidation. The NDC was considered the worst offender in this regard by 44 respondents from the North and 20 from the South, followed by the NPP (8 from the North and 5 from the South). The CPP was cited by only one respondent from the South.

Election Violations

It is now common knowledge that, even though the elections were generally adjudged free and fair, there were many violations in many constituencies across the country. The Okaikoi constituencies were no exception.

Twenty-four respondents from the South and 62 from the North were able to identify some instances of electoral violations. Topping the list is intimidation by the military and NDC supporters (11 and 37 from the South and the North respectively), followed by insults (4 and 8 respectively) and multiple voting (4 and 7 respectively).

Pattern of Voting in the 2000 Elections

The overwhelming majority of respondents were unhesitant in disclosing the parties they voted for in the 7 December elections. Only 3 in the North and 6 in the South did not respond.

Presidential Election

The NPP topped the list with 74 in the North and 68 in the South voting for it. The NDC came a poor second by garnering 17 and 10 votes respectively. The votes for the other parties were distributed as follows: *PNC* — North: 3 and South 7; *UGM* — North: 3 and South: 6; *CPP* — North: 1 and South: 7; and *NRP* – North: 2 and South: 1. The GCPP obtained none.

The foremost reasons given by respondents for voting for a specific party were that, first, the party had good policies to ensure the country's development (41 in the North and 33 in the South); and, secondly, the national leadership must be changed (34 and 38 respectively).

Parliamentary Election

Just as in the presidential election the largest number of respondents (72 in the North and 66 in the South) voted for the NPP. The NDC came a distant second with 16 and 10 respectively. The first most significant reason for voting for a particular party was the same as the first of the reasons given as regards the presidential election but with different scores, namely, 40 in the North and 36 in the South. The second reason turned on a party having a good and honest candidate (28 and 17 respectively).

Election Issues

In Survey I respondents identified the economy as the foremost of the three most significant national development issues. The scale of priorities rather changed with those interviewed after the elections. Respondents in the North ranked the three most crucial national development issues: employment, education and crime control. The economy hardly featured. For Southern respondents it was education, employment and the economy. It must be emphasized that these were among the priority national development issues, with the economy given pride of place, which all the parties promised in their various manifestoes to tackle. The most significant constituency development needs were also similar. In the North the list comprises, first and foremost, a good road network, then sanitation followed by toilet (KVIP), while in the South it encompassed sanitation, a good road network and street or security light.

A number of studies on Ghanaian politics since independence have underscored a preoccupation with local issues to the near exclusion of national issues (as, for example, Austin, 1964; Dunn and Robertson, 1973). The cumulative evidence would seem to confirm this perspective. It is perhaps, refreshing to note that some respondents in Okaikoi may be moving in a rather different direction.

When asked which types of issue most influenced how they voted on 7 December, more than half of respondents in the North (56) and about one-third (32) in the South singled out national issues contrasted with barely 3 and 12 respectively who cited constituency issues. But one-third in either constituency identified both local and national issues, and thus struck a balance between the two types of issue. To the majority of respondents (76 in the North and 68 in the South) the party which best articulated the most crucial national development issues and constituency development needs was the NPP. The NDC was again, ranked a distant second by 13 and 10 respondents respectively.

Evaluation of the Electoral Process

Introduction

In early November 2000 President Rawlings at a Kumasi NDC rally made the flesh-creeping remark that he and his party would "only hand over power [to an opposition party] at the second coming of Christ" (*The Independent*, 5 November 2000). This confirmed the fears of the opposition parties and numerous political commentators that the NDC was determined to entrench itself in power by rigging the 2000 elections.

The EC, which was itself under a thick cloud of suspicion compounded by its inept handling of a simple matter of setting the election date, took certain significant steps to allay these fears. These included replacing voter thumb-print identification (ID) cards with photo ID cards (to be discussed presently) and ensuring that the right election officials were appointed and properly trained. Besides, in an important statement issued in September 2000 by its chairman, the EC promised to encourage more domestic election observer groups to operate, insisting that "election observation is not a witch hunt but a fact-finding EC mission". In the statement the EC revealed that it was designing a check-list of "dos" and "don'ts" which, inter alia, would make polling stations restricted areas that could be accessed only on the EC's authorization and would bar party chairmen, District Chief Executives (DCEs) and other people in authority from entering the polling stations. The statement concluded by significantly urging "party agents to be extra vigilant and not go and sleep at polling stations" (*The Evening News*, 21 September 2000). In effect, one of the most crucial antidotes to election rigging is unremitting vigilance by the citizenry.

Respondents' Assessment of the Elections

In the estimation of a resounding majority of respondents in each constituency, 95 compared with a mere 4 in the North and 91 compared with 6 in the South, the 2000 elections were generally free and fair. Only 1 and 3 respectively did not know. The national scores are: positive — 92.5% and negative — 3.3%. This was also the verdict of a number of the domestic election observer groups like Ghanalert and the Coalition of Domestic Election Observers (CODEO) comprising over twenty civil society organizations (CSOs) like the Ghana Bar Association (GBA), the Ghana National Union of Teachers (GNAT), the National Union of Ghana Students (NUGS) etc. (*The Evening News*, 3 January 2001; *The Independent*, 18 December 2000).

Media Coverage

As many as 93 compared with 4 in the North and 95 compared with none in the South agreed that the state-owned print and electronic media adequately covered the elections. And to a slightly reduced majority, 85 as against 7 and 89 as against 9 respectively, the coverage was fair to all the parties and candidates.

It may be interjected here that the state-owned media in pre-election times generally favoured the ruling NDC. Thus, both honoured Article 5(1) of the 1992 Constitution more in breaching, than in observing, it. It states that: "The State shall provide fair opportunity to all political parties to present their programmes to the public by ensuring equal access to the state-owned media". Even the stories which the state-owned media found convenient to carry on the activities of the opposition parties were so slanted that they turned out to be unfavourable to the public image of such parties.

However, in the run-up to the 2000 elections the state-owned media strenuously tried to cover all the parties reasonably fairly and objectively. In this respect, the performances of the *Daily Graphic* and the Ghana Broadcasting Corporation (GBC) were impressive; and the former for the first time ever went to the extent of designing guidelines for equal, adequate and objective reporting on the parties (CDD, 2000:4-5).

Problems at Polling Stations

On election day there were various media reports of late opening of polling stations, shortage of election materials, poor quality of the indelible ink, voters' names missing from the voters registers etc. All this may have cast doubts on the EC's preparedness for the elections.

In Okaikoi, however, only a few respondents, 7 in the South only, encountered any such problems; but only 4 of these respondents described the nature of the problems they encountered: 3 did not find their names and one had to wait for a long time for lack of ballot papers. Seventy-one respondents as against a significant 25 in the North and nearly all (96) compared with a mere 3 in the South found the election officials helpful; and barely 6 and 4 respondents respectively admitted being intimidated by some people.

On the kind of the security personnel present at their polling stations, slightly under half of respondents in the North and two-thirds in the South spotted the police, 14 and 8 soldiers, 14 and 5 prison warders respectively. Thus the police presence was more heavily felt than that of soldiers. In the North 82 respondents and almost all (97) in the South were happy to see such security personnel around.

The largest number of respondents, 94 in the North and 92 in the

South, were emphatic that voting at their polling stations was orderly. But to 1 and 4 respectively it was disorderly; while 2 in the South only found it chaotic. At national level 95.8% of respondents described it as orderly, 6.3% as disorderly and 0.4% as chaotic (Political Science Department, March 2001: 21).

Thumb-print versus Photo IDs

During the run-up to the December elections the EC supported by segments of the opposition, especially the NPP, decided to convert the voter thumb-print identification (ID) cards into photo ID cards in order to check impersonation. Hell nearly broke loose when the ruling NDC threatened fire and brimstone if the thumb-print ID cards were phased out of existence. It was argued that the execution of this policy would result in a huge proportion of registered voters being disenfranchised because the conversion period was too short.

In the event, a "concerned citizen", Mr P. K. Apaloo, took the matter to the Supreme Court which ruled, inter alia, that both types of ID card should be used in the elections (*Daily Graphic*, 1 December and 5 December 2000; *The Chronicle*, 3-4 December, 2000). Although opposition parties like the GCPP, NRP and CPP accepted the ruling because it finally put a seal on the controversy, the NPP and some CSOs like the GBA considered it a serious blow against democratization (*The Evening News*, 5 December 2000).

When Okaikoi respondents were asked whether they used photo ID cards to vote, their responses were overwhelmingly positive: 93% in the North and 89% in the South; only a few (9% and 1% respectively) voted with thumb-print ID cards. The national averages are: positive — 92.6% and negative — 3.9%. A scant 1% in the South only had a problem with voting with the thumb-print ID card because of being questioned by the election officials but the problem was resolved to his/her satisfaction.

If these findings on Okaikoi and at national level are representative, then the EC's claim that the greatest number of registered voters succeeded in obtaining photo ID cards was justified. In that case, as Ghanalert correctly observed, "the debate over whether only those with photo ID cards should cast their ballots appeared to be insignificant on election day" (Ghanalert, reported in *The Independent*, 18 December 2000 and *The Guide*, 19 December 2000–2 January 2001).

Results of 7 December Elections in Okaikoi

It will be recalled that the largest group of respondents in Survey I intended to vote for the NPP in the presidential election (49% in the South and 42.7% in the North) as well as in the parliamentary poll (49% and 44.5% respectively). In Survey II the largest proportion of respondents actually voted for the NPP in the presidential election (74% in the North and 68% in the South) as also in the parliamentary election (72% and 66% respectively). The actual results reflected respondents' pattern of voting, although the NDC performed a little better than the scores for the NPP would suggest. The number of registered voters in the South was 92,026 and in the North 111,701.

Table 6.8: Presidential Election

	NPP	%	NDC	%	TURNOUT %
North	38,863	55.9	24,989	36.0	62.2
South	35,589	65.6	16,948	31.2	58.9

Source: Electoral Commission, *7 December Presidential Results Sheets*, 13 December 2000.

Table 6.9: Parliamentary Election

	NPP	%	NDC	%	TURNOUT %
North	36,511	55.5	24,466	37.2	59.4
South	34,179	64.5	16,460	31.1	58.2

Source: *Ghana Gazette*, 5 January 2001.

Presidential Run-off Election

At national level the results were inconclusive because no presidential candidate obtained more than 50% of the votes cast. Kufuor obtained 3,131,739 (48%) and Mills 2,895,575 (45%). A presidential run-off became inevitable, as the Constitution demanded; and it involved the front-runners, the NPP and NDC.

Opinion in Okaikoi on whether or not a run-off was more likely in 2000 than in 1996 was about evenly split, with a slight majority in the South discounting it, as we have seen. In the event it was the sizeable minority in the South who were proved right.

Interestingly, some people including the NPP presidential candidate objected to the holding of the run-off largely because of the huge expenditure involved. In a commercial broadcast, Kufuor reasoned that "it is debatable whether our country, with its current economic hardships, should be called upon to spend as much as 15 billion *cedis* for a second round election in which the outcome is obvious". He therefore, called on Mills, his NDC competitor, "in the spirit of reconciliation . . . to concede [defeat] without putting the nation to further expense and unnecessary tension" (reported in *The Weekend Statesman*, 15–21 December 2000).

It is regrettable that Kufuor and those who shared his position forgot that democracy is a very expensive enterprise. Fortunately the majority opinion prevailed and the run-off came off. But the build-up to the election was haunted by the spectre of a possible volcanic eruption of violence across the country if either of the two contending parties, notably the NDC, lost the election. They traded accusations and counter accusations against each other, with the NPP rightly accusing the NDC of pitting some other ethnic groups against the Asantes or Akans (*The Evening News*, 18 December, 2000). All this threatened to bury the real issues at stake. In the end the good sense of Ghanaians triumphed.

Voter Participation in the Run-off

Respondents in Okaikoi voted overwhelmingly in the run-off (95 in the North and 90 in the South). Eighty-two and 78 respectively voted for Kufuor; while 17 and 10 respectively opted for Mills. Of those who explained why they voted for Mills, 10 in the North and 8 in the South did so for the sake of continuity; 4 and 1 respectively because of his good policies; and 2 apiece in the North only because he represented or was the leader of their party and because they followed the majority in their area.

Forty-five in the South and 41 in the North voted for Kufuor because he represented a change or they wanted a change; 22 and 9 respectively because he was a better candidate or the right person for the job; 1 and 10 because his policies were good; 9 in the North only because they wanted to try him also; and 6 in the South only for his humility and tolerance. It is revealing that in both constituencies none voted for Kufuor because they followed the example of the majority of their tribesmen and women. The consistent pattern of voting by respondents in either constituency is evident in the great majority, 78 as against 13 in the South and 84 as against 11 in the North who said that they voted for the presidential candidate in the first round.

On the whole the overwhelming number of respondents, 94 in the South and 88 in the North, found voting at their various polling stations orderly. A mere 1 and 5 found it disorderly and chaotic respectively. This most favourable opinion is confirmed at national level as follows: orderly — 89.7%; disorderly — 0.2%, and chaotic — 5.2% (Political Science Department, March 2001: 27).

Results of the Run-off

Nationally, Kufuor won the run-off with 3,631,263 (56.9%) votes to Mills's 2,750,124 (43.1%). He also defeated Mills in both Okaikoi contituencies: in the North by a wide margin — 39,153 (61.7%) to Mills' 24,272 (38.3%); and in the South by a whopping margin — 37,669 (72.3%) votes to Mills' 14,398 (27.7%). The additional votes for Kufuor nationally and in Okaikoi were certainly due partly to the support of the other opposition parties. The combined total percentage the other opposition presidential candidates obtained in the first round presidential election was 8.1 in the North and 3.1 in the South. Interestingly, the percentage turnout in the run-off fell from that in the first round by 5.2 in the North and 2.1 in the South, presumably partly because some voters may have thought that the results of the run-off in Kufuor's favour were already a foregone conclusion.

Conclusions

The conclusions to be drawn from the analyses of the two surveys, some of which have been indicated already, are many. But because of space limitation only a few will be highlighted. First, nearly all respondents were registered voters who voted in large numbers in the 2000 elections. However, this did not translate into higher turnouts in either constituency. This may have been due to either the voters' register being possibly bloated or some voters refusing to exercise their franchise. If the latter was the case, the parties, NCCE, EC and human rights advocacy CSOs will have to step up the political education of the electorate.

Secondly, of the 410 respondents in the two surveys slightly more than one-third (136) were registered party members. Here, also, the parties must intensify their membership drive campaigns. In any case the NPP claimed the lion's share of the number of such respondents as well as of the non-registered ones. The majority of respondents preferred the NPP to any other party. In the actual elections the Okaikoi electorate as a whole very strongly rooted for the NPP as well, followed by the NDC. This consistent pattern of voting since 1992 has made the two constituencies NPP strongholds. Indeed, a two-party, rather than a multiparty, system has been developing both in Okaikoi and in the country as a whole since then.

Thirdly, despite the paucity of registered party members, a sizeable number of respondents accepted party politics as a necessary constitutive element of democratic governance, which is very healthy for democratization. But a minority were afflicted by the "cynicism syndrome", as already noted. This quixotic stance is dangerous to democratization. Hence, the necessity for party politics cannot be over-emphasized. Such is "the human condition" that a world without conflict/antagonism, as envisaged by Karl Marx and some communitarians, is an impossibility. According to one political thinker, in our present circumstances "it is preferable to give [social antagonisms] a political outlet within a pluralistic system. The great strength of liberal democracy . . . is precisely that it provides the institutions [like political parties] that, if properly understood, can shape the element of hostility in a way that defuses [their] potential (Mouffe, 1993: 4–5).

In the opinion of numerous respondents two of the afflictions of the opposition parties were the inadequate finance and logistics at their disposal; and they believed that ruling parties always "have an undue advantage over the opposition parties". But they simultaneously rejected state funding of all the parties. The rationale behind the demand for state funding is to reduce to a tolerable level the incumbency advantage. The debate on state funding and incumbency advantage must be re-opened; for there is an urgent need to design "ground rules" towards the emergence of a level playing field for all the parties.

Fourthly, most respondents relied more heavily on the media for political information; and they considered the private radio stations as the most trustworthy media source to tell the truth. Besides, many correspondents agreed that the media fairly and adequately covered the campaigns of all the parties. That the media, especially the private radio stations and newspapers (excepting the pro-NDC papers) played a cardinal role in the 2000 elections cannot be over-emphasized (see, e.g., *The Chronicle*, 31 October–1 November 2000). On election day particularly, the private radios relayed across the country as a whole news of acts of commission and omission which in no small way may have helped to reduce irregularities and malpractices in many constituencies.

Fifthly, the overwhelming majority of respondents considered the elections generally free, fair and orderly, and they were satisfied with the EC's conduct of the elections. But opinions on its independence from the government were about evenly split between the two constituencies, with the South being more sceptical. The lack of a clear picture on the issue in Okaikoi may be explained in terms of the problems attendant on the voter registration exercise like shortages of materials, its clumsy handling of fixing a date for the first round elections; and its inability to clean the bloated voters' register thoroughly, among other issues. On the credit side, the EC, *inter alia*, provided campaign vehicles to all the parties, converted thumb-print ID cards into photo ID cards despite opposition from some NDC leaders and created the congenial environment for more domestic election monitoring groups to emerge. On balance the EC's management of the electoral process has progressively improved since 1992. It must, however, continue to reform the process with the support of IPAC by, *inter alia*, radically reviewing the bloated voters' register, completing the conversion exercise, and re-demarcating the constituencies to ensure justice for the overpopulated ones.

Sixthly, it was found that development issues dominated the electoral calculations of a great many respondents in Okaikoi. In fact, most of them voted for "positive change" largely because of their poor opinion of the performance of the economy, with significant implications for democratization. Such respondents yearned both for democracy and for the upliftment of their living standards. Therefore, the new state managers must so co-ordinate political and economic reforms that the two reinforce, rather than conflict with each other (Luckham and White, 1996: 9). And, for emphasis, the Bretton Woods financial institutions and the international donor community should not force down the throat of the new government such unreasonable economic conditionalities (like privatization of water) as to undermine continued democratisation in Ghana.

Finally, the majority of respondents in Okaikoi and in the country (Political Science Department, February 2001:11) opined that Ghana could be described as a democracy which has improved since 1996. This opinion confirms the findings of several surveys on the issue (as, e.g., Bratton *et. al.*, 1999: 1–18). At first glance such a view is unexceptionable. After all the formal democratic institutions have been established; they have appeared to be operating fairly well. And only the benighted would deny that Ghanaians as a whole have experienced some measure of civil and political rights and competitive elections since the dark days of the Provisional National Defence Council (PNDC).

But at a deeper level of scrutiny, what was evolving in Ghana under Rawlings during (1993–2000) may at best be characterized as "low intensity democracy" (Gills *et. al.* eds, 1993, quoted in Luckham and White eds, 1996: 1–10 and *passim*) or "façade" or "Canada-dry" democracy serving as a cosmetic cover for the operation of neo-patrimonial practices. These include "[over] centralization of power in the hands of the president, personal loyalties, pervasive clientelism [and] . . . corruption, an unofficial presidential control of the armed forces [and other security institutions] — all these informal [neo-patrimonial] institutions [and practices] undercut [through manipulation] the formal democratic institutions [constitutionally mandated] to monitor, check and discipline the government . . ." (Sandbrook and Oelbaum, 1999:12). There was pervasive systemic corruption. This was not what the pro-democracy forces as a whole bargained for.

Since independence, if not well before it, a fairly solid constituency for genuine constitutional-democratic governance has been building up, even if by fits and starts, as opposed to the anti-democratic hardliners of the "political lunatic fringe". This largely explains why the fanciful experiments with other systems of rule launched by such hardliners after their coups have not lasted beyond two decades in Ghana. The 2000 elections have hopefully ushered in a new dawn of genuine democratisation in Ghana. But, as is well known, there have been too many false dawns in the country's post-independence history. It is hoped, and expected, that the current new dawn will not be another false one.

REFERENCES

Austin, D. (1964) *Politics in Ghana: 1946–1960*, London: Oxford University Press.

Bratton, M, P. Lewis and E. Gyimah-Boadi (1999) *Attitudes to Democracy and Markets in Ghana*, Afobarometer Paper No. 2, Department of Political Science, Michigan State University, USA.

Centre for Democracy and Development, Ghana (December 200) *Democracy Watch*, Accra, Vol. 1, No. 4.

Commonwealth Secretariat (1997) *The Presidential and Parliamentary Elections in Ghana, 7 December 1996: the Report of the Commonwealth Observer Group*, London: Creative Base Europe Ltd.

Daily Graphic (Accra) 21 September 2000; 20 November 2000; 1 December 2000; and 5 December 2000.

Drah, F. K (1996) "Rapporteur's Report", in K. Kumado (ed.) *Funding of Political Parties in West Africa*, Accra: Friedrich Ebert Foundation.

Drah, F. K (1996) "The Concept of Civil Society in Africa: A Viewpoint" in F.K. Drah and M. Oquaye (eds.) *Civil Society in Ghana*, Accra: Friedrich Ebert Foundation (printed by Gold Type Press).

Drah, F. K (1998) "The 1996 Elections and Democratisation: A Case Study of Okaikoi", in J. R. A. Ayee (ed.) *The 1996 General Elections and Democratic Consolidation in Ghana*, Accra: Department of Political Science, Legon.

Department of Political Science, Legon (February 2001) *Pre-Elections Survey: 2000 Elections (National): Summary of Pre-Elections Survey*.

Department of Political Science (March 2001) *Post Elections Survey: 2000 Elections (National): Summary of Pre-Elections Survey*.

Dunn, J. and A. F. Robertson (1973) *Dependence and Opportunity: Political Change in Ahafo*, Cambridge: Cambridge University Press.

Electoral Commission (13 December 2000) *7 December Presidential Results Data Sheets*.

Free Press (Accra) 26 April 2000.

Ghana Gazette (12 January 2001) *Results of the 28 December, 2000 Presidential Run-off Election*.

Ghana Palaver (Accra) 27 September 2000 and 13–14 November 2000.

Ghana Statistical Service (1997) *Core Welfare Indicators Questionnaire (CWIQ) Survey*, Accra.

Gills, B. et. al; eds. (1993) *Low Intensity Democracy: Political Power in the New World Order*, London: Pluto.

Hart E. and E. Gyimah-Boadi (January 2000) *Business Associations in Ghana's Transition* (Critical Perspectives No. 3), Centre for Democracy and Development, Accra.

Hess, H. (1994) *Party Work in Social Democratic Parties: A Practical Handbook*, Bonn: Friedrich Ebert Foundation.

Kumado, K (1996) "Financing of Political Parties in Ghana: The Case for Public Funding" in K. Kumado (ed.) *Funding of Political Parties in West Africa*, Accra: Friedrich Ebert Foundation.

Luckham, R. and G. White (eds.) (1996) *Democratisation in the South: The Jagged Wave*, Manchester: Manchester University Press.

Mouffe, C. (1989) *The Return of the Political*, London: Verso.

National Democratic Congress, *Constitution*.
New Patriotic Party, *Constitution*.
Public Agenda, (Accra) 20-26 November 2000.
Sandbrook, R. and J. Oelbaum (June 1999) *Reforming the Political Kingdom: Governance and Development in Ghana's Fourth Republic*, (Critical Perspectives No.2), Centre for Democracy and Development, Accra.
The Chronicle, (Accra) 31 October–1 November 2000; 3–4 December 2000; 3–4 January 2001.
The Evening News (Accra) 3 January 2000; 12 May 2000; 21 September 2000; 5 December 2000; and 18 December, 2000.
The Guide (Accra) 19 December 2000–2 January 2001.
The Independent (Accra) 5 November 2000; 18 December 2000; and 11 January 2001).
The Weekend Statesman (Accra) 24–30 November 2000; and 15–21 December 2000.

CHAPTER 7

Survey Pattern and Election Outcomes in the Mfantseman West and Cape Coast Constituencies

KWAME BOAFO-ARTHUR

Introduction

Elections serve as an effective barometer that gauges the moods, propensities and preferences of electorates. More importantly, elections symbolize the spirit of popular participation, which is crucial in any democratic setting. This applies to the 2000 elections just like earlier ones held during the 4th Republic in Ghana.

The uniqueness of Ghana's 2000 elections lies in the fact that it led to a peaceful change of government. Even though the New Patriotic Party (NPP) won the parliamentary and presidential elections in the Cape Coast constituency, the same cannot be said for the Mfantseman West Constituency. In the main elections the National Democratic Congress (NDC) won both the parliamentary and presidential elections in the Mfantseman West constituency. Nonetheless, the NPP won the run-off in both constituencies.

Many issues arise out of these outcomes. What explains the preferences of the electorate in the two constituencies? Why was there a shift of support to the NPP in the run-off? Were the electorate fully cognizant of the main issues at stake?

The foregoing and many other issues are tackled in this chapter with reference to the survey patterns and the electoral outcomes in the Mfantseman West and Cape Coast constituencies.

Profile

Cape Coast, the capital of the Central Region, has been a political hot spot since the inception of the Fourth Republic. Political contestation for the parliamentary seat since 1996 has always been intense and acrimonious. This has been the case because the incumbent MP, Christine Churcher, who also won the 1996 parliamentary election to represent the constituency, turned out to be a political firebrand for the NPP and all attempts by the NDC to win the seat in the 1996 and 2000 elections failed. Paradoxically, Ms Churcher was once a Provisional National Defence Council (PNDC) Secretary. Her defection from the PNDC and teaming up with the opposition raised the stakes in both the 1996 and 2000 elections.

In political terms, Cape Coast also has a very rich history. It was formerly the capital of Ghana until the colonial administrators deemed Accra to be strategic enough and thereby moved the capital to Accra. Apart from that Cape Coast is known far and wide as the cradle of education in Ghana. It boasts numerous first class secondary schools and a University and most of the inhabitants are politically well informed. Cape Coast castle that served as the seat of government when Cape Coast was the capital is equally a topnotch tourist attraction. Being the final point where captured slaves were transferred unto slave ships bound for the new world has its own emotive impact on tourists, especially African-Americans who never hesitate to visit the castle chamber to see how their forefathers were kept before transshipment to the new world. Its apparent elite status gives the impression that decisions by the electorate would be the result of deep reflection on several relevant variables.

The Mfantseman West constituency with Saltpond as its capital has a rich political pedigree of its own. The United Gold Coast Convention (UGCC) was formed at Saltpond. Dr Kwame Nkrumah also formed the Convention Peoples' Party (CPP) at Saltpond after breaking from the United Gold Coast Convention (UGCC). In terms of political sophistication, the constituency can easily rank second to the Cape Coast constituency in the Central Region.

In terms of the politics of the Fourth Republic, the constituency has produced its own form of political drama or theatrics. In the 1996 elections, the candidate of the NPP dramatically defected to the NDC in a run-off election and actually campaigned with the NDC candidate much to the chagrin of the top brass of the NPP. The run-off became necessary as a result of a mix up of ballot papers with the contiguous Mfantseman East constituency. More importantly, the NDC has been winning the constituency since the inception of the Fourth Republic.

From the foregoing, it is not difficult to fathom why the two constituencies were selected for the election survey. In terms of representation, the two constituencies straddle both coastal fishing and inland farming communities. Both have long coastal stretches of fishing communities and inland farming communities apart from the large dose of blue-collar workers and numerous educational institutions. Thus, the survey in the two constituencies clearly captured representative samples of government workers, private entrepreneurs, farmers, fishermen and artisans.

Demographic Data

Gender Distribution

In the pre-election survey 61 male respondents and 39 female respondents were interviewed in the Mfantseman West constituency. Corresponding figures for the Cape Coast constituency were 50 male and 50 female. However, in the post-election survey there were 64 male and 36 female respondents for the Mfantseman West constituency and 57 male and 43 female respondents in the Cape Coast constituency. It was difficult to get an equal number of respondents because of the unwillingness of most women to participate in the interviews.

Age Distribution

The age distributions of the respondents in both the pre- and post-election surveys were equally interesting. In the pre-election survey respondents aged 31–40 years accounted for 25 per cent and 24 per cent in the Mfantseman West and Cape Coast constituencies respectively. The same 25 per cent of the age bracket were interviewed in the post-election survey in Mfantseman West whilst the corresponding figure for the Cape Coast constituency was 29 per cent. For those within the age group of 18-25, 20 per cent were interviewed in the Mfantseman West constituency and 25 per cent were interviewed Cape Coast constituency. In the post-election survey 14 per cent of that age group responded in the Mfantseman West constituency and 24 per cent in the Cape Coast constituency.

Overall, 80 per cent and 91 per cent of respondents in the Mfantseman West and Cape Coast constituencies were between the ages of 18 to 50 in the pre-election survey. For the post-election survey 66 per cent and 80 per cent of respondents in the Mfantseman West and Cape Coast constituencies respectively were within the age group 18 to 50. The implication is that a majority of respondents were relatively young even though those polled in the Cape Coast constituency were younger than in the Mfantseman West constituency.

Another interesting feature of the demographic data is the educational background of the respondents. Should one attribute the ability to analyze issues to those who are highly educated or to all the electorate? Can those having only primary education be seen as being well informed and therefore capable of making an informed political judgement?

In both the pre-election and post-election surveys, the percentage of those with university and technical or teacher training educational background was low. For instance, whilst respondents with university education constituted one per cent and 3 per cent in the Mfantseman West and Cape Coast constituencies respectively, the corresponding figures for the post-election survey were 5 per cent and 11 per cent respectively. The majority of respondents had a primary school background. In the pre-election survey, those with primary school education constituted 50 per cent and 51 per cent of respondents in the Mfantseman West and Cape Coast constituencies respectively whilst in the post-election survey, 57 per cent were interviewed in the Mfantseman West and 50 per cent in the Cape Coast constituencies. Nonetheless, numbers of respondents with secondary school background were quite appreciable. In the pre-election survey, 24 per cent in the Mfantseman West constituency and 25 per cent in Cape Coast constituency were interviewed. The percentages for the post-election survey in the Mfantseman West and Cape Coast constituencies were 23 and 25 respectively.

Occupation

The occupational background of respondents points to a preponderant number being artisans. For instance, in the pre-election survey, 27 per cent of respondents in Mfantseman West and 32 per cent in the Cape Coast constituency were artisans. In the post-election survey, 17 per cent and 61 per cent in the Mfantseman West and Cape Coast constituencies respectively were artisans. Whereas 12 per cent respondents in the pre-election survey in Mfantseman West were farmers, in the Cape Coast constituency farmers constituted only 2 per cent. The corresponding figures for the post-election survey for the two constituencies in that order were 11 per cent and 0 per cent for Mfantseman West and Cape Coast respectively. The unemployed constituted 15 per cent and 13 per cent in the Mfantseman West and Cape Coast constituencies respectively. For the post-election survey, 12 per cent and 11 per cent of the interviewees in the Mfantseman West and Cape Coast constituencies respectively claimed to be unemployed.

Religion

With regard to religion, most respondents in both the pre-election and post-election surveys were Christians. In the pre-election survey, 84 per cent and 85 per cent of respondents in the Mfantseman West constituency and the Cape Coast constituency respectively were Christians. Muslims formed 11 per cent in Mfantseman West and 12 per cent of respondents in the Cape Coast constituencies. In the post-election survey, 22 per cent in the Mfantseman West constituency and 15 per cent in the Cape Coast constituency were Muslims while 73 per cent in the Mfantseman West constituency and 81 per cent in the Cape Coast constituency were Christians. Numbers of animists or traditional religionists in both pre- and post-election surveys were quite low.

Income

The incomes of respondent clearly depicted the dire economic situation in the country. In both the pre-and post-election surveys, many respondents were on very low incomes. For example in the pre-election survey, 64 per cent in the Mfantseman West constituency and 72 per cent in the Cape Coast constituency had annual an income of less than ¢5 million. For the post-election survey, 53 per cent in the Mfantseman West constituency and 27 per cent in the Cape Coast constituency had a monthly income of less than ¢100,000. In all, 96 per cent of post-election respondents in the Mfantseman West constituency and 86 per cent of those in the Cape Coast constituency earned below ¢400,000 per month. A sizeable percentage of 11 for the Mfantseman West constituency and 19 per cent of those in the Cape Coast constituency had no form of income whatsoever.

Political Participation

In simple terms, political participation involves the process of how and why people get involved in politics. Chilcote (1981) makes it clear that mass mobilization and participation are essential to democracy. From a different perspective, Luckham and White (1996) also contend that without political participation and public awareness, the virtues of democratic governance embracing transparency, responsiveness, accountability, official propriety and tolerance cannot be achieved. Thus the essence of political participation in a democratic setting cannot be gainsaid.

In the two constituencies under review the extent of participation especially in the areas of voting in the district, parliamentary and presidential elections was gauged. In addition, respondents were asked about their involvement in political party activities such as attending meetings, rallies, financial contributions to party activities and the holding of party positions.

In the pre-election survey 100 per cent of those interviewed in both the Mfantseman West and Cape Coast constituencies were registered voters. However, in the post-election survey, 94 per cent and 98 per cent of respondents in the Mfantseman West and Cape Coast constituencies respectively were registered voters. Most of the respondents in the two constituencies voted in the 1996 and 2000 parliamentary and presidential elections. Interestingly, most of those polled were not registered members of political parties. In the pre-election survey, 62 per cent and 68 per cent in the Mfantseman West and Cape Coast constituencies respectively were not registered members of political parties. In the post-election survey, 58 per cent and 66 per cent of those interviewed in the Mfantseman West and Cape Coast constituencies respectively were not registered members of political parties. Nonetheless, the percentages that voted in both the 1996 and 2000 elections were very high in both constituencies. For instance, in the pre-election survey, 84 per cent of the respondents in the Mfantseman West constituency and 86 per cent in the Cape Coast constituency voted in the 1996 presidential and parliamentary elections. In the post-election survey, 92 per cent and 93 per cent of respondents in the Mfantseman West and Cape Coast constituencies respectively voted in the 2000 presidential and parliamentary elections.

What could be said about the low registration as party members and the high voter turnout in the two constituencies is that even though there are many floating voters in the constituencies their sense of political participation is high. As such, none of the constituency is a safe seat for any political party since there is no serious commitment to party activities such as being a registered member of a political party would seem to imply. It further implies that winning either of the seats calls for intense campaigning by the contestants. Incidentally, respondents could not give any credible reason for not being a registered member of a political party. Whereas 29 per cent in the Mfantseman West claimed ignorance of the registration procedure, 19 per cent in Cape Coast constituency felt they disliked party politics hence their refusal to register with a political party. It is instructive to note however that 50 per cent of those who had not registered with any political party in the Mfantseman West and 52 per cent of those in Cape Coast were inclined towards the New Patriotic Party while 8 per cent in the Mfantseman West and 16 per cent in Cape Coast constituency were sympathetic towards the National Democratic Congress respectively.

Voter Perception of the Economy

Economic development presents the single most important challenge to governments. It turns out to be also the single most important barometer for the assessment of the performance of a government. The nature of the economy affects everybody in a political system irrespective of education or social standing. It is further argued by some that economic development also determines the lifespan of various regimes. In Ghana, various military regimes have capitalized on economic hardships to overthrow a government in power. In a democratic setting, the economy is bound to be the most important yardstick for assessing regime performance.

Thus, the economy was bound to be of immense significance in the 2000 elections since its performance was bound to influence the mode of voting by the electorate. In the pre-election survey when respondents were asked what they thought about the state of the Ghanaian economy today, the responses in the two constituencies were as in Table 7.1.

Clearly, voter perception of the economy was negative in both constituencies. Whilst 56 per cent in Mfantseman West constituency and 66 per cent in Cape Coast constituency felt the economy was very bad, only 2 per cent in Mfantseman West and 1 per cent in Cape Coast constituencies were of the view that the economy was very good. Altogether, 80 per cent in Mfantseman West constituency and 83 per cent in Cape Coast constituency indicated that the economy was not in very good shape.

An appreciable number of respondents in both constituencies also felt the economy had not improved in any way since the last elections in 1996. In the Mfantseman West and Cape Coast constituencies, 68 per

Table 7.1: The State of the Economy

	Mfantseman West Frequency	Mfantseman West Percentage %	Cape Coast Frequency	Cape Coast Percentage %
Very Good	2	2	1	1
Good	11	11	11	11
Bad	24	24	17	17
Very bad	56	56	66	66
Neither good or bad	6	6	5	5
Don't know	1	1	–	–
TOTAL	100	100	100	100

cent and 69 per cent respectively felt the economy had become worse. At the same time, 16 per cent in Mfantseman West and 12 per cent in Cape Coast constituency were of the view that the economy had just improved since the 1996 elections. In addition, 11 per cent in Mfantseman West constituency and 17 per cent in Cape Coast constituency felt that there had been a sharp economic deterioration since the last elections in 1996.

The views of respondents on the living standards of individual households were also dismal. To the question: "Has your household's standard of living improved since the last elections?" The responses were as in Table 7.2.

Table 7.2: Household

	Mfantseman West Frequency	Mfantseman West Percentage %	Cape Coast Frequency	Cape Coast Percentage %
Much better		2	6	6
A little better	21	21	20	20
A little worse	42	42	28	28
Much worse	33	33	45	45
Don't know	2	2	1	1
TOTAL	100	100	100	100

In the Mfantseman West constituency 75 per cent of the respondents felt the economy was not in any better shape. Of this group, 42 per cent were of the view that the economy was a little worse whilst 33 per cent felt the economy was much worse. In the Cape Coast constituency 73 per cent perceived the economy in a bad shape. Whilst 28 per cent felt the economy was a little worse, 45 per cent were of the view that the economy was much worse. However, 21 per cent in Mfantseman West constituency and 20 per cent in Cape Coast constituency believed that the economy was a little better. Altogether, the economy was perceived by a higher percentage as being in trouble.

Respondents perceived unemployment as the major economic problem in Ghana today as Table 7.3 clearly shows in answer to the question "What do you consider to be the major economic problem in Ghana today?"

Table 7.3: Major Economic Problems

	Mfantseman West Frequency	Mfantseman West Percentage %	Cape Coast Frequency	Cape Coast Percentage %
Inflation	24	24	12	12
Competition from cheap imports	–	–	3	3
High interest rates	1	1	–	–
Don't know	–	–	–	–
Unemployment	50	50	54	54
Lack of private investments	–	–	–	–
Depreciation of the *cedi*	23	23	26	26
Other	1	1	2	2
Missing	1	1	3	3
TOTAL	100	100	100	100

As noted above, respondents see unemployment as the major economic problem facing the country. In the Mfantseman West constituency 50 per cent of respondents as compared to 54 per cent in the

Cape Coast constituency see unemployment as a major problem. Whilst 24 per cent in Mfantseman West constituency perceive inflation as the second major problem, 26 per cent in Cape Coast constituency see depreciation of the *cedi* as the second major economic problem. Altogether, unemployment, inflation, and the depreciation of the *cedi* were seen as major developmental constraints that have impacted negatively on the economy of the nation.

Democratic Process

Another issue of importance is the perception by the electorate of the democratic process which includes the perception of the political system, press freedom, and the freedom of political groups in the political system. In both constituencies, an overwhelming majority were of the view that Ghana could be aptly described as a democratic country. In the Mfantseman West and Cape Coast constituencies 70 per cent and 75 per cent of the respondents respectively were of this view.

Table 7.4: Has Democracy Improved Over the Last Four Years?

	Mfantseman West		Cape Coast	
	Frequency	Percentage %	Frequency	Percentage %
Yes	60	60	68	68
No	24	24	23	23
Don't know	15	15	9	9
Missing	1	1	–	–
TOTAL	100	100	100	100

Similarly, 60 per cent in the Mfantseman West constituency and 68 per cent in the Cape Coast constituency indicated that democracy had improved since the last elections in 1996. However, 24 per cent in Mfantseman West constituency and 23 per cent in Cape Coast constituency were of the opinion that there had not been any appreciable improvement in democracy since the last elections. These were responses to the question whether over the past four years democracy had improved in Ghana. Table 7.4 gives a pictorial view of the responses.

Freedom of the press is equally crucial in any democratic setting. Respondents were of the view that the press in Ghana has been free since the last elections. In the Mfantseman West and Cape Coast constituencies 71 per cent and 76 per cent respectively hold the view that the press in Ghana has more freedom now than four years ago. Similarly, respondents in the two constituencies were of the view that political parties and other associations have more freedom now than four years ago. In Mfantseman West, 73 per cent were of this view whilst 80 per cent in Cape Coast constituency share the same opinion.

Electoral Process

Freedom to exercise one's franchise without fear of intimidation underlies the electoral process. In situations where the electorate fear to express themselves or are coerced to vote in a particular line, the true feelings as well as the electoral preferences of the people are stifled. Thus the electoral process indicates the general political climate in which elections are conducted.

It is clear from the responses of those interviewed in the two constituencies that generally the electoral climate was propitious for the genuine expression of citizen preferences in the 2000 elections. A greater percentage of respondents in both constituencies felt a free atmosphere existed for free and fair elections in the 2000 elections. In Mfantseman West, 69 per cent of interviewees were of the view that free and fair conditions existed. For Cape Coast constituency 53 per cent were of similar view. What was baffling was an equally high percentage in both constituencies who could not tell whether conditions propitious for free and fair elections existed. In Mfantseman West the percentage was 21 whilst in the Cape Coast constituency it was as high as 34 per cent. The implication, in my view, is that a sizable number of the respondents could not pinpoint what amounts to free and fair conditions for democratic elections. This calls for intensive education by the National Commission for Civic Education (NCCE).

A higher percentage of respondents also felt that the 1996 elections had been conducted in a free and fair atmosphere. For instance while 50 per cent in the Cape Coast constituency felt the elections had been conducted in a free and fair atmosphere, 28 per cent felt otherwise. In the Mfantseman West constituency 39 per cent as opposed to 30 per cent felt the 1996 elections had been conducted in a free and fair atmosphere.

In spite of the free and fair atmosphere that characterized the 1996 and 2000 elections, the majority of respondents were convinced that the Electoral Commission was not truly independent of the government. Whether they thought the Electoral Commission was independent of government control elicited the following responses in Table 7.5.

Table 7.5: Independence of the Electoral Commission

	Mfantseman West		Cape Coast	
	Frequency	Percentage %	Frequency	Percentage %
Yes	30	30	23	23
No	36	36	47	47
Don't know	33	33	29	29
Missing	1	1	1	1
TOTAL	100	100	100	100

In the Mfantseman West constituency a high 36 per cent were of the view that the EC was not independent of the government as against 30 per cent who were firmly convinced that the EC was independent. In the Cape Coast constituency 47 per cent felt the EC was not independent of the government as against 23 per cent who felt the EC was independent. As many as 33 per cent in Mfantseman West and 29 per cent in Cape Coast constituencies felt however that they could not tell whether the EC was independent of the government or not.

Interestingly, many felt that apart from the EC there was no other effective way of influencing the outcome of the elections. In the Mfantseman West constituency 49 per cent felt that there was no other mode of influencing electoral outcomes. The corresponding figure for Cape Coast constituency was 48 per cent. Again, a high 38 per cent for Mfantseman West constituency and 35 per cent for Cape Coast constituency indicated they did not know whether there existed other avenues for influencing electoral outcomes. What the responses tell us simply is that the EC is still perceived in a negative light and must still work on improving its image.

Another point of interest is the relative advantages carried by contesting parties into the electoral fray. Respondents were of the view that incumbency carried undue advantages. In the Mfantseman West constituency 51 per cent as against 21 per cent and in the Cape Coast constituency, 62 per cent as against 24 per cent were of the view that the party in power got undue advantage over the parties in opposition during elections.

Party System

For almost twenty years, Ghana was under the iron rule of the PNDC. Many were those who felt very strongly that for an opposition party to wrestle power from the NDC was not possible. However, in the pre-election survey it became evident that an opposition party could wrest political power from the ruling government. Responses to the question about the chances of an opposition party winning the presidential elections make it clear as Table 7.6 shows.

Table 7.6: Chances of an Opposition Party Winning the Presidential Election

	Mfantseman West		*Cape Coast*	
	Frequency	*Percentage %*	*Frequency*	*Percentage %*
Very good	38	38	42	42
Good	19	19	32	32
Not so good	21	21	16	16
Don't know	22	22	10	10
Missing	–	–	–	–
TOTAL	100	100	100	100

Respondents were of the view that the opposition had the chance of winning the presidential elections. In the Mfantseman West constituency 38 per cent of respondents felt the opposition could win the presidential elections. A high 42 per cent in the Cape Coast constituency were of the same opinion. However, 21 per cent in Mfantseman West constituency and 16 per cent in Cape Coast constituency believed that the chances were not too good. A sizable percentage of 22 in Mfantseman West constituency and 10 in Cape Coast constituency could not predict. Correspondingly, the respondents felt the chances of the Progressive Alliance made up of the NDC, EGLE, and DPP were not so good in answer to whether the Progressive Alliance had good chances of winning the elections as table 7.7 indicates.

Table 7.7: Chances of the Progressive Alliance Winning the Elections

	Mfantseman West		Cape Coast	
	Frequency	Percentage %	Frequency	Percentage %
Very good	20	20	22	22
Good	22	22	18	18
Not so good	34	34	42	42
Don't know	24	24	17	17
Missing	–	–	–	–
TOTAL	100	100	100	100

34 per cent of respondents in Mfantseman West constituency and 42 per cent of respondents in the Cape Coast constituency were of the opinion that the chances of the Progressive Alliance winning the presidential election were not so good. Whilst 20 per cent in the Mfantseman West constituency and 22 per cent in Cape Coast constituency were convinced that the alliance had very good chance of winning the presidential election, 22 per cent in the Mfantseman West and 18 per cent in Cape Coast were of the view that the alliance's chances were good. As many as 24 per cent in Mfantseman West and 17 per cent in Cape Coast constituency indicated that they did not know which party was going to win the elections.

However, respondents could not predict that there was going to be a run-off in the presidential elections. While 21 per cent in Mfantseman West constituency and 29 per cent in Cape Coast constituency believed a run-off was likely, 64 per cent in Mfantseman West and 64 per cent in Cape Coast were of the view that run-off was unlikely.

The issue of the financing of political parties has been the subject of intense debate in Ghana. Whilst the government of the NDC had been adamant on the issue of parties funding their own campaigns, those in the opposition preferred some form of state funding for political parties. Respondents in the two constituencies favoured state funding of political parties. Asked whether parties should be financed by the state, the responses were:

Table 7.8: Should the State Finance Parties?

	Mfantseman West Frequency	Mfantseman West Percentage %	Cape Coast Frequency	Cape Coast Percentage %
Yes	58	58	65	65
No	39	39	32	32
Don't know	3	3	3	3
Missing	–	–	–	–
TOTAL	100	100	100	100

A very high percentage of 58 in Mfantseman West constituency and 65 in the Cape Coast constituency expressed preference for the state funding of political parties. Those opposed to funding of political parties in the Mfantseman West constituency and Cape Coast constituency were 39 per cent and 32 per cent respectively.

The modes of selecting candidates to stand on various party tickets in the constituencies were found to be very democratic. In the Mfantseman West constituency 67 per cent found the process democratic and the same percentage in the Cape Coast constituency were of the same view.

Running Mates

The criteria for the selection of running mates were also crucial. However, respondents were of the view that the most important variable was the political experience of the running mate. In both the Mfantseman West constituency and the Cape Coast constituency experience was ranked very high. For the former 86 per cent of respondents felt experience was crucial and for the latter, 90 per cent felt experience was very important. In spite of that, a majority of respondents in both constituencies were of the conviction that the choice of a running mate was not going to influence their votes for particular parties. In Mfantseman West constituency 83 per cent and 95 per cent in Cape Coast constituency expressed such views.

Opinion on the issue of regional balance in the selection of the president and the running mates was divided in the two constituencies. Whereas in Mfantseman West constituency 31 per cent were in support, an overwhelming 64 per cent were convinced that it was not necessary. However, those in the Cape Coast constituency thought otherwise. 56 per cent favoured regional balance while 43 per cent were indifferent to that. Respondents in the two constituencies did not favour ethnic balance in the selection of the president and his vice. In Mfantseman West constituency 29 per cent believed it was important to have an ethnic balance while 66 per cent felt it was not necessary. In the Cape Coast constituency 45 per cent favoured ethnic balanced while 54 per cent were not in favour.

Media

Dissemination of information through the media is very important not only in educating the people on their rights but also influencing their voting patterns at times. Respondents made it clear as Table 7.9 shows that radio is an effective means of reaching the people. The following responses were in answer to the question which source they have found to be the most useful in deciding whom to vote for in their constituency.

In Mfantseman West constituency 61 per cent of respondents regularly listened to radios through which they followed political events. In the Cape Coast constituency 74 per cent were regular listeners to the radio. However, 17 per cent in Mfantseman West constituency and 14 per cent in Cape Coast constituency also patronized the television. With regard to the veracity of information from the media a majority of respondents in the Mfantseman West constituency (35 per cent) believed private radio stations could be relied upon for accurate information on political events. In the Cape Coast constituency 23 per cent of respondents were of the view that state-owned public radios were more trustworthy even though 20 per cent felt that private radios are more reliable in their reportage.

Table 7.9: Most Useful Media Source on Information

	Mfantseman West		Cape Coast	
	Frequency	Percentage %	Frequency	Percentage %
Television	17	17	14	14
Newspaper	4	4	6	6
Friends and family (word of mouth)	5	5	4	4
Candidate rallies	2	2	1	1
Radio	61	61	74	74
Magazines	–	–	–	–
Posters/Fliers	2	2	1	1
Don't know	6	6	–	–
Other	–	–	–	–
Missing	3	3	–	–
TOTAL	100	100	100	100

Run-off

All the respondents in the two constituencies voted in the run-off. In the Mfantseman constituency 84 per cent voted for Mr J. A. Kufuor whilst 16 per cent voted for Professor Mills. In the Cape Coast constituency 83 per cent voted for Mr Kufuor and 17 per cent voted for Professor Mills. Those who voted for Professor Mills did that for the sake of continuity while those who voted for Kufuor did so because he was an embodiment of change. Others indicated that his policies were good. The overwhelming majority of respondents (90 per cent in Mfantseman West and 91 per cent in Cape Coast constituency) indicated that they voted for the same candidate in the first round of voting.

Conclusion: Lessons

The survey of voter attitudes and perceptions brings out very interesting findings. First, the electorates in the two constituencies could not predict the eventual run-off between Mr Kufuor and Professor Mills. Secondly, respondents clearly underlined the imminent defeat of the ruling party in their responses. The conviction of respondents was strengthened by their overall perception of the performance of the economy. They were concerned about the high unemployment in the country, high inflation and the rapid depreciation of the national currency. The study therefore underlines the critical link between the economy and voting behaviour. The lesson then is that a government that aims to retain power must tackle the nagging economic problems with all seriousness.

Another interesting finding is the continued mistrust of the EC. The fact that respondents believed the electoral commission was not independent of the then ruling government is a serious indictment that ought to concern all peace-loving and democratically minded Ghanaians. Even though respondents could not substantiate the basis of the mistrust, democratically minded people should not allow suspicion of the EC to remain. It is up to the EC to work hard to improve on its image. One believes, however, that the successful change of government through the ballot box should be enough to convince sceptics that the EC is of age and calls and dances to its own tune.

Sustaining or consolidating democracy, among many other things, is also a function of the commitment to democratic principles as well as the acceptance of functional democratic structures by the electorate. The survey pointed to the general belief in the two constituencies that democratic practices had improved since the last elections. The desire to continue in this strain was uppermost in the minds of respondents. This has to be maintained and the best way to carry this along is for those in authority to allow democratic structures to operate in a transparent and accountable manner. By so doing, all citizens could end up being zealous defenders of the democratic ethos.

Finally, a solution has to be found for the gross inequity in party resources so as to bring some degree of fairness to political contestation. When the NPP was in opposition, it made a lot of argument on the need for state funding of political parties. The privileged position of the NDC, most probably, blinded them to the need for sober reflection on the issue. The roles of the parties have changed and since most respondents support the idea of state funding of political parties, it remains to be seen whether the status quo will be maintained or there will be a positive change along the lines of political party funding.

REFERENCES

Chilcote, R. H. (1981) *Theories of Comparative Politics: The Search for a Paradigm* (Boulder, Colorado: Westview Press).

Chazan, N. *et al.* (1992) *Politics and Society in Contemporary Africa* (Boulder, Colorado: Lynne Rienner Publishers).

Luckham, R. and Gordon White (1996) *Democratization in the South: The Jagged Wave* (Manchester: Manchester University Press).

CHAPTER 8

Survey of the 2000 Elections in Berekum and Wenchi East Constituencies

KWASI ANSU-KYEREMEH

Introduction

Both the Berekum and Wenchi constituencies are located in Brong-Ahafo Region which with 17 NDC parliamentary seats out of a total of 21, was the "second world bank" for the ruling NDC. But while the Berekum had an incumbent NDC MP, Wenchi East had a sitting NPP MP.

The choice of Berekum and Wenchi East for this survey was informed though, by prevailing and previous political circumstances. Joseph Henry Owusu-Acheampong, the incumbent Berekum NDC MP, was the Minister of Agriculture and immediate past Majority Leader/Minister of Parliamentary Affairs, in both cases as a member of Cabinet, in the NDC government. During the rule of the PNDC (NDC's antecedent military government), he was the Brong-Ahafo Regional Secretary.

Thus, Owusu-Acheampong was a towering political figure in the Brong Ahafo Region. As the "democrat" Popular Front Party (PFP), precursor to the NPP, Berekum MP in the Third Republic, he had crossed over to join the authoritarian administrations of Rawlings whose coup had removed the parliament to which Owusu-Acheampong had belonged. With the opposition cry for change in the 2000 elections, it was important to observe political events associated with the campaign in his constituency.

The Wenchi East constituency, on the other hand, represented the status quo. The only exciting thing about it was to see whether the sitting NPP minority MP would be able to retain the seat. It would also be interesting to see if as the former constituency of the Prime Minister of the Third Republic, Dr K. A. Busia, its electorate would stick with its incumbent NPP MP to achieve the change in government that the NPP was campaigning for.

Political Violence and the Mood of the Constituencies

Observations during the pre-election survey provided another stark contrast between the two constituencies, which further justified their selection for this study. Berekum was tense. There was evidence of political violence. A twenty-seven-year-old woman had been brutalised by NDC supporters because she would not allow them to paste election posters on an electricity pole in front of her house.[1]

In an interview, the first victim said she had not reported the assault to the police because the she and her family saw MP Owusu-Acheampong as so influential that no successful legal action could be contemplated against any NDC supporter. Also, the victim could not afford to throw away the ¢22,000 the local hospital was charging for the completion of a police injury report form. A second assault (allegedly including a DCE) of a 17-year-old JSS student by NDC supporters had been reported to the police but the complainant had requested the police to discontinue prosecution.

Until contradicted by his detectives, the Chief Inspector of Police would not confirm this act of political violence. Thus, it was no surprise when bloody clashes occurred in Berekum between NDC and NPP supporters later in the campaign. Dissatisfied with police ability to protect them NPP supporters had, accordingly decided to defend themselves.[2]

Indeed, fewer respondents in Berekum (14%) felt parties were equally enabled in terms of logistics (cars, loudspeakers) than Wenchi East (48%). The intimidation in Berekum alluded to earlier was confirmed by a 67% "Yes" response to the question: "Was there intimidation of some party members and supporters by others in the 2000 elections?" Wenchi East responses were 15% "Yes." In both constituencies, respondents found the NDC (55% Berekum and 11% Wenchi East) "guilty of such intimidation" compared to the NPP (17% Berekum and 8% Wenchi). Berekum respondents (36%) found "intimidation by the military/NDC supporters" compared to 12% of their Wenchi East counterparts.

Far from the Berekum situation, no violence was reported in Wenchi by any party officials or the police. Thus, once again, as Berekum violently struggled for change from NDC to NPP, Wenchi East had changed its status quo since 1996 and was waiting only to reaffirm its local politics to achieve the change sought nationally by the NPP to enable it to form a government.

Closure of *CHRIS FM* Radio Station

The influence of Minister/candidate Owusu-Acheampong on local politics was thought to have been brought to bear on the closure of the local *CHRIS FM* radio station by soldiers on 8 November 2000. The Regional Security Council closed the station when the MP blamed a bloody clash between NPP and NDC supporters on "incitement" by the station.

This particular action of the incumbent NDC MP for Berekum appeared to have backfired against him as the National Media Commission (NMC), Commission on Human Rights and Administrative Justice (CHRAJ) and the Ghana Journalists Association (GJA) descended on Berekum and caused the reopening of the station on 21 November 2000.

On 7 and 28 December 2000, the question, then, was whether the events of the period leading to the election as described above would have had an impact on voters' decisions. That is, while no particular drama was expected in Wenchi East, many wondered how the Owusu-Acheampong factor would affect the outcome of the election in Berekum. The answer could not be captured by the survey. But respondents' answers to the pre-election survey, in addition to those of the post-election survey as described in an earlier paragraph, could give some indications. The survey, its responses and how they compared to the results of the elections are described and analysed in the following sections.

The Pre-election Survey

Between Monday, 23 October 2000 and Sunday, 29 October 2000, a seventy-eight-item questionnaire was administered in face-to-face interviews to a sample of 100 respondents in the Berekum and Wenchi East constituencies (total of 200 in the Region). Coordinated by research assistants with post-graduate qualifications, the interviewers were graduates, mostly senior secondary school teachers.

The Sample

Besides questions which related to political variables as pertained to the 2000 elections, the survey also sought knowledge of the characteristics of respondents. These characteristics included gender, age, educational background, occupation, religion and income. In both Berekum and Wenchi

East, there were more male respondents (60% and 51% respectively) than female respondents (39% and 48%). This reflected the more male (58.1) and fewer female (40.7) national percentages.

Three quarters (75%) of respondents in the Berekum constituency belonged to the 18–40 age bracket. A similar figure (71%) was recorded in the Wenchi East constituency. The national figure for that age group was 61.7%. However, while in both Berekum (26%) and Wenchi East (22%) either the age group 18–25 was second to the 31–40 group (29% in each case), at national level, there were more of the 26–30 (20.1%) than the 18–25s (16.9%). In all three cases though, the 31–40 age group constituted the largest (29%, 29% and 26%) age cohort in the sample. The two constituencies (61–70 group at 0.1% and 0.1%) also differed from the national least represented group which was age 71+ (2.5%).

Respondents' educational background indicated that, while at national level the largest group was those with secondary education (23.0%), in both Berekum (50%) and Wenchi East (47%) the largest group was the primary level educated. Those with university education were either not represented in the Wenchi East sample (0.0%) or were the least represented and at the national level (3.9%). The least represented among the Berekum constituency respondents, however, were those respondents with teacher training/technical college education.

The largest group of Berekum respondents claimed to be unemployed (23%), but in Wenchi East, they were farmers (25%) as was the case at national level where they tied with traders at 18% each. Least represented in all three cases was the managerial class: just about half a per cent (0.6%) at the national level, and none (0.0%) in either Berekum or Wenchi East.

It was surprising that no respondent (0.0%) belonged to African traditional religion in either Berekum or Wenchi East. The practice would be expected to have greater presence in rural communities above the five per cent (4.4%) who claimed nationwide to hold that belief. Close to four-fifths (76.2%) described themselves as Christians. In Berekum, the figure for Christians was close to nine-tenths: a whopping 87%. Wenchi East came very close to this at 83%. For the Islamic faith, a tenth (10%) claimed it in Berekum, 14% in Wenchi East, and 16.8% among all respondents nationwide.

Just over half (55%) of the respondents in the Berekum constituency did not disclose their income. Over a third (39%), though, indicated they earned less than five million *cedis* in a year. Another twentieth (6.0%) earned five to ten million *cedis*. As in Wenchi East, no one from the Berekum constituency indicated they earned above ten million *cedis*. In Wenchi East, where about 32% would not disclose their income, over half (53%) earned less than five million *cedis* and 15% between five and ten million *cedis*. Nationally, virtually half (49.2%) of the respondents earned less than five million *cedis*, and 5.7% earned five to ten million *cedis*. Less than one per cent (0.7%) earned more than ten million *cedis* while as many as 44% of all respondents did not indicate how much they earned.

Findings

The above characteristics may have influenced respondents' answers to the rest of the questions summaries of which are provided here under the sub-headings political participation, voter perceptions, and evaluation of the democratic process as relate to elections and party organization. Others are media and the presidential run-off election.

Political Participation

This variable was measured using indicators such as party membership and support including activism and voting behaviour. Less than half (45%) of respondents from the Berekum constituency were registered members of political parties. But this was more than in Wenchi East where just above a quarter (29%) belonged to parties. The national response was 40.1%. Of the 49 holding party cards in Berekum, 40 belonged to the NPP, seven to the NDC, one to CPP and one to UGM.

A similar picture emerged in Wenchi East. And of the 29 out of the one hundred respondents who disclosed their party affiliation, 21 were for the NPP, four for NDC and one for UGM. Nationally, there were 41 identifications with various parties with the percentages: NDC 17.6, NPP 16.0, PNC 2.9, CPP 2.3, NRP 1.8, and UGM/DPP 0.1 each.

The two constituencies differed in their participation in "keep-fit" or "jama."[3] To the question: "Do you participate when your party holds a rally/keep fit/Jama in your town or village?" Nearly two-thirds (64%) of Berekum respondents indicated they participated in the activity against virtually a third (33%) who did not. In contrast among Wenchi East respondents, 30% did while 64% did not.

As to whether parents' party choices affected offspring preferences, while just over a tenth (13%) were influenced by their parents in Berekum, 16% were in Wenchi East. However, almost four-fifths (75%) and over two-thirds (68%) in Berekum and Wenchi East respectively said voting was their personal decision. Only one per cent in each case were influenced by their peers.

Voting

Political participation was also measured in terms of voting during elections. In Berekum, well over three quarters of respondents (88%) voted in the 1996 presidential and parliamentary elections while in Wenchi East as many as nine-tenths (90%) did. About three quarters of respondents (87.1%) voted at national level. Respondents tended to vote for presidential and parliamentary candidates from the same party.

The Horse Race

The first three parties they were going to vote for were nationally: NPP 41.6%, NDC 30.9%, and CPP 4.3%. In Berekum, the pattern was NPP 76%, NDC 12% and PNC 0.3%, while Wenchi East recorded NPP 74%, NDC 10% and CPP 0.4%. Less than a tenth (8.4%) nationally as well as a mere five per cent in the Berekum constituency were undecided.

Participation in local government elections tended to be lower. When respondents were asked whether they had voted in the 1998 District Assembly Elections, their answers were: Berekum 74%, Wenchi East 83% and nationally 75.5%.

The Issues

It is often believed that elections are fought over issues or ought to be so. Election surveys, therefore, endeavour to measure voter concerns about various issues. In this survey, the issues included the economy.

The Economy

The main issue of concern to the electorate seems to have been the state of the Ghanaian economy. About three-fifths (77.4%) of respondents nationally saw it as "bad" (18.3%) or "very bad" (59.1%). The figures for the constituencies were Berekum 83% (11% "bad" and 72% "very bad") and Wenchi East 89% (8% "bad" and 81% "very bad"). Only 4.3% (national), 2.0% (Wenchi East) and 0.0% (Berekum) believed the Ghanaian economy was "very good."

Unemployment (41.3% nationally) was the most mentioned economic problem. Inflation (23.5%) and depreciation of the *cedi* (22.3%) were next of greatest concern. Constituencies responded similarly: unemployment (Berekum 47%, Wenchi East 58%) and inflation/depreciation of the *cedi* (Berekum 24%/24% and Wenchi East 22%/13%).

In hard times, one expects people to seek support. Social relationships and interdependence were such that in the event f having to seek help to enable the household to survive, respondents (59% in Berekum and 62% in Wenchi East) would rather turn to family members.

Views on State of Democratic Governance

A general question was posed: "Do you think Ghana today could be described as a democratic country?" Two thirds (67.2%) of all respondents, nationally, answered in the affirmative while about a fifth (22.5%) responded in the negative. This compares to Berekum's just over half (58%) who said yes and the third (36%) who said no. Wenchi East responses (52% yes and 31% no) were more in line with those of Berekum than nationally.

Regarding media freedom about two-thirds (62.6%) thought there was greater press freedom than four years earlier, while about a fifth (19.4%) thought the opposite. Responses from Wenchi East (53% yes and 26% no) shared this national pattern. In Berekum though, and apparently before *CHRIS FM* radio station was closed, almost three quarters (72%) thought there had been greater press freedom while only 17% did not.

Berekum and Wenchi East respondents differed in terms of the "most useful" information source "in deciding who to vote for in your constituency." For Berekum respondents the sources were television 46%, radio 22% and candidate rallies 18% compared to Wenchi East (66% radio, 16% television and 5.0% each for newspaper, friends/family and candidate rallies). It has already been stated that Berekum was the only constituency where the local radio station (*CHRIS FM*) was closed by the NDC government for part of the election campaign period. The national responses were radio 43.1%, television 29.6% and newspaper 9.8%. Berekum (state-owned public television 39%, private radio 22%, private newspapers 16%) and Wenchi East (private radio 44%, state-owned television 16%, and 11% don't know).

Respondents were also not in total agreement on which of the media they trusted most to tell the truth. Among respondents nationwide, radio was again mentioned most often (46.6%) as "the source found most useful in deciding who to vote for in a respondent's constituency." It was followed by television 19.3%, and candidate rallies 12.8%.

With respect to the medium most trusted by respondents to tell the truth, the findings from Berekum respondents were state-owned television (39%), private radio (22%) and private newspapers (16%). There had been speculation that the closure of the private radio station *CHRIS FM*, might have cost the ruling NDC some votes in this constituency. The high rating of this medium, second only to television both as the medium found useful in deciding which way to vote and as the most trustworthy to tell the truth, seems to lend credence to that speculation.

In Wenchi East, respondents actually found the private radio most (44%) trusted to tell the truth with state-owned television (16%) and private newspapers (9.0%) following in that order. Perhaps the Wenchi East respondents were also sourcing their election information from the two private radio stations located at nearby Techiman (only 20 kilometres away). In both Wenchi East and Berekum, though, one needs to be reminded about high illiteracy rates which would have minimized newspaper readership.

And in terms of freedom of association, by a margin of three-to-one, respondents across the nation thought political parties and other associations had more freedom (67.5%) than four years before the study. Only 17.3% did not think so. Once again, respondents from Berekum held a highly optimistic view. Seven times as many (77%) felt freedom of association as did not (10%). About a fifth (19%) of respondents from Wenchi East though, had no opinion on this issue. But of those who did, 32% believed there was freedom of association while a virtual fifth (19%) saw things differently.

A question sought responses on the confidence of the electorate in the impending 7 December elections. Fewer people contemplated free and fair elections in Wenchi East (55%) than Berekum (63%). An absolute fifth (20%) thought the elections would not be free and fair in either constituency. In fact, a large proportion of respondents seem to have sided with the opposition that the 1996 general elections had not been free and fair.[6]

A finding which should be of concern to the National Electoral Commission (NEC) was about perceptions of its independence by respondents. In both the Berekum and Wenchi East constituencies, more respondents doubted its independence. Although there were large proportions of "don't knows" (23% Berekum and 27% Wenchi East), in both cases, those who thought the Commission was independent (28% and 31%) were fewer than those who thought otherwise (48% and 41%).

Whatever advantage the ruling party enjoyed over the opposition parties was to be realistically assessed against what respondents' perceived to be "the chances of an opposition party winning the presidential election." The numbers were larger in Berekum (57% "very good"/21% "good") and Wenchi East (53% "very good"/21% "good"). In contrast, less than half (43.8%–25.4% "very good"/18.4% "good") saw the incumbent Progressive Alliance (NDC, EGLE, DPP) winning. The latter coalition was given a winning chance of only 24% in Berekum and a mere 13% in Wenchi East.

There was a general agreement among respondents that "most of the parties in Ghana" were not "financially sound." In Berekum, close to two-thirds (62%) responded negatively while in Wenchi East the response was over two-thirds (65%) of respondents.

Internal party democracy was another important concern for this study. A question sought to establish the observance of democratic procedures in the selection of candidates to stand for elections for respondents' parties. Around three-quarters of respondents in Berekum (78%) and Wenchi (72%) thought the process was "democratic." An insignificant number (0.2% in Berekum and 0.4% in Wenchi East) thought the process was "not democratic." The rest of the respondents in the two constituencies could not pass judgement.

It had taken some time for the various presidential candidates to nominate their running mates. The time lapse led to all kinds of speculation with regional, ethnic and even religious factors overplayed and personal qualities and capabilities relatively underplayed as criteria for selection. This study therefore, sought to determine whether in the minds of potential voters, the running mate was a factor to be considered in casting their ballots.

A crucial question in this respect was: "Will the presidential running mate chosen affect the party you will vote for?" The answers provided by the Berekum and Wenchi East constituency respondents suggested the media were wasting precious news and other space on the issue. Political parties could also have spent energy and resources devoted to that issue on other more important strategic things. In Berekum and Wenchi East, 71% and 78% of respondents indicated a presidential running mate would not affect the substantive candidate they were going to vote for.

An element of the personality cult in Ghanaian politics which the study sought to measure was not confirmed by findings of the two Brong-Ahafo constituencies. In Berekum, just about half (48%) of the respondents answered negative to the question "Do parties in Ghana project personalities more than their policies?" In Wenchi East, the "No" answer was as high as 79%. But nationally, respondents were not so sure. While 47.6% responded in the negative, 35.2% responded in the positive.

In the case of the Ghanaian electorate (with some estimates of illiteracy as high as half the population), separation of party and candidate may be the exception rather than the rule.[7] Some may argue that, in certain cases, it is even the party symbol that matters most.[8]

Local Government and Issues of Representation

There was some evidence about reliance upon district assembly representatives in seeking solutions to community problems. Respondents were asked about the *most* effective means of seeking such solutions. Among Berekum respondents, "contacting your own representative on the District Assembly" (60%), "going through your member of parliament" (12%) and "contacting officials of the district assembly itself" (8.0%) were top of the order. Responses from Wenchi East were: "contacting your own representative on the district assembly" (74%), "contacting officials of the district assembly itself" (9.0%), and "going through your church or religious organization" (4.0%).

The Presidential Run-off

Respondents hardly expected a second round of voting in the presidential election. Berekum respondents (39%) and Wenchi East (17%) thought "a second round presidential run-off is more likely in the 2000 elections than in the 1996 one." The split of 39% "Yes" and 39% "No" among Berekum respondents, however, differed from the huge gap between the Wenchi East (17% "Yes"/57% "No") "more likely" numbers.

In the findings of the pre-election survey presented above, respondents in the Berekum and Wenchi East constituencies (and even nationally) were not expecting a second round of voting to choose a president. This, however, was exactly what happened after the official 7 December vote tally. The run-off voting took place on 28 December after which a follow-up survey to the first one sought the views of the electorate about that particular election. The turn-out, according to respondents' answers was 97% in Berekum and 92% in Wenchi East. Perhaps, the most interesting finding here is the comparison of votes in the first round presidential voting and the run-off (see Table 8.1).

Table 8.1: Voter Preferences for President in Percentages

Constituency	Survey 1 NPP	Survey 1 NDC	December 7 NPP	December 7 NDC	December 28 NPP	December 28 NDC	Survey 2 NPP	Survey 2 NDC
Berekum	82	15	64.4	33.4	71.1	28.3	83	14
Wenchi East	63	35	58.2	37.8	65.4	34.2	76	22

In the two constituencies, the votes for the NPP candidate increased in the second round. The questions, however, asked for party to be voted for (for president) in the pre-election survey while respondents were asked to indicate which presidential candidate they voted for by name (supplied) in the post-election survey.

Only a handful of respondents (10% in Berekum and 32% in Wenchi East) were willing to give reasons why they voted for Professor Mills, the NDC candidate. Half of these in Berekum voted for him because he represented their party and was the party leader, while three felt he was "better candidate/honourable."

In the case of John Agyekum Kufuor, the NPP presidential candidate, 83% of Berekum respondents assigned reasons for voting for him. Virtually half of them stated the reason that "he represented a change/want a change." The largest group of Wenchi East respondents (36%) out of the 68% who gave reasons why they voted for him cited the same change as their reason, while 16% of them felt "his policies are good."

Answers to two questions, as set out in Table 8.2, seem to offer some explanation for the voting pattern for president in the two constituencies. Respondents' believed the NPP candidate to have better articulated the most important national issues. In their own constituencies, they also felt the NPP candidate best articulated their most important development needs. This combination ought to have translated into more votes for the NPP flagbearer, John Agyekum Kufuor as one could hardly have expected otherwise.

Table 8.2: Issues Influencing Presidential Votes in Percentages

Issue	Berekum		Wenchi East	
	NPP	NDC	NPP	NDC
Best articulation of most important national issues	86	13	64	23
Best articulated most important development need in constituency	86	13	67	30

It is also interesting how consistent respondents had been in casting their ballots in the two presidential elections as shown in Table 8:1. To the question: "Did you vote for the same presidential candidate in the first round?" Answers were overwhelming "yes" in both constituencies (89% in Berekum and 96% in Wenchi East).

Conclusion

This study set out to probe the extent of progress of western-style democracy in Ghana using the conduct of and participation by electors in the 2000 presidential and parliamentary elections as indicators. Accounts of the two constituencies selected from the Brong-Ahafo Region for the study indicate reasonable progress in the "new" democratic dispensation using the conduct of elections as a measure. There was some violence in Berekum leading to the closure of a local FM station upon which potential voters depended for information about the election campaign. And there were some other incidents of violence.

But all told, whatever pre-election problems were experienced in the Brong Ahafo Region, as represented by the Berekum and Wenchi East constituencies, were not enough to seriously obstruct the achievement of a free and fair election. To this end, one may conclude that there was evidence of improvement of democratic practice. One may accordingly expect less violence (probably violence-free elections as happened in Wenchi East constituency) and a greater advancement in democratic practice in the two constituencies.

NOTES

1. One will recall the Inspector General of Police (IGP) had ordered political parties not to do this and had actually sent police personnel to remove all political party posters from electricity poles in the capital city.
2. Seventeen NPP polling assistants are alleged to have been arrested and detained at the Third Batallion military barracks at Sunyani without charge on the eve of 1996 election day and released only after the election.
3. Early morning jogging during which party songs and slogans were sung.
4. The issue of whether the NDC has a tradition is contentious since its past is more of a military adventurism than a political organization.
5. The Prime Minister of the Second Republic, Dr Kofi Abrefa Busia, hailed from Wenchi constituency.
6. This seems to somehow confirm the NPP's contention, as stated in its documentation of what it perceived as election malpractices, *The Stolen Verdict*.
7. In actual fact, the survey questionnaire ensured all three as categories of choice alternatives in answer to survey questions.
8. Dr Kwesi Nduom (CPP candidate for Komenda, Edina, Eguafo and Abirem) blamed his loss on spoilt ballots resulting from uneducated voters who for each ballot paper (presidential and parliamentary) thumb-printed **twice** on the *Oson* (elephant) symbol of the NPP presidential candidate and his own CPP party symbol of the *Akoninini kokoo* (red cockerel). He had campaigned for voters to vote for the NPP presidential candidate and himself for MP.

CHAPTER 9

The 2000 Elections in Bawku Central and Nabdam Constituencies

DANIEL A. SMITH[1]

Introduction

On the morning of 8 December 2000, following Ghana's first round of presidential and parliamentary elections, the volatile mix of electoral politics and ethnic tensions exploded in Bawku, Upper East Region. The town was under a state of siege for several days. Fighting in Bawku was not arbitrary; it entailed calculated military-like campaigns, replete with AK-47s and other sophisticated assault weapons. The resulting bloodshed left as many as 50 people dead, hundreds of homes and business destroyed, and thousands of lives shattered. The conflict only subsided when military reinforcements from the Regional Security Committee (REGSEC) arrived from Tamale with their armoured vehicles and heavy artillery. While indeed an anomaly, the violence in Bawku clearly belies the widespread understanding of Ghana's 2000 elections as a "peaceful" consolidation of democratic governance.

Even though the post-election violence in Bawku received national headlines, Upper East (or "Lower-Upper Volta," as on occasion it is derisively dubbed) remains largely an enigma for most Ghanaians residing in the southern swath of the country. Among those inhabitants who live in the south, political knowledge of Upper East generally begins and ends with the assassination attempt on President Nkrumah during his state visit to Kulungugu in August, 1962. During the myriad post-election analyses, numerous media personnel exposed their ignorance of the people and places in the north. Following the first round of electoral returns, for example, an otherwise knowledgeable *Choice FM* radio presenter repeatedly peppered an increasingly dumbfounded field reporter stationed in Wa (the regional capital of Upper West), querying, "We've heard there have been some problems in Wa Central with Hawa." But the problems "with Hawa" — Madam Hawa Yakubu, who was contesting a parliamentary seat — were occurring in Bawku, Upper East, more than 300 kilometers and a hard day's drive from Wa. Arising out of their own ignorance, the mayhem in Bawku came to symbolize for those living in the south the supposed backwardness of the ignorant and tribalistic people living in Upper East.

In particular, newshounds in Accra tended to reduce the cause of the violence in Bawku to one factor: innate hatred between two ethnic groups, the Kusasi and the Mamprusi. On *Joy FM*, another popular radio station in Accra, a pundit stated categorically of the post-election violence in Bawku, "It's not an electoral problem, it's a tribal problem." Print journalists too tried to de-politicize the violence, focusing instead on the ethnic or "tribal" angle of the conflict. In one of the first full-length commentaries on the "8 December War at Bawku," the state-owned *Daily Graphic* ran a piece by Chris Okyere in early January. Okyere (2001) asked rhetorically:

> But who was the cause of the war? Hei man, Stop it! This is not the time to apportion blame. This is not the time to point [an] index finger at people. Neither will it be in anyone's interest to use the Bawku Central Parliamentary election as a premises for explanation, irrespective of how comprehensive and unbias[ed] the explanation may be, to what happened on December 8, 2000. It is still a factor of ethnicity; everything boils down to [the] chieftaincy dispute, and nothing else.

Presaging the conflict, Okyere (2000) observed two months prior to the 7 December election that, "one can simply say that, Bawku is a place where a mere argument or fight between two people can result in an uncontrollable inferno."

Okyere, though, was not the only journalist who discounted the role of politics in the Bawku conflict by highlighting the ethnic dimension. Nearly every post-election dispatch on the conflict apportioned blame to innate ethnic hatred between the Mamprusi and the Kusasi. Following the conflagration, one columnist called Bawku "the topmost violent area in the region" (David 2001), with another contributor contending that "tribal wars are devastating Bawku, and with no feasible solution, it will not be surprising if the next tribal war annihilate[s] Bawku and its surroundings beyond repairs, and beyond human habitation" (Apkena 2001). Well after the conflict, a journalist for the privately owned *Ghanaian Chronicle* commented how, "The Kusase tribe of Bawku, in the Upper East Region, has been embroiled in a bitter chieftaincy dispute with the Mamprusis, another tribe in the town for years, which easily generates into deadly clashes at the least provocation" (Nsefo 2001).

The failure of the journalistic community to investigate, or even to acknowledge, how political factors have contributed to the ethnic tensions in Bawku is deeply troubling. Rather than viewing politics as a possible catalyst, journalists have instead reified ethnicity. Their take on the matter tends to be both reductionist and essentialist: the Bawku conflict is a tribal and only a tribal matter.

Perhaps this oversimplification of the situation in Bawku by journalists (and more generally, their ignorance of the political history of Upper East) is due in some small part to the paucity of scholarly studies on northeastern Ghana. While several scholars have examined the region's cultural, ethnic, and economic dimensions (Syme 1932; Fortes 1945; Manoukian 1951; Goody 1967; Iliasu 1971; Bening 1975; Drucker-Brown 1975; Chambas 1980; Davis 1987; Roncoli 1994; Chalfin 1996; 2000; Scholottner 2000), the foremost political study on the north by Ladouceur (1979) is now quite dated. Upper East Region did not even come into existence until January, 1983 when President Jerry Rawlings and the Provisional National Defense Council (PNDC) bisected the Upper Region for administrative purposes and political expediency. Compared with the other regions of Ghana, there is strikingly little scholarship on the politics of Upper East. The region was even excluded from a national public opinion survey of the 1996 elections (Ayee 1997).

Drawing from pre- and post-election public opinion surveys as well as interviews with leading political officials and party activists, this chapter examines the political attitudes and voter behaviour of residents of two constituencies in Upper East —Bawku Central and Nabdam. Despite their proximity, the two constituencies provide a rich cross-section of the Upper East Region. Taking into account the demographic dimensions of the two constituencies, one-stage, stratified pre- and post-election random public opinion surveys of 100 respondents were conducted in each constituency in late October 2000 and early January 2001. Although some notable similarities exist between the two constituencies, the survey data expose some of the variation within the region. The purpose of this study is not to provide a full-fledged inquiry into the causes of the violence in Bawku.[2] Rather, by drawing on the survey data, the study sheds some light on the politics of Upper East in the context of the 2000 elections as well as exploring the political complexities of the region. The analysis presented here is but a first step in generating a more scholarly dialogue about the political experiences of those residing in Upper East.

A Demographic Profile of Bawku Central and Nabdam Constituencies

To an outsider, much of Upper East Region is likely to appear the same. Labyrinthine compound houses, roofed with thatch or zinc litter the rural savanna. Most residents do not have access to electricity or running water. The region has one of the highest mean household sizes and one of the lowest school attendance rates in the country (GSS 2000a: 1–10). Literacy rates in Upper East Region, according to a recent study, were the lowest in the country, with only 26.3% of adults functionally literate. In 1999, poverty for the region was the deepest in the country; 88% of residents officially were living below the poverty line and 80% were living in "extreme poverty" (GSS 2000b: 13; 40). While national poverty declined during the 1990s, it worsened in Upper East. The mean annual per capita income of those living in the region in 1999 was just ¢321,000, nearly ¢200,000 less than the national average and far less than $100 per annum (GSS 2000a: 102). Approximately two-thirds of average household income in the region was derived from agriculture. Not surprisingly, the formal economic sector remains quite sparse, as less than 13% of average household income in Upper East comes in the form of wage income (GSS 2000a: 104). Despite (or perhaps because of) the abject poverty, the population of the region continued to grow during the 1990s. According to the provisional 2000 census, 917,251 people resided in the region, up from 772,700 in 1984. Although the geographically compact Upper East Region has the second lowest number of residents, its population density is the fourth highest in the country (behind Greater Accra, Ashanti, and Eastern Regions); over 100 persons live in every square kilometre in the region (GSS 1998).

Yet in many ways, Bawku Central and Nabdam constituencies represent opposite ends of the demographic spectrum in Upper East. The two constituencies — while similar in terms of geographic territory — are vastly different along a range of variables. Nabdam constituency, with one of the smallest populations in all of Ghana, is ethnically homogenous, extremely impoverished and entirely rural. The constituency, one of three administered by Bolgatanga District (the other two being Bolga and Talensi), has almost derisory economic and education opportunities for its residents. Most of the public facilities in Nangodi, the largest "town" in the constituency, have been abandoned; an electric water pumping station off the main Bolga-Bawku road lies dormant, waiting for electrification to reach the area. In Nabdam in late October, less than two months before the 7 December elections, the wheelchair-bound Paramount Chief of Nangodi whispered to me in Nabit, the dominant local language of the area, "We have nothing."

While only 30 miles north-east of Nabdam, Bawku Central, relatively speaking, is a cauldron of economic activity. While suffering acute fuel shortages (due to the smuggling of subsidized petrol to neighbouring Francophone countries), Bawku is a major centre (along with Bolgatanga) of regional and international commercial activity (Chalfin 2001). The constituency rests in Bawku East District along with Binduri and Garu/Timpani constituencies. According to the 2000 census, Bawku East District had a population of 307,162, making it the largest of the six administrative districts in the region. By several estimates, Bawku Central constituency has a population close to 150,000, and along with its vibrant mix of ethnicities, has a growing formal economy and middle class due to the presence of a regional hospital, district administration offices, a polytechnic and several schools.

Identities, Social Capital, and Perceptions about the Economy

The survey data are useful in fleshing out the previously sketched picture of Upper East using aggregate data from the GSS. The questionnaire probed how respondents identified themselves, as well as how they assessed their social and economic resources. Again, there are both similarities as well as differences in how those residing in Nabdam and Bawku Central constituencies think about themselves and their available resources.

Of those surveyed in Nabdam constituency, 94% of respondents said they grew up in a rural area, with 71% saying that they were strongly attached to their region. This sense of community identity is reinforced by the ethnic and religious sentiments that are strongly held among the residents of Nabdam; 79% of those responding said they felt attached to their ethnic group and 75% said they felt strongly about their religion. Not surprisingly, as the GSS aggregate data suggest, 60% of those surveyed said that their household income was not really enough to survive on and another 29% claimed that their household was just enough on which to survive; only 1% of those surveyed in Nabdam said that their household earned enough to achieve good standard of living. For those in the constituency, the dire economic conditions are nothing new; only 22% of respondents said that the standard of living of their household had got much worse over the past five years, compared with the national survey response of 45%. Over two-thirds of those surveyed in Nabdam said that if their household could not manage on its income, they would seek assistance from their neighbours (68%), with another 27% saying they would get help from members of their family. Both figures are much higher than the national averages. With a percentage close to the national mean of 77%, 73% of those surveyed in Nabdam said they thought the state of the Ghanaian economy was currently very bad (49%) or bad (24%), with 55% of those surveyed saying that the economy had become worse (49%) or sharply deteriorated (6%) over the last four years. Yet those surveyed were not wholly pessimistic about their futures. Nearly three-quarters of those who responded said they thought their household's standard of living would become either a little better (24%) or much better (50%).

In contrast with Nabdam, 56% of those surveyed in Bawku Central said they were strongly attached to the Upper East, with 12% saying they were weakly attached. This is consistent with the perception that Bawku is an outpost of economic activity that attracts a considerable number of outsiders who come to conduct business transactions. Instead of regional attachment, roughly two-thirds of those responding to the survey claimed strong attachment to their religion (66%) or to their ethnic group (64%); both figures are higher than the national averages. Again, reflecting the harsh economic conditions facing those in the area, 85% of those surveyed in the constituency said their household income was either not really enough to survive on (51%) or only just enough to survive on (34%). Assessing the past five years, 26% and 27%, respectively, of those who responded in Bawku Central said the standard of living of their household either became a little worse or much worse. However, 69% of those surveyed were optimistic that their standard of living would become much better or a little better over the next five years. Over 90% of those polled said they would turn to either neighbours (54%) or family members (39%) if they could not survive on their household income. Consistent with these household level figures, nearly three-quarters of those surveyed said the state of the Ghanaian economy was very bad (46%) or bad (26%), with 70% saying that the state of the Ghanaian economy had become worse (51%) or sharply deteriorated (19%) over the past four years.

Political Participation and Party Affiliation

While they may be poor and living on the margins, residents of Upper East are not apolitical. In both constituencies, 94% of those surveyed said they planed to vote in the 2000 elections. Over half (54%) of the survey respondents in Bawku Central and 72% of those in Nabdam claimed in late October that they had attended a political rally in connection with the 2000 elections. Of those responding to the survey, 82% and 74% of those in Bawku Central and Nabdam, respectively, said they were following the activities of the political parties in the media. A relatively high percentage of respondents in both constituencies (88% in Bawku and 79% in Nabdam) also professed to have voted in the 1996 presidential and parliamentary elections.

The high registration rates for both constituencies reflect the Electoral Commission's (EC) 2000 election figures. Based on the provisional 2000 census figures and the EC's registration data, 52.4% of the total population in Upper East was registered to vote in 2000. Furthermore, according to the pre-election survey, 95% of those surveyed in Bawku Central and 96% of those in Nabdam claimed they were registered to vote, which was only slightly lower than the national average (98.6%). The impressive registration figures for Nabdam and Bawku Central constituencies, despite their remoteness (especially Nabdam), go a long way to debunking claims made by functionaries of the National Democratic Congress (NDC) in the days leading up to the 7 December election that as many as 2.5 million people, primarily in rural areas, would be disenfranchised because they could not obtain photo IDs from the EC. In Nabdam, for example, none of those surveyed said they were unable to exchange their thumb-print IDs for photo IDs; only one person claimed this to be the case in Bawku Central.

While the percentage of registered voters is similar in the two constituencies, the absolute number of registered voters in Bawku Central and Nabdam is quite disparate. According to the EC, 480,853 voters were registered in Upper East in 2000, with an average of 40,071 voters in each of the 12 constituencies in the region. The regional average is considerably lower than the national average of 53,509 voters per constituency, but there is significant variation across the constituencies in Upper East. Compared with the national average, two of region's constituencies — Bawku Central and Bolgatanga — are severely underrepresented in parliament in terms of the "population quota;" Bawku Central had 77,459 registered voters and Bolga had 68,823 registered voters in 2000. In stark contrast, Builsa South constituency had only 14,733 registered voters, easily the smallest of the country's 200 constituencies; Nabdam constituency follows closely, with 16,104 registered voters (Smith 2001b). (See Figure1)

Prior to the 2000 elections, many political pundits predicted that Upper East would once again fall solidly into the NDC camp (Ephson 2000). Indeed, the region voted strongly for Rawlings and the NDC in 1996 (Ayee 1997), as the party had swept all 12 constituencies in both the presidential and parliamentary races. In his re-election bid, President Rawlings won the region with 69% of the vote (winning 66% in Bawku Central and 77% in Nabdam). In contrast, John Kufuor, the NPP's 1996 flag bearer won just 17% of the

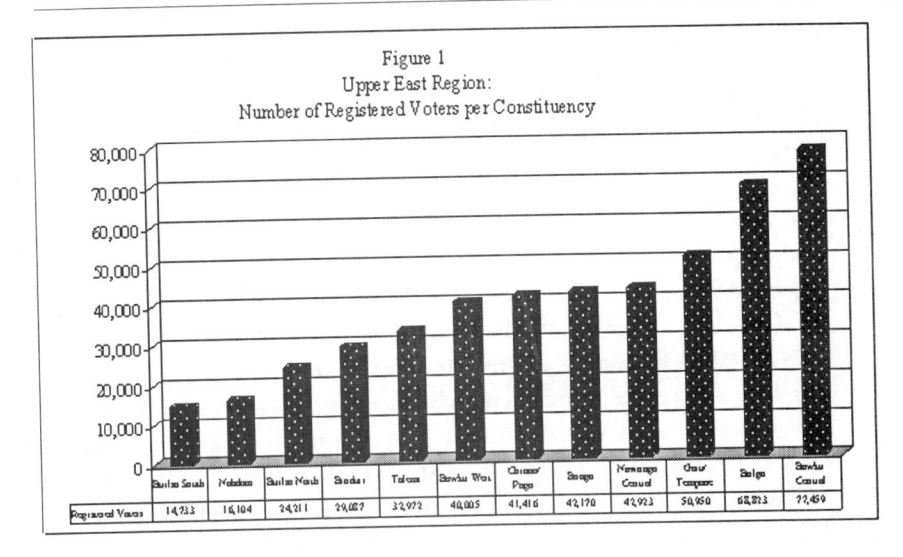

Figure 1
Upper East Region:
Number of Registered Voters per Constituency

Constituency	Registered Voters
Builsa South	14,733
Nabdam	16,104
Builsa North	24,211
Bodua	29,027
Talom	32,972
Bawku West	40,005
Chiana Paga	41,416
Bongo	42,170
Navrongo Central	42,923
Chau Tempane	50,950
Bolga	68,823
Bawku Central	77,459

vote in Upper East, with Edward Mahama of the People's National Convention (PNC) winning the remaining 14% (Smith 2000a). The 1996 parliamentary contests also had the NDC's Hajia Fati Seidu unseating Hawa Yakubu, the Independent Member of Parliament for Bawku Central, and Moses Asaga of the NDC easily winning the Nabdam constituency.

Regarding party membership, the survey revealed that a substantial percentage of residents in the two constituencies claimed to be registered members of political parties. In Bawku Central, 41% of those surveyed said they were party members, and somewhat surprisingly, 63% of those in Nabdam said they were registered party members. Both figures are higher than the national survey average (40%). When asked whether or not they thought an opposition party had a chance to win the presidential election, only 23% and 26% of Bawku Central and Nabdam respondents, respectively, replied "very good," which was much less than the more optimistic national average of 38%. Furthermore, compared with the national survey results (35%), considerably more respondents in Bawku Central (59%) and Nabdam (44%) thought that parties in Ghana project "personalities more than their policies."

When disaggregated along partisan lines, the strong party membership of the voting-age respondents in the region reveals some interested patterns. In Nabdam, the survey found that 37% of those polled said that their parents belonged to the NDC tradition, if it may be called that, with another 17% and 16% percent, respectively, saying that their parents belonged to the CPP and NPP/UP traditions. But among those who were actually surveyed, two political parties — the NDC and the PNC — clearly dominate the partisan leanings of those living in Nabdam. A high percentage of those who claimed to be members of a political party belonged to either the PNC (43%) or the NDC (40%); only 11% of those surveyed who claimed to belong to a party said they were members of the NPP. There is also a clear gender differentiation in party membership in Nabdam constituency. Women who said they belonged to a party were much more likely than men to be members of the NDC (67%), and much less likely to be members of either the PNC (25%) or NPP (8%). Both male and female older respondents (those over the age of 50) were three times more likely to be members of the PNC than the NDC, with twice as many of those under 30 claiming membership of the NDC rather than the PNC. Those surveyed who had either primary or no formal education were nearly twice as likely to be members of the PNC as the NDC; however, those who had at least a secondary education were much more likely to support the NDC than any other party. Of the 47% of the respondents in Nabdam who were not members of a political party, 38% said they were inclined to support the NDC, with 31% and 19%, respectively, saying they leaned towards the PNC and the NPP.

The high percentage of membership and party inclination towards the PNC in Nabdam, especially among men, should not come as too much of a surprise. Both Mahama — the PNC's presidential flag bearer whose mentor, ex-president Hilla Limann, headed the erstwhile People's National Party (PNP — and Nicholas Nonlaht Nayebil, the PNC parliamentary candidate and a popular educator, have strong personal followings in the area. In 2000, Mahama bumped his 1996 vote tally in Nabdam constituency from 18% to 29%. While the PNC faces some serious obstacles to expanding its presence nationally (and even in Bawku Central), the party has a substantial following in much of Upper East. In the first round, Mahama won 19.9% of the vote in the region (just 2% less than Kufuor's 21.9%[1]), and in half of the 12 constituencies in Upper East, Mahama and PNC parliamentary candidates placed at least second and won more than 25% of the vote. (In Bolga, PNC candidate David Apasera won the constituency, tallying over 50% of the vote). The impressive showing by Mahama and PNC parliamentary candidates in the region, combined with the continued praise and respect for Limann by many of those living in Upper East, belies the assertion that the support in the north for Limann and the PNP in 1979 was "highly conditional" and "evanescent" (Nugent 1995: 30).

In contrast to Nabdam, party membership rates and party inclination in Bawku Central more closely mirror the national trends. Nationally, the survey revealed that of those who were registered with a party, 43% were members of the NDC, 39% were members of the NPP, 7% were members of the PNC, 6% were members of the CPP, with the other parties accounting for the remaining 5%. In Bawku Central, 42% of card-carrying party members were affiliated with the NDC, with 34% members of the NPP, 17% with the PNC, and 5% with the National Reform Party (NRP). It should not come as a surprise that support for the NDC among the Bawku Central respondents was stronger than that of their parents, as 32% of those surveyed said their parents belonged to the CPP tradition, compared with only 27% saying their parents belonged to the NDC tradition. Slightly more than 25% said their parents were aligned with the UP/NPP ideological tradition, which was very close to the national figures (27%). Of those surveyed, the strength of the NDC in terms of party membership cuts across all strata of gender, age and education, with the notable exception that those with either no education or only a primary education were more likely to support the NPP. Of those respondents who were party members, nearly three-quarters (73%) with at least a secondary education were affiliated with the NDC. In terms of party inclination, similar patterns held, although a majority of those surveyed with less than a secondary education were aligned with the NDC, with those between the ages of 41 and 60 being more likely to lean towards the NPP.

With respect to ethnicity, the survey data reveal that Nabdam constituency is indeed fairly ethnically homogenous and that Bawku Central is quite heterogeneous. Two thirds (66%) of the respondents in Nabdam said their "mother tongue" was Nabit, with another 17% replying Mosi. In contrast, 13 different mother tongue languages were cited in Bawku Central; 40% of the respondents said Kusaal was their mother tongue, but several other languages had significant numbers, including Bisa (19%), Hausa (9%), Mampruli (8%), and Mosi (6%). Notably, ethnicity — as measured by one's native language — does not seem to heavily influence one's partisan leanings. In Nabdam constituency, of those who cited Nabit as their native language, 41% were either members or supporters of the PNC, with another 38% favoring the NDC. In Bawku Central constituency, there was a slight correlation between "native tongue" and partisanship, but not nearly as strong as the press insinuated after the 8 December violence. While nearly 60% of native Kusaal speakers were either members or supporters of the NDC, 24% were members or supporters of the PNC, with 14% likewise members or supporters of the NPP. Of Mampruli native speakers, 57% said they were either members of or supported the NPP, with the other respondents split evenly (14% each) between the NDC, Reform, and PNC. Native Bisa speakers were even more scattered across the partisan spectrum, with 47% either members or supporters of the NPP, 24% members or supporters of the NDC, 18% with the PNC, and 12% aligned with the NRP.

7 December Voting Patterns

The pre-election survey asked respondents whom they were likely to support in the 2000 presidential and parliamentary elections. The survey correctly predicted that the NDC's presidential candidate, John Atta Mills, would win in both constituencies, although it overestimated the strength of the PNC in both Bawku Central and Nabdam constituencies. On election day, PNC sympathizers in Bawku Central (and to a lesser degree in Nabdam) apparently decided not to "waste" their votes on Mahama of the PNC, who had little national appeal. On 7 December, a majority (52%) of voters in Bawku Central voted for Mills, with Kufuor coming in a distant second with 36% of the vote. While the survey was fairly accurate with respect to the support for Mills, the survey found that 24% of the respondents said they would support Mahama for the presidency; in actuality, he won just 7% (See Table 9.1).

Table 9.1: Bawku Central and Nabdam Constituencies: Percentage of Vote for Presidential and Parliamentary Candidates

	Survey Predictions [October 2000]			*Actual Results* [7 December 2000]			*Difference* [Actual – Survey]		
	NDC	NPP	PNC	NDC	NPP	PNC	NDC	NPP	PNC
Bawku Central									
Presidential	39	32	24	52	36	7	13	4	(17)
Parliamentary	40	39	18	47	49	3	7	10	(11)
Nabdam									
Presidential	33	14	42	51	13	29	18	(1)	(13)
Parliamentary	41	11	41	54	12	32	13	1	(9)

In the hotly contested parliamentary race, voters narrowly rejected incumbent Hajia Fati Seidu, as she won 46.4% of the vote. Instead, a slim plurality (48.3%) of voters returned Madam Hawa Yakubu — the "Iron Lady" — to Parliament, following her four year absence from public life. The four other parliamentary candidates from the UGM, PNC, CPP, and Reform parties split the remainder of the vote. Although Seidu had the power of incumbency and the sizeable NDC bankroll working for her, many voters were upset that the Deputy Minister of the Upper East Region never made a single statement on the floor of Parliament during her term in office. More importantly, many of the party faithful were disappointed with the lack of internal democracy in the NDC, as the National Executive Council of the NDC party refused to hold primaries even though there were several party members who wanted to challenge Seidu. According to the October survey, 35% of those in Bawku Central who said they had voted for Seidu in 1996 criticized the NDC for how it selected its parliamentary candidate in 2000, saying that the process was not democratic (See Table 9.1).

In the lead up to the 7 December elections, Yakubu campaigned much as she did in 1992 and 1996 — as an independent — despite the fact that she was a leading member of the NPP. Although she was eventually bypassed, Yakubu had flirted with the possibility of joining Kufuor's as his running mate over the summer (Obeng 2000). Standing on principle, though, Yakubu boycotted Kufuor's only campaign rally in Bawku after he was persuaded by local NPP party functionaries not to greet the Bawku Naaba, Azoka Abugdago II, the Kusasi chief of the Bawku Traditional Area (and known supporter of the NDC). Prior to the rally, Yakubu had personally met the Bawku Naaba, assuring him that Kufuor would greet him when his entourage arrived in town (Yakubu 2001). Because she lost face when Kufuor did not greet Naaba Azoka, and because of the perceptible anxiety among many electors in the district with the Ashanti-dominated NPP, Yakubu further distanced herself from the NPP and ended up financing most of her campaign with her own money.

The "Declaration of Results" for Bawku Central constituency was approved by the EC's Returning Officer (and signed by the NPP, NRP, and UGM party agents, but not the NDC's agent) on 9 December at 9:30pm. However, due to the continuing carnage the EC decided to wait until 11 December to officially announce Yakubu's victory. Following her defeat, Seidu immediately took legal action. She challenged the official vote count — which showed Yakubu winning by a mere 874 votes out of 45,822 cast in the High

Court in Bolgatanga — but her suit demanding a recount of the collated results as well as of all the ballots cast at the 151 polling stations in the constituency was eventually thrown out by the Supreme Court (Seini 2001; Asamoah 2001).

In Nabdam, Mills tallied 51% of the vote, topping Mahama's 29% and dwarfing Kufuor's 13% (the EC provisional results incorrectly declared that Kufuor won only 1.75% of the vote). While the survey incorrectly predicted that Mahama would outpoll Mills on 7 December it accurately assessed the lack of support for Kufuor in the constituency, as only 14% of the respondents said they intended to vote for the NPP presidential candidate (See Table 9.1).

In the parliamentary race in Nabdam, which like Bawku Central received the bulk of attention of those living in the constituency, Moses Asaga managed to retain his seat. The October survey predicted a dead heat between Asaga, the Deputy Minister of Finance, and the PNC candidate Nicholas Nonlaht Nayebil. At the time, there was talk in the constituency that the NPP parliamentary candidate, Boniface Gambila Adagbila, would bow out of the race and throw his support behind Nayebil. The PNC/NPP alliance, however, never materialized. As a result, the race did not end up being as close as the pre-election survey indicated, although Asaga won in less than convincing fashion. The incumbent parliamentarian won with 54% of the vote, with Nayebil winning 32%, Adagbila winning 12%, and the CPP candidate, William Tampugre, winning just 2% of the vote (See Table 9.1).

To solidify his win, Asaga and the NDC pulled out all the stops. Soon after announcing his intention to challenge Asaga, Nayebil of the PNC coincidentally was transferred by the Ministry of Education to Tamale in Northern Region from his post at Kongo Senior Secondary School, so as to make campaigning in Nabdam more difficult. According to several leading opposition party members, including one who once was an active member of the "revolutionary cadre" under the PNDC, the NDC allegedly allocated at least ¢350 million (roughly $50,000) to Asaga, who then dispersed the money to party operatives in the constituency. Party agents of the NDC allegedly gave every household in the constituency ¢20,000 in the days leading up to the election, along with two gallons of *pito* (local millet beer), one bottle of *akpeteshi* (local gin), and a bowl of smoked herrings. Some NPP activists were reportedly even bought off by the generosity of the NDC party agents, including one man who was given ¢2 million to defect to the NDC. Finally, in addition to Asaga's Ministry of Finance Toyota Land Cruiser, the party mobilized a Nissan 4x4 pick-up truck to Nabdam to assist with electioneering in the hard-scrabble district. In contrast, the NPP only sent nine bicycles to the Nabdam party chairman; the promised vehicle never arrived. The PNC constituency chairman received only two bright red bicycles from party headquarters with which to campaign.

Evaluation of Running Mates

Several months prior to the first round of elections, the suspense over the selection of the parties' running mates was closely followed by the media. Despite efforts by NDC and NPP party leaders to downplay the regional dimension of the selection of their presidential running mates, many pundits argued that Mills (a Fanti) and Kufuor (an Asante) needed to look to the north in order to round out their tickets so as to capture an important "electoral bloc" of voters. In their analyses though, the media often oversimplified the "northern" question, conflating regionalism with both ethnicity and religion. In the end, Mills and the NDC chose Martin Amadu, the Deputy Attorney General, a Catholic who was born and partially schooled in Bawku. Kufuor and the NPP countered by selecting Alhaji Aliu Mahama, a Muslim contractor from Tamale.

The pre-election survey sheds some light as to whether all the fuss over regionalism and ethnicity in the selection of the vice presidential candidate really mattered to the electorate. The national survey results show that regional (15%) and ethnic (4%) considerations in the selection of the Presidential running mate were not as important as experience (56%). Close to 85% of those polled nationally said that a party's presidential running mate would not affect their vote for President, although 38% replied that it was important to have a regional balance on the ticket, and 28% said it was important to have an ethnic balance.

In sharp contrast, 40% of those surveyed in Upper East (Nabdam and Bawku Central combined) stated that a regional balance was the most important consideration in the selection of a Presidential running mate, although only 6% cited ethnicity as being the most important factor. Nearly one in five voters in Upper East (19%) said that the selection of a presidential running mate would affect their vote, with 70% saying that it was important that the presidential ticket was regionally balanced, and 59% saying that the ticket should be ethnically balanced. These figures from the residents of Upper East underscore the latent feelings of many of those living in the region (and more generally, those living in the north), that their interests may be marginalized by southern orientation of the NDC and NPP.

Presidential Run-off

In both constituencies, the presidential run-off was anti-climatic. Running counter to the national results, Mills defeated Kufuor in Upper East, 57% to 43%. In Bawku Central and Nabdam, Mills won 58% and 59% of the vote, respectively. Although Kufuor again lost both constituencies, he nearly doubled his share of the vote in the region between the first round and the run-off election, from 22% to 43%. In contrast, Mills only bettered his 7 December total in the second round by 5% in the region. Interestingly, the October pre-election survey found that 42% of those in Bawku Central thought a presidential runoff election was likely, while only 27% of those surveyed in Nabdam thought a second round was likely.

While there were no run-off election incidents to report in Nabdam, the heightened tensions in Bawku following the first round were still palpable. To quell the conflict, the Regional Security Committee (REGSEC) imposed a dusk-to-dawn curfew on the town. According to several sources in Bawku, the military troops were even given the mandate to "shoot and kill" any would be rabble-rousers. The curfew was lifted temporarily for the second round of voting, which fell during the Christmas and El Faid holidays, but it was reinforced the next day. Fighting nearly resumed on 30 December when jubilant NPP supporters who were celebrating Kufuor's victory near the taxi rank in the centre of town, were allegedly harassed and beaten by military personnel.

Conclusion: Lessons

It is interesting to speculate what might have happened had the post-election violence in Bawku occurred anywhere in the south of the country. If such election-related violence had taken place in a less peripheral area, it is possible that the whole election exercise would have been brought into question; at the least, domestic and international observers would likely have removed their "free, fair, and transparent" seal of approval. This is the underlying irony of the violence in Bawku. The marginalization from the political mainstream of residents in Bawku, and those in Upper East more generally, feeds upon itself. Every time opinion leaders in the south either ignore or misunderstand the problems in Upper East, the region becomes increasingly isolated and dislocated from the rest of Ghana. The widespread ignorance about "Lower Upper Volta" among southerners only serves to further marginalize those residing in the north.

Following the violence, Madam Hawa Yakubu, the newly elected Member of Parliament for Bawku Central, portrayed the events in her constituency "not as a tribal war as is being made to seem" (Bansah 2000), but rather as an "ethnic misunderstanding in the area" (Yakubu 2000). This "ethnic misunderstanding" in Bawku was as much attributable to the political machinations of partisan elites as it was to an innate hatred between ethnic groups. It is no coincidence that the shooting on 8 December that sparked the violence in Bawku began outside Community Centre where the parliamentary vote count was taking place. Had Yakubu opted again to run for Parliament as an independent, it is likely she would have won the Bawku Central seat without much difficulty. But by hitching her horse to the NPP wagon, she enabled the NDC to play the "ethnic card" and engender fear among the Kusasi that an NPP government would revert control of the Bawku skin back to the Mamprusi. While Yakubu genuinely tried to quell these sentiments during her campaign, vocal partisans of the NDC (both locally and nationally) preyed upon this underlying ethnic uncertainty and insecurity in Bawku so as to dissuade the electorate from voting for the NPP.

Unfortunately, to date, those who have written about the violence in Bawku have not dared to challenge the essentialist ethnic explanation of the conflict. While no one would disagree that there is a tangible ethnic dimension to the hostility in Bawku, it is far too simplistic to view it as just a chieftaincy turf battle between the Kusasi and the Mamprusi. In Bawku, as well as Nabdam, the ethnic landscape is continually being shaped by the contours of national politics, chronic poverty and a pervasive feeling of exclusion and marginalization. Only by cultivating an appreciation of the quotidian attitudes of those residing in the region will a more nuanced understanding of the politics of Upper East be realized.

NOTES

1. I would like to thank Nachinaba Abugri at the Institute of African Studies, University of Ghana for his invaluable assistance interviewing political and party officials in Upper East as well as my superb team of field enumerators, Jerimiah Awini, Dorcas Bengah, Joyce Mamattah, and Mumuni Sherazu. I would also like to thank Brenda Chalfin, E. Gyimah-Boadi, and Will Reno for their helpful comments on an earlier draft.

2. The basic chronology of events in Bawku following the voting is a matter still under dispute. According to several reports, around 10am on 8 December gun shots pierced the air. The shots apparently came from a nearby Kola nut house, owned and frequented by Kusasi traders. The handful of security personnel on detail at the community center responded with their own warning shots, dispersing the large crowd from the park in front of the Community Center. Widespread arson and gunfire ensued, with supporters of the NPP and NDC looting and setting ablaze the businesses and homes of their alleged rivals (including Hawa Yakubu's house on the Bawku-Pusiga road). While the battle lines were drawn largely along ethnic divisions, the fighting was concentrated more along partisan lines, as Kusasi "boys" targeted not only Mamprusi "boys", but also fellow Kusasi who dared to support Yakubu and the NPP. Likewise, the Mamprusi "strongmen" who were involved in the fighting were driven by partisan interests as much as ethnic ones, as they burnt the NDC headquarters and other businesses owned by known financial backers of the NDC. The fighting continued through to Saturday, 10 December.
3. Kufuor's actual regional tally of 21.9% differs from the Electoral Commission's (EC) provisional results. For Nabdam constituency, the EC recorded Kufuor's vote as 171, which was in fact Goosie Tanoh's vote total. Kufuor actually won 1,297 votes in the constituency (Electoral Commission of Ghana 2000b).

REFERENCES

Ampratwum-Mensah, A. (200 "Bawku Central NDC committee formed," *Daily Graphic*, 11 October, p.11.
Apkena (2001) "Bawku: The Way Out." *The Guide*. 28 February–5 March, p. 4.
Asamoah, A. (2001) "NDC Thrown Out," *The Guide*. 17–23 January, p. 1.
Ayee, J. R. A. ed. (1998) *The 1996 General Elections and Democratic Consolidation in Ghana*. Accra: University of Ghana, Legon.
Bansah, S. (2000) "Police knows serial killers!" *The Crusading Guide*, 21–27 December, p.1.
Bening, R. (1975) "Foundations of the Modern Native States of Northern Ghana," *Universitas* 5: 116–38.
Chalfin, B. (1996) "Market Reforms and the State: The Case of Shea in Ghana," *Journal of Modern African Studies* 34: 421–440.
Chalfin, B. (2000) "Risky Business: Economic Uncertainty, Market Reforms and Female Livelihoods in Northeast Ghana," *Development and Change* 31: 987–1008.
Chalfin, B. (2001) "Border Zone Trade and the Economic Boundaries of the State," *Africa*, 71: 7–32.
Chambas, M. (1980) "The Politics of Agricultural and Rural Development in the Upper Region of Ghana: Implications of Technocratic Ideology and Non-participatory Development." PhD Dissertation in Political Science, Cornell University.
David, A. (2001) "Minister Denounces Violence in Bawku East," *Free Press*, 25 April–1 May, p.8.
Davis, D. (1987) "Then the White Man Came with his Whitish Ideas," *International Journal of African Historical Studies*, 20: pp. 628–46.

Drucker-Brown, S. (1975) *Ritual Aspects of the Mamprusi Kingship*. Cambridge: African Studies Centre.

Electoral Commission of Ghana (2000a) "Declaration of Results for the Office of Member of Parliament from Bawku Central." 12 December. Mimeograph.

Electoral Commission of Ghana (2000b) "Declaration of Results for the Office of President of Ghana from Nabdam." 8 December. Mimeograph.

Ephson, B. (2000) "Parliamentary Opinion Polls," *The Dispatch*, 29 November–5 December, p.1.

Fortes, M. (1945) *The Dynamics of Clanship Among the Tallensi*. London: Oxford University Press.

Ghana Statistical Service (GSS) (1998) "Quarterly Digest of Statistics." Accra: Ghana Statistical Service. March.

Ghana Statistical Service (GSS) (2000a). "Poverty Trends in Ghana in the 1990s." Accra: Ghana Statistical Service. October.

Ghana Statistical Service (GSS) (2000b) "Ghana Living Standards Survey: Report of the Fourth Round (GLSS 4)." Accra: Ghana Statistical Service. October.

Goody, J. (1967) *The Social Organization of the Lowiili*. London: Oxford University Press for the International African Institute.

Iliasu, A.A. (1971) "The Origins of the Mossi-Dagomba States," *Research Review* (University of Ghana). 7: 95–113.

Ladouceur, P. (1979) *Chiefs and Politicians: The Politics of Regionalism in Northern Ghana*. London: Longmans.

Manoukian, M. (1951) *Tribes of the Northern Territories*. London: International African Institute.

Nsefo, J. M. (2001) "Malam Isa's sack scuttled his people's chance in government." *The Ghanaian Chronicle*, 23–24 April, p. 8.

Obeng, K. W. (2000) "Why Kufuor rejected Hawa," *Public Agenda*, 11–17 September, p.1.

Okyere, C. (2000) "Bawku saved from war!," *Daily Graphic*, 19 October, p.7.

Okyere, C. 2001. "The December 8 War at Bawku," *Daily Graphic*, 10 January, p.9.

Roncoli, M. C. (1994) "Managing on the Margins: Agricultural Production and Household Reproduction in Northeastern Ghana." Ph.D. Dissertation in Anthropology, State University of New York and Binghamton.

Scholottner, M. (2000) "We Stay, Others Come and Go: Identity Among the Mamprusi in Northern Ghana." In Carola Lentz and Paul Nugent, eds., *Ethnicity in Ghana: The Limits of Invention* (NY: St. Martin's Press), pp. 49–67.

Seini, I. (2001) "Court orders re-count of Bawku Central votes," *Daily Graphic*, 8 January, p.24.

Smith, D. (2001a) "Ghana's 2000 Elections. *Electoral Studies*. (forthcoming).

Smith, D. (2001b) "The Structural Underpinnings of Ghana's December 2000 Elections." *Critical Perspectives*, No. 6, Ghana Centre for Democratic Development (CDD-Ghana), Accra.

Syme, J. K. G. (1932) *The Kusasis: A Short History*. Mimeograph.

Yakubu, H. (2000) "Hawa Yakubu's Press Statement." *Accra Mail*. 21 December, p.9.

Yakubu, H. (2001) Interview by the author. 3 April Accra.

CHAPTER 10

The 2000 Elections in Ellembelle and Jomoro Constituencies

BEATRIX ALLAH-MENSAH

Introduction

The 2000 general elections and presidential run-off in Ghana are indeed test cases for the country's avowed commitment to democratic governance, its institutionalization and eventual consolidation. Consequently, the factors that determine a fair and free elections, political parties strategies and voters decision-making are as crucial as the eventual outcome of the elections. To establish the facts, figures and the fiction of the elections, pre- and post-election surveys were carried out by the Political Science Department nationwide. This chapter examines the above issues with particular reference to the Ellembelle and Jomoro constituencies.

Profile of the Ellembelle and Jomoro Constituencies

The Ellembelle and Jomoro constituencies are in the Western region where Nzema is the main language of the indigenes. Though there are three constituencies in the area of this study, there are only two districts. Ellembelle is one of the two constituencies in the Nzema East District, the other is Evalue Dwira. As in any part of the country there are different ethnic groups, which enhance and enrich the multi-ethnic diversity in the constituencies.

The Ellembelle constituency is between the Jomoro and Nzema East district with Aiyinase as the constituency capital but Axim as the district capital. This has created a kind of tense relationship between residents from the two districts. In fact, in the light of the confusion, people from the Ellembelle constituency have been advocating their own district so that there would be 3 districts and 3 constituencies in that part of the region. This constituency was selected for the study for a number of reasons.

First, Nkroful, the home town of the late Dr Kwame Nkrumah is in the constituency. Secondly, it is one constituency with a kind of agreement between the Convention People's Party (CPP) and the New Patriotic Party (NPP) in order to capture (or is it maintain?) the parliamentary seat for the CPP and ensure a change in government. Supporters of the NPP were to support the CPP parliamentary candidate who was the incumbent the Honourable Freddie Blay against especially the NDC parliamentary candidate, Kaku Korsah, the immediate past Metropolitan Chief Executive (MCE) for Shama Ahanta East Metropolitan Assembly (SAEMA) and other candidates whilst CPP supporters were to support the NPP flag bearer for the presidential slot. As a result, it was the only constituency in the country in which the NPP did not field any parliamentary candidate. The third reason was to ascertain the tenacity of tradition in politics; that is whether people from Ellembelle were staunch CPP members or whether the wind of change got to their doorsteps. The major occupation of the people is farming and coconut oil extraction.

The Jomoro constituency is coterminous with Jomoro district with Half Assini as the district capital. Due to its proximity to the Ivory Coast there are movements of people, goods and services between the two countries. The choice of the constituency for the survey is firstly due to its proximity to the Ivory Coast. Again the constituency is considered an NDC stronghold and therefore makes interesting case when the clarion call from the people is for change. In addition, the constituency was also chosen to ensure that people in that part of the country were not excluded from such an important survey. There is also the contested view that Jomoro is not only an NDC stronghold but also a controversial constituency/ district and with the cry for change, it would be interesting to monitor events in the constituency.

Demographic Data on Ellembelle and Jomoro

The demographic information will cover the gender, age and educational distribution of respondents from the two constituencies (see Tables 10.1, 10.2, and 10.3). Other aspects will be the occupation, religion and incomes of respondent (see for example, Table 10.4).

With the exception of the post-election survey in the Ellembelle constituency, in all other cases, the male respondents outnumbered the females. Even though the intention of the survey was to capture a 50%

Table 10.1 Gender Distribution of Respondents

		Pre-Election %	Post-Election %
Ellembelle	Male	59	46
	Female	41	54
	TOTAL	100	100
Jomoro	Male	54	58
	Female	46	42
	TOTAL	100	100

Source: Survey data

Table 10.2: Percentage Distribution of Age

		Pre-election %	Post-Election %
Ellembelle	18–25	30	20
	26–30	26	22
	31–40	13	19
	41–50	14	16
	51–60	8	10
	61–70	5	10
	71 /above	4	3
	TOTAL	100	100
Jomoro	18–2	21	17
	26–30	26	22
	31–40	23	32
	41–50	17	14
	51–60	8	10
	61–70	3	3
	71/above	2	2
	TOTAL	100	100

Source: Survey data

Table 10.3: Percentage Distribution of Educational Background

		Pre-Election %	Post-Election %
Ellembelle	None	9	15
	Primary	33	33
	Secondary	34	32
	Tr. Training/Technical	11	8
	Polytechnic/Vocational	12	12
	University	1	0
	TOTAL	100	100
Jomoro	None	13	14
	Primary	43	49
	Secondary	31	22
	Tr. Training/Technical	5	7
	Polytechnic	4	5
	University	4	3
	TOTAL	100	100

Source: Survey data

gender balance this was not possible due to the unwillingness of women to respond to questions especially where the husband or even a brother was around, particularly if these men were educated irrespective of the extent of their education. Of those who agreed to respond, the majority did not have answers to simple information required and ended up utilizing the "don't know" option. This was a bit frustrating but it all points to the fact that women, on the average are less politically conscious and psychologically less involved in politics than men. This is supported by Randall's assertion that the most solidly founded charges among numerous other charges preferred against women's political behaviour is that "they know less about politics, are less interested and less psychologically involved in it than men" (1982: 56). This should be a concern for all who believe in genuine participatory and egalitarian democracy.

From Tables 10.1 and 10.2, it is obvious that the politically active groups are those between the ages of 18 and 40 years. This is not surprising.

Table 10.4: Employment Distribution of Respondents

	Pre-election %	Post-election %
Ellembelle		
Unemployed	25	23
Teacher/Professional	11	20
Businessman	2	3
Manager	1	–
Farmer	13	19
Trader/Artisan	38	34
Public Servant	2	–
Other	8	1
TOTAL	100	100
Jomoro		
Unemployed	20	14
Teacher/Professional	12	11
Businessman	5	10
Manager	2	–
Farmer	25	20
Trader/Artisan	25	30
Public Servant	5	6
Other	6	9
TOTAL	100	100

Source: Survey data

In all cases the percentages are about twice those of the 41 and above age group meaning that their role in the political process is crucial.

Table 10.3 indicates the low educational status of respondents in the two constituencies. Perhaps its effect on the constituencies led them to mention education as one of the most important need in the areas.

In Table 10.4 only the major variables were used for the assessment. Generally those in employment are more than those who are unemployed in both constituencies, yet the unemployment rate is quite high giving rise to some labour concerns. Farming, though recognized as the mainstay of the economy of the constituencies under study, is clearly from the data presented giving way to other jobs. Some respondents' comments that the farmlands are diminishing and yields are far below expectation coupled with low returns from farming activities in the constituency may serve as the reasons for the change in labour trends. This is reflected in the annual incomes declared by respondents. Whilst some were reluctant to disclose their annual incomes others could not readily calculate theirs since they claimed they did not have regular incomes or due to insufficiency they hardly have anything left. In Ellembelle for instance, over 68% were unwilling to disclose their annual income. However from the post-election data 80% claimed they had less than and up to five hundred thousand (500,000) *cedis* as annual income. Similarly, in Jomoro as many as 69% were not forthcoming with details of their annual income, whilst post-election data indicated that 65% earned less than and up to five hundred thousand (500,000) *cedis*.

On religion, it was noted from the constituencies that over 93% claimed they were Christians with less than 7% claiming to be Moslems.

Political Participation/voter Perception

In both constituencies, almost every respondent was a registered voter, that is 95–99%. Yet only 32% from Ellembelle and 43% from Jomoro were members of political parties and the major reasons given for their stand were mainly personal which accounted for between 29% and 34% of responses. The second reason for the low response of 14% was that the significance of party politics in Ghana had been relegated to the background. Of those who disclosed their party, 15% indicated they belonged to the CPP, followed by the NDC with 11% and the NPP with 8% in Ellembelle. In Jomoro the CPP had 13%, NDC 12% and NPP 19%. In Jomoro as many as 56% of respondents and an even higher percentage of 65% in Ellembelle did not disclose their party affiliation.

These high percentages of unwillingness to disclose party affiliation may be linked to the rumours during the pre-election campaign period that the party that won the election would harass those who voted for the losers. In fact, there were threats of beatings and intimidation and actual confrontation between CPP and NDC supporters and members in Ellembelle and NPP and NDC supporters and members in Jomoro constituencies. This is a very disturbing development in these constituencies and of such threats the implications are not good for the process and consolidation of democracy, which should exhibit tolerance of diverse and opposing ideologies and views.

Respondents who claimed they did not belong to any party, however, indicated the party they were sympathetic with. In the Ellembelle constituency the highest percentage of 28 supported the CPP whilst the party's support in Jomoro was 19%. The NDC had 11% each in the two constituencies and the NPP had 28% in Jomoro and 14% in Ellembelle. Putting these together whilst there was 42% support for the opposition in Ellembelle, it was only 11% for the ruling party, the NDC. In Jomoro, the situation was not different for the ruling party, which had 11%. For the opposition, there was 47% support from floating voters. Thus, together with their party membership of 11% in Ellembelle the NDC had a total support of 22% and in Jomoro the total came up to 23%. For the opposition parties, this came up to 65% in Ellembelle and as high as 79% in Jomoro.

These figures reveal some interesting trends and changes and highlight the level of enlightenment and perhaps sophistication of the Ghanaian voter. From data collected, it appears that the Jomoro constituency is more of an NPP than even a CPP area. This scenario is a little bit surprising in the sense that in the past two elections the constituency has been an NDC stronghold probably because the NDC party won both the parliamentary and presidential slots in the 1992 and 1996 elections. In the 2000 elections there were some changes. The allegiance to parties shifted strongly in favour of the opposition in general and the NPP in particular. What was to be expected was that the victory would be for both the party and the parliamentary candidate. This did not turn out to be the case.

Whilst the NPP flag bearer won in the constituency, its parliamentary candidate failed to get the votes of the same electorate who voted for his president. This raises some queries especially when as many as 68% of voters in the constituency said they would vote for both party and candidate. According to observers from the constituency, the NPP candidate, an architect from Elubo was not "known" in the constituency and had not done anything for the constituency and therefore was not that popular. In addition, some of the electorate described him either wrongly or rightly as an arrogant person who may push them around if voted for. Probably, that could account for the close race between the incumbent NDC parliamentarian and the independent candidate, a transport owner/driver apparently rich and popular. In effect, the absence of a likeable competitor for the parliamentary seat of Jomoro led to the returning of the incumbent to power in spite of respondents' perception that their MP had not adequately represented them in the last parliament. The respondents' vote for the NPP flag bearer, however, supported their wish for change in government.

In Ellembelle, voting patterns indicated that the unofficial alliance between the CPP and NPP at both parliamentary and presidential levels made some headway. The arrangement though unofficial was that supporters of NPP would throw their weight behind the CPP parliamentary candidate whilst the CPP supporters would back the NPP presidential candidate. This is interesting for a number of reasons. First, this happened against the backdrop of the last failed official alliance between the opposition parties and one may wonder why the need for this unofficial alliance. Secondly, did the CPP as a party and its supporters heed the admonition that their presidential candidate did not stand a good chance of winning the elections in 2000? And thirdly, was it the clamour for change at all costs that led to the teaming up of the two opposition parties to outvote the incumbent NDC government? There is no gainsaying the fact that Ellembelle is a CPP "stronghold". If that is the case, then why did the CPP not believe in its party and support strength and go on its own "strength"?

One answer, perhaps hypothetical, is that the CPP was not sure of itself and did not want to take any chances especially when it appeared that opposition from the NDC leading to some pre-election clashes between the two parties. It could also be that the CPP was playing politics on the basis that nothing is sure in politics and that there are no permanent friends or enemies in politics. Indeed, even though 15% of respondents affirmed their membership of the CPP and 28% claimed they were sympathizers of the party, a total of 43%, the CPP parliamentary candidate still needed the 8% NPP party members and 22% sympathizers to ensure total victory and counteract any NDC threat, real or imagined. The loose alliance or memorandum of understanding was important in that the 14% of NPP sympathizers were "floating" and could shift allegiance any time to any party.

It is interesting to note that a majority of 64% of respondents in Ellembelle and as many as 84% in Jomoro joined parties of their own accord. This denotes independence of mind and judgement by voters.

This explains why some sceptics have questioned the strength of the Nkrumah tradition in these two constituencies especially when the politically active groups are the youth who indeed cannot associate with the vision and achievements of Nkrumah except to read them as history with little or no contact with the actuality on the ground. For instance, about 69% and 61% of respondents from Ellembelle and Jomoro respectively are between the ages of 18 and 40. This scenario brings out the sensitive character of voters and even their volatility. In other words, because they did not claim to have any serious attachment to any political tradition and joined parties on their own accord and not through any unworthy influences, voters would not just follow the crowd but would consider the issues at both the national and the constituency level before casting their vote. This gives some food for thought as far as political trends in the country is concerned.

It cannot be categorically affirmed however, that the absence of a similar alliance between the CPP candidate in Evalue Gwira's constituency accounted for his inability to overcome the challenge from the NDC parliamentary candidate. But that could be one of the numerous reasons why the CPP candidate failed to retain his seat in Parliament. It needs emphasizing here that the number of CPP seats in parliament dropped instead of increasing as expected and that does not augur well for the party's avowed resurgence.

The media's role in the political process was supported by attendances at political rallies and the following up of political events in the news media, which were as high as 75% in Ellembelle and 61% in Jomoro. What can be deduced from this is that the people were not just interested in casting their votes in a fashionable way, but they deemed it a national and patriotic duty that should be performed on the basis of information and education: both important in election situations. As noted, voters in the main are rational and can define their individual self-interest and seek to maximize their self-interest when deciding for which candidate and /or party they should vote (United Nations 1997: 10).

Voter Perception on the Economy

The state of the Ghanaian economy appeared to be the main determining factor of the outcome of the 2000 elections. The clarion call for change was not only an end in itself but a means to an end. The end was to bring about positive growth and visible enhancement of all sectors of the economy to be experienced by the ordinary Ghanaian at expectedly different levels and in different ways. As a result, at national and constituency levels the economy took centre stage.

Asked about their perception of the state of the economy, just about 10% and 12% respondents from Ellembelle and Jomoro respectively were of the view that the economy was either good or very good. This compares with the national total percentage on the issue, which was 14%. However and not surprisingly, a whopping 82% from Ellembelle and 79% from Jomoro compared with about 77% nationally did not mince words on the deplorable state of the economy, which had consequentially led to deterioration in the standard of living for themselves and their family members. In addition respondents identified unemployment as the major economic problem facing the country among other variables, which included inflation, competition from cheap imports, high interest rates, lack of private investment and depreciation of the cedi. In Ellembelle the percentage of unemployment was as high as 65% whilst a modest 36% complained about the issue in Jomoro. The difference in the unemployment figures as the most serious economic problem and those who laid bare their unemployed status could be attributed to the fact that even though some respondents identified themselves as traders and artisans, they categorically mentioned in discussions related to but not part of the survey that their incomes are so negligible that they consider themselves unemployed.

Similarly, the rate of inflation attracted comments from some respondents. One interesting point worth noting was that a respondent stated that the inflation problem had been compounded by the plight of the marginally employed and worsened that of the unemployed. He decried the apparent change in governmental strategy with respect to price increases and sarcastically surmised that "now parliament does not pass major laws in Ghana and that these have been left to those who are in those sectors. For instance, budget reading, which is an annual ritual, has now become a daily affair and instead of it to take place in parliament, it now takes place in shops and market places; and government endorses them by not acting and everybody does what he likes with respect to pricing of goods and services".

The unemployment problem is obviously exacerbated by the equally aggravating problem of inflation. Even those who insisted that unemployment was the biggest economic problem support this. They noted that workers could not afford to buy their basic needs and therefore could not afford to help the unemployed in society. In any case, they could not ignore them. This means that, for every single worker, there was at least one employable unemployed sharing the meagre income with him or her. One respondent from Jomoro also made this unfortunate but open and factual statement that, if there were no jobs, there was no money, and because life must go on, we would employ all the survival strategies there are to live. These two comments are very sobering and sum up the implications and effects of unemployment and related economic problems in the country. Since many could not alter their conditions by themselves, they believed that their power to change their situation is the opportunity offered by democracy, through the ballot box, as a system of governance.

Evaluation of the Democratic/Electoral Process, the Party System and the Media

Democracy and elections are bedfellows in spite of the contention as to the exact kind of relationship that exist or should exist between the two. It is indeed, true that all democratic processes should necessarily have an element of elections but that does not translate into electoral processes being democratic or translating into democracy. Elections serve as the critical determinants of democratization and democracy. In Ghana, however, elections are the biggest issues when it comes to the generality of democracy where the ordinary eligible citizen exercises his/her franchise.

Democratic governance in Ghana has overstepped the primary stage and is gradually taking root. This is supported by an average of 44% of respondents from both constituencies who thought that Ghana could be described as a democratic country and an average 28.5% who had contrary views. Breaking these down, those from Ellembelle who thought Ghana is not democratic were more than those from Jomoro. They also accredited an improvement in democracy over the past four years. What may be noted from these responses vis-à-vis the economy during the same period is that whilst a majority of respondents from the two constituencies noted an increase in the democratic status of the country, this did not apply to the economy where they reported of deterioration and poor living standard. This could be interpreted as the apparent lack of correlation between democracy and development.

This scenario may be superficially seen to vindicate those who propose that economic development is not necessarily dependent on democratic structures as in the case of the Asian Tigers. In this connection, Joseph (1999: 6) puts forward two views. He states that, whilst Mkandawire considers the linkage between democratization and economic liberalization to be generally harmful in its consequences, Bates views this nexus as fundamental and unavoidable. In addition, for Bates to say that democratization is connected to a broader process of economic reform is not an accidental occurrence. It also tends to raise the issue as to which one should come first; the economy or politics. What may be the panacea is a simultaneous attention to democratic development and economic enhancement since both are processes and means and never ends in themselves. This could be facilitated by democratic structures and their operation.

Ake's position on this nexus (1996: 127) is also worth considering. To him, the end of development should be the people. If this is the case then their well-being must be the supreme law of development. But this can only be the case if the people have some decision-making power. In addition the only way of ensuring that social transformation is not dissociated from the well-being of the people is to institute democracy. Thus, in spite of its shortcomings democracy must achieve, in the final analysis, some accepted degree of efficacy (Apter 1991: 463). The above gives credence to the idea of a relationship between democracy and development. It is therefore not surprising that the economy ranked highest among other issues with regard to determinants for voting in the 2000 general elections.

The media have a major and challenging role to play in ensuring that the conduct of elections is free and fair in all respects. Although it may be argued that an incident-free election is utopian, one can also advocate a secure and safe atmosphere devoid of any form of intimidation by any group, party or institutions.

It is interesting to note that a positive assessment of democracy corresponded with increase in press freedom and quite significantly increase in the number of private media houses especially FM stations. Also on coverage of the elections, respondents felt that it had been adequate and fair to all the parties. An impressive 82% from Ellembelle and 95% from Jomoro stated that the elections had been free and fair whilst an equally impressive 75% from Ellembelle and 81% from Jomoro said the coverage had been adequate during the campaign period. However, respondents in the Jomoro constituency observed a worrying scenario where though they are Ghanaians they could not have Ghana television reception but rather had Ivorian television reception.

This has complex implications. First, the consequences of having access to a foreign country like the Ivory Coast especially in a politically extremely volatile situation, as witnessed on television can deter would-be dissidents on one hand and on the other, it could pipe up sentiments of a "we-no-go-sit down" kind which could lead to civil and political unrest. On the existence of conditions for free and fair elections, Jomoro recorded 69%. This represented a marked improvement over the 36% who acknowledged that the 1996 elections were free and fair. This cannot be taken for granted due to the importance and functions of elections in general and free and fair elections in particular. It is reiterated that free and fair elections help the people to choose their own leaders. Additionally, they address the concern with legitimacy through regular and transparent processes whilst opening avenues for political parties especially the opposition to compete by offering their respective political visions for socio-economic development (Kieh 1999: 106).

Parties, Elections and Outcomes

Respondents from the two constituencies predicted interesting outcomes. Between the two, 65% believed that the opposition had a chance of winning the elections whilst only 26% vouched for the victory of the progressive alliance. It is instructive to note however that an average of only 18.5% felt there could be a presidential run-off with 50% of respondents from both constituencies confident of a one-round victory for the winning party, which was predicted to be a party from the opposition. This sure stance partly stems from the confidence the electorate had in their parties and their candidates. This confidence was affirmed when respondents stated that they had no qualms with the process of nominating parliamentary candidates, which had been democratic. This was also reflected in the perception that parties in Ghana project personalities more than policies. In Ellembelle 44% and 57% from Jomoro had this inclination. Whether this is right or wrong is debatable.

Nonetheless, the danger is that this scenario could lead to personality cults and personalization of parties. This cannot be blamed much on the parties. One plausible reason could be the financial inadequacies of most of the parties and the concentration of power in the hands of a few who may be the backers of the party. It may also be a reflection of the absence or weakness of internal party democracy. Projecting personalities more than the party may create a scenario where the exit of that or those people from office or the party could trigger disintegration of the party concerned. On the other hand, weak or absent internal party democracy does not augur well for enhancing democratic governance which could also be due to the financial weakness of the parties which compels them to accord high regard to personalities who have been the financial backbone and sustenance of the party. This leads to the contentious issue whether there should be state funding of political parties activities or not.

The issue of state funding of political parties has come up for discussion and debate on several occasions and in many circles with the general perception being that parties should obtain some form of state funding. The amount of and the formula for such funding have not been too clear to all stakeholders. Views on this matter varied in both constituencies. Forty-one per cent from Jomoro and 63% from Ellembelle felt there should be state funding. The majority of those who supported state funding of political parties activities cited fairness as the cardinal basis since to them there was no gainsaying the fact that the party in power has undue advantage over the opposition parties. The seriousness attached to funding of political parties is re-echoed in the response on the inadequacy of logistics of the parties. At both constituency and national levels respondents identified funding as the main challenge to political parties. Interestingly, the percentages varied quite substantially. Jomoro's 51% contrast sharply with Ellembelle's 73%. This confirms the position that anything that was likely to jeopardize or affect the image of the NDC party received a lower percentage response with the opposite happening in the Ellembelle constituency. Interpretation of this is quite tricky because, there appear to be more NPP supporters in the constituency yet some responses did not correlate with this assertion. There is controversy around the constituency's clear position with regard to party lines.

The Presidency and Running Mates

Five main variables were identified as important for the choice of presidential running mates. From these, respondents from the two constituencies settled on experience as the most important factor to consider, although the percentages varied slightly (see Table 10.5).

Table 10.5: Percentage Distribution of Variables for Presidential Running Mates

Variables	Ellembelle %	Jomoro %
Ethnic Background	1	1
Regional Balance	11	13
Gender Balance	6	9
Experience	66	41
Party Loyalty	10	22
Other	6	14
TOTAL	100	100

Source: Survey data.

One crucial issue worth considering here is that respondents from the two constituencies were categorical on the irrelevance of ethnicity as a factor to be considered in presidential running mates. It can be deduced that this holds not only for running mates but also for presidential candidates and indeed in politics in Ghana generally. Reiterating this, Diamond emphasized that although ethnic pluralism and cleavage was a central fact of political life in Africa, the heterogeneity in their demographic balances varied greatly giving rise to explosive ethnic conflicts in some countries and no clashes or less explosive clashes in others like Ghana. Quite interestingly, Diamond states "even though ethnicity has been a continual source of political tension in Ghana, it has not consistently polarized the polity as it has in Nigeria, Uganda or Zimbabwe because of the more decentralized and demographic and cultural profile. This undoubtedly is a good omen for Ghanaian politics due to the potential destructive nature of enthnicized politics.

On a more sobering note is the point that gender balance was the second least important factor to be considered after ethnicity. Between the two constituencies, the average percentage for gender balance was 7.5% just a little below the percentage of women represented in the 200-seat parliament. The obvious interpretation is that though efforts are being made to overcome this low representation, there are still more miles to cover in order to generate smiles on the faces of those concerned. At national level, it was the least important factor getting just 2.3% of approval. From the parties' perspectives, they are committed to gender issues and will ensure that they give them the needed attention. But utterances from some party members make these "commitments" somehow bleak. It is quite disturbing to note that people are making efforts to trivialize the importance of gender, which permeates all aspects of socio-economic and political life without consideration of its unpleasant and boomerang effect. It is time to ensure that "gender fashionable" gives way to "gender functional", this will ensure enhancement in development at all levels.

Other issues that came up were the criteria for electing the presidential candidate. Most respondents from the two constituencies indicated that both national and constituency matters were the decisive factors for their vote in the December 2000 elections and that the political party that best articulated their concerns was the NPP followed by the NDC (see Tables 10.6 and 10.7).

Table 10.6: Percentage Distribution of Issues Influencing Choice of President

Issue	Ellembelle %	Jomoro %
National	26	5
Constituency	6	4
Both	66	84
Don't know	2	7
TOTAL	100	100

Source: Survey data

The figures in Tables 10.6 and 10.7 partially explain the reasons for the success of the NPP party at presidential level. It is worthy of note that, in spite of its NDC support, respondents from Jomoro did not cover up the fact that it was the NPP that best articulated their concerns. This may appear contradictory with regard to some figures already quoted on other issues. But the important thing to note is that, after the first round of the election, the reality was laid bare and there was no reason for pretence; it was time to face matters as they appeared. The respondents' predictions of the presidency and the presidential run-of are contained in Tables 10.8 and 10.9.

Table 10.7: Percentage Distribution of Party which best Represent Respondents Interests

Party	Ellembelle %	Jomoro %
NDC	27	14
NPP	56	77
PNC	5	–
CPP	12	3
NRP	–	1
TOTAL	100	100

Source: Survey data.

Table 10:8 Percentage Distribution of Respondents' Party Preference

Party	Ellembelle %	Jomoro %
NPP	5	33
NDC	16	18
CPP	54	25
UGM	–	2
Don't Know	12	15
No Response	13	7
TOTAL	100	100

Source: Survey Data

Elections and Development Issues

At national level, the main election issue identified by respondents was the economy, which accounted for 90% of respondents' answers, followed by change and development with continuity trailing the variables. The quest for change was for development, which many felt, had not been visible in their constituencies. The respondents from the two constituencies had different and similar needs (see Table 10.10).

Table 10.9: Percentage Distribution of Respondents Preference for Presidency in the Run-off

Candidate	Ellembelle %	Jomoro %
J. A Kuffour	58	13
J. E. A. Atta-Mills	22	83
No Response	20	4
TOTAL	100	100

Table 10.10: Development Concerns in the Constituencies

	Development Issue	Percentage
Ellembelle	Toilet (KVIP)	24
	Employment	23
	Education	16
Jomoro	Employment	19
	Education	16
	Electricity	15
	Water	13

Source: Survey data.

The closeness of the percentages indicates the need to deal with all those developmental issues raised. In fact, some respondents had difficulty mentioning only three claiming that there were more than three most important developmental needs. This was particularly evident in the Jomoro constituency even though it is the constituency that was openly supportive of the NDC and against anything that appeared to discredit the NDC government. What is striking is that from both constituencies, respondents mentioned education and employment though with slight differences between the constituencies. Other respondents did not answer at all claiming that nothing would be done even if they did. This accounts for the shortfall in percentages for both constituencies.

One major and rightly identified problem in the two constituencies is education at all levels. Most schools at all levels glaringly lack adequate and safe structures, teachers and other logistics. Another identified problem is the low enrolment and support for girls in schools beyond the senior secondary level. The situation at Nsein Secondary School, which is found in the same district as Ellembelle constituency, depicts this state of affairs. It is noted that even though more girls enroll at SSS level than boys, by the time they reach SSS three, there are fewer girls than boys and the latter also excel in the end of year exams more than the former. This in general has affected the number of children from the two constituencies who make it to the tertiary level. One reason for this unfortunate situation of dropping school rates is lack of funds, a condition that pushes parents to pressurize their girls to get married. This raises concern on issues of identity and social capital to which we now turn.

From the survey, respondents from Jomoro stated that their main source of help was family members, which accounted for about 60% followed by neighbours accounting for 26% and then friends with 6%. In the Ellembelle constituency, it was the opposite. For them, assistance from neighbours accounted for 61.6% followed by family members with 34% and trade unions with 2%. The differences may be explained as follows. In the Jomoro constituency, most people have relations in the Ivory Coast who often remit money to them and also due to the proximity of the constituency to the Ivory coast, they are able to get to them with relative ease and hence able to reduce their financial burden. Secondly, Jomoro is more ethnically diverse than Ellembelle. Furthermore, due to the proximity of the constituency to the Ivory Coast, a lot of traders are attracted to the area whilst there are more government agencies and branches for jobs than in Ellembelle especially at Half Assini because of its status as the district capital.

In Ellembelle, the scenario is slightly different where families are together as a result of the localized nature of the constituency. Although there are some people from different parts of Ghana in this constituency as well, the number is not that high in comparison with Jomoro. By and large, neighbours and relatives stay in the same locality. As to why family members do not help is a matter of concern but one explanation is that those family members are genuinely without and therefore not in a position to help. Probing on why some relatives would not help, a few respondents stated that they might have been struck by "donor fatigue"; consequently people have no choice but to turn to their neighbours for assistance. It is therefore not surprising that unemployment was higher in Ellembelle than it was in Jomoro.

Conclusion: Lessons

The importance of elections has been underscored in this study supported by the power of the electorate to seek information, assess situations and consider party and candidate programmes of action as the determining factor for directing political decision making. The urgency for a change in government to ensure some positive change not only in governance for its own sake but as a means of achieving social and economic development will would be visible in the lives of the people was the underlying principle and determining factor for political decision making in the Ellembelle and Jomoro constituencies in particular and at national level in general. It is indeed true that election as a process has some limitations, but it does not diminish its inevitable functions as the vehicle through which first, the electorate expresses its trust in the persons elected, secondly, a representative parliament is chosen and thirdly, the government of the day can be controlled, re-elected or defeated (Nohlen 1996: 6). This is exactly what happened in the election 2000.

In this regard all stakeholders in the political game must realize that politics is dynamic and so are the underlying economic and social variables. Just as Ake notes that the people are the end of development and therefore the supreme law of development, this study equally acknowledges, based on the above analysis, that the voice of the people is the ultimate in political decision making. Taking the people for granted whilst in or out of office could spell political disaster and even doom for the party, agency, institution or government concerned because of the power of democratic governance.

REFERENCES

Ake, Claude (1996) *Democracy and Development in Africa* (The Brookings Institution, Washington D.C)

Apter, David E. (1991) " Institutionalism Reconsidered", *International Social Science Journal: Rethinking Democracy*, No. 129 (August).

Diamond, Larry (1996) "Introduction: Roots of Failure, Seed of Hope" in Diamond, Larry;

Linz, Juan J.; and Lipset, Seymour M. (eds) *Democracy in Developing Countries: Africa*, (Lynne Rienner Publishers, Boulder, Colorado).

Hyden, Goran and Bratton, Michael (1995) "Introduction", in Hyden, Goran and Bratton Michael (eds) *Governance and Politics in Africa* (Lynne Rienner Publishers, Boulder, Colorado).

Joseph, Richard (ed.) (1999) *State, Conflict and Democracy* (Lynne Rienner Boulder, Colorado).

Kieh, George Klay; (1999), "Democratization in Africa: A balance Sheet" in Mbaku, John Mukum, *Preparing Africa for the Twenty-First Century: Peaceful Co-existence and Sustainable Development* (Ashgate, Aldershot).

Nohlen, Dieter (1996) *Elections and Electoral Systems* 2 edn (Macmillan, Delhi).

CHAPTER 11

The 2000 Elections in Choggu-Tishigu, Tolon and Kumbungu Constituencies

DAN McKWARTIN

Introduction

In December 2000 and January 2001, the Department of Political Science of the University of Ghana embarked on pre- and post-election field surveys which covered all the ten regions of Ghana. These comprehensive surveys sought to explore, among other things, the determinants of political participation, voter perception of, and involvement with institutions such as political parties and the mass media, voter perception of the economy and other issues, evaluation of the democratic process, and identities and social capital.

Between 1981 and 2000, politics in Ghana was centred on one person — Flight Lieutenant Jerry John Rawlings. From 1981 to 1992, Ghana was an effective authoritarian state under the auspices of the Provisional National Defence Council (PNDC) headed by Rawlings who seized power through a military coup d'état on 31 December 1981. As a result of internal and external pressures, popular elections were conducted in 1992 pursuant to the Fourth Republican Constitution adopted earlier in the year. This began Ghana's transition from authoritarianism to liberal democracy.

In the November 1992 Presidential elections Rawlings who ran as the flag bearer of National Democratic Congress (NDC) party, won 58.4% of the votes against four other candidates — Adu Boahen of National Patriotic Party (NPP) 30.3%, Hilla Limann of People's National Convention (PNC) 6.7%, Kwabena Darko of National Independence Party (NIP) 2.9% and Emmanuel Erskine of People's Heritage Party (PHP), 1.8%.

Pursuant to a two-term limit of four years each mandated by the 1992 Constitution, Rawlings ran again in 1996 and won with 57.4% of the votes against two other candidates — J. A. Kufuor of NPP 39.6% and E. N. Mahama of PNC 3.0%. In addition to winning the presidency, Rawlings's NDC also fully controlled Parliament from 1982 to 2000.

The December 2000 elections however resulted in dramatic changes in NDC's control of the presidency as well as Parliament. The presidency was keenly contested by seven candidates — J. E. A. Mills of NDC, G. Hagan of Convention People's Party (CPP), D. Lartey of Great Consolidated Popular Party (GCPP), C. W. Brobby of United Ghana Movement (UGM), G. Tanoh of National Reform Party (NRP), J. A. Kufuor (NPP) and E. N. Mahama (PNC). None of the presidential candidates received a majority of the votes in the 7 December 2000 elections. In which case, run-off elections between the two top candidates, J. E. Mills and J. A. Kufuor, were held on 28 December 2000. NPP's Kufuor won with 56.9% of the votes against NDC's Mills 43.1%.

In the 2000 parliamentary elections, the NDC won 92 seats compared with 133 seats that it won in 1996, constituting a net loss of 41 seats. On the other hand, the NPP which won only 61 seats in 1996 captured 100 seats in 2000, constituting a net gain of 39 seats. The PNC increased its 1 seat in 1996 to 3 in 2000, and CPP won 1 seat. Regionally, the NDC fully controls four regions (all the 7 seats in Upper West; 8 of the 12 seats in Upper East; 18 of the 23 seats in Northern; all the 19 seats — including the 2 independents who support NDC — in Volta; and marginally controls two regions (10 of the 19 seats in Western; and 9 of the 17 seats in Central). On the other hand, the NPP fully controls four regions (16 of the 22 seats in Greater Accra; 31 of the 33 seats in Ashanti; 14 of the 21 seats in Brong Ahafo; 18 of the 26 seats in Eastern) and has a weak presence in Northern (3 of the 23 seats) and Upper East (2 of the 12 seats).

What accounts for the hegemonic decline of the NDC and the emerging dominance of the other opposition parties, particularly the NPP in the 2000 elections? We examine these political changes based on our observations of three constituencies — Choggu-Tishigu, Tolon, and Kumbungu — of Northern region. To what extent do our findings in these constituencies reflect national patterns? Are these constituencies microcosms or aberrations of macro-political dynamics in Ghana? Do constituency matters explain what goes on at national level? Or do national matters explain what goes on at constituency level? We specifically examine the linkages between constituency electorate decisions and national electorate decisions along the following lines:

1. The impact of campaign theme;
2. Advantages and disadvantages of incumbency;
3. Saliency of issues;
4. Candidate image; and
5. Relevance of partisanship.

It is our contention that there is a direct relationship between micro-political electorate expressions or preferences and national electoral outcomes.

Elections, Candidates and Voters

According to Flanigan and Zingale (1994) and Polsby and Wildavsky (1991), elections are not mandates on issues but rather indirect means of citizen control over public officials. This power of citizen control over public officials is rooted in Lockean representative government based on consent and liberal democratic theory which privileges, among other requirements, popular participation and public contestation (Dahl, 1971; Riker, 1988; Bibby, 1995). Party identification has been found to have a long-term influence on voter's choice (Campbell et al., 1960; Flanigan & Zingale, 1994) whereas candidate images have both positive and negative effects in the short-term (Asher, 1992). Indeed, the relationship between saliency of issues and voting choice is well established (Key, 1966; Kramer, 1971, RePass, 1971; Alt & Chrystal, 1983; Tufte, 1980; Abramson et al., 1994). However, in recent times, there is a trend towards candidate-centered elections (Wattenberg, 1971). Finding a campaign theme that resonates with the voters is also found to enhance a candidate's electoral success (Nelson, 1993; Pomper, 1993). Our present study is grounded in these theories of elections.

Profile of Choggu-Tishigu and Tolon-Kumbungu Constituencies

Choggu-Tishigu, Tolon, and Kumbungu are three of the twenty-three constituencies that make up the Northern region, the largest region in terms of land mass (70,384 square kilometres) in Ghana. According to the Provisional Results of the 2000 Population and Housing Census, the Northern region has a population of 1,854,994 and a population density of 26 persons per kilometer. Choggu-Tishigu with Tamale as the constituency headquarters is considered urban in terms of population and infrastructural (health, schools, electricity, water, roads) distribution. This constituency is composed of thirty-eight electoral areas of which two — Moshie Zongo and Hilltop — were randomly selected for this study.

Six candidates representing six of the seven political parties competed for the Choggu-Tishigu constituency parliamentary seat. The youngest of the candidates was 26 years old who was at that time pursuing a master of philosophy degree at the University of Cape Coast; the oldest was 54 years old and a lawyer by profession. Three of the candidates representing the NPP,

NRP, and CPP were selected through primary elections supervised by the Regional Electoral Commission. These candidates were first selected by party delegates drawn from the wards in accordance with their party's constitution. The other three representing the PNC, NDC, and UGM did not go through any primaries but were recommended through introductory letters from the party's headquarters. All the candidates were male.

Tolon and Kumbungu constituencies are rural in terms of infrastructural distribution. Tolon is the constituency headquarters. This constituency consists of 16 electoral areas of which Nyankpala South was randomly selected for this study. Five candidates (NDC, NPP, CPP, PNC, UGM) representing five of the seven political parties competed for the Tolon constituency parliamentary seat. The youngest of the candidates were two 28 year olds with polytechnic (electrician) and agricultural college (teacher) qualifications respectively; the oldest was 57 years old with a bachelor of arts degree and a politician by profession. There were no primaries for selecting the candidates. All the candidates were male.

Kumbungu is the constituency headquarters of Kumbungu constituency. This constituency consists of 25 electoral areas of which Dalung was randomly selected for this study. Six candidates (NPP, NDC, UGM, CPP, PNC, NRP) representing six of the seven political parties competed for the Kumbungu constituency parliamentary seat. The youngest of the candidates was 25 years old unemployed with a senior secondary school qualification; the oldest was a 51 years old lawyer. Primary elections were not used to select the candidates. All the candidates were male. Table 11.1 summarizes the background of the parliamentary contestants.

Virtually all the presidential candidates spent a lot of time campaigning in the Northern region, which indicated that the north would be a crucial region for determining the outcome of the presidential contest. Our initial field observation of billboards and posters prior to the elections on 22 October 2000 showed that the north was "NDC country." The three constituencies that were surveyed were blitzed with NDC posters. There were few NPP posters. The symbolic presence of the other parties — PNC, UGM, CPP, NRP, GCPP — in terms of political advertisements was insignificant. On 26 October 2000, a long convoy of cars with NDC supporters was observed in Tamale. We were told that President Rawlings, campaigning on behalf of the NDC, had arrived in town on his way to Walewale for a political function.

Our guess that the north was "NDC country" was confirmed by the 7 December 2000 presidential results whereby NDC's Mills received the majority of the votes in 16 constituencies except seven (Damango/Daboya, Yendi,

Table 11.1: Parliamentary Candidates and Their Background

Constituency	Candidate	Party	Age	Sex	Qualification	Profession
Choggu-Tishigu	Alhaji M. Haroon	NRP	41	M	B.Ed.	Teacher
	Gamel N. Adam	CPP	44	M	Ph.D.	Lecturer
	Issah Ahmed	PNC	35	M	Secondary	Farmer
	Alhaji A. Sumani	NDC	54	M	LLB	Lawyer
	Yunus Macdana Adam	UGM	29	M	'A'3 Post Sec	Teacher
	Mohammed Amin	NPP	26	M	M.Phil.	Student
Tolon	Alhaji A. Salifu	NDC	57	M	B.A.	Politician
	Alhassan A. Baako	NPP	48	M	M.S.L.C.	Farmer
	Samson H. Salifu	CPP	44	M	Cert. 'A'	Accountant
	Mohammed N. Togmah	PNC	28	M	Polytechnic	Electrician
Kumbungu	Alidu B. Talhat	NPP	35	M	GCE 'O'	Teacher
	Dawuda Ibrahim	NRP	25	M	S.S.S.	Unemployed
	Issahaku Huzeru	UGM	43	M	GCE 'O'	Self-employed
	Umar M. Hashim	PNC	26	M	S.S.S.	Unemployed
	Iddrisu Iddi	CPP	36	M	—	Teacher
	Alhaji M. Mumuni	NDC	51	M	Graduate	Lawyer

Source: Northern Region Electoral Commission

Chereponi, Gukpegu/Sabongida, Choggu/Tishigu, West Mamprusi, and Nalerigu). NPP's Kufuor received the majority of the votes in only one constituency (Yendi) of the 23. None of the other parties received more than fifty percent of the votes in any of the constituencies.

However, in the 28 December 2000 run-off, in addition to Yendi that he won on 7 December NPP's Kufuor received a majority of the votes in five constituencies (Mion, Gukpegu/Sabongida, Choggu/Tishigu, Tolon, and West Mamprusi). The Northern region had earlier overwhelmingly voted for NDC in the parliamentary elections (18 out of the 23 seats).

What explains this seemingly dichotomous electoral choice of the president and parliamentarians?

Hypotheses

We hypothesize the following in our empirical study of the linkages between constituency political behavior and national political behavior in the context of the 2000 elections:

> *Hypothesis 1a:* A campaign theme that resonates with the public contributes to a candidate's electoral chances.

Conversely,

> *Hypothesis 1b:* A campaign theme that does not resonate with the public will hurt a candidate's electoral chances.
>
> *Hypothesis 2a:* Incumbency associated with positive developments will gain the support of voters.

Conversely,

> *Hypothesis 2b:* Incumbency associated with disappointments will not gain support of voters.
>
> *Hypothesis 3:* The party with more voter identification or support is more likely to win an election.
>
> *Hypothesis 4:* Voters informed and concerned about an issue will positively or negatively affect a candidate's electoral chances.
>
> *Hypothesis 5:* A candidate's image may positively or negatively influence the voters' choice.

Methodology

The research project covered two phases — the pre-election phase and the post-election phase — and employed both qualitative and quantitative techniques. The qualitative dimension of the research project entailed informal face-to-face discussions with the declared candidates, opinion leaders, party officials, electoral officials, law enforcement officers and some non-randomly selected voters in the three Northern region constituencies of Choggu-Tishigu, Tolon, and Kumbungu.

The quantitative dimension of the research project entailed the administering of a carefully designed questionnaire to four hundred voters randomly selected from these constituencies — two hundred in the pre-election survey and two hundred in the post-election survey.

Analysis

The unit of analysis is the constituency. Throughout almost all of this study, we compare the responses of the respondents in the three Northern region constituencies with the nation-wide responses to determine whether or not linkages exist between constituency political behaviour and national political behaviour. Because of the statistically insignificant votes obtained by the other political parties and their candidates in both the parliamentary and presidential elections as depicted in Tables 11.2 and 11.3, our focus is mainly on the two major political parties — NPP and NDC.

Hypothesis 1a: A campaign theme that resonates with the public contributes to a candidate's electoral chances.

The campaign theme of the NPP was "Positive Change" and that of the NDC was "Stability and Continuity." We examine how these campaign themes influenced the choices of the electorate. In testing this hypothesis, we look at the post-election responses of the electorate to the question: "If you voted for Mr. Kufuor of the NPP or Prof. Mills of the NDC, give reasons for your answer."

In the three constituencies, 11% of voters voted for stability and continuity compared to 43% who voted for positive change as depicted in Table 11.4. Nationally, 13% of voters voted for stability and continuity compared to 41% who voted for positive change. Clearly, NPP's campaign

Table 11.2: Constituency/Parliamentary Election Results in Choggu-Tishigu, Tolon, and Kumbungu of Northern Region, 7 December 2000

Constituency	Candidate	Party	Votes Obtained
Choggu-Tishigu	**Alhaji M. Sumani**	NDC*	18,937 (35.4%)
	Adam M. Amin	NPP	18,585 (34.7%)
	Gamel N. Adam	CPP	13,816 (25.8%)
	Issah Ahmed	PNC	1,293 (2.4%)
	Alhaji M. Haroon	NRP	682 (1.3%)
	Yunus Macdana	UGM	185 (0.3%)
Tolon	**Alhaji A. Salifu**	NDC*	11,740 (49.3%)
	Alhassan A. Baako	NPP	8,701 (36.5%)
	Sampson H. Salifu	CPP	2,751 (11.5%)
	Mohammed N. Togmah	PNC	420 (1.8%)
	Adam Alhassan	UGM	208 (0.9%)
Kumbungu	**Alhaji M. Mumuni**	NDC*	12,477 (60.4%)
	Alidu B. Talhat	NPP	3,699 (17.9%)
	Iddrisu Iddi	CPP	3,555 (17.2%)
	Issahaku Huzeru	UGM	456 (2.2%)
	Umar M. Hashim	PNC	399 (1.6%)
	Dawuda Ibrahim	NRP	127 (0.6%)

* Winner
Source: Electoral Commission

theme of positive change resonated with the public and contributed to the electoral success of their presidential candidate, Mr Kufuor.

Hypothesis 2b: Incumbency associated with disappointments will not gain the support of voters.

We test this hypothesis by examining the voters' attitudes about and perceptions of the economy. Many respondents cited the economy as the main issue facing the country. Were the voters satisfied with the way that the

Table 11.3: Constituency Presidential Election Results in Choggu-Tishigu, Tolon, and Kumbungu in Northern Region, 7 December and 28 December 2000

Constituency	7 December Candidate	Elections Votes received	28 December Candidate	Run-off Elections Votes received
Choggu-Tishigu	Lartey (GCPP)	607 (1.1%)	Mills (NDC)	20,474 (38.6%)
	Mills (NDC)	20,701 (38.9%)	Kufuor (NPP)*	32,601 (61.4%)
	Hagan (CPP)	9,984 (18.8%)		
	Brobby (UGM)	102 (0.2%)		
	Mahama (PNC)	1,766 (3.3%)		
	Tanoh (NRP)	385 (0.7%)		
	Kufuor (NPP)	19,631 (36.9%)		
Tolon	Lartey (GCPP)	440 (1.9%)	Mills (NDC)	10,876 (47.2%)
	Mills (NDC)	12,031 (50.6%)	Kufuor (NPP)*	12,143 (52.8%)
	Hagan (CPP)	2,009 (8.4%)		
	Brobby (UGM)	142 (0.6%)		
	Mahama (PNC)	373 (1.6%)		
	Tanoh (NRP)	156 (0.7%)		
	Kufuor (NPP)	8,625 (36.3%)		
Kumbungu	Lartey (GCPP)	591 (2.8%)	**Mills (NDC)***	**12,690 (61.8%)**
	Mills (NDC)	12,344 (59.5%)	Kufuor (NPP)	7,848 (38.2%)
	Hagan (CPP)	3,494 (16.8%)		
	Brobby (UGM)	142 (0.6%)		
	Mahama (PNC)	373 (1.6%)		
	Tanoh (NRP)	150 (0.7%)		
	Kufuor (NPP)	3,717 (17.9%)		

* Winner
Source: Electoral Commission

incumbent NDC party handled the economy? We validate this hypothesis by looking at the responses of respondents to the question: "Would you say that over the past four years the Ghanaian economy has improved or become worse?" in the pre-election survey.

Table 11.4: If you Voted for Prof. Mills of NDC or Mr Kufuor of NPP, Give Reasons for Your Answer

	Frequency	
	Stability and Continuity (NDC)	Positive Change (NPP)
Choggu-Tishigu/Tolon/Kumbungu Constituencies*	11 (11%)	43 (43%)
National**	499 (12.9%)	1576 (40.6%)

*Sample size: 200 **Sample size: 3,878
Source: Survey data.

Table 11.5 shows that 56% of voters in the three constituencies stated that the economy became worse during the tenure of the NDC and another 49% nationally stated that the economy became worse. Indeed, the majority of voters were disappointed with the way that the economy functioned during the tenure of the NDC, resulting in the loss of NDC's bid for the presidency. In addition to the bad economy, the respondents also faulted the incumbent NDC for high inflation, unemployment and depreciation of the national currency.

Table 11.5: Would You Say that Over the Past Four Years the Ghanaian Economy has Improved or Become Worse?

Response	Frequency	
	Choggu-Tishigu/Tolon/Kumbungu Constituencies*	National**
Considerably improved	35 (35%)	301 (7.5%)
Become worse	56 (56%)	1970 (49.2%)

* Sample size: 198 ** Sample size: 4004
Source: Survey data.

Hypothesis 3: *The party with more voter identification or support is more likely to win an election.*

You cannot win an election in a competitive democratic polity if a large portion of the voters do not identify with or support the candidate or the political party. We test the voter identification/electoral success hypothesis by looking at the voters' responses to a post-election survey question: "If you are not a registered member of any political party, which of the following parties do you have an inclination towards?"

Table 11.6 shows that 32% of the voters in the three constituencies identified with or supported the NPP compared with 28% for the NDC. Nationally, 41% of the voters identified with the NPP compared with 21% for the NDC. Even though the incumbent NDC captured all the parliamentary seats in these constituencies as shown in Table 11.2, the party did not have much support in its presidential bid. Tables 11.7 and 11.8 reveal the dichotomy or what we may describe as the divided loyalty of the voters.

Table 11.6: If you are not a Registered Member of any Political Party, which of the following Parties do you have an Inclination Towards?

Party identified with	Frequency	
	Choggu-Tishigu/Tolon/ Kumbungu Constituencies*	National**
NPP	64 (32%)	1,572 (40.5%)
NDC	55 (27.5%)	801 (20.7%)

*Sample size: 200   **Sample size: 3,878
Source: Survey data.

We observe a consistent increase in support for the NPP and decrease for the NDC at both constituency and national levels. For example, 36% the voters in the three constituencies stated in the pre-election survey that they *would vote* for the NPP but in actuality, 46% said that they *had voted* for the

Table 11.7: Distribution of 7 December 2000 Presidential Support by Intended Votes, Actual Votes, and Political Party in Choggu-Tishigu, Tolon, and Kumbungu Constituencies

	NPP	NDC	PNC	CPP	NRP	GCPP	UGM	NR	TOTAL
Intend to Vote for*	68 (36.2%)	86 (45.7%)	5 (2.7%)	20 (10.6%)	2 (1.1%)	0 (0.0%)	0 (0.0%)	7 (3.7%)	188 (100%)
Voted for**	91 (46.4%)	71 (36.2%)	30 (15.3%)	3 (1.5%)	1 (0.5%)	0 (0.0%)	0 (0.0%)	0 (0.0%)	196 (100%)

NR = No Response *Pre-election **Post-election

Source: Survey data

Table 11.8: Distribution of 28 December Presidential Run-off Elections by Intended Votes, Actual Votes, and Political Party Nation-wide

	NPP	NDC	PNC	CPP	NRP	GCPP	UGM	NR	TOTAL
Intend to Vote for*	1,665 (41.6%)	1,239 (30.9%)	171 (4.3%)	180 (4.5%)	134 (3.3%)	8 (0.2%)	15 (0.4%)	150 (3.7%)	4,004 100%
Voted for**	2,329 (60.1%)	1,156 (29.8%)	66 (1.7%)	151 (3.9%)	59 (1.5%)	3 (0.1%)	10 (0.3%)	104 (2.7%)	3,878 (100%)

NR = No Response *Pre-election **Post-election

Source: Survey data.

NPP. On the other hand, 46% of the voters stated that they *would vote* for the NDC but in actuality, only 36% said that they *had voted* for the NDC, as shown in Table 11.7. Nationally, 42% of voters stated in the pre-election survey that they *would vote* for the NPP but in actuality, a whopping 60% said that they *had voted* for the NPP compared to 31% who said that they *would vote* for the NDC but in actuality, 30% said that they *had voted* for the NDC.

Table 11.9 provides more compelling evidence for the tremendous voter support that NPP's Kufuor has. His average of 30.4% votes in the three constituencies in the 7 December elections increased to an average of 50.8% in the 28 December run-offs. Kufuor's average of 29.6% in the Northern region in the 7 December elections increased to 48.9% in the 28 December run-offs. In the case of NDC's Mills, his vote averages for both elections remained flat or statistically the same.

Hypothesis 4:   Voters informed and concerned about an issue will positively or negatively affect a candidate's electoral chances.

Were the Ghanaian voters concerned about certain issues in the elections? What were the issues? What were the positions of the candidates on the issues? Did the voters distinguish between the candidates on the issues? Spatially, what were the relative positions of the voters and the candidates on the issues?

Table 11.10 depicts the issues that the three constituencies identified as the most important nationwide.

Table 11.11 depicts the issues that the three constituencies identified as the most important in their Constituencies

Asked which issues, national or constituency, influenced their vote the most in the December 2000 elections, 79% of respondents in the three constituencies mentioned both national and constituency issues.

Tables 11.12 and 11.13 summarize how the voters implicitly juxtaposed the positions of the political parties on the issues.

Tables 11.14 and 11.15 summarize the issues identified by the national electorate and the perceived positions of the political parties on the issues.

Tables 11.12 and 11.14 present interesting similarities between the perceptions of the voters in Choggu-Tishigu/Tolon/Kumbungu and those of the national electorate, with respect to the articulation of issues by the political parties. Forty-nine percent of the voters in the three constituencies stated that

Table 11.9: 7 December and 28 December 2000 Distribution of Average Presidential Votes in Choggu-Tishigu/Tolon/Kumbungu Constituencies, Northern Region, and Nation-Wide

	7 December Votes		28 December Votes	
	Mills (NDC)	Kufuor (NPP)	Mills (NDC)	Kufuor (NPP)
Choggu-Tishigu/ Tolon/Kumbungu Constituencies Average	15,025 (49.7%)	10,658 (30.4%)	14,680 (49.2%)	17,531 (50.8%)
Northern Region Average	12,444 (50.7%)	55,608 (29.6%)	12,045 (51.1%)	11,525 (48.9%)
Nation-wide Average	289,558 (44.5%)	313,174 (48.2%)	275,012 (43.1%)	363,126 (56.9%)

Source: Computed from Electoral Commission results.

Table 11.10: The most Important Development Issues at National Level Identified in Choggu-Tishigu, Tolon, and Kumbungu Constituencies

Issue*	Frequency	Percentage %
Education	141	25
Hospital	75	14
Agriculture	84	15

*Multiple issues identified, only those high frequencies included in table, hence percentages do not add up to 100.

Source: Survey data.

Table 11.11: The most Important Development Issues at Constituency Level Identified in Choggu-Tishigu, Tolon, and Kumbungu Constituencies

	Issue*	Frequency	Percentage %
Choggu-Tishigu	Education	35	12.3
	Good road network	54	19.0
	Sanitation	48	16.9
Tolon/Kumbungu	Hospital	56	18.9
	Education	46	15.5
	Water	38	12.8

*Multiple issues identified; only those with high frequencies included in table, hence percentages do not add up to 100.

Source: Survey data.

Table 11.12: In Your View (Choggu-Tishigu, Tolon/Kumbungu voters), which of the Political Parties Best Articulated the Most Important National Development Issues?

Party	Frequency	Percentage %
NPP	97	49
NDC	72	36.4
PNC	26	13.1
CPP	3	1.5
TOTAL	198	100

Source: Survey data.

Table 11.13: In Your View, Which of the Political Parties Best Articulated the Most Important Constituency Development Issues in Choggu-Tishigu, and Tolon/Kumbungu?

Party	Frequency	Percentage %
NPP	95	48.2
NDC	71	36.0
PNC	27	13.8
CPP	4	2.0
TOTAL	197	100

Source: Survey data.

Table 11.14: In Your View (National Electorate), Which of the Political Parties Best Articulated the Most Important National Development Issues?

Party	Frequency	Percentage %
NPP	2,417	62.3
NDC	1,077	27.8
PNC	129	3.3
CPP	72	1.9
NRP	68	1.8
GCPP	25	0.6
UGM	15	0.4
No response	75	1.9
TOTAL	3,878	100

Source: Survey data.

Table 11.15: In Your View (National Electorate), Which of the Political Parties Best Articulated the Most Important Development Need in Your Constituency?

Party	Frequency	Percentage %
NPP	2,376	61.3
NDC	1,057	27.3
PNC	125	3.2
CPP	109	2.8
NRP	65	1.7
GCPP	3	0.1
UGM	9	0.2
No response	134	3.5
TOTAL	3,878	100

Source: Survey data.

NPP best articulated the most important national development issues compared to 36% for the NDC, as shown in Table 11.12. Over 62% of voters nation-wide stated that the NPP best articulated the most important national development issues compared to 28% for the NDC, as shown in Table 11.14. With respect to the articulation of constituency issues, 48% of the voters in Choggu-Tishigu and Tolon/Kumbungu stated that the NPP best articulated the development issues facing them compared to 36% for the NDC, as shown in Table 11.13. At national level, 61% of voters stated that the NPP was the party that best articulated the development issues in their constituencies compared to 27% for the NDC, as shown in Table 11.15.

Clearly, not only were the voters in the three constituencies and across the nation concerned about the issues, they also positioned the political parties relative to theirs on the issues. And indeed, the voters found the NPP's position closer to their own in determining which party to vote for in the elections.

Hypothesis 5:   A candidate's image may positively or negatively influence the voters' choice.

Here, we look at the normative dimension of the calculus of voting. In contrast to party identification which very often has a long-term influence, candidate's image is found to have a short-term influence on elections (Bibby, 1995; Asher, 1992). There are certain personal characteristics of candidates that voters find important. For example, the voters may perceive a candidate as weak or strong, experienced or inexperienced, competent or incompetent, gullible to whims and caprices of special interests, or one who can bring about needed change.

Tables 11.16, 11.17, 11.18, 11.19, 11.20 and 11.21 provide summaries of response on some of these normative considerations. We see in Table 11.16 that 64% of voters in Choogu-Tishigu, Tolon and Kumbungu voted for NPP's Kufuor compared to 34% NDC's Mills in the Presidential run-offs. Nationally, as shown in Table 11.17, 68% of voters voted for NPP's Kufuor compared to 27% for NDC's Mills.

Tables 11.18 and 11.19 summarize the reasons for voting for either Mills or Kufuor. A large number of respondents did not answer this question. However, for the few who answered this question, 6% voted for Mills because his policies were good compared to 17% for Kufuor; another 6% voted for Mills for the sake of continuity compared to 22% who voted for Kufuor

Table 11.16: Which of the Candidates did you Vote for in 28 December Presidential Run-off Elections in Choggu-Tishigu, and Tolon/Kumbungu Constituencies?

Candidate	Frequency	Percentage %
J. E. A. Mills (NDC)	67	33.5
J. A. Kufuor (NPP)	127	63.5
No response	6	3
TOTAL	200	100

Source: Survey data.

Table 11.17: National Electorate, Which of the Candidate's Did You Vote for in the 28 December Presidential Run-off Elections?

Candidate	Frequency	Percentage %
J. E. A. Mills (NDC)	1,044	26.9
J. A. Kufuor (NPP)	2,648	68.3
No response	186	4.8
TOTAL	3,878	100

Source: Survey data.

Table 11.18: Choggu-Tishigu, Tolon/Kumbungu Constituencies, Why did You Vote for Mills (NDC)?

Reason	Frequency	Percentage %
Better candidate/ Honorable & honest	16	8
Leader of my party	3	1.5
His policies are good	11	5.5
Continuity	11	5.5
Capable of doing the job	21	10.5
No response	137	68.5
TOTAL	200	100

Source: Survey data.

because they wanted a change from the status quo and that Kufuor represented that change. Nation-wide, as depicted in Tables 11.20 and 11.21, 13% of voters voted for Mills because they wanted continuity compared to 41% who voted for Kufuor because they wanted a change from the status quo.

Table 11.19: Choggu-Tishigu, Tolon/Kumbungu Constituencies, Why Did You Vote for Kufuor (NPP)?

Reason	Frequency	Percentage %
Leader of my party	32	16
Represented change/ Want a change	43	21.5
Better candidate	7	3.5
His policies are good	34	17
No response	83	41.5
TOTAL	199	99.5

Source: Survey data

Table 11.20: National Electorate, Why Did You Vote for Mills (NDC)?

Reason	Frequency	Percentage %
Better candidate/ Honorable & honest	250	6.4
Leader of my party	104	2.7
His policies are good	45	1.2
Continuity	499	12.9
I followed the bandwagon	7	0.2
I was intimidated	3	0.1
Capable of doing the job	75	1.9
Belong to my tribe	1	0.0
No response	2,894	74.6
TOTAL	3,878	100

Source: Survey data

Table 11.21: National Electorate, Why Did You Vote for Kufuor (NPP)

Reason	Frequency	Percentage %
I like	83	2.1
Leader of my party/ Member of my party	115	3.0
Represented change/ Want a change	1,576	40.6
Better candidate/ Right person for the job	381	9.8
His policies are good	250	6.4
We want to try him	51	1.3
I was cheated (conned)	15	0.4
His humility & tolerance	48	1.2
He became popular	1	0.0
Because of the alliance	11	0.3
I followed the bandwagon	7	0.2
From my tribe	–	–
No response	1,340	34.6
TOTAL	3,878	100

Source: Survey data.

Indeed, NPP's Kufuor was perceived as the candidate to bring about the change that the voters in the three constituencies as well as nation-wide wanted. In spite of the experience of Mills as the incumbent Vice-President, his appeal in terms of handling both constituency and national development issues was limited.

Conclusions

Our empirical study of voting behavior depicts some striking similarities between constituency political behavior and national political behavior. Our analysis focused on five dimensions — impact of campaign theme, disadvantages of incumbency, saliency of issues, relevance of partisanship and candidate image. We observed linkages between constituency electorate decisions and national electorate decisions. It is our contention that the political expressions in Choggu-Tishigu, Tolon, and Kumbungu constituencies of Northern Region of Ghana are a microcosm of rather an exception to macro-political dynamics in Ghana in the context of the 2000 presidential and parliamentary elections. Both the constituency and national survey data confirm the hypotheses advanced in this study.

The NPP won the presidency and fifty percent of the parliamentary seats because:

1. Their campaign theme of "Positive Change" resonated with the public compared with the campaign themes of the other political parties;

2. Disappointments such as high unemployment, depreciating national currency, high inflation associated with the incumbent NDC negatively affected the NDC;

3. More voters identified with the NPP than with the other political parties;

4. The relative position of the NPP on the issues was closer to the positions of the voters;

5. The voters wanted a change, and the NPP was perceived as the party that could bring about this change.

REFERENCES

Abramson, Paul R., John H. Aldrich, and David W. Rohde, *Change and Continuity in the 1992 Elections*. Washington, DC: Congressional Quarterly Press, 1994.
Alt, James E. and K. Alec Chrystal, *Political Economics*. Berkeley and Los Angeles: University of California Press, 1983.
Asher, Herbert B., *Presidential Elections and American Politics: Voters, Candidates and Campaigns Since 1952, 5th Edition*. Pacific Grove, CA: Brooks/Cole, 1992.
Bibby, John, *Governing by Consent: An Introduction to American Politics, Second Edition*. Washington, DC: Congressional Quarterly Press, 1995.
Campbell, Angus, Philip E. Converse, Warren E. Miller, and Donald E. Stokes, *The American Voter*. New York: Wiley, 1960.

Dahl, Robert A., *Polyarchy: Participation and Opposition*. New Haven, CT: Yale University Press, 1971.
Flanigan, William H. and Nancy H. Zingale, *Political Behavior of the American Electorate, 8th Edition*. Washington, DC: Congressional Quarterly Press, 1994.
Key, Jr. V. O., *The Responsible Electorate*. Cambridge, MA: Harvard University Press, 1966.
Kramer, Gearald H., "Short-Term Fluctuations in U.S. Voting Behavior, 1896–1964," in *American Political Science Review*. Volume 65 (March 1971): 131–143.
Nelson, Michael, *The Elections of 1992*. Washington, DC: Congressional Quarterly Press, 1993.
Polsby, Nelson W. and Aaron Wildavsky, *Presidential Elections: Contemporary Strategies of American Electoral Politics, 8th Edition*. New York: Free Press, 1991.
Pomper, Gerald, ed., *The Elections of 1992: Reports and Interpretations*. Chatham, NJ: Chatham House, 1993.
RePass, David E., "Issue Salience and Party Choice," in *American Political Science Review*. Volume 65 (June 1971): 389–400.
Riker, William H., *Liberalism Against Populism: A Confrontation Between the Theory of Democracy and the Theory of Social Choice*. Prospect Heights, IL: Waveland Press, Inc., 1988.
Tufte, Edward R., *Political Control of the Economy*. Princeton, NJ: Princeton University Press, 1980.
Wattenberg, Martin P., *The Rise of Candidate-Centered Politics*. Cambridge, MA: Harvard University Press, 1991.

CHAPTER 12

Determinants of Political Choice in Koforidua and New Juaben North Constituencies in the 2000 General Elections

GILBERT K. BLUWEY

Introduction

There is no gainsaying that elections are the central institution of democratic governments. This is because in a democracy, the authority of the government derives from the consent of the governed. And the principal mechanism for translating that consent into governmental authority is the holding of free and fair elections.

Although all modern democracies hold elections, not all elections are democratic. Right-wing dictatorships, single-party politics and the erstwhile Marxist regimes hold elections (which they carefully manage) to give their rule the aura of legitimacy. In such elections, there may be only one candidate or a list of candidates, with no alternative choices. Such elections may offer several candidates for each office, but ensure through intimidation or rigging that only the government-approved candidate is chosen. Other elections may offer genuine choices — but only within the incumbent party.

Ghana had experienced this kind of electoral farce in 1960 and in 1965. In the presidential election/constitutional referendum held in 1960, state machinery including the security services was used to intimidate the electorate and whip it in line to vote for Kwame Nkrumah and the Republican constitution. In 1965, the incumbent President Nkrumah was a candidate; he was also the Electoral Commissioner and the Returning Officer at the same time. As both the life chairman and the general secretary of the incumbent Convention People's Party — the only legal party in Ghana — Nkrumah received and vetted applications from presidential and parliamentary aspirants. In the end, he declared those he selected as elected unopposed. Indeed, he personally assigned several parliamentarians to constituencies of his own choice. Certainly, Ghana in the first Republic experienced no democratic election.

According to Jean Kirkpatrick, an eminent American scholar and diplomat, democratic elections "are not merely symbolic. . . . They are competitive, periodic, inclusive, definitive elections in which the chief decision makers in a government are selected by citizens who enjoy broad freedom to criticize government, to publish their criticism and to present alternatives". In his view, democratic elections are competitive because opposition parties and candidates, as indeed the incumbents, enjoy equal freedom to speak and publish their views on the issues and so offer alternatives both in personnel and policy to the electorate. In the same way, democratic elections are periodic because democracies do not elect incumbents for life. Elected officials are accountable to the people and must return to the voters at prescribed intervals to renew their mandate. Public officials in democracies therefore accept the risk of being voted out of office.

Democratic elections are inclusive because the franchise is freely available to all adults irrespective of sex, religion, ethnic origin, or political affiliation. A very large proportion of the populace therefore enjoys the franchise in a democracy. Democratic elections are also definitive because the outcome of the elections is the emergence of legitimate public officials. Finally, democracies may also refer certain critical issues to be decided directly by the populace. Resort to the electoral process in this way is called a plebiscite or referendum.

Again, Breton and Galeotti (1985) assert that elections "are primarily, instruments in the hands of the public to signal particular preferences or opinions to competing representatives. . . ." Thus while in office, governments must seek to meet the preferences of the electorate or risk being thrown out of office at the next polls. In line with this thinking, Muller (1982) asserts that "both the voters and the representative are rational economic men bent on maximizing their utilities." That is to say, voters use the available good information to assess the closeness or otherwise of their preferences, hopes an aspirations to those of the candidates and parties and vote accordingly. But misinformation and voting by habit may obstruct rational choice. The election campaign is meant to prevent such negative forces from impacting on voter choice.

Finally, as Anthony Downs (1957) asserts, "parties formulate policies in order to win elections, rather than win elections in order to formulate policies." It is logical therefore to ask, "to what extent was political choice (the elections) influenced by the issues raised during the electioneering campaign?" or " to what extent was choice influenced by rational factors dictated by manifestos and party programmes?" The answers to these and other similar questions will help us identify the major determinants of the political choices made by the people of Koforidua and New Juaben North constituencies in the December 2000 elections.

Demographic Data on the Respondents

The following data represent the socio-political and economic background of the respondents in the two surveys. As demographic data, they project the spread or coverage of respondents across the myriad of core groups within the areas covered by the survey.

(i) Gender	Koforidua	New Juaben North
Male	47	60
Female	53	40
TOTAL	100	100

(ii) Age		
18–25	21	23
26–30	18	20
31–40	26	23
41–50	19	10
51-60	7	14
61-70	5	8
71 and above	2	2
TOTAL	100	100

(iii) Educational Background		
No education	4	12
Secondary	20	17
Polytechnic	7	3
Primary	51	64
Teacher Trg./Technical Coll.	15	2
University	3	2
TOTAL	100	100

	(iv) Region of Birth	Koforidua	New Juaben North
	Ashanti	6	1
	Central	2	3
	Greater Accra	4	–
	Upper East	1	2
	Volta	8	2
	Brong Ahafo	3	2
	Eastern	72	85
	Northern	1	4
	Upper West	–	1
	Western	3	–
	TOTAL	100	100
	(v) Religion		
	Christian	93	79
	African Traditional	–	6
	Muslim		15
	TOTAL	100	100

The picture above shows a fairly cosmopolitan voting population in each of the two constituencies. Koforidua recorded 71% indigenes and only 15% non-indigenes. The Christian population is very high, recording 93% and 79% in Koforidua and Effiduase respectively.

The survey paid great attention to gender balance, recording 47% male and 53% female in Koforidua. In Effiduase, the figures for the respondents were 60% male and 40% female. The survey also revealed an intolerable level of adult illiteracy at Effiduase, recording 12% in this regard. In Koforidua, it was a mere 4%.

Profile of the Constituencies

The two constituencies are in the Koforidua Municipal Assembly area. According to the 2000 national population census, the two constituencies have a combined population of 139,370 people. The electoral registers for the two constituencies however gave a total of only 77,250. Out of this number, the Koforidua constituency had 55,137 registered voters at 30 polling stations, while the New Juaben, North Constituency had 22,113 registered voters at 18 polling stations.

Both constituencies are cosmopolitan in demographic composition. Almost every ethnic and religious group within Ghana and in the neighbouring countries of Togo, Cote d'Ivoire, Burkina Faso, Benin and Nigeria is represented in Koforidua and Effiduase. It must be of interest to note that although Effiduase is the capital of the New Juaben North Constituency, in all things particular, it is part and parcel of Koforidua.

The names of some of the electoral areas of Koforidua clearly attest to the ethnic heterogeneity of the town. First there are typical Akan names, which attest to the Ashanti origins of the indigenous people. Some of these are: Adweso Estate, Asuofiriso, Ohemaa Park, Janofo to mention only a few. Next are those with typical Ewe names such as: Anlo Town (north and south) and Klu town. Finally, there are Oguaa Town, Ada Town and the Zongo areas.

The myriad Christian religious denominations, which span the length and breadth of Ghana are found in the numerous tiny communities of Koforidua. The Moslems and traditionalists are no less conspicuous, either.

By a system of random selection, the 100 respondents for each round of survey in the Koforidua constituency were selected from the following electoral areas:

Adweso	Nsukwaoso
Akwoasu Asebi	Klu Town
Anlo North Town	Oguaa Town
Central Market Area	Ohemaa Park
Debakrom	Social Welfare Area

A total of 6 candidates, all sponsored by political parties, contested the Koforidua parliamentary seat. We observed that each of the 6 political parties in the contest had an office in Koforidua designated as both the District and Regional Office. In addition, each of the candidates had a field office in each of the 30 electoral areas in the constituency. The presidential candidates were associated with the District and Regional offices of their respective parties. The Great Consolidated Popular Party (GCPP) of Dan Lartey was the only political party that was only barely visible in Koforidua. All the others had their banners and their symbols widely distributed and hanging all over the town. In addition to these, the Tee shirts were conspicuous in the market and all public areas.

The parliamentary candidates and their sponsoring parties were as follows:

Hon Yaw Barimah (incumbent)	NPP
George Freeman Boateng	NDC
Nana Boadu-Sarpong	CPP
Kwaku Marfo-Frimpong.	PNC
Stephen Oduro-Boakye	NRP
Prince B. Aboagye	UGM

Four of the candidates were in their fifties while one of them was only 30; another one, at 49 was also close to fifty. A look at the educational background of the candidates showed impressive attainments. Three of them had university degrees while one, the incumbent, was on the roll of the Supreme Court of Ghana as an advocate. There were two others with middle level technical qualifications. Only one had an "Ordinary Level" certificate.

We were surprised that there was no female parliamentary candidate although the Regional Minister for the past four years had been a female with a post-tertiary educational qualification. We tried to find out if the presence of a female regional minister in Koforidua over a period of four years made no impact (as a role model) on the women of the Region. Respondents were either evasive or indifferent.

My pre-election survey notes sums up the political climate in the Koforidua constituency as follows:

> The general mood of the people of this constituency is clearly one of anger against the NDC government for what they alleged as its total neglect of Koforidua in terms of development infrastructure. The town roads and the market are in advanced stages of disrepair, there is no reliable system of water supply for the entire area and the buildings and furniture at the Ghana Secondary School which serves the area are in a poor state. Other general complaints were on the economy, the high cost of medical care, the cash and carry system and the myriad fees being levied by the authorities of the public schools.

We also noted that "on the whole, Koforidua is a violence-free constituency. The party operatives are friendly in their inter-personal relations. We did not pick up any allegation or counter-allegation of unfriendly utterances or behaviour towards one another among the leadership of the various political parties. . . . This is certainly an exciting political arena exhibiting a healthy contest between wills and brains."

The New Juaben, North constituency is not very different in demographic composition from Koforidua. The constituency headquarters is Effiduase which also houses the nationally renowned Catholic Hospital for orthopaedic surgery and also two highly rated public senior secondary schools: the Pope John Senior Secondary School and the Ghana National Secondary School. It shares the same ethnic heterogeneity with the Koforidua constituency in which the Asante component predominates.

The New Juaben North Constituency had 22,113 registered voters distributed to 18 polling stations each representing an electoral area. On the basis of random sampling, the 100 respondents in each of the two surveys were selected from the following 9 electoral areas:

Aburodua	Oguaa
Adumasa	Suhyen
Akwandum	Zongo (Asokore)
Jumapo	Zongo (Ghanass)
Zongo (Oyoko)	

Two of the seven political parties did not contest the parliamentary seat: the GCPP of Mr Dan Lartey and the UGM of Dr Wereko Brobbey. Indeed, the GCPP was notable for the conspicuous absence of its banners and posters throughout the constituency. We were not able to identify any of its offices or field operatives. The UGM, on the other hand, had an office where several activists converged regularly for strategic sessions in respect of the presidential campaign. The line-up of the parliamentary candidates was:

Hon. Hackman Owusu-Agyeman (incumbent)	NPP
Samuel Machel Nimo	NDC
Yaw Oti-Dankese	CPP
Samuel Effah Krofah	PNC
Joseph Obeng	NRP

Two of the candidates were in their fifties, while two others were in their forties. The remaining candidate who described himself simply as a farmer was 37 and had only a Middle School Leaving Certificate. The incumbent MP was the only candidate with a higher tertiary educational background. Indeed, Hon. Hackman Owusu-Agyemang is a retired UN executive with considerable business and public service experience. Of the remaining three, two are first cycle public school teachers and one is a middle-level civil servant.

The New Juaben North Constituency, like its twin neighbour, had no female parliamentary aspirant. This should be a source of worry for all proactive feminists because as part of the Koforidua municipality, New Juaben North should share the impact of feminine political sophistication, which should flow from the presence of a female Regional Minister only a few kilometres away.

On the whole, the New Juaben, North constituency exhibited a violence-free campaign period. Its socio-political problems were identical to those of its neighbour, Koforidua. The bad state of town roads, the absence of a dependable source of water supply, the poor state of the Koforidua central market and the hard economic conditions of daily life, were issues widely shared throughout the constituency. In short, both the Koforidua and New Juaben, north constituencies exhibited heavy leanings towards the New Patriotic Party and its presidential and parliamentary candidates.

The Survey

This paper explores in a systematic way, the determinants of the results of the 2000 elections in the Koforidua and New Juaben North constituencies. It is part of an electoral survey conducted before and after the December 2000 General Elections in Ghana under the auspices of the Department of Political Science, University of Ghana, Legon. Two separate surveys were conducted. The first was before the elections and the second was about a week after the run-off election.

The two surveys (the pre-election and the post-election) covered the following issue-areas: a) general political participation (b) voter perception of, and involvement with, political parties (c) evaluation of democratic institutions and process and (d) election issues. Each survey also gave demographic data on the respondents. Finally, the post-election survey carried a section on factors that influenced choice in the "man-to-man" presidential, run-off.

General Political Participation of Voters

An overwhelming percentage of the voters indicated that they were regular voters and active participants in political events. In Koforidua, as many as 99% of respondents said that they were registered voters. Again, a high percentage of 97% responded that they had voted in the 2000 parliamentary, presidential and presidential run-off elections. This represents about an 8% increase over the 1966 responses, which put the percentage of participation at 91%. The figures correspond almost exactly with the responses given during the pre-election survey when 98% said they would definitely vote in the impending elections.

The picture was fairly different in the New Juaben North constituency. There, 95% of respondents said they were registered but only 84% said they had actually voted in 1996. In the 2000 elections, however, 98% said they had actually voted. The questionnaire did not provide a clue to determine the reason for this higher rate of participation. My guess is that the issues, the tenor of the campaign and the issuing of photo ID cards induced greater participation than in 1996.

Voter Perception of, and Involvement with, Political Parties

Responses under this heading show that in each constituency, the percentage of regularly registered party members is only about half of the politically active. In Koforidua, 36% were registered party members and 64% said they were not. In New Juaben North, 35% had party cards, while 65% of the politically active had no card.

Again, in Koforidua 24% said they carried NPP cards, while 17% said they had NDC cards. This is very well reflected in the presidential and parliamentary elections of 7 December 2000, where the distribution was, NPP 59%, NDC 36% with the remaining 5% going to the remaining parties in the field. In New Juaben North, however, there was a wide difference between those who carried NDC cards (19%) those who carried NPP cards (10%). The PNC and the NRP had 3% card-carrying members among respondents, while the UGM, GCPP and the CPP recorded none.

It is interesting to note that in both constituencies, most respondents actively followed the activities of the various political parties. 90% said so in Koforidua, while 87% also said so in New Juaben North. 52% and 67% in Koforidua and New Juaben North respectively, said they attended all the campaign rallies organized by the various political parties in connection with the elections.

The low percentage of respondents, who regularly paid party dues and made contributions to their parties, corresponds with the equally low percentage of card-carrying party members. Most voters did not know who provided the money for the running of their political parties. However, around 30% of respondents thought that big business, including government contractors provided the money needed for the operations of the political parties.

The regular party members overwhelmingly complained of inadequate financial support and such logistics as vehicles and dependable equipment for public address. Many agreed that campaign materials such as scarves, Tee shirts, caps and posters were in adequate in supply.

Koforidua respondents registered a fairly high opinion of politics, parties and politicians. Sixty-six per cent thought that party politics had "improved the quality of living of Ghanaians"; 68% think that political parties are doing a good job while a whopping 91% **rejected** the view that "irrespective of the party in power, there is no difference to what happens at the national level".

In New Juaben North, on the other hand, only 49% thought that party politics "have improved the quality of living of Ghanaians". But a high number of 87% responded that "political parties are doing a very good job" (in Ghana). Of Juabeng North respondents 98% also reject the notion of "obiara ba a saa". Certainly, voters in both constituencies are of the liberal democratic persuasions. They have no misgivings about politics and political leaders and they also believe that parties and individuals can make a difference in the ability of government to improve upon the living conditions of the people.

In both constituencies, respondents thought that the playing field was fairly level, except in the wide differences in the capability of parties to procure money and logistics. But respondents rejected by as much as 80% any suggestion that there were instances of intimidation of political opponents. The final voting figures for the parties/candidates reflected fairly accurately the pre-election options of the respondents. We identified both constituencies as clearly pro-NPP. But the NPP success may be due more to the calibre of its parliamentary candidates than to a traditional pattern of voting (by habit). This will be explained further in subsequent surveys. We would however, note that over 60% of respondents observed that (compared to the other parties) the NPP had a "good and honest candidate" and also had "good policies to ensure the development of the country."

Evaluation of Democratic Institutions and the Process

The frequency and manner of interaction between the Member of Parliament and respondents were used as the means of voter-evaluation of the structures instituted by the constitution for democratic political practice in Ghana. The point is that in general terms; the MP is the first and the most accessible point of contact between the political authorities and the individual voter. The MP is also the primary representative of his/her political party among voters and he/she is also the prime beneficiary of the political activity of voting engaged in by the people. As a candidate therefore, his/her general extent of acceptance is almost invariably reflected in the ultimate fortunes or reverses of the party and its presidential candidate. There are, indeed far too few occasions where there are significant differences between the fortunes or reverses of the parliamentary candidate and those of the presidential candidate. Where the parliamentary candidate has also been a popular, highly personable incumbent, the race is sealed for his party and presidential candidate.

In this regard, it is amazing that although 33% of Koforidua respondents say they had interacted with the incumbent Hon. Yaw Barima during the four years of his tenure as many as 69% gave him an approval rating for being "very helpful" and able "to bring development to the area". The incumbent must here be advised that closeness to the electorate is as important as helping build infrastructure within the constituency.

Hon. Hackman Owusu-Agyemang had a different more acceptable story to tell in this regard. Fifty-eight per cent of respondents had interacted with him, 46% of whom had done so at meetings and his approval rating was a whopping 82%. Of course, at the personal level, the MP for New Juaben North is better resourced than his counterpart in Koforidua. The former may be advised that a drastic fall in the popularity of the NPP in the more populous Koforidua could have adverse effects on his own safe seat.

Evaluation of the Electoral Process

The electoral progress received overwhelming endorsement in both constituencies for being transparently free and fair (95-98%), for receiving balanced coverage from the state media (91–96%), for being transparently free of undue obstacles (88–92%), for the able and helpful disposition of election officials (93–94%) and for the absence of elements that would intimate the voter either to turn away from voting, or to vote as directed by someone else (87–89%). In other areas of evaluation, 99% said the voting was orderly and 90% in Koforidua and 94% in New Juaben North said they voted with photo ID cards.

Indeed, incidents of impersonation and other irregularities were unrecorded throughout the two constituencies. This should not be surprising because during our pre-election survey, we noticed that party activists engaged in frantic efforts to educate voters on the electoral process. We attended a forum organized at Koforidua and Effiduase by the National Commission for Civic education (NCCE) and the political parties. The obvious pay-off was the smooth, uneventful voting in both constituencies. The Electoral Commission also presented disciplined and highly committed staff. Officials turned up punctually and the proverbial shortage of election materials was minimal this time, or at least in these two constituencies.

Election Issues

The survey covered three broad issue areas. The first consisted of social services such as education, health care, water, good roads and street lights and employment opportunities. The second effort was to match national issues against local and constituency issues and the third was to determine which party's promises sounded most credible to voters. In addition to obtaining these responses, we conducted open-ended interviews with the respondents about such other factors as the special qualities of both the presidential and parliamentary candidates, the factor of traditional party alliances, the impact of the presidential running mate on a particular presidential ticket and the general perception of the respective parties' potential for competence in government. These will be discussed in the next section. Respondents generally agreed that parents would contribute to the provision of educational opportunities. However, many thought that parent-teacher levies and their corresponding outputs left much to be desired. Many also advocated expansion of places in the universities but at costs that are easily within the reach of the lowest income group in the country.

The cash-and-carry system at the nation's health institutions, coupled with the high cost of drugs made health an item of high concern to respondents. Between 60 and 75% in both constituencies rated cheap and accessible health care as top priority.

The bad state of Koforidua town roads and the equally deplorable state of the roads connecting Koforidua and Effiduase to the outlying villages were also of serious concern to the electorate. In addition, many queried why Koforidua, as a regional capital should not have street lights. The erratic power supply to the municipality made the Electricity Company of Ghana (ECG) an issue.

The daunting problems posed by the inefficient delivery of basic services to the Koforidua and Effiduase municipality has been compounded by the absence of a reliable water supply system. Voters saw this as evidence of NDC's (incumbent's) lack of interest in Koforidua and its environs. Others we spoke to thought that the NDC leadership in the area was to blame because they lacked the vigour to drive home their plight to the national leadership. Thus, a whopping 74-81% responded that Hon. Hackman Owusu-Agyemang and his colleague Hon. Yaw Barima offered the best hope for better attention to the needs of Koforidua through an NPP victory. Thus, J. A. Kufuor netted 63% in Koforidua and 73% in new Juaben North.

The Presidential Run-off

For the second time in Ghanaian political history, there was a presidential run-off because none of the candidates received the mandatory majority of more than fifty per cent of the valid votes cast. This is in accordance with Article 63(3) which states that:

> A person shall not be elected as President of Ghana unless at the presidential election the number of votes cast in his favour is more than fifty per cent of the total number of valid votes cast at the election.

Accordingly, a run-off presidential election was held on 28 December 2000 between Professor John Atta-Mills, the NDC candidate and Mr J. A. Kufuor, the NPP candidate. This is also in accordance with Article 673(4) of the 1992 constitution which states that:

> Where at a presidential election there are more than two candidates and no candidate obtains the number of percentage of votes specified in clause (3) of this article a second election shall be held within twenty-one days after the previous election.

The enthusiasm of voters in the two constituencies for the run-off presidential elections was high. Officials and supporters of all the non-incumbent (non-NDC) parties responded firmly to the decision of their national leaders to support Mr J. A. Kufuor, the NPP candidate. Within days, it became clear that the NDC candidate would have very little chance in the run-off against Mr J. A. Kufuor of the NPP. Day after day and night after night, only NPP campaign records sounded at the various popular entertainment spots in the twin cities of Koforidua and Effiduase. Indeed, in the closing days of the campaign, it was obvious that the NDC itself had given up.

The final figures released by the Electoral Commissioner vindicated our predictions. In Koforidua, the overall percentage of voter turnout dropped from 67.6% (45,556). However, Mr J. A. Kufuor of the NPP registered an increase in both the number of votes cast for him (29,512 against 28,232) and the percentage of the votes in his favour (68.2% as against 62.7%). In the same way, Professor Atta-Mills, who originally had 15,414(32%) dropped to a low of 13,738 (31.8%) in the run-off.

The reversal of fortunes was more dramatic in the New Juaben North constituency. Mr Kufuor swung up to 14,976 votes (77.6%) while Professor Atta-Mills slumped to a mere 4,311(22.4%) of the votes. Again, it must be noted that voter turnout in the run-off presidential elections in the New Juaben North constituency was also lower than in the original election. The turnout was 19,382 (68.7%) in the presidential run-off. These figures clearly depict Koforidua and Effiduase as indisputable NPP strongholds.

Observations and Conclusions

Certain conclusions obviously flow directly from the data produced by the surveys in Koforidua and Effiduase. These conclusions seek to explain the choices made by the electors of the two constituencies in the December 200 elections. It is important to state that in addition to the data revealed by the surveys, we were also influenced by our observation of the political events in the areas during our field trips. We also had the benefit of conversing with individuals during which we gathered facts outside the framework of the survey.

First, we tried to address the issue of voting by habit and /or bandwagon voting. This refers to voter behaviour induced either by belonging to a given political tradition and/or trying to belong to "the winning side". In either of these situations, issues and personalities do not matter to the voter. He/she either votes faithfully to support the party of his/her tradition or votes for the party that demonstrates a higher potential for winning the elections and forming the government at national level.

In our survey, we observed very strong anti-NDC feelings in the two constituencies. This is borne out by the crushing defeat in 1996 of the NDC candidates who were also senior and nationally very popular ministers in the NDC government. In 1996, Mr D. S. Boateng, a cabinet minister lost to

Mr Yaw Barima, a legal practitioner by 18,648 votes (40.1%) to 26,025 (56.0%). In New Juabeng North, Mr Hackman Owusu-Agyemang beat Mr Samuel Nuamah Donkor of the NDC by a whopping 11,629 (59.6%) to 7,494 votes (38.4%). It may therefore seem that the voters of the two constituencies have developed a habit of pro-NPP voting.

However, the second element in our observations seem to be more relevant to the voting pattern in the two constituencies. This is the element of the personal standing of the candidates. This refers to the performance records of the two NPP candidates both of whom swept the polls. Although they both belonged to a non-incumbent party, each one did very well in the provision of amenities out of the MPs' Common Fund. In addition, both MPs reached out to several international NGOs which yielded appreciable development assistance in several forms. During the campaign, Hon. Hackman Owusu-Agyeman produced and distributed widely, a brochure entitled, *Four Years of Change: New Juaben North*. In this brochure, the candidate gave a detailed breakdown of his past services, full expenditure on the MPs' Common fund and the promise which a possible NPP government held for the Koforidua municipality-including Effiduase, the entire Eastern region and Ghana. The figures were quite credible and constituted a formidable wall of defence for candidate Hackman Owusu-Agyeman and the New Patriotic Party in the two constituencies.

In the Koforidua constituency itself, the relatively younger but equally robust campaigner, Hon. Yaw Barimah also had several completed social projects to his credit. He had provided drainage on the Koforidua mortuary road to provide an unimpeded drive from the town centre to the public cemetery. For a people who have a deep-seated emotional attachment to funeral protocols, that was a project that stood high among voters for performance. Mr Barima was also a conspicuous donor at funerals for both the prominent and the lowly placed in society. Several bags of cement and pieces of furniture to carefully selected schools — reflecting full coverage of the electoral areas of the constituency — went out from Mr Barima's arsenal. Thus, when the Hon. MP for Koforidua ran into trouble with the NDC-appointed Municipal Chief Executive over the release of his share of the Common Fund to pay for projects, he won the sympathy of the people against the MCE who was then seen as being vindictive and unresponsive to the needs of the common people.

These various forms of negative perception of the incumbent NDC by the people were also extended to the absence of water to the Koforidua municipality, the bad state of the roads in and outside Koforidua and the general state of poor delivery of services in the area. Most first cycle schools were in deplorable states of disrepair.

But above all, to a people whose main source of income is derived from the proverbial "buy and sell", Ghanaian economic activity, the fluctuations in prices occasioned by the ever-depreciating *Cedi*, was a matter of great concern. Even those who had no appreciation of how the stability of a national currency reflects on prices, the ever-galloping prices of commodities including transport fares, were of serious concern.

Finally, not a few complained bitterly about the cash and carry system in the nation's health institutions. Indeed, the escalating cost of drugs and medical care in general was of considerable concern to these voters.

These conditions generally strengthened the voters in the two constituencies in their rejection of the NDC and its platform. It rendered the electorate more ready to accept that a change in the personnel of government as promised by the NPP would reverse the socio-economic plight of the people. In this regard, the two NPP candidates as non-incumbents sounded more credible than the NDC.

But why was the choice seemingly situated between the NDC and the NPP? Where were the CPP, the PNC, UGM and NRP and what about Mr Dan Lartey and the UGCPP? First, these parties, new as they were in the field along with their presidential and parliamentary candidates lacked name and ideological recognition. Against either the NPP or the NDC, none of these parties had any visible hold on the electorate in the two constituencies. The poor showing of both the CPP and the PNC however, could be attributed more to poor organization and appeal than to name and ideological recognition. The names, Kwame Nkrumah and the old CPP (1949-1966) were still fresh in several homes and hearts. In the same way, the Zongo residents are numerous in the two constituencies. But Professor Hagan registered a paltry 275 (0.6%) in Koforidua and 77 (0.4%) in Effiduase. Dr John Mahama on the other hand, registered 522 (1.2%) in Koforidua and 241 (1.2%) in New Juabeng North. It is possible that the inclusion of Alhaji Aliu Mahama on the NPP presidential ticket swayed the Zongo/Muslim voters to the NPP at the expense of Dr Mahama, a Christian. Professor Hagan, on the other hand, failed to touch the people as a true CPP and an Nkrumahist candidate.

In sum, this survey concludes that voter choice in these two constituencies was based on rational decisions rather than on habit or bandwagon voting.

REFERENCES

Bell, David V. J., Deutsch, Karl W., Lipset, Segmour, M., *Issues in Politics and Government* (Boston: Mutton, 1970).

Bluwey, Gilbert K., *Political Science: An Introduction* (Accra: Ananse Publishers, 1993) Chapter 8.

Bluwey, G. K. "The Opposition in Democratic Government", in K. A. Ninsin and F. K. Drah, eds., *Political Parties and Democracy in Ghana's Fourth Republic* (Accra: Woeli Publishers, 1993): 207–223.

Bluwey, G. K. "Determinants of Political Choice in the Agona-West and Effutu Constituencies", in J. R. A. Ayee, ed., *The 1996 General Elections and Democratic Consolidation in Ghana* (Legon: Department of Political Science, 1998): 341–354.

Breton, A. and Galeott, G., "Is Proportional Representation Always the Best Electoral Rule?", *Public Finance* (1985): 40.

Dennis, C. M., *Public Choice II* (London: Cambridge University Press, 1989).

Dye, Thomas R., and Zeigler, Harmon L., *The Irony of Democracy: An Uncommon Introduction to Politics* (North Duxbury Press, 1978).

Ghana, Republic of *The Constitution of the Republic of Ghana, 1992* (Accra: Ghana Publishing Corporation, 1992).

Kousoulas, George D., *On Government and Politics* (North: Duxbury Press, 1975).

Lamb, Karl A., *The People, May Be* (North Duxbury Press, 1978).

La Palombara, Joseph, *Politics Within Nations* (Englewood Cliffs, N.J.: Prentice-Hall, 1974).

Sherrill, Kenneth S., and Vogler, David I., *Power, Policy and Participation* (New York: Harper & Row, 1977).

Wittman, Daniel A., "Parties As Utility Maximizers" *American Political Science Review* (June 1969).

CHAPTER 13

Election 2000 Politics in Komenda-Edina-Eguafo-Abirem and Agona West Constituencies

A. ESSUMAN-JOHNSON

Democracy and Good Governance[1]

Democracy has been defined variously as "government of the people, by the people and for the people". It can also be seen as a society in which everyone counts for one and no one counts for more than one. It is also seen as a society in which the effective political power of the majority prevails. It is also a society in which the consent of the people is the basis of the power and authority of the government. A democratic system of government lays down a framework of democratic principles and guidelines for political leaders to follow in their dealings with the people. A democratic society on the other hand is one in which, in addition to enjoying a democratic system of government, the bulk of the people observe democratic practices in their dealings both with their leaders and with one another.

A democratic society is thus a creation of its people and leaders and it grows and develops over a long period of time. Democracy is therefore something to be nurtured by the people and the leaders. To a large extent the democratic culture of a country depends on the democratic culture of the leaders. The people will usually not know the kind of democratic culture that its leaders posses. Society usually puts in mechanisms by which the people can restrain their leaders from abusing and misusing their power. Ultimately, the citizens of a country are its best laws, its best institutional constraints, and its best referees, because it is the people who can exercise control over their leaders by defining what they can or cannot do. A civic minded people, conscious of their rights and determined to preserve them, can exercise considerable control over their leaders through periodic elections, judicial and constitutional provisions against the abuse and misuse of power, the pressure of public opinion, and as a last resort, open resistance. By the power of their vote, people can change their leaders at regular intervals. Where elections are free fair and impartially conducted, they constitute an effective check on leaders, because any elected leader who proves to be unresponsive to popular feeling among the electorate risks defeat at the next elections.

Another way of exercising control over leaders is through the pressure of public opinion. Public opinion reinforces and strengthens the other two ways of controlling leaders, for an elected leader who outrages the conscience of the public risks defeat in the next elections, and it is much easier to apply and enforce institutional sanctions against a leader if it is known that the public will readily welcome such action. Public opinion may be defined such a strong feeling of the majority of the members of a group about an issue that they are prepared to act on it. We can thus speak of public opinion reference to both national and sectional issues, for example the results of free and fair national election are taken to indicate public opinion among the citizens of a country, whereas a resolution by an organization represents public opinion among its members. Also public opinion is not mere sentiment popular feeling. Usually public opinion is directed at influencing policy, but in general leaders do not care much about what a people think or feel they will not act on it. Under representative government, politicians are interested in public opinion only in so far as it may affect their policies and programmes or their chances of winning elections or both. Representatives who act in the name of the people need to listen to public opinion. But it would be impossible to go round asking everybody in his or her constituency his opinion about an issue. They try to determine what the public feeling on a particular issue is by reading the newspapers, talking to people and reading letters on the matter sent to them by the people in their constituency.

The pillars of democracy has included a constitution with the rule of law enshrined, a bill of rights, the existence of political parties, a government chosen by the people and that rules by the mandate of the people, a free press and periodic elections to enable the government renew its mandate to rule. a government is concerned about the exercise of its mandate it would be concerned about the opinion of the governed about its policies. Democratic governments are thus very concerned about their standing in the eyes of the governed, because at the appropriate time they will go back to the people for a renewal of their mandate to govern.

The Theoretical Perspectives

Three theoretical issues that political scientists have raised in the discussion of elections in Africa have been 1) voter choice 2) voter turnout and 3) political participation.[2]

Voter Choice

The fact that an elections usually entails some degree of choice for the electorate — between candidates, parties and perhaps policies — raises the issue of the factor or factors determining the choice made. The issue for the student of elections is "why did candidate A win and candidate B lose?" In African election studies the answer to the question has been found less in quantitative methods, but in what W. G. Runciman[3] has argued as the need to subordinate quantitative methods to a sense of political history. This has been classed as a "loose" theoretical framework, which has made possible a number of judgments explaining election outcomes in terms of leadership popularity (charisma), regime support, ideological commitment or ethnic loyalties. The most important theoretical principle underlying most African election studies has been a consensus that African voters tend to make their electoral choice as communities rather than as individuals. Taking the key community of orientation to be an ethnic one for the great majority of Africans, most observers have seen group identity as determining the individual's choice; electoral contests as being a vying for ethnic community support; and electoral success as usually based on ethnic coalition building. The primacy of the constituency over the individual has been seen as far more important than party orientation, issue orientation, social class or ideology as a determinant of voting behaviour.[4] Austin despite his concern with these other issues has done some very illuminating electoral analysis in looking at individual constituencies.[5] He found that generally, the support of the traditional holders of authority was all-important in winning, that the manipulation of traditional loyalties and conflicts to secure voter support was the substance of the campaign and that the election was perceived by most as voters as a contest between rival kin-based communities. The case studies of four Ghanaian districts in the 1969 General Election found little change in this situation.[6] Other studies of Ghana's elections have included those in which Chazan and LeVine (1979), Chazan (1987), Jeffries (1980) Oquaye (1995), Nugent (1995), Gyimah-Boadi (1997), Ayee (1997) examined voting behavior of the Ghanaian electorate from various points of view.[7] The most encompassing study of a Ghanaian election has been Ayee (ed.) (1998), which looked at the social, institutional and normative basis of Ghanaian politics and how they could shape democratic practice and stabilize democratic institutions.[8] This work is a study of the elections in two constituencies in the central region of Ghana

The Third Election

Ghana has been a long way towards finding its niche in a stable democracy in a continent where stable democratic systems are few and far between. Among the few cases that Africa can point to, have been Botswana, Senegal and Benin. Ghana's democratic politics very closely mirror that of Benin. Benin had been through a long period of military intervention in politics. The incumbent military leader, Mathew Kerokou in 1991 returned his country to democratic politics and lost the first election after a period of military rule to Nichephore Soglo. Kerokou accepted the election results and went into opposition. In the next election in 1996, Kerokou won the election and came back as a civilian president. That was the first time in an African country when an incumbent government had been defeated in an election and the defeated leader has gone into opposition and won back the presidency. [9]

As in Benin, Ghana's third republic was overthrown by the military on 31 December 1981 and an undemocratic government — the Provisional National Defence Council (PNDC) — led by Flt Lt Jerry John Rawlings was set up to rule the country. After pressures from internal sources e.g. the activities of the Movement for Freedom and Justice (MFJ) as well as the linking of continued external donor assistance to democratization, the PNDC moved to democratic politics in 1992. In the 1991 general elections, the PNDC metamorphosed into a political party — National Democratic Congress (NDC) led by Rawlings — to contest the elections for which the PNDC set up an uneven political playing field in they set the rules of the game, took an unassailable lead and asked the opposition parties to compete. The opposition contested the presidential election won by Jerry Rawlings, but after seeing the election malpractices, they boycotted the parliamentary election. The NDC won the uncontested parliamentary election hands down with 187 seats out of 200 with other parties in alliance with the NDC winning the other seats. Through this, a semi-military government civilianized itself and thus became "democratic". The NDC presidential candidate, Flt Lt Jerry Rawlings sought re-election in 1996. In the presidential elections, Rawlings was returned with 57.4% of the vote. His party's dominant position in Parliament was reduced. The distribution of seats in Parliament was as follows: NDC 133, NPP 61, PCP 5, PNC 1. The election was generally thought to have been influenced by the incumbent President and his party and it was thought that the political playing field was still not even given the events of the 1991 elections. The 1992 Constitution bars a President from seeking a third term in office and this meant that the incumbent president, Rawlings who had served two terms was disqualified from seeking re-election in the 2000 presidential election. It is against such a background that this paper looks at the election in the KEEA and Agona West constituencies in the 2000 general elections.

Background to the Election in KEEA and Agona West

The elections in the two constituencies in the central region were contrasting. The main commercial town of Agona West is Agona Swedru with Agona Nyarkrom as the traditional capital as it is the seat of the paramount chief of the Agona traditional area. The Agona district of which it is a part has a population of 158,678[10] The KEEA, which has a population of 111,985,[11] is made up of the four main towns of the constituency, namely Komenda, Edina (Elmina), Eguafo and Abirem. The main town is Edina (Elmina) due to its tourist attraction of the first slave castle to be built on the coast. Komenda is the next main town, which has the only institution of higher learning in the district, a teacher training college and which used to have a sugar factory. Eguafo and Abirem are small rural farming towns.

The election was much more vigorously contested in KEEA than in Agona West due in part to the profiles of the candidates in the two constituencies. In the KEEA parliamentary elections the contest was between the following: Dr Ato Quarshie (NDC) Dr Kwesi Nduom (CPP) George Manso-Howard (NPP) John Assifuah-Nunoo (PNC) and Robert Mensah (NRP). The contest was however mainly between the sitting NDC MP, Dr Ato Quarshie and the CPP candidate Dr Kwesi Nduom. Even though Dr Nduom was only an assembly member in the KEEA, he had developed a national profile as a management consultant and an outspoken critic of the NDC government. He was widely seen as biding his time to seek to be the flag bearer of the CPP in the future. Dr Nduom's contest for a seat in the district assembly in the 1997 District assembly elections turned out to be a contest against the full strength of the NDC (notwithstanding the non-partisan nature of the DAs) and he prevailed. Both candidates are natives of Elmina and this brought the youth of Elmina very much into the contest on the side of the two candidates.

The contest in Agona West was between the following: Abu Hamid Wanzam (PNC), Samuel Oppong (NDC), Samuel Kweku Obodai (NPP), Kojo Anan (NRP), and Mathew Cawrie (CPP). The contest was however mainly between the NDC candidate Samuel Oppong, the sitting MP, and the NPP candidate Samuel K. Obodai. The politics of the constituency is such that preference tends to be given to candidates who are natives of Agona Nyarkrom because it is the seat of the Agona paramountcy. For this reason it is instructive that the two leading candidates were natives of Agona Nyarkrom.

The Pre- and Post-election Survey

It is against this background that the survey took place. Pre-election and post-election surveys were taken from a sample of 100 respondents randomly chosen in the constituency. The survey sought to find out the extent of political participation among respondents. Asked if they were registered members of political parties, the majority 62% said no in Agona West, while in KEEA it was 57%. The explanation for this seem to be that even though people have inclinations towards particular parties, they were not registered card carrying members. For those who were registered members of parties 20% indicated they belonged to the NDC in Agona West and 29% in KEEA. For those who indicated the NPP it was 21% in Agona West and 13% in KEEA. Political rallies were not popular in the two constituencies; 70.4% in Agona West and 61% in KEEA indicated they were not attending political rallies. What the parties were using was early morning gatherings of the youth of the parties in what was called "Keep Fit". A very high percentage of the sample had also voted in the 1996 elections, 90.8% in Agona West and 87% in KEEA. Party allegiance had been high, as 89.8% in Agona West and 85% in KEEA indicated that they voted for the same party in the 1996 general elections. Further evidence of the active political participation of the electorate is provided by their participation in the 1998 District Assembly elections. 73.5% of voters in Agona West and 80% in KEEA said they had voted in the local elections.

On partisan political affiliation, in Agona West 33.7% indicated the NDC as the party of their parents, 25.5% indicated the UP/NPP group and 11.2% indicated the CPP. In the KEEA, 28% indicated NDC as the party of their parents followed by 27% indicating the CPP and 14% indicated the NPP. This seems to suggest that the NDC and NPP dominate the politics of Agona West while the NDC and the CPP dominated the politics of the KEEA.

Political Participation

A very high proportion of respondents had also voted in the 1996 presidential elections with 90.8% in Agona West and 87% in KEEA indicating they had voted in the 1996 presidential election. Fifty-two per cent voted for the NDC and 33.7% voted NPP in Agona West. In KEEA 47% voted NDC and 36% voted NPP. In the parliamentary elections, 53.15 voted NDC and 33.7% voted NPP in Agona West. In KEEA 48% voted NDC and 36% voted NPP. Nearly all of them (99%) in both constituencies indicated they would vote in the 2000 elections. In the presidential elections 38.6% indicated they would vote for the NPP, 30.6% would vote for the NDC in Agona West. In KEEA, 41% indicated they would vote for the NDC, 31% would vote NPP and 9% would vote CPP. In the parliamentary elections, in Agona West, 36.7% would vote for NPP and 34.7% would vote NDC. In KEEA 45% would vote NDC, 24% would vote NPP and 14% would vote CPP.

The Economic Situation

The survey sought to find out respondents views on the economy. Asked what they thought about the state of the Ghanaian economy 85.7% in Agona West said either bad or very bad. In KEEA the response was 90% saying either bad or very bad. In Agona West, 61.2% said the economy had worsened over the past four years, while in KEEA 81% said the economy had worsened. Asked whether their standard of living had improved since the last election, 46.9% in Agona West said their standard had become much worse and 30.6% said a little worse. However 19.4% said things had become a little better. In KEEA, 66% said their standard of living had become much worse, 19% said it had become a little worse and 12% said it had become a little better. Against this economic situation respondents were asked to indicate what they consider to be the major economic problem in Ghana today. In Agona West they indicated the following: 58.2% indicated unemployment and 10.2% indicated depreciation of the *Cedi*. In KEEA 65% indicated unemployment and 15% indicated the depreciation of the *Cedi*. The general economic situation in the two constituencies prior to the elections was very poor with unemployment being the single major important problem facing the country.

The Democratic Process in the Constituencies

The survey also sought to evaluate the democratic process in the two constituencies. Asked if they thought Ghana could be described as a democratic country, 72.4% in Agona West answered in the affirmative and 75% in KEEA answered in the affirmative. The majority of respondents (78.6% in Agona West and 83% in KEEA) also thought democracy had improved in the in the country. Press freedom was also thought to have improved over the past four years. Some 87.8% of respondents in Agona West and 98% in KEEA thought political parties and other associations had more freedom now than four years ago. Against this background respondents were asked if they thought conditions existed in Ghana for free and fair elections in the 7 December 2000 elections. Responses indicate that people were highly confident of the fairness of the elections. 79.6% of Agona West and 79% from KEEA were confident that conditions existed for free and fair elections. Asked if they thought, apart from the Electoral Commission there were any other ways to influence the elections, 65.3% in Agona West and 77% in KEEA said no. This is an indication that people were confident of the Electoral Commission's ability to run free and fair elections. Respondents were equally confident of the way the district office of the Electoral Commission was performing; 75.5% in Agona West and 77% in KEEA thought so. The District Police Commanders provided evidence of inter-party cooperation in the two constituencies.

In interviews the District Police Commander in Agona West[12] explained that the political atmosphere in the district during the run-up to the elections was not turbulent in Agona Swedru. This he attributed to the formation of a "Peace Committee" made up of the chairmen or representatives of all the political parties. The committee discussed and revolved problems arising out of the political campaigns, which did not attract court action. He related the story of a head teacher of a primary school who removed NDC posters, which had been posted on the walls of his school. Under the Political Parties Law it is an offence to tamper or remove such posters. The "Peace Committee" accepted the head teacher's explanation that he removed the posters in good faith because the posters should not have been posted in the school in the first place. The Divisional Police Commander also put in place a "Peace Task Force" which included the NCCE, the Electoral Commission, the police and the prisons. He reiterated that the police would not like to be drawn into settling political conflicts, hence the "Peace Committee". Up to the date of the interview the political parties had conformed to the law by informing the police about when and where they were going to hold a political activity. The police followed up to check on all such political activities in the same area at the same time. As a result of these measures there had not been any political conflicts in the constituency.

In a similar interview in KEEA, the District Police Commander,[13] explained that there had not been any serious conflict in the constituency over the election campaign. There had however been complaints from all the parties to the police. This was due to the fact that the election in the constituency has been polarized between the NDC and the CPP. The parties had been expecting the police to effect arrests as a result of these complaints, but the District Commander explained that there had not been any arrests. The police instituted weekly inter-party meetings. There was another meeting of the security agencies (Police, BNI and Prisons) and representatives of the parties. This meeting saw to the easing of tension among the parties during the week. Among the complaints of the parties were: the removal of party flags, tearing up of flags, removal of posters, and the wearing of party T-shirts to the rally or keep-fit of a rival party. These things created tensions and were the cause of petty squabbles among the parties in the constituency. The police had solved these problems through dialogue with the parties.

Some reports had been made to the police by party members themselves. Some party members especially the fisher folks removed flags positioned in town to use as souvenirs or hoisted them on their boats when they went to sea. The supporters of the NDC and the CPP were all involved in this kind of activity. The Police Commander reported that during meetings, party members saw the police as friends, but the NDC supporters saw the CPP candidate, Dr Kwesi Nduom, as a major threat to the wining chances of their candidate, Dr Ato Quarshie, and this was one major source of antagonism between the two parties.

Generally, people were of the view that the electoral process had been free and fair. About 80% of the electorate from each constituency indicated that the elections had been free and fair. Similarly when asked what they thought of the last (1996) elections, 82% in KEEA and 68% from Agona West thought those elections had been free and fair. In this regard the survey sought the views of the people about the Electoral Commission. The Commission had come under some suspicion particularly from the opposition who had feared that the Commission was cozying up to the ruling government. Some 61% in KEEA and 65% from Agona West thought the Commission was sufficiently independent of government control. Asked if they thought the ruling government had had undue advantage over opposition parties, 54% in KEEA and 46% in Agona West answered in the positive. This would suggest that in the eyes of the people the ruling government was making an unfair use of incumbency. Given this advantage of the ruling government, the survey sought to assess the chances of the opposition winning the elections. On the chance of the opposition wining the presidential elections, 53% in KEEA and 61% in Agona West said it was either very good or good. This suggests that there was a fairly good confidence that the opposition could win the elections. Interestingly most people surveyed didn't think there was the possibility of a run-off in the elections. Asked if they thought a run-off was likely 71% in KEEA and 76% in Agona West answered in the negative.

The survey also sought to measure the kind of projection political parties made during the campaign. The assumption of the survey was that Ghanaian political parties projected personalities more than their policies. When asked if they thought parties in Ghana project personalities more than their policies, the overwhelming majority in both constituencies (77% in KEEA & 78% in Agona West) answered in the negative. This suggests that the electorate thought the parties projected their policies or the party rather than the individual candidates. It would seem that the parties projected themselves more than the candidates. This may stem from what this author would call the Rawlings-NDC and NPP-Kufour syndrome. By this is meant the fact that as a party, the NDC had been projected much more on the apron strings of Flt Lt Rawlings who seemed larger than the party. In the case of the NPP, it was the image of the party that projected Mr J. A. Kufour. This may also explain the poor showing of the NDC in the election, as the NDC candidate Prof. J. E. A. Mills could not match the image that Rawlings had projected for the NDC in previous elections. The NDC itself seem to have been aware of this, as they did all they could to use Flt Lt Rawlings in the campaign and succeeded in dwarfing the image of Prof. Mills. The NPP on the other hand used the party's carefully crafted image as the most credible opposition party to sell their candidates.

On financing the parties, over half (55%) in KEEA and 44% in Agona West said they didn't think parties were financially sound even though 19% and 36% from the two constituencies felt the parties were financially sound. The electorate in the two constituencies was generally opposed to the state financing the parties. Asked if they thought the state should finance parties, 54% and 61% respectively from the two constituencies answered in the negative. The implication here is that people generally want the state to stay out of the financing of political parties. On the process of candidate selection, the view from the two constituencies is that they were satisfied with it. First the two constituencies indicated an overwhelming liking for the candidates nominated by their parties. In KEEA it was 78% and 79% in Agona West.

Similarly 76% in KEEA and 71% in Agona West described the selection process of the candidate as democratic. It was not very clear what they meant by democratic, because none of the parties held a party congress at constituency level. The lack of primaries especially for the NDC raises issues about what the electorate meant when they answered that the process for the selection of the party candidate was democratic.

Election Issues

Asked to name the three issues at national level in the 2000 elections, 80.6% of respondents in Agona West named the Economy, 12.2% named Continuity and Stability and 2% named Change and Development. In KEEA 90% named the Economy, 5% indicated Continuity and Stability and 2% named Change and Development. This indicates the importance that the state of the economy had in the election issues. In the Agona West constituency, the three most important development issues in the elections were Education 31.6%, Employment 27.6% and Electricity 7.1%. In KEEA the development issues were Education 18%, Employment, 16% Toilet (KVIP) 16% and Market 16%. What stands out is the general concern about education and unemployment, which relates very much to the larger issue of the economy. Asked what they would vote for in the presidential election, 70.4% in Agona West said they would vote for "both party & candidate" while in KEEA 77% said they would vote for "both party & candidate". For the parliamentary elections 72.4% in Agona West indicated they would vote for "both party & candidate" and 67% in KEEA said they would vote for "both party and candidate" This indicates that for both the presidential and the parliamentary elections what influenced the electorate was what the parties had to offer and the candidates standing on the party ticket.

Identities and Social Capital

The survey also sought to provide insights into identities and issues of social capital. Asked what they felt strongly attached to, 49% in Agona West indicated the family followed by the region where they lived (20%) and region where they grew up (18%). In KEEA, 50% indicated the family, followed by the region where they grew up (23%) and the region where they lived (10%). This is an indication that respondents were very strongly attached to their families and the region where they grew up and live. Asked about the adequacy of their household incomes, 81.65 in Agona West and 86% in KEEA said they did not have enough to survive on. This spoke volumes about the dire economic situation of the electorate prior to the elections. This was further confirmed when respondents were asked to assess what their household standard of living has been like, 49% in Agona West and 63% in KEEA indicated it has been "much worse" followed by 30.6% in Agona West and 23% in KEEA who indicated "a little worse". Asked to assess what their household standard of living would be like in the future, 29.6% in Agona West and 56% in KEEA said it would still be "much worse". On where they would look for assistance to supplement their income, 45.9% in Agona West and 35% in KEEA indicated they would approach their family members. 34.7% in Agona West and 50% in KEEA would approach their neighbours. Most respondents however (67.3% in Agona West and 71% in KEEA) expected that most of the help to supplement their household income was expected to come from family members.

The survey tried to assess how the electorate related to their District Assemblies (DA) on social issues. Asked about the most effective way of getting the DA to take action on a problem in the district, 57.1% in Agona West and 47% in KEEA said "contacting officials of the DA itself" and 39.8% in Agona West and 50% in KEEA said "contacting representatives on the DA." Of these options, the most effective method was indicated as "contacting the representative on the DA". The interesting thing though was that when asked if over the past five years they had been concerned about any problems that could have been solved by their DA, 73.4% in Agona West and 61% in KEEA answered in the negative. What this suggests is that the electorate are largely passive and are not very much engaged with their DA about issues of development in their area.

Most respondents (85.7%) in Agona West and (85%) in KEEA were aged 18–50. The education background of most of them, 64.3% in Agona West and 59% in KEEA is primary education. This is an indication of a relatively young electorate with primary education. The occupational background of respondents gives a further indication of the dire economic situation within which the election took place. In Agona West, 25.5% indicated they were traders, 18.4% were unemployed and 13.3% were farmers. In KEEA, 34% were unemployed, 19% were traders and 14% were farmers. This means that most of the electorate are either unemployed or are in the informal sectors of farmers and traders.

Table 13.1: 1st Round Presidential Elections in the Central Region

	Mills	Hagan	Mahama	Kufour	Tandoh	Lartey	Brobey
Votes	237,227	17,295	2,791	269,501	7,291	6,887	1,449
%	43.73	3.19	0.51	49.68	1.34	1.27	0.00

Source: Electoral Commission of Ghana.

Explaining the Results

Against this background the results of the election in the two constituencies were interesting. In the first round of the presidential election there was no clear-cut winner, as the Central Region voted nearly half (49.68%) for J. A. Kufour and 43.73% for J. E. A. Mills. However in the second round of voting things were much more decisive. The Central Region (see Table 13:2) voted 60.31% for J. A. Kufour as President, which must have contributed in no small way to the victory of Mr Kufour. In the two constituencies studied, both voted for Kufour with Agona West and KEEA voting 70.12% and 52.62% respectively for Kufour. In the parliamentary elections, the NPP candidate Samuel Kweku Obodai with 57.5% of the vote won Agona West. The NDC candidate Samuel Oppong with 36.9% of the vote followed him in second place. The NDC candidate, Dr Ato Quarshie with 46.3% of the vote won KEEA. The CPP candidate Dr Paa Kwesi Nduom with 43.7% of the vote followed him closely in second place. What this also indicates is that while the NPP turned out to be strong in Agona West and was able to carry home the quest for change and defeat the incumbent NDC candidate, it was not to be in KEEA.

Table 13:2 Presidential Run-Off Results in the Central Region

	J. E. Attah-Mills	J. A. Kufour
Votes	199,006	302,414
%	39.69	60.31

Source: Electoral Commission of Ghana

The incumbent NDC candidate Dr Ato Quarshie won the election in the KEEA against the strong CPP candidate Dr Kwesi Nduom. The defeat of Dr Nduom in KEEA raises other issues about the ability of new candidates to defeat incumbents. There were very strong grounds for people thinking and believing that Dr Nduom would defeat the incumbent NDC candidate. An interview with a resident of Elmina[14] suggested that the people of Elmina were embittered about what they considered as the loss of the Fishing Harbour to Sekondi. The people feel that the incumbent NDC MP should or could have done something about it but did nothing. Furthermore the people of the constituency claim the sitting MP did not attend parliamentary sessions and they had not seen or heard him speak in parliamentary debates. In addition to this Dr Nduom was seen to have created jobs and job opportunities in the area, through his hotel (Coconut Grove) and also that fishmongers sell fish to the hotel and pineapple farmers sell to the hotel.

Even though interviews in the constituency suggested that the people wanted a change of the incumbent NDC candidate, he won the seat. The explanation seems to come from an interview held with an NDC organizer in Elmina.[15] According to him, the winner of the election would depend on the past development projects carried out in the constituency. These include the provision of street lights, roads and markets. He argued that even though the youth in the constituency saw Dr Nduom as a very formidable opponent to the incumbent NDC candidate, they thought the CPP presidential candidate (Prof. Hagan) would not win and this would go against Dr Nduom. The reasoning here is that a candidate must have his presidential candidate win to help him realize the programmes he has lined up for his constituency. The things going for the incumbent, Dr Ato Quarshie, were (1) that they thought his presidential candidate (Atta-Mills) was likely to win and (2) that he was responsible for the road network in the constituency and the provision of street lights.

Conclusion

The 2000 parliamentary and presidential elections have proved to be a defining moment in the election politics of Ghana. For the first time in the political history of the country, one civilian government has been changed through the ballot box. The people of Ghana were given a meaningful political choice to make and decided to make a change based on the their assessment of the political and economic situation of the country under the governance of the

National Democratic Congress (NDC). The country effected a change through the ballot box from the NDC to the NPP in a free and fair election.

Of the two constituencies studied in the Central Region Agona West effected an change of the incumbent NDC candidate in favour of the NPP candidate while in the KEEA constituency, the electorate retained the incumbent NDC candidate. The elections in KEEA seem to have been influenced more by the local politics of Elmina where the two leading candidates came from. Even though local politics did not particularly favour either of the two leading candidates, the incumbent seems to have had the edge over the main challenger, by being seen to have been responsible for the development of roads and street lights in Elmina which the main opponent could not match notwithstanding the fact that he has a good hotel that was providing jobs for the locals. In the Agona West constituency there were not so many local political issues, but the influencing factor for the electorate was the national mood for a change.

NOTES

1. Much of the discussion on democracy & good governance has benefited from the following sources: Henry W. Ehrmann (ed) (1963) *Democracy in a Changing Society* Vakils, Feffer & Simons Private Ltd. Bombay, pp. 3–26 and Kwadwo Afari-Gyan (1991) *Understanding Politics*, Asempa Publishers, Accra, pp. 56–69.
2. Denis L. Cohen "Elections and Election Studies in Africa", in Yolamu Barongo (ed.) (1985) *Political Science in Africa* Zed Books, London, pp. 72–94.
3. *Ibid.*, p.80.
4. *Ibid.*
5. Denis Austin, "Elections in an African Rural Area", in *Africa*, Vol. XXIX, pp. 1–17. See also Denis Austin, *Politics in Ghana 1946–1960* (London, Oxford University Press, 1964).
6. Denis Austin and Robin Luckham (eds.), *Politicians and Soldiers in Ghana* (London, Frank Cass, 1975).
7. See Chazan, N. & Le Vine, V. "Politics in a Non-Political System: the March 30, 1978 Referendum in Ghana", *African Studies Review*, Vol. XXII Vol. 1, pp. 177–208. Gyimah-Boadi, E, (1997) "The Challenges Ahead", *Journal of Democracy*, Vol. 8 No. 3 (April) 78–91, Nugent, Paul (1995) *Big Men, Small Boys and Politics in Ghana*, London & New York, Pinter. Oquaye, M. (1995) "The Ghanaian Elections of 1992: A Dissenting View", *African Affairs*, Vol. 94: 259–275; Ayee, J. R. A. (1997) "The December 1996 General Elections in Ghana", *Electoral Studies*, Vol. 16, No. 3 (September): 416–427; Jeffries, R. (1980) "The Ghanaian Election of 1979" *African Affairs*, Vol. LXXIX No. No. 316: 397–414.
8. Ayee, J. R. A. (ed.) (1998) *The 1996 General Elections and Democratic Consolidation in Ghana*, Department of Political Science, University of Ghana, p.3.

9. Riley, S. P. "The Democratic Transition in Africa: An end to the One-Party State?" *Conflict Studies*, 245.
10. Government of Ghana (2000) *2000 Population & Housing Census (Provisional Results)* Ghana Statistical Service, August, 2000.
11. *Ibid.*
12. Interview with Supt. Justice K. Asante, District Police Commander, Agona West. Agona Swedru 23 October 2000
13. Interview with Chief Inspector Amankwaa-Simpson, District Police Commander, Elmina 25 October 2000.
14. Interview with Mr French, Teacher St. Ann School, Nkontrodo, Elmina, 24 October 2000.
15. Interview with Anthony K. Eshun, NDC Youth Organizer, 24 October 2000.

CHAPTER 14

Explaining Voter Behaviour in the Ho Central and Ho East Constituencies of Volta Region in Ghana's 2000 Elections

STEVENS K. M. AHIAWORDOR

Introduction

Elections in Ghana since independence have sometimes produced results that are difficult to explain. Since 1992 when Ghana's Fourth Republic was born, three elections have been held in 1992, 1996 and 2000. The 2000 Presidential and Parliamentary elections were held on 7 December 2000 with a presidential run-off election on 28 December. In spite of the impressive win for the opposition New Patriotic Party (NPP) in almost every region of Ghana, the Volta Region once again recorded over 90% support for the National Democratic Congress (NDC). In the parliamentary elections for instance while the region as a whole voted over 75% for the NDC, the Ho Central and Ho East constituencies recorded 83.3% and 85.6% respectively for the NDC candidates *(Electoral Commission: Gazetted Result of 7 December, 2000 Parliamentary Elections)*. Similarly, the two constituencies recorded 88.4% and 91.8% respectively for the NDC presidential candidate on 7 December and 90.4% and 93.7% respectively in the 28 December presidential run off *(Electoral Commission: Gazetted Results of 7 December and 28 December 2000 Presidential Elections)*. Interestingly, it was only in the Volta Region that NPP did not win a single constituency in either the presidential or parliamentary elections.

This paper, which is the result of surveys conducted in the two constituencies before and after the 2000 elections, attempts to explain why voters in the two constituencies voted the way they did. The paper begins with an introduction, the methodology adopted by the survey, the profile of the two constituencies and the demographic characteristics of the respondents. The paper also looks at the social, political and economic factors that influenced voters in their selection of parties and candidates. The paper finally makes observations and draws conclusions for Ghana's democratic consolidation.

Methodology

Two separate surveys were conducted in October/November 2000 and January 2001. The first survey, termed the pre-election survey, was conducted to ascertain the views of the electorate prior to the elections on pertinent national and local issues and how these issues were likely to affect their voting behaviour. The post election survey was conducted to confirm some of the responses obtained in the pre-election survey.

In all, 100 questionnaires each were administered in each of the two constituencies for both the pre- and post- election surveys. In the Ho East constituency, 18 villages and towns (6 from Adaklu traditional area, 4 from Ziope traditional area and 8 from Agortime traditional area) were covered. During the pre-election survey 37 questionnaire were administered in Adaklu area, 41 in Agortime area and 22 in Ziope while in the post- election survey 34 questionnaire were administered in Adaklu area, 33 in Agortime and 33 in Ziope. The survey covered all the 11 electoral areas in the constituency. On the whole 38 respondents were interviewed in the three urban settlements of Adaklu Waya, Agortime Kpetoe and Ziope townships. In the case of Ho Central, 18 out of the 23 electoral areas were covered in both the pre- and post-election surveys. Whereas 48 respondents were interviewed in the Ho township 52 were interviewed from the outlying villages in both surveys.

In addition to the questionnaire administered, the views and opinions of some community and opinion leaders, ordinary citizens, party officials, election officials, the press and a cross section of the security agencies were solicited to enrich the final outcome of the study.

Rationale for the Choice of the Constituencies

The reasons for the choice of the two constituencies are varied. First in 1996, a similar study of Ketu South and North constituencies which lie in the southern part of the Volta region was carried out (Ayee, 1998: 461–478). It is therefore only appropriate to do a similar study in the central part of the Volta region to find out what the people in that part of the region also felt about the 2000 elections. Secondly before the 2000 elections, there was an intense political agitation for the change of the Ho Central constituency parliamentary candidate. The study in this constituency was, therefore, intended to find out how the refusal of the NDC to change the parliamentary candidate would affect voter choice. Thirdly since the 1992 elections, virtually every regional capital had fallen into the hands of the opposition except a few nationwide, including Ho, the Volta Regional capital (Anebo, 2000: 272). It was therefore necessary to find out why Ho Central constituency alone among many regional capitals still followed a certain trend and also to find out whether the trend would change in the 2000 elections. Fourthly for Ho East, it was of interest to find out how the electorate viewed the elevation of their member of parliament, Hon. Steve Akorli to the high office of Minister of State. It was also to find out whether this gesture by President Rawlings would be reciprocated through an extensive vote for the NDC or not. Finally, the choice of the two constituencies is to find out how the voters in the two constituencies who have remained Rawlings's loyalists were going to vote when their idol was no longer a candidate in the elections.

Profile of the Two Constituencies

Three constituencies, namely, Ho Central, Ho East and Ho West constitute the Ho District. The Ho East constituency comprises three traditional areas, namely, Adaklu, Agortime and Ziope traditional areas. It is generally a rural constituency with Ziope, Agortime Kpetoe and Adaku Waya being the only semi-urban settlements within the constituency. The constituency is made up of 11 electoral areas, namely, Abuadi, Ablonu, Waya, Xelekpe (Adaklu traditional area) Kpetoe, Afegame and South Agortime (Agortime traditional area) and Ziope, Keyime, Bedzame and Takuve (Ziope traditional area).

The Ho Central constituency, on the other hand, is made up of the Ho township which is urban and, in fact, the seat of Volta Regional Administration, and a number of outlying villages which include the following: Sokode, Akrofu, Klefe/Ziave, Taviefe, Matse/Lume, Tokokoe/Tanyigbe, Shia/Nyive, Takla/Hodzo and Akoefe. In all, the constituency has 23 electoral areas. Apart from Ho township, all the other settlements are rural.

The two constituencies are ethnically homogeneous; comprising mostly Ewe speaking people with only a few non-indigenes who are mainly found in the public and civil sectors as well as in the business sector. Whereas the Ho East constituency is inhabited largely by farmers and petty traders with little or no economic diversification, Ho Central is made up of farmers, artisans, civil and public servants, and a variety of other occupational groups. On the whole, the two constituencies are characterized by limited socio-economic diversity and therefore may be considered as socially and economic unsophisticated and homogeneous.

The Demographic Profile of the Constituencies

Gender Distribution

For the pre-election survey, the sample was made up of 63 males and 37 females for Ho East and 54 males and 46 females for Ho Central. Even though the original intention was to have equal number for both sexes, this could not materialize for the following reasons. First, many females in both constituencies refused to answer questions with the excuse that they did not have the time or were not knowledgeable in political issues. Secondly, some females who reluctantly agreed to be interviewed ended up giving either evasive answers or responses that were not relevant to the questions. Thirdly, some females claimed that they had not been following political activities as they had been busy in the market selling their wares to ensure the survival of their families. The unbalanced gender distribution in the pre-election survey did not change much during the post-election survey. Generally, the political consciousness of women and their participation in politics in both constituencies were observed to be very low perhaps due to the extensive illiteracy and the high number of female school drop outs in both constituencies.

Table 14.1: Gender Distribution

Gender	Ho East Frequency	Ho East Percentage %	Ho Central Frequency	Ho Central Percentage %
Male	63	63	54	54
Female	37	37	46	46
TOTAL	100	100	100	100

The results of the survey shows that whereas respondents of the ages of 18–40 constituted 57% in the Ho East constituency, 59% of the same age group was captured in Ho Central.

It is clear from the age distribution of respondents that majority belong to the youthful age of 40 years or below. This group is most active in politics in the two constituencies because they consider themselves as having greater stake in the political system. Most of the elderly people interviewed did not see any reason for engaging in politics since their entire life had not improved in spite of many promises by politicians under whom they had lived. The age distribution clearly demonstrates the enthusiasm and interest that youth in the two constituencies have in political activities in the contemporary youth-driven Ghanaian society.

Table 14.2: Age Distribution of Respondents

Age Group	Ho East Frequency	Ho East Percentage %	Ho Central Frequency	Ho Central Percentage %
18–25	17	17	12	12
26–30	13	13	23	23
31–40	27	27	24	24
41–50	20	20	18	18
51–60	14	14	14	14
61–70	8	8	3	3
71 –	1	1	4	4
No Response	–	–	2	2
TOTAL	100	100	100	100

Table 14.3: Educational Background of Respondents

Educational Background	Ho East Frequency	Ho East Percentage %	Ho Central Frequency	Ho Central Percentage %
None	11	11	8	8
Primary	39	39	41	41
Secondary	16	16	26	26
Polytechnic	4	4	8	8
Training/Technical	23	23	17	17
University	2	2	–	–
No Response	5	5	–	–
TOTAL	100	100	100	100

The educational background of the respondents indicates that whereas only 11% and 8% respectively had no formal education in the Ho East and Ho Central constituencies, an almost negligible percentage of 2% and 0% respectively for both constituencies had University education. The data also reveal that the majority of respondents in both constituencies had either primary, teacher training/technical or secondary education. It is therefore clear from the data that majority of respondents had attained some appreciable level of education and were therefore capable of understanding basic political and economic issues.

Occupational Background

On the occupational distribution of respondents, 5% and 11% respectively for Ho East and Ho Central were unemployed. For Ho East, the major occupational groups were teachers 21%, farmers 32%, traders 10% and businessmen 9%. In the case of Ho Central, teachers constituted 6%, farmers 2%, traders 28%, artisans 12% and others 21%.

The high percentage of 21% for others in Ho Central may explained by the fact that being a more urban constituency people engage in many more variety of occupations some of which have not been captured by the questionnaire. Whatever the case, it is clear that most people in both constituencies are engaged in one occupation or another. Unemployment is therefore relatively low.

Table 14.4: Occupational Distribution

Occupation	Ho East Frequency	Ho East Percentage %	Ho Central Frequency	Ho Central Percentage %
Unemployed	5	5	11	11
Teacher	21	21	6	6
Businessman	9	9	4	4
Manager	–	–	4	4
Professional	6	6	4	4
Farmer	32	32	2	2
Trader	10	10	28	28
Artisan	5	5	12	12
Public Servant	8	8	8	8
Others	4	4	21	21
TOTAL	100	100	100	100

Income Distribution

Closely related to the occupational distribution is income distribution of respondents. In terms of income distribution the majority of the respondents earn annual incomes that fall below five million *cedis*. This implies that most employed people in both constituencies fall within the low income group.

Table 14.5: Income Distribution

Income level (¢) Per Annum	Ho East Frequency	Ho East Percentage %	Ho Central Frequency	Ho Central Percentage %
0 – 4.9 million	62	62	71	71
5 – 10 million	9	9	5	5
Above 10 million	2	2	–	–
No Response	27	27	24	24
TOTAL	100	100	100	100

The data reveal that whereas 62% of respondents in Ho East earn less than 5 million *cedis* per annum, 71% of respondents in Ho Central fall within the same category. The 27% and 24% respectively that did not give their income either did not know their exact incomes or were unwilling to reveal them for obvious reasons. Normally, people in the rural areas fear disclosing their incomes when they are not sure of the identity of the researcher or his motives. The data also reveal that poverty in the two constituencies is deep since only 11% in Ho East and 5% in Ho Central earn incomes above 5 million *cedis* per annum.

Religious Background of Respondents

The majority of respondents from the two constituencies are Christians who belong to various Christian religious denominations. For Ho East, 3% were traditional religion practitioners and no Moslems with 96% of the respondents belonging to the Christian religion. In the Ho Central constituency 89% are Christians, 6% traditional religion practitioners and 2% Moslems.

Region of Birth and Region of Residence of the Respondents

On the region of origin, 93% of the respondents in Ho East indicated that they had been born in the Volta Region while 90% from Ho Central also claimed the same. In Ho East 3% of respondents had been born in Ashanti region, 3% in the Western region and 1% in Brong Ahafo. For Ho Central, 1% had been born in Greater Accra, 2% in Brong Ahafo region, 2% in Northern region, 2% in Western region and no response was received from 3%. Similarly, on the region of residence, 99% of respondents in the East constituency resided in the Volta region while 98% from Ho Central resided in the same region. The data on region of origin and residence are important because since 1992, election results in Ghana particularly for the Volta and Ashanti Regions have followed an ethnic or regional pattern. Whereas the NPP, which is generally considered as Akan party, has always dominated the polls in Ashanti region, the NDC has always drawn its overwhelming support and votes from the Volta region which is considered as its "World Bank". It has always been argued that the few odd votes, which are cast for opposition parties in the two regions come from people who do not originate from those regions. Hence the Volta region, which is less cosmopolitan, records higher percentages for the NDC as compared to the more cosmopolitan Ashanti region.

The State of Political Party Activities

In both constituencies, political party activities including campaigns were vigorous and vibrant prior to the 7 December elections. The Ho Central Constituency, for example, hosted the national congress of the NDC and NPP respectively. One significant development however was that the campaigns were generally devoid of mass rallies. On the contrary all the parties resorted to house-to-house campaigns at dawn and in the evenings. An NPP activist interviewed at Ho revealed that this approach was more cost-effective for the party while at the same time it afforded the electorate the opportunity to interact with party officials and candidates more intimately.

As far as campaign posters of political parties and candidates were concerned, the NDC had a domineering presence. In fact in some villages in the Ho East constituency, only NDC posters were on display as there appeared to be no opposition sympathisers or supporters around.

At the close of nominations for parliamentary candidates, seven contestants had filed their nomination for Ho East (see Table 14.6) while six had filed for Ho Central (see Table 14.7).

Table 14.6: Parliamentary Candidates: Ho East Constituency

Name	Age	Party	Profession
Gati Raymond Yao	39	UGM	Teaching
Kathryn Susan S. Akatey	27	PNC	Administrator
Sek Evans Donyo	47	CPP	Ex-Soldier
Bright Kobla Kudiabor	35	NRP	Self-Employed
Francis Kumedzro	52	NPP	Teaching
Steve Senu Akorli	52	NDC	Accounting

Table 14.7: Parliamentary Candidates: Ho Central Constituency

Name	Age	Party	Profession
John Nelson K. Akorli	46	NPP	Teaching
Mathias S. Adom	51	UGM	Farming
Eli Kotoku Elikem	45	CPP	Food Specialist
Kofi Attoh	46	NDC	Public Servant
Alfa Anas Hamidu	40	PNC	Electrician
Cousin Doamekpor	42	NRP	Media Practitioner
Stephen B. Ashun	59	IND.	Rtd Army Officer

The seventh candidate for Ho Central, Lt Col (Rtd) Stephen Brekum Ashun who failed in his nomination bid on NPP ticket and who therefore decided to go independent stepped down just before the elections. From all indications, the NDC candidates for the two constituencies were the most popular of all the candidates. It was however obvious that their popularity did not stem from any personal attributes they had but rather because of the popularity of the political party for which they stood. Even though Steve Akorli was quite popular with the electorate, Kofi Attoh faced some opposition during the period of the pre-election survey. The reasons for the opposition were twofold. First, Mr Attoh was regarded as a "stranger" because he came from a minority sector of he constituency, Taviefe; something the indigenous people from Ho opposed vehemently. Second, was the general feeling (whether rightly or wrongly) that for all the eight years that he had been in Parliament, Ho Central constituency had seen no positive development. The people's anger was based on the fact that since Mr Attoh was not only an MP and a leading member of the ruling NDC party but also the Deputy General Secretary of the party, he was someone with easy assess to the Executive and could therefore have influenced the allocation of resources to Ho.

Political Participation

Generally, political participation by the electorate was very high. Whereas 96% of the registered voters interviewed in Ho East claimed to have registered as voters, 100% from Ho Central had also registered to cast their votes. Only 4% of voters from Ho East claimed they did not register as voters (see Table 14:8).

Table 14.8: Frequency Distribution of Voter Registration in the Ho East and Ho Central Constituencies

	Ho East		Ho Central	
	Frequency	Percentage %	Frequency	Percentage %
Registered voters	96	96	100	100
Not registered	4	4	–	–
TOTAL	100	100	100	100

It was, however, difficult to get people indicate which party they effectively belonged to. Only 40% of respondents in Ho East claimed they were registered members of the NDC while 30% also claimed the same in Ho Central. Whereas 50% for Ho East refused to say which party they belonged to, 62% in Ho Central also refused to disclose their party membership. Similar responses were obtained when the respondents were asked to indicate their party affiliation. While 46% in Ho East said they were affiliated to NDC, 51% from Ho Central indicated their affiliation with NDC. Interestingly, only very few people in either constituency wanted to be identified with any of the opposition parties. The refusal of many respondents to indicate their party membership and/or affiliation may have been due to fear of intimidation by political opponents or lack of confidence in the researchers. Indeed they were sceptical about the motives of the researchers and in spite of all attempts to convince them that it was just an academic exercise, most of them refused to be convinced. This state of affairs may be attributed partly to illiteracy among a large segment of voters and partly to their past experiences.

It was clear from the survey that many voters in both constituencies had been following political party activities in the media. This is because whereas 88% indicated that they closely followed political party activities in the media in Ho East, 91% indicated that they did same in Ho Central. At the same time 60% in Ho East attended political rallies while 40% did not attend. For Ho Central, 40% frequently attended political rallies whereas 60% did not. The implication of this is that political rallies are gradually losing their essence as a major campaign strategy. The proliferation of modern means of communication such as radio, TV, FM stations and newspapers is providing the alternative means for educating the electorate on political issues.

Voter Perception of the Economy

On voter perception of the nature of the economy, many respondents were objectively frank. In Ho East, only 43% said it was either good or very good whereas 17% in Ho Central also felt the same. For Ho East, 47% felt the economy was either bad or very bad while 71% felt the same in Ho Central. Only 7% felt it was neither good nor bad in either constituency (see Table 14.9). Indeed, the majority of respondents in both constituencies were of the opinion that their standard of living had worsened. In all 53% of respondents in Ho East agreed that their standard of living had fallen with only 6% indicating that their standard of living had improved. Similarly, in Ho Central 62% indicated that their standard of living had fallen whereas only 4% felt that their standard had improved. On the issue of the most important national economic problems, the majority of respondents from both constituencies named unemployment, inflation and depreciation of the *cedi* as most significant. Even though they admitted that their economic conditions had worsened since 1996, more than 90% in Ho East and about 80% in Ho Central still expressed their unflinching support for the NDC.

One revealing aspect of the survey was that most respondents and those interacted with blamed the state of the economy on external factors such as the falling price of cocoa and gold, rising crude oil prices and other external economic pressures. Equally amazing was how even rural people, most of

Table 14.9: Voter Perception of the State of the Economy

Peerception	Ho East Frequency	Ho East Percentage %	Ho Central Frequency	Ho Central Percentage %
Very good	7	7	2	2
Good	36	36	15	15
Bad	19	19	35	35
Very bad	28	28	36	36
Neither good nor bad	7	7	7	7
Don't know	2	2	4	4
Missing	1	1	1	1
TOTAL	100	100	100	100

whom could neither read nor write, could understand such issues. It was quite obvious that NDC activists and members of other political and non-political groups affiliated to the NDC have been educating the electorate on the causes of the poor performance of the economy. Rather than blaming the NDC for the economic woes of the country, most respondents praised the NDC government for ensuring peace and stability and also guaranteeing the availability of goods on the market.

Evaluation of the Democratic Process

When respondents were asked to evaluate the democratic process, 91% in Ho East and 96% in Ho Central described Ghana as a democratic state. In a similar vein, 79% in Ho East and 94% in Ho Central agreed that the democratic process had improved since 1992 (see Table 14.10). The respondents attributed improvement in the democratic process to amongst other factors improved press freedom in Ghana. In fact, whereas 77% in Ho East and 85% in Ho Central agreed that press freedom had improved in Ghana, 4% for Ho East indicated that press freedom had not improved. The remaining 23'% in Ho East and 15% in Ho Central did not know whether press freedom had improved or not. This number may be made up of people who either had no access to any medium of communication or were very illiterate and therefore

Table 14.10: Opinion on Description of Ghana as a Democratic Country

Opinion	Ho East Frequency	Ho East Percentage %	Ho Central Frequency	Ho Central Percentage %
Yes	91	91	96	96
No	5	5	3	3
Don't know	4	4	1	1
TOTAL	100	100	100	100

could not follow issues in the press. The positive perception about Ghana's democratic process by the respondents contributed to a high turnout during the 2000 elections.

Evaluation of the Electoral Process

Perception of the neutrality of the Electoral Commission (EC) and its ability to organize free and fair elections was neither too positive nor too negative. In Ho East 46% felt the EC was independent while 48% could not vouch for its neutrality with only 4% declaring that it was not neutral. In the case of Ho Central 41% felt it was independent, 18% said it was not while 39% did not know (see Table 14.11). Interactions with some voters in both constituencies

Table 14.11: Frequency Distribution of the Independence of the Electoral Commission

Opinion	Ho East Frequency	Ho East Percentage %	Ho Central Frequency	Ho Central Percentage %
Yes, Independent	46	46	41	41
No, not independent	4	4	18	18
Don't know	48	48	39	39
Missing	2	2	2	2
TOTAL	100	100	100	100

however revealed that some voters were not satisfied with the performance of the EC. In most of the villages in the Adaklu traditional area in the Ho East constituency the people complained that electoral officials came only once to register them and issue voter ID cards to them. Even then, they claimed that the day chosen was Ho market day therefore many people especially the women had not been available to register and/or obtain voter ID cards. There were also allegations of electoral fraud in the Agortime Kpetoe and Agortime Afegame areas of Ho East constituency. The complaints centred mostly on multiple registration of voters and registration of aliens from Togo. Two people against whom such allegations were made at Kpetoe admitted that they had registered in some other parts of the country where they lived but were currently residing at home i.e. Kpetoe. They did not go through the formal process of voter transfer because, to them, it was too cumbersome in terms of cost, distance and time involved. It was clear that the people were ignorant about the process of voter transfer and consequences of multiple registration. They rightly blamed their ignorance on the EC's inability to adequately educate them.

On the issue of alien voters it became clear that since a number of villages in the Ho East and Ho Central constituencies share borders with Togo, some people in such villages as Agortime Afegame, Kpetoe, Sh'ia, Nyive, Takla and Hodzo who have migrated to Togo usually crossed over to register and to vote during elections. Because of the nature of the borders and the relationship that exists among the people along the borders, it is difficult to distinguish between genuine Ghanaian emigrants and their Togolese counterparts. In a chat with Customs and Excise officials at Nyive, Shia and Kpetoe, they maintained that since most of them were also strangers transferred to such places, it was difficult to distinguish the indigenes from the non-indigenes. Besides, it was not part of their duty to check such infiltrators. It was thus clear that the problem of alien voters which has existed since independence cannot be easily solved without the collaboration and co-operation of governments of both countries, the Electoral Commission and all public institutions that operate along the borders.

Evaluation of the Party System

Even though quite a good number of respondents felt that political parties were not financially sound, many were equally opposed to state finding of political parties. Quite significant was the relatively high number who did not know whether political parties were financially sound or not. For Ho East, whereas 36% felt that political parties were not financially sound, 43% did not know. Similarly, in the case of Ho Central 50% felt that political parties were financially weak while 29% did not know (see Table 14.12). The ignorance about the financial status of political parties is understandable since most party supporters are not registered party members and therefore do not attend party meetings nor do they ask for the financial statements from their constituency executive. Those opposed to state funding of political parties have argued that it would not only impose a further burden on the over stretched budget of the state but would also result in the proliferation of many non-viable political parties.

Table 14.12: Opinion on whether political parties in Ghana are Financially Sound or Not

Opinion	Ho East Frequency	Ho East Percentage %	Ho Central Frequency	Ho Central Percentage %
Yes, there is	15	15	21	21
No, there isn't	36	36	50	50
Don't know	43	43	29	29
Missing	6	6	–	–
TOTAL	100	100	100	100

Election Issues

At national level a majority of the respondents in both constituencies identified the economy as the mot important election issue. Indeed 88% of those interviewed in Ho East and 97% in Ho Central were of the view that the economy was crucial. While 8% from Ho East mentioned continuity and stability, only 2% from Ho Central felt that continuity and stability was an essential issue. Ironically, while they conceded that the economy was generally bad, they still indicated their intension of voting for the NDC for various other reasons.

At local level, respondents from both constituencies emphasized employment, education, good roads, and markets as their major needs. According to them, good roads would facilitate the marketing of their products most of which are agricultural. In the more rural areas of the two constituencies the respondents were equally concerned about the extension of electricity and the provision of income-generating activities that would prevent the youth from drifting to the urban centres. Generally, in most of the communities visited, complaints were made about the lack of basic amenities such as water, schools, buildings, good roads, toilets and teachers. Asked why they would still vote for the NDC even though these amenities had not been provided, they replied that the NDC was not to blame but the District Assemblies were. They complained about the ineffectiveness of the District Assembly and their assemblymen in providing them with the basic amenities.

Evaluation of the Presidential Running Mate

As far as the criteria for the choice of presidential running mates were concerned, respondents from both constituencies were divided between the need for experience and regional balance. Of the respondents in Ho East, 78% felt that experience should be the main consideration while 9% opted for regional balance. For Ho Central, 54% were of the view that regional balance should be considered while 43% believed in the need for experience (see Table 14.13). Interestingly, none of the respondents from the two

Table 14.13: Frequency Distribution on the most Important Factors in the Choice of Presidential Running Mates

Factors	Ho East Frequency	Ho East Percentage %	Ho Central Frequency	Ho Central Percentage %
Ethnic background	2	2	–	–
Regional balance	9	9	54	54
Gender balance	–	–	–	–
Experience	78	78	43	43
Party loyalty	7	7	1	1
Others	4	4	2	2
TOTAL	100	100	100	100

constituencies felt that gender balance was necessary in spite of the fact that there were a good number of female respondents. Interactions with voters from a number of communities in both constituencies revealed that neither men nor women considered the need for women to be selected as presidential candidates or running mates. They were of the view that the two top positions are so demanding that women may not be able to cope with the physical rigours that are involved.

Evaluation of the Media and Political Education

Most respondents from both constituencies indicated that radio was their main source of information regarding the elections. While 48% from Ho East obtained information through radio, 56% from Ho Central did same. In Ho Central 17% of respondents relied on television while only 5% from Ho East, which is a more rural constituency, relied on television. Whereas posters of political parties, the Electoral Commission and NCCE were relied upon by 8% from both constituencies only 3% in Ho East and 2% in Ho Central relied on newspapers (see Table 14.14). Obviously, the cost of news-

Table 14.14: Frequency distribution of the most useful media as source of Information

Media	Ho East Frequency	Ho East Percentage %	Ho Central Frequency	Ho Central Percentage %
Television	5	5	17	17
Newspaper	3	3	2	2
Friends and family	5	5	10	10
Candidate rallies	19	19	4	4
Radio	48	48	56	56
Magazine	2	2	-	-
Posters/fliers	8	8	8	8
Don't know	2	2	1	1
Others	7	7	1	1
Missing	1	1	1	1
TOTAL	100	100	100	100

papers coupled with extensive illiteracy makes newspapers a very rare source of information to most respondents.

Most of the electorate in Ho Township indicated that they had benefited substantially from the programmes on the local FM station, Volta Star Radio, which is their main source of information. In addition, they had access to the national dailies. They however did not have access to the private newspapers, which hardly reach Ho. Beyond the Ho township, many of the electorate rely on public radio, candidates, assemblymen, unit committee members, the Electoral Commission, the NCCE, the 31st December Women's Movement, the ACDRs and PVOs for political education. It must be emphasized that with the predominance of public radio which generally expresses the views of the ruling party and the above named institutions, most of which are affiliated to the NDC, there is no doubt the information flow would tilt in favour of the NDC. It was therefore not surprising that the one-sided information flow gave the NDC a clear advantage over the rest of the contesting political parties in the two constituencies.

The Presidential Run-off

The presidential run-off which was held on 28 December 2000 was won by the NPP presidential candidate, John Agyekum Kufuor. The NDC presidential candidate J. E. A. Mills who won in four regions; Northern 51.10%, Upper East 57.17% and Upper West 61.97% obtained the highest vote of 589,719 representing 88.47% from the Volta Region. Whereas the NDC increased its total votes from 40,165 to 50,346 in Ho Central and from 22,421 to 29,025 in Ho East, the NPP recorded just a slight increase of 3,727 to 5,345 in Ho Central and from 866 to 1,967 in Ho East for the 7 December and 28 December presidential elections respectively (Electoral Commission, Gazetted Result of 7 December and 28 December 2000).

For the presidential run-off elections, 92% of respondents from both constituencies voted while 5% from each constituency refused to vote.

With regard to candidates of their choice, 68% from Ho East and 96% from Ho Central voted for the NDC candidate whereas 27% from Ho East and 4% from Ho Central voted for the NPP candidate. Thirty nine per cent of those who voted for Prof. Atta Mills in Ho East said they voted for him for the sake of continuity while 5% said he represented the party they belonged to. Only 3% voted for him because of his policies. While 34% did not say why they voted for him, 5% claimed that he was capable of doing the job. In the case of Ho Central, 96% indicated that they voted for Prof. Mills because his policies were good while 4% failed to give reasons for their choice.

For the NPP presidential candidates 19% of respondents from Ho East who voted for him did so because they wanted a change while 2% felt he was the right man for the job. Interestingly, only 2% from each of the two constituencies voted for J. A. Kufuor because of the alliance of opposition forces.

Many respondents voted for the same presidential candidates on 7 December and during the run-off. In fact 82% in Ho East and 96% in Ho Central voted for the same presidential candidate. 13% from Ho East and 4% from Ho Central voted for different presidential candidates during the two elections.

Virtually all respondents described the presidential run-off elections as free from problems with election official being very fair. The elections were also free from intimidation with a well-organized security arrangement.

Conclusion: Lessons

Very useful lessons and conclusions may be drawn from the study of the 2000 elections in the Ho East and Ho Central constituencies. First, the study revealed that there is generally a very high level of illiteracy in both constituencies especially in Ho East. This had a negative effect on the people's understanding of the democratic process. Indeed, such is the level of ignorance that some of the electorate did not even know that other political parties apart from the NDC exist. It was also revealed that the weapon of misinformation was adopted by some political parties to influence the electorate. In most rural areas voters were told not to vote for any other party especially the NPP as they stood the risk of being expelled from Ghana to Togo.

Again, the issue of evolving a very credible electoral process in which aliens would not be able to vote must be given serious attention. This is because the study revealed that the present system gave opportunity to Togolese nationals to vote in Ghana. The study also underscored the dominant role of ethnicity in Ghana's electoral process and the need to take measures to reverse the trend. Indeed, considering the negative impact of ethnicity on national cohesion and unity efforts must be made by government and relevant institutions to address the issue. Furthermore, it was clear that the NDC remains the strongest political force in the two constituencies and that any political party that intends to win any of the two constituencies has to work extra hard. So extensive is the support for the NDC in both constituencies that the electorate were not prepared to accept any charge of non-performance against the NDC.

Finally, one unique revelation of the study has been that for the first time, the elections were generally free and fair with the security agencies acting as neutral agents of the state. Indeed, all political parties in the two constituencies expressed satisfaction with the performance of the EC, the security agencies and the electorate for being tolerant and impartial throughout the elections.

REFERENCES

Anebo, F. K. G. (2000) "Voting Patterns and Electoral Alliance in Ghana", in Okwadiba Nnoli (ed.), *Government and Politics in Africa — A Reader*, AAPS Books, Harare, Zimbabwe.

Ayee, J. R. A. ed. (1998) *The 1996 General Elections and Democratic Consolidation in Ghana*, Department of Political Science, Accra.

Kontoh Emmanuel (1998) "The Impact of Ethnic Politics on the 1996 General Elections: The Case of the Kumasi District", unpublished B.A. (Hons) Dissertation presented to the Department of Political Science, University of Ghana, Legon.

Smith D. (2001) "The Structural Underpinnings of Ghana's December 2000 Elections", *Critical Perspectives*, The CDD, Accra, Ghana.

The Electoral Commission: Gazetted Results of Ghana's 2000 Presidential Elections held on 7 and 28 December 2000.

The Electoral Commission: Gazetted Results of Ghana's 2000 Parliamentary Elections held on 7 December 2000.

The Electoral Commission: Survey Data on Ho Central and Ho East Constituencies.

The Electoral Commission: Daily Graphic, 29 May 2000.

The Electoral Commission: Profile of Ho District Assembly.

CHAPTER 15

Democratic Pluralism, Electoral Processes and Grassroots Participation in the Gukpegu/ Sabongida and Savelugu Constituencies

TOGBIGA DZIVENU

Elections are an important part of restoring the political process of the country. Successful elections can also help strengthen our democratic institutions and encourage greater political participation among the people.

Dr Kwadwo Afari-Gyan, Chairman,
National Electoral Commission
Daily Graphic Wednesday, 6 December 2000

Introduction

Elections cannot be free and fair by themselves without the necessary democratic institutions and supporting structures charged with overseeing such responsibility. In which case, vibrant civil institutions and the effective roles they play behind the scenes produce successful elections and consequent successful democratisation processes. Thus, a healthy public perception of these institutions and how they play out their roles is fundamental. The question is: what are these democratic institutions and how do their interplay encourage greater political participation among the people sufficient to ensure free and fair elections?

For one thing, political power derives from the ballot box in democratic pluralism. In other words, elections lend voice to the citizenry to express their political will. So, in pluralistic democracies, it is elections that validate political legitimacy. It is in this context that elections are regarded as primary manifestations of the people's voice (IBRD, 1997: 111). Within this framework, elections become key instruments for broadening, deepening and strengthening grassroot participation and democratic governance. Successful elections, therefore, not only demonstrate a successful democratisation process but also guarantee a peaceful transfer of political power in a democratic polity

(Lind eke and Wanzala, 1994: 5; Dumor, 1998: 23). However, to ensure the peaceful transfer of power, elections must be transparent, credible, free and fair. That they must be necessarily perceived so is instructive (Ayee, 1998: 53). For, what invalidates electoral outcomes and jeopardizes peaceful transfer of power is electoral fraud or doubtful electoral results. More often than not, the incidence of electoral fraud occurs at the grassroots. Ensuring an enduring process of democratic governance inevitably demands putting in place effective grassroots structures and vibrant civil institutions. It is against this background that this chapter examines the role of grassroots institutions in enhancing political participation and subsequent free and fair elections. Furthermore, the chapter also investigates the influence of these institutions on voter behaviour in the 2000 elections. The concern here is to determine voter behaviour in these settings and how it compares with the national situation.

Constituency Profile

Two constituencies in the Northern Region, Gukpegu[1] and Savelugu, form the basis of the study. Both constituencies are two of the 23 constituencies making up the Northern Region. They both share a common language, Dagbani, and belong to the Dagbon dynasty. Within the Dagbon dynasty, there are two houses that ascend to the Ya Na skin: the Abdu and Andani Gates. However, the advent of western democracy has sharply divided the two houses along traditional political party lines. The result is that the Andani lineage supports Nkrumah's CPP whilst the Abdu Gate prefers the UP/NPP or the Danquah-Busia tradition. Thus, grassroots support for either political party over the years depends on the lineage of the reigning Ya Na in Yendi, the traditional capital of Dagbon.

The choice of the two constituencies was dictated by a number of socio-economic and psycho-political factors. The socio-economic factors were determined in the context of types of economic activity: commercial and agrarian. Psycho-political factors were however, measured in the context of past voter behaviour and local geopolitics. For practical purposes, the voting pattern that emerged during the 1996 elections indicated that rural constituencies voted extensively for the NDC government (Jonah, 1998:239). It would be interesting to gauge voter behaviour in the 2000 elections against the 1996 elections results to determine whether feelings remained the same. Besides, the Region is the home of some political juggernauts like Alhaji Huudu Yahaya, NDC; the Vice President, Aliu Mahama, NPP; and Mary Salifu Boforo, the

Region's only sitting female MP. It would be noteworthy to appreciate the contributions of all these factors.

The geographical location of the constituencies also meets the urban-rural dichotomy. Gukpegu's location within the Tamale metropolis renders it commercial, urban, and rural or partly agrarian. Thus, it provides urban and urban-rural (peri-urban) voter perspectives. Similarly the setting of Savelugu constituency within the Savelugu District, a rural district, makes it typically agrarian and partially commercial in nature. In this way, it also presents the rural and rural-urban or peri-urban voter viewpoints.

Methodology

The primary objective in selecting the two constituencies for study was to examine voter behaviour in urban and rural settings. Even within this urban-rural categorization, there is a further stratification in the two constituencies — categorized as urban, peri-urban and rural. The intention here is to capture that segment of population falling outside the two defined urban-rural categories. Voter behaviour can then be determined and examined within the context of urban, urban-rural/rural-urban, and rural as well as the dynamics and stimuli to which voters respond. To achieve this end, five electoral areas were randomly selected from a list of electoral areas specified in each of the selected two constituencies — as notified in the Gazette of 7 August 1992, Act 455, PNDCL 284, (2). The selection criteria include four electoral areas in an urban milieu, two in urban-rural or rural-urban — otherwise described as "peri-urban" — and four in typical rural localities. In all, 10 electoral areas were altogether randomly selected to reflect the categorizations stated above (see Table 15.1).

Table 15.1: The Randomly Sampled Electoral Areas

Electoral Area	Gukpegu	Savelugu	Total
Urban	Dakpema; Zogbeli	Limanfong; Kugafong	4
Peri-urban	Nyohini	Nayilifong	2
Rural	Kontingli; Pagaza	Kpatuli; Yong	4
TOTAL	5	5	10

Source: The Gazette 7 August 1992.

In each of the 10 electoral areas, 20 respondents were selected using a simple random sampling technique. Two surveys were conducted. The first one, labelled "Pre-elections", was conducted before the 7 December elections within the period 23 October 2000 to 7 November 2000. The second one or the "Post-elections" survey was carried out after the 28 December presidential run-off between 6 and 20 January 2001. A total of 200 respondents were interviewed within each of the two constituencies during each survey — making a grand total of 400 respondents.

Demographic Profile

In both constituencies, the results show more male respondents than the female. There were 42% female respondents as against 58% male in Gukpegu and 38% female respondents against 62% male in Savelugu in the pre-elections survey. Similarly, in the post-elections survey, Savelugu recorded 66% male respondents and 34% female whilst Gukpegu documented 66% male and 33% female. The emergent picture of the low record of women respondents in both cases was not a case of gender favouritism. Rather, it was due to the limitations of rural research in which timing is a critical factor. For in certain communities, women are not easily available for interview. They are either away in the market, on the farm or, during an off-season, away for funeral observances in another village. On market days also, due to lack of transportation, women usually set out for the market very early and return home late. Sometimes, by the time the researcher gets to the community, the women are in the middle of doing one thing or the other and would not be available for interviewing. The choice then falls on those readily available: the men.

Over 80% of respondents identified with Islamic religion. 18% and 17% of respondents in Gukpegu and Savelugu proclaimed Christianity and only 2% indicated affiliation with African traditional religion. The survey revealed that Muslims in the rural areas are more strongly attached to their religion than those in the urban settings. Sixty-eight per cent of respondents in the Savelugu constituency were strongly attached to their religion whilst only 18% in Gukpegu indicated so. Again, over 90% of respondents were born and have continued to live in the Northern Region. These people also demonstrated strong attachment to both their region and ethnic group. Those who were born outside the region were less committed. Most people were unwilling to disclose their incomes. Apart from those in the urban areas, the general income of most respondents in the rural areas was less than ¢500,000.

The politically active groups also varied from rural to urban constituency. In Savelugu constituency, the most politically active group fell within the 31–40 age group — contrasting with the 26-30 in the Gukpegu constituency. Respondents from age 18 to over 71 took part in the survey in Savelugu constituency whilst some of 18 to 50 participated in Gukpegu. It is noteworthy that in the rural constituency, all age groups were actively involved in issues concerning the community. Perhaps, this has to do with the cultural practices in the rural areas where elders decide on community issues. Again, in contrast with the urban constituency, one does not just walk into a rural community and conduct any research without first meeting the community elders.

Literacy is comparatively lower in the Savelugu constituency. A high 69% of respondents could neither read nor write in Savelugu constituency whilst a low 39% was recorded in Gukpegu. The literacy rate is accordingly much higher in the Gukpegu constituency, 61%. Again, 69% of respondents in the Savelugu constituency indicated farming and its related activities[2] as their occupation whilst Gukpegu recorded 44%. The literacy rate appears to go in tandem with the type of occupation pursued in the two constituencies. In other words, farming and its related activities seem to be the preserve of people with low or no formal education.

It is important to note that the term "unemployment" has different connotations for both rural and urban respondents. In the urban constituency, "unemployment" means "absence of waged-labour". To those in the rural constituency, or in rural agrarian communities, "unemployment" refers to the disabling effects of government's policy on agriculture. Thus, to the rural folks, "unemployment" insinuates government's removal of subsidies, lack of agricultural inputs and shrinking available compound farmland. It is in this context that they regard the government as responsible for their poor economic plight. The Chief Farmer at Nyohini, Mr. Baako Napari, summed it up thus:

> The absence of agricultural inputs was due to the removal of farm subsidies and non-availability of credit facilities for smallholder farmers. It was also argued that due to rapid population growth, the available cultivable compound farmlands have given way to erection of new households. The result is that farmers have to travel longer distances to eke out living from the land but couldn't obtain bank loans to procure bicycles. Furthermore, the removal of the agricultural inputs left the farmers to their own devices and so made them poorer[3] (Chief Farmer, Baako Napari, 2000).

In this way, "unemployment" was defined not in its conventional economic sense but in a functional agrarian context. Similarly, "inflation" was simply interpreted as "high cost of living". Such differentials could also bias assessing household living standards in urban-rural dichotomy.

Political Participation

Elections ensure a fair degree of grassroots political participation and create room for a fair representation of the electorate in multiparty balloting. In other words, the process of elections provides the assurance that the people have made a choice and that the chosen representative is accountable to them. In this way, elections epitomize key features of eliminating oligarchy and instituting democracy (Ibrahim, 1994:24). In all, seven political parties contested the 2000 elections at national level. Without ranking them, these were the NDC, NPP, NRP, CPP, PNC, UGM and the GCPP. The GCPP did not, however, participate in the electoral process at constituency level. However, only four got representation in Parliament. In both constituencies, it was a straight fight between NDC and NPP[4]. Only the NDC and NPP secured over 40% of the popular votes cast (see Tables 15.2 and 15.3).

Both Gukpegu and Savelugu constituencies demonstrated a high degree of political consciousness and participation. Two things strongly evidenced this assertion: the consistent high rate of voter registration and voter turnout in 1996, 1998 and 2000 elections. For example, the 1996 elections recorded a high voter turnout rate of over 80% in both constituencies. As well, the 1998 District Assembly elections saw a high voter participation rate of 70% and 81% respectively in both Gukpegu and Savelugu constituencies. Similarly, voter registration during the 2000 "Pre-elections" survey was 97% in the Gukpegu constituency and 99%in Savelugu. Voter turnout rates in both constituencies during the 2000 elections were again as high as 96%. All this compares favourably with the national voter registration rate of 98.6% and voter turnout rate of 96.4% in the 2000 elections (see Tables 15.3–15.5). Thus, both constituencies have time after time recorded a high participation rate in the voter registration exercise and in the actual exercise of their franchise. In which case, the 2000 elections were clear attestations of the broadening and deepening of grassroots democratic practices and expectations in both constituencies (Frazer, 1994: 3). The inference here is that both constituencies exhibit a high rate of political awareness and demonstrable grassroots participation within a pluralistic democracy — which must be nurtured.

Table 15.2: 2000 Elections: Parliamentary Nomination and Election Results

Constituency	Name of Candidate	Party	Age	Sex	Qualification	Profession	Votes Obtained
Gukpegu/ Sabongida	Mustapha Ali Adris	NPP	45	M	B.A. (Political Science & Sociology)	Lecturing	24,819 (45.5%)
	Abdul-Nashiru Issahaku	NDC	39	M	PhD	Lecturing	22,255 (40.8%)
	Iddrisu Hussein Ayuba	CPP	43	M	Dip. Agric.	Agriculturalist	6,764 (12.4%)
	Wahab Ali	NRP	38	M	"A" 3-Year Post-Sec	Teaching	463 (0.8%)
	Amusa Fuseini	PNC	28	M	GCE 'O' Level	Contractor	–
	Mumuni Fatawu	UGM	27	M	SSCE	Teaching	190 (0.3%)

Table 15.3: 2000 Elections 2000: Parliamentary Nomination and Election Results

Constituency	Name of Constituency	Party	Age	Sex	Qualification	Profession	Votes Obtained
Savelugu	Mary Salifu Boforo	NDC	49	F	NVTI	Farming	13,725 (63.9%)
	Alhassan Abdulai Abubakari	NPP	48	M	MSLC	Driving	6,029 (28.1%)
	Yakubu Abdulai	CPP	30	M	B.A. (Integrated Development Studies)	Teaching	1,097 (5.1%)
	Mahama Iddrisu	PNC	39	M	SSSC	Mechanic	308 (1.4%)
	Ahmed Shani Yakubu	NRP	38	M	GCE 'O' Level	Teaching	225 (1.0%)
	Mohammed Yussif	UGM	32	M	Cert. 'A' 4-Year	Teaching	102 (0.5%)

Sources: Regional Electoral Commission, Tamale; Ghana Gazette, 5 January 2001

Table 15.3: Voter Registration in the 2000 Elections

Responses	National %	Gukpegu %	Savelugu %
Yes	98.6	97	99
No	1.3	3	1
Missing	0.1	–	–
TOTAL	100	100	100

Source: Pre-election Survey data: 2000 Elections

Table 15.4: Voter turnout: 2000 Presidential and Parliamentary Elections

Responses	National %	Gukpegu %	Savelugu %
Yes	96.4	96	96
No	2.0	–	3
Missing	1.7	4	1
TOTAL	100	100	100

Source: Post-election Survey data: 2000 Elections

Table 15.5: Voter turnout in 1996 Parliamentary Elections

Responses	National %	Gukpegu %	Savelugu %
Yes	87.1	80	90
No	11.4	11	8
Missing	1.5	9	2
TOTAL	100	100	100

Source: Pre-election Survey data: 2000 Elections

Voter Perception of, and Involvement with, Political Parties

The political history of Ghana has produced two major political opponents: the Nkrumah and Danquah-Busia traditional political groupings — or the CPP and the UGCC/UP/NPP political parties. The political philosophies of these two early parties have left undying legacies of political rivalry on Ghana's political arena. As such, most of the areas that usually support either of these two parties are known as their traditional homes or strongholds. Not even the series of military interregnums littering Ghana's political history have been able to dissipate this political legacy or alter the political scene. Consequently, most of the new emergent political parties try in various forms to identify with these early political groups to gain popular acceptance.

Nevertheless, most respondents did not demonstrate support for either traditional party simply because their parents did. In fact, during the pre-election survey, only 5% and 21% of respondents in Gukpegu constituency declared that their parents identified with either traditional party. The picture in the Savelugu constituency was no different. Only 8% and 14% of the respondents in the constituency exhibited any party loyalty to either the CPP or the UGCC/UP/NPP. For one thing, attraction to political parties was on the basis of the particular political party's enunciated policies and not by tradition. Responding to whether the respondents were "registered members of a political party", only 13% and 27% in Savelugu and Gukpegu respectively agreed. On how the respondents became members or sympathizers of the political parties, 75% and 63% of them in both constituencies claimed by "personal decision"[5].

Neither did most respondents register as members of any political party nor publicly identify with any. At national and grassroots level, the registration of members of political parties was low. Only 40.1% at national level actually registered with any particular party. Similarly, only 36% and 34% respectively actually identified with a specific political party at constituency level. The low rate of membership registration is in a way consistent with the 1996 elections survey where only 31% of respondents registered as "members of a political party" (Allah-Mensah, 1998: 262). Thus, the figures 61% and 64% theoretically represent those who do not belong to any political party at all or the non-partisan group (see Table 15.6).

These figures do not necessarily represent numbers of undecided voters, either. In other words, these figures embody both those hiding their party affiliations for "personal reasons" and non-active party adherents. For, when

Table 15.6: 2000 Elections: Statistics of Political Party Membership

Responses	National %	Gukpegu %	Savelugu %
Yes	40.1	36	34
No	58.6	61	64
Missing	1.3	3	2
TOTAL	100	100	100

Source: Pre-election Survey data: 2000 Elections

probed further to know whether they had any inclination towards any political party, a different picture emerged. Twenty-one per cent of respondents identified with NDC, 14% with NPP and 1% with the CPP in the Gukpegu constituency. In addition, 21%, 11%, 1% and 1% in Savelugu variously endorsed NDC, NPP, CPP and UGM (see Table 15.7).

Table 15.7: Statistics of Inclination towards Political Parties

Constituency	NDC %	NPP %	CPP %	UGM %	Total %	Missing %
Gukpegu	21	14	1	—	36	61
Savelugu	21	11	1	1	34	64

Source: Pre-election Survey data: 2000 Elections.

Thus, putting together the 44% of the decided respondents of NDC and the 21% of those inclined towards NDC in Savelugu totalled 65%. Whilst 9% of the decided respondents of NPP and 11% of those inclined towards NPP amounted to 20%. Incidentally, the NDC candidate obtained 63.9% of the popular votes cast in the Savelugu constituency during the 2000 elections whilst the NPP candidate had 28% (Ghana Gazette, 5 January 2001). The connotation here is that not registering party membership does not necessarily imply being non-partisan or an undecided voter. For, most of the non-partisan group may be hiding their party affiliations for personal reasons. For example, in Gukpegu and Savelugu constituencies 20% and 43% of the respondents respectively attributed their non-registration of membership to the fear factor. The non-registration of membership could also be deliberate in order to benefit from the vote-buying overtures.

Various factors may explain this phenomenon. These include the fear of political victimization, ignorance of membership registration procedures and simply apathy. These are corroborated in the following observation:

> The non-membership registration is a fallacy. Every one of us has a party preference and is accordingly a member of a political party. The main problem is fear: fear of political victimization and fear of not benefiting from the ongoing vote buying exercise! On one hand, identifying with a particular party often exposes one to the wrath of others who may not like that particular party. On the other hand, there is a vote buying exercise going on and no one knows who comes round to buy one's vote. So, declaring one's party affiliation means losing on the benefit from the overtures of other party agents. Don't you see each house displays posters of all the parties? So you see, it's all part of the strategy! Elections time becomes our season for free cash.[6]

The incidence of poverty also created room for the pecuniary inducements. Electoral favours were sought and bought as need be — in different forms. It was reported that as much as ¢500,000 was given as agricultural loans to men in groups of three whilst women took ¢140,000 in some electoral areas. In others, counterfeit ¢5000 notes were used to buy the votes. In some cases, money was given to the voters in opponents' strongholds to release their voter ID cards. These cards were in turn submitted to the EC as cards of the deceased and these names were accordingly deleted from the voters' register. This explains why some voters could not find their names during the presidential run-off — and so, could not vote.

The District Electoral Commission

The conduct and supervision of public elections (parliamentary and presidential) and referenda in Ghana is the function of the National Electoral Commission (NEC). Established under the 1992 Constitution, Article 42 (1) and vested with that power under Article 45 (c) of the Election Act 1993, the NEC carries the responsibility of supervising the conduct of both parliamentary and presidential elections. To enhance its effectiveness and activities, the EC is decentralized to cater for the electorate at the grassroots. As elections are conflictual in nature, the credibility and independence of the EC is critical. It is in this context that the EC must act and be seen as credible, independent, competent and above reproach (Ayee, 1997: 41; Dumor, 1997: 29). Curiously enough though, most elections studies tend to focus on the outcomes and consequently ignore the civil institutions and supporting structures. It is, therefore, imperative to examine the roles of these institutions at the grassroots whilst evaluating the success of Ghana's 2000 elections.

Article 46 of the 1992 Constitution provides for the independence of the EC. Under this Article, the EC "shall not be subject to the direction or control of any person or authority". Voter perception on the ground is, however, not consistent with this provision. Public perception of the EC remains doubtful and questionable. Even at national level, there was a considerable ambivalence about its credibility. Only 32.5% of respondents at national level believed that the EC was independent of government control whilst 34.1% thought otherwise. Similarly, opinions were divided at national level on whether there were other ways to influence the elections apart from the EC. Only 22.2% agreed that there were other ways to influence the elections and 38.5% of respondents thought EC as the only institution that could. The uncertainty was no different at constituency level. When asked whether the EC was independent of government control, a mere 46% and 57% of the respondents in both Gukpegu and Savelugu constituencies respectively thought so. Most respondents talked to in the two constituencies also doubted the independence of the EC. Their logic was that since the incumbent government appointed and paid the EC staff, it could not easily be free of government control. It was a question of "He who pays the piper calls the tune".

The Role of Grassroots Civil Institutions

When asked whether the EC had been fair to all the parties, 46.1% of respondents at national level agreed. However, at the grassroots, 69% and 71% of respondents in Gukpegu and Savelugu respectively approved of its performance. The question is what has made the difference and why? The difference may be due to the role of the civil institutions in both constituencies. For the effective performance and coordination of these functions, Articles 51 and 52 of the 1992 Constitution provide for the establishment and appointment of district representatives of the EC. These district representatives had been appointed as required and accordingly assigned these responsibilities. To further enhance the effectiveness of the EC at the grassroots, the assistance of other institutions was sought. These include the media (e.g. radio), National

Commission for Civic Education (NCCE) and Ghana Private Road and Transport Union (GPRTU). All these organizations work within a clearly defined rules and regulations as enshrined in the 1992 Constitution and in the Electoral Act 1993 (Act 451).

The Media

Elections are often organized around issues and democratic governance. As such, elections provide opportunities for communicating information about societal issues and preferences in a democratic society (IBRD, 1997: 113). These issues invariably affect directly or indirectly the socio-economic well-being of the citizenry and generally form the basis of public debate and government policies in parliament. It is in this way that election issues largely contribute to participatory democracy and help determine and shape the political will of the people. Thus, an even flow of information provides hope for meeting people's expectations and creates room for good governance (Clausen, 1998: 187). Similarly, election issues also occasion scrutiny of the incumbent government and, so, have the capacity of influencing electoral outcomes (Ayee, 1998: 279). An available effective source of information is therefore, a necessary condition.

The FM Radio

Throughout the country, the radio remained the most widely used and effective source of information. At national level, 43.1% of respondents identified the radio as the source of information about election issues. 29.6%, 9.8% and 8.8% of respondents indicated television, newspaper and word-of-mouth as alternative sources of information. Sixty-four per cent and 18% of respondents in Savelugu and Gukpegu constituencies respectively however, chose the radio as their most effective source of information about the elections. The use of television and newspaper appears to be restricted to the urban areas. Eleven per cent and 58% of respondents in Savelugu and Gukpegu constituencies respectively depended on the television whilst only 5% in Gukpegu opted for the newspaper. Thus in the rural areas, the radio was the most reliable source of information whilst the television was chosen as the most trusted source in the urban area. The preference for newspapers appears to correlate with the prevailing literacy rate in each constituency. The high illiteracy rate of 69% in the Savelugu constituency may have resulted in no one opting for the print media there (see Table 15.8).

Table 15.8: Most Effective Source of Information about the 2000 Elections

Source	Gukpegu %	Savelugu %
Radio	18	64
Television	58	11
Friends (word-of-mouth)	21	11
Newspaper	5	0

Source: 2000 Elections: Post-election Survey

In both constituencies, the role of the FM radio stations proved indispensable to the democratisation process. Championed by the Ghana Danish Community Programme (GDCP), special radio programmes on voter education and political tolerance were channelled through the Region's local radio stations. This involved daily radio talk shows and dramatization of the concepts in democratic practices, namely political participation and tolerance. The GDCP stations were very effective in communicating both issues in the national debate and messages of participation to both constituencies. Most respondents were very pleased with the radio talk shows and broadcasts — as it made them feel part of the national debate (Boadu-Ayeboafoh, 2001b: 7). In addition, with the radio stations, most people became aware of their democratic rights, responsibilities and expectations and so felt part of the democratic process. In this way, these radio stations contributed immensely to establishing better understanding of the issues, the expectations and in bringing the various communities closer. This largely helped reduce the attendant tensions incident to general elections (Boadu-Ayeboafoh, 2001a: 7). Hence, 85% and 93% of respondents in Gukpegu and Savelugu constituencies respectively felt adequate media coverage had been provided in the 2000 elections.

The National Commission for Civic Education

To complement the contributions of the radio stations, the District Assembly also set up an "Anti-Party Task Force". The objective was to educate the voters on avoiding violence during and after the elections. In addition a series of one-day workshops was organized for party candidates, community leaders, party representatives, assemblymen and women, unit committee members and opinion leaders on political tolerance. This was further strengthened by the establishment of Civic Education Clubs in the various electoral areas in the Savelugu-Nanton district by the NCCE. The objectives of this initiative were to educate the people on the constitution, their civic rights and responsibilities and democratic practices and expectations. Membership was open to the youth — especially those in the JSS and the SSS — who formed the focal groups. They were trained and sent back to their various communities to disseminate the knowledge on the "new way of doing politics"[7].

The GPRTU

The local GPRTU also assisted in the supply and the distribution of the logistics to various polling stations in both constituencies during the 2000 elections. The only cost to the EC was in the provision of fuel to cover the trip. To facilitate easy access to and use of their vehicles, the GPRTU put in place a system described as "priority loading arrangements". With the "priority loading arrangements", vehicles could be commandeered to undertake political errands. On their return, such vehicles were given priority to load first[8]. Political parties were also encouraged to take advantage of these arrangements to convey their party adherents to political rallies. According to Mr Abdulai, only the NDC and the NPP had taken advantage of such arrangements. Thus, the high participation rate demonstrated in the two constituencies evidenced the effective roles played by the instituted civil institutions and structures.

Conclusions: Lessons

The 2000 elections marked one more of Ghana's transitions: a peaceful transfer of power through the ballot box. Ensuring a free and fair electoral process guarantees a free and fair representation of the people in pluralistic elections. It is for this reason that the electoral process is often described as the cornerstone of the democratic process. In other words, the 2000 elections were critical to Ghana's nascent democratisation process. By way of a retroactive performance assessment, the 2000 elections were a form of referendum about the continuance of the NDC rule. The results consequently presented a damning indictment of the NDC government.

Safeguarding electoral outcomes demands putting in place effective institutions and structures to enhance the legitimacy of the electoral process and its outcomes. The role of the EC and the civil institutions at the grassroots is, therefore, crucial. For, it is the grassroots that largely determine the success or failure of elections. It is therefore, imperative that much attention is paid to staffing at the grassroots as much as the staffing at national or regional levels. At the moment, the principal limitations of these grassroots institutions include inadequate staffing, poor allocation of resources and logistics. For them to function efficiently, they must be adequately resourced.

One hundred per cent and 99% of respondents in Gukpegu and Savelugu respectively, believed that the 2000 elections had been free and fair. The high voter turnout and participation rate of over 90% showed a significant improvement on the 1996 elections. In addition, the change of government has also indicated a shift in the voting pattern. Thus, the results in both constituencies have shown that the basic constitutional arrangements put in place were responsible for the high grassroots political participation in the 2000 elections. Not only did their interplay ensure an adequate flow of information but it also guaranteed the high political participation rate and the subsequent free and fair elections. That is, the 2000 elections gave voice to the electorate to speak for change and the results certainly mirrored this consensus. Thus, the results of the 2000 elections presented a healthy demonstration of the broadening and deepening of Ghana's incipient democratic culture.

NOTES

1. For the purposes of this study, only Gukpegu will be used to represent Gukpegu/Sabongida.
2. Farming activities are not limited to food production alone. Even those in the buy-and-sell activities consider themselves farmers as they also participate in the food production process. Notably, buy-and-sell activities ran next to farming countrywide.
3. Personal interview the researcher had with Chief Farmer, Baako Napari at Nyohini on 25 October 2000.
4. Even at national level, it was a straight fight between the incumbent NDC and the NPP. Ultimately, the NPP won the presidential election and gained the parliamentary supremacy as well.
5. "Personal decision" here refers to policies of the particular political party.
6. Personal interview the researcher had with Mohammad Alhassan, Savelugu 10 January 2001.
7. This was culled from personal interview with NCCE officials: Messrs Alhassan Imora, Assistant Field Officer, and Alhassan Iddrisu, Accounts Officer, on 9 January 2001 — corroborated by the Assemblyman for the Limanfong, Carr.
8. Personal interview the researcher had with Dickson Abdulai, GPRTU Secretary, Savelugu Branch, on 28 October 2000.

REFERENCES

Allah-Mensah, B. "Politics, The Economy and Voting Behaviour in the 1996 Elections", in Ayee, J. R. A. ed. *The 1996 General Elections and Democratic Consolidation in Ghana.* Accra: Gold-Type Ltd., 1998.

Ayee, J. R. A. "Measuring Public Opinion on Key and Economic Issues: A Survey of the December 1996 General Elections in the Keta and Anlo Constituencies", in Ayee, J. R. A. ed. *The 1996 General Elections and Democratic Consolidation in Ghana.* Accra: Gold-Type Ltd., 1998.

Blunt, K. "Mills not to blame-Ex MP" *The Ghanaian Chronicle* Monday, 2 July 2001.

Boadu-Ayeboafoh, Y. "Press freedom and ethics: The Ghanaian experience" *Daily Graphic* Tuesday, 26 June 2001.

Clausen, T. "State-Civil Society Relations in Ghana's Fourth Republic", in Ayee, J. R. A. ed. *The 1996 General Elections and Democratic Consolidation in Ghana.* Accra: Gold-Type Ltd., 1998.

Dumor, E. "Keynote Address: The 1996 Elections Democratic Consolidation", in Ayee, J. R. A. ed. *The 1996 General Elections and Democratic Consolidation in Ghana.* Accra: Gold-Type Ltd., 1998.

Frazer, J. "Electoral Success: Harbingers of Hope? *Africa Today* Vol. 41 No. 3 1994. Ghana Gazette. *Notice of Publication of a Constitutional Instrument* Accra: Ghana Publishing Corporation, 5 January 2001.

Ibrahim, J. "Political Exclusion, Democratization and Dynamics of Ethnicity in Niger", *Africa Today* Vol. 41, No. 3, 1994.

IBRD. *World Development Report: The State in a Changing World.* New York: Oxford University Press, 1997.

Jeffries, R. (1996) "He Who Cares Wins: Electoral Politics in Ghana" SOAS, London (mimeo).

Johnston, A. M. and R. W. Johnson. "The Local Elections in Kwazulu Natal", *African Affairs* Vol. 96 No. 384, 1997.

Jonah, K. "Agency and Structure in Ghana's 1992 and 1996 Presidential Elections", in Ayee, J. R. A. ed. *The 1996 General Elections and Democratic Consolidation in Ghana.* Accra: Gold-Type Ltd., 1998.

Lindeke, W. A. and Winnie Wanzala. "Regional Elections in Namibia: Deepening Democracy and Gender Inclusion", *Africa Today*, Vol. 41 No. 3, 1994.

CHAPTER 16

The 2000 Elections and Politics in Manhyia and Obuasi Constituencies

KOFI BAKU

Introduction

In his seminal study of politics in Ghana, Austin (1970) suggests that election studies must concern themselves broadly with five principal questions. These are: who are the competitors; what are the issues; how are the elections conducted; who won and who did not win and what is the effect of the election on the general direction of politics at the time. These concerns which were differently formulated in a seventy-eight item questionnaire which was administered to samples of 100 respondents in each of the constituencies of Manhyia and Obuasi, form the basis for this chapter.

The crucial importance of the general elections of December 2000 could hardly be exaggerated. For the first time in the history of Ghana an incumbent president had concluded his constitutional term in office and was leaving office for a new elected president. More than that the said incumbent, Jerry John Rawlings, had dominated politics in Ghana for nearly two decades. Given that he was personally exceedingly charismatic and held considerable appeal for the rural populace, urban poor and the lowly placed in Ghanaian society, the burning question was whether or not his exit would end the era of the National Democratic Congress's (NDC) two electoral victories since the return to constitutional rule in 1993. Would his successor, Professor John Evans Atta Mills, hold similar appeal and ensure victory for the NDC? Would the main opposition party, the New Patriotic Party (NPP), riding on the tide of the cry for "positive change", wrestle power from the hands of the NDC? Would a new government emerge from the uneasy coalition, even if not openly declared, of minority and opposition groups whose principal bond of unity was a common dislike of Rawlings and the NDC? These questions and several others made it difficult to predict the national results of the 2000 general elections. This difficulty notwithstanding, there was largely some certainty that the NPP would win in the Ashanti Region, but with what majority?

Ashanti Region in Ghanaian Politics

Ever since the National Liberation Movement (NLM) was launched on 19 September 1954 at the source of the Subin River in Kumasi, the capital of the Ashanti Region (Austin 1970; Allman 1993), the Region has remained the stronghold of all parties that trace their descent from the United Gold Coast Convention. These parties include, the Ghana Congress Party, the United Party, the Progress Party, (PP), the Popular Front Party (PFP), and the NPP. The descent is more recently known as the Danquah/Busia tradition. The pre-eminence of this tradition in the Ashanti Region was however, not always translated into votes and national electoral victory. In the pre-1966 era, Kwame Nkrumah's Convention People's Party (CPP), dominated politics in rural Ashanti between 1951 and 1966. (Austin and Luckham, 1975). Thus, in the 1956 general elections, the NLM won only 12 out of the 21 seats in the Ashanti Region, which at the time included the present-day Brong Ahafo Region. With the overthrow of the CPP in 1966 however, the Danquah/Busia tradition assumed a dominating position in the Ashanti Region. In 1969, the PP swept all the seats in the Ashanti Region with 79.2% of total votes cast and in 1979 PFP won 19 out of the 22 seats as against two which were won by the People's National Party (PNP) which claimed to be the successor of the CPP.

The post-1966 domination of politics in the Ashanti Region by the Danquah/Busia tradition has also been reflected in the choice of their national leaders. In 1979 Victor Owusu, an Asante from Kwabre, led the PFP. In 1992, 1996 and 2000 the NPP fielded Professor Albert Adu Boahen, and John Agyekum Kufuor both Asante[1] from Juaben and Nkawie respectively as presidential candidates. Not surprisingly therefore, even with "a stolen verdict" in 1992, Professor Boahen polled 431,380 votes in the Ashanti Region well ahead of the 234,237 for Jerry John Rawlings, who won the presidential election. In the 1996 elections, the story remained the same. NPP's John Agyekum Kufuor polled 827,804, twice the 412,474 votes that Jerry John Rawlings of the NDC polled in the Ashanti Region.

This apparent show of "Asante nationalism" in recent times in favour of the NPP notwithstanding, there have been interesting national and local developments worthy of the attention of any student of elections and politics in Ghana. First there has been the rebirth of the CPP, the nemesis of the Danquah/Busia tradition in the Ashanti Region. Would this rebirth, even if only in name, fracture the NPP dominance in the Ashanti Region? Would the array of political heavyweights of Asante origin such as Nana Konadu Agyeman-Rawlings, Paul Victor Obeng, Daniel Ohene Agyekum, Kwame Peprah, Nana Akuoku Sarpong and Nana Akwasi Agyeman of the royal house of Asante paraded by the NDC shore up their showing in the region and cause interesting surprises? These intriguing issues made the Ashanti Region in general and the Manhyia and Obuasi constituencies in particular interesting and worthy of study. But before turning to the main questions raised at the outset, we must look at the pre-election scene in the Ashanti Region in general and in the Manhyia and Obuasi constituencies in particular.

The Ashanti Region occupies a total land space of 9,417 square miles the third largest in the country, coming after the Northern and Brong Ahafo Regions. It however, has the largest population of 2,290,537 people according to 1987 figures and the largest number of 33 parliamentary seats. Ashanti Region is fabulously rich in agricultural, natural and mineral resources. Cocoa, timber and gold have given the region significant surplus wealth as evidenced in the several enormous multi-storey buildings in Kumasi particularly in its more indigenous suburbs of Manhyia and Bantama. The Asante have a proud history and heritage stretching back at least two centuries. In recent years their power and glory have been epitomised in the Golden Stool and its occupant, the Asantehene; the Asante accord beatified veneration and emotional attachment to both. It is in this last respect that we should view two incidents that directly or indirectly affected Asante attitudes to the 2000 election.

In 1999, the long reigning Otumfuo Opoku Ware II, the Asantehene who had been enstooled in 1970, died. In keeping with the Asante constitution and custom a successor had to be named from eligible nephews of the deceased King in the royal family. Ordinarily, this was purely the domain of the Asante, or indeed, the domain of only the royal household led by the Queenmother. However Asante sensibilities were highly offended when it was widely speculated that the government of the NDC was interfering with the constitutional process of choosing and enstooling the occupant of the golden stool. It was rumoured that government strongly favoured Nana Akwasi Agyeman one of the frontrunners for the stool. Nana Akwasi Agyeman was a member of the governments of the Provisional National Defence Council (PNDC) and the NDC as the Chief Executive of the Kumasi Metropolitan Assembly, a special ambassador and a deputy minister for the environment.

The second incident was closely related to the first. Soon after his enstoolment Otumfuo Osei Tutu II visited the seat of government in Accra to confer with the political leadership of the country. Again, there was outrage among the Asante who were scandalised by what was considered the use of undignified and undiplomatic language and mannerism by President Rawlings when he received and addressed Otumfuo and his entourage.

The merits or otherwise of these two incidents were emotionally discussed nationally in both the print and electronic media soon after they occurred. In Kumasi, the FM stations, which operate for most of the time in Asante twi, were inundated with calls condemning what was considered a show of gross disrespect to the hallowed office of the Asantehene and the Asante in general. So strong were the sentiments expressed by the Asante in Kumasi that the then Ashanti Regional Minister, Mr Kojo Yankah, had to apologise on behalf of the President. To some, the government of the NDC was on a collision course with the Asante and their sentiments were to be expressed in the ensuing elections.

The Attraction of the Manhyia and Obuasi Constituencies

For different reasons Manhyia and Obuasi constituencies hold attractions of their own. They are both urban and cosmopolitan. Manhyia lies in the heart of Kumasi and it houses the golden stool, the soul and spirit of the Asante nation and the symbol of their unity. It is also the seat of the Asantehene, the powerful king of Asante. This notwithstanding, Manhyia has a large non-Asante population, particularly persons from the northern part of Ghana but has surprisingly remained a traditional Asante community. It has since 1992 consistently recorded extensive support for the NPP whose parliamentary candidate in 1996 and 2000 was Dr Addo Kufuor, a sibling of the NPP presidential candidate. In 1996 it recorded 93,078 registered voters, second only to Bantama which had 126,810 registered voters. These facts would point to the maintenance of the *status quo ante*, that is, the Manhyia constituency would continue to rally behind the NPP particularly in view of Dr Addo Kufuor's blood relationship with the flag bearer of the party. But we were cautioned in our fieldwork not to rush to conclusions, as there were convinced supporters of the NDC in the royal household in the Manhyia palace.

Obuasi constituency on the other hand consists of the Obuasi town itself, which has been described as an urban industrial town, and a few adjoining villages and lies in the heart of Adansi, the cradle from which all

Akans trace their origins and migrations. In Obuasi is located one of the world's oldest, largest and richest gold mines operated by the Ashanti Goldfields Company Limited (AGC). As of now, the mine in Obuasi has proven gold reserves of 21 million ounces and it is inextricably bound with the lives of the people of the constituency as evidenced in the pithy statement of one respondent that "Obuasi is AGC and AGC is Obuasi". The town also has a large collection of migrant mine workers of all ranks and stations in life from all over Ghana with nothing but their labour to offer. In addition, it has also attracted a large non-indigenous population in search of a fortune. Thus, by all accounts Obuasi is a lot more ethnically diverse and cosmopolitan than Manhyia and its social and economic relations intricate and complex.

Even though Obuasi generates a great deal of wealth and it is directly connected to the global economy via the gold industry, it has its gloomy side too. The social and economic infrastructures of the town are poor. Obuasi town roads in particular are in an extremely deplorable state. At the time the research for this chapter was conducted, the roads were unmotorable and generated considerable dust that worsened the unacceptable levels of pollution in the town. Worse still, gold prices had been plummeting since 1999 causing considerable strain on the industry that sustains the town. Several employees of AGC have had to be laid off. There was also a costly and misguided lawsuit by Adryx Mining and Metal Company Limited against AGC believed to have been engineered by the government of the NDC to compel AGC to change its board of directors in the early part of 2000. The news of the lawsuit against AGC, the only Ghanaian company to be listed on the New York and other international stock exchanges, hit national and international headlines plummeting further the company's share value. Sentiments ran high as the end of the Obuasi mine was thought to be imminent. Workers at the Obuasi mine, therefore, displayed open hostility to both President Rawlings and Vice President John Evans Atta Mills and demonstrated against them when they visited Obuasi on different occasions to address political rallies.

The sentiments expressed in Obuasi were therefore much more than the parochial "national" sentiments expressed by Manhyia and Ashanti Region as a whole. They were sentiments that went to the root of the town's livelihood and were expressed by both Asante and non-Asante alike. The question, then, was whether the lowly placed workers at the mine who had hitherto thrown in their lot with the NDC would repeat that in 2000? Would they register their protest against lack of social infrastructure and perceived or real governmental interference in the management of their company by joining hands with the opposition and thereby indirectly exerting political pressure for a change in their circumstances?

The Candidates and their Performance in the 2000 Elections

It is against this background that we must address the main issues raised at the outset. Firstly, we must turn our attention to the candidates. In 1996 there was a straight fight between Dr Kwame Addo Kufuor for the NPP and Yaw Addai Boadi for the NDC, both incidentally Asante, for the seat of the Manhyia constituency. In contrast, Obuasi reflected its ethnic diversity and a non-Asante also competed for the seat of the constituency. Anthony Bright Boadi-Mensah (NPP), Peter Kenneth Owusu (NDC), Kwabena Appiah-Pinkrah for the Peoples Congress Party (PCP), and Quarcoo Thomas Aduah for the National Convention Party (NCP), were all Asante while Peter Alhassan for the Peoples National Convention, (PNC) hailed from Northern Ghana.

The picture in Manhyia was however, different in 2000 when there were four candidates in contention for the seat. The NDC candidate was Samuel Bofa Donkoh, a 49-year old Barrister-at-law. Educated at the University of Ghana and the Ghana School of Law, S. B. Donkoh hails from Mim in the Brong Ahafo Region but was born and bred in Manhyia, Kumasi. He is an Akan but not an Asante. Then there was Nana Owusu Boateng, who stood on the ticket of the CPP. A real doyen of the old order of the days of the CPP and NLM in which the local farmer of substance and modest education staked claims to national political office, Nana Owusu Boateng is a 61-year old farmer and middle school leaver who completed his formal education in 1956. He hails from Brofoyerdru-Kodie, in the Ashanti Region. Salifu Mumuni, a 45-year old farmer from Daboya in the Northern Region who was born in Alabar in the Manhyia constituency was the PNC candidate. Mumuni, as his colleague candidates for the PNC in Obuasi in 1996 and 2000 was non-Asante from the Northern Region. Finally, there was the incumbent MP, Dr Kwame Addo Kufuor, a native of Nkawie seen as a true son of the soil having been bred in Kumasi with a long tradition of membership of the NPP and its predecessor parties. Dr Kufuor is a 60-year old graduate of the University of Cambridge in the United Kingdom and a medical officer by profession who until his election to Parliament in 1996 practised his profession in his own clinic: the Kufuor Clinic, which is located in the constituency.

In view of the great deference the Asante have for the legal profession,

S. B. Donkoh was the only serious challenger to Dr Kufuor in the line up. Even so, he was no match for Dr Kufuor's intellectual image and qualities as a mature professional. Nana Owusu Boateng, on the other hand, was severely handicapped by his modest education. A Middle School Leaving Certificate obtained in 1956 without more would hardly meet the challenges of a modern sophisticated parliament and this must have been paramount in the minds of the electors. In the good old days, however, Nana Owusu Boateng's age and wealth would have stood him good stead, age being synonymous with sagacity and economy of language rather than the rhetoric and long speeches on the soap box and on the floor of parliament.

By far then, Dr Kufuor was the best known of the candidates, not least because of the credentials enumerated above, but also because he was readily associated with his clinic in the constituency and also because he was the incumbent MP and the direct brother of the NPP presidential candidate. Gentle, affable and handsome, Dr Kufuor is widely acclaimed by his constituents as eminently qualified to be the leader of the NPP. Clearly, as a favourite local son of ability, substance and influence it was not doubted that he would be given a senior cabinet position in a future NPP government, possible charges of nepotism notwithstanding. Already, as the shadow Minister for Health in the 1996–2000 parliament, he had discharged himself creditably and had achieved personal popularity. Not surprisingly, as many as 70% of all respondents surveyed in the constituency indicated that they voted for the NPP in 1996 and 68% indicated that they would vote for that same party in 2000. Eventually, Dr Kufuor won over 80% of the votes in the constituency. The final results were Samuel Bofa Donkoh (NDC) 12,244; Nana Owusu Boateng (CPP) 493; Salifu Mumuni (PNC) 1,614 and Dr Kwame Addo Kufuor, (NPP), 64,067.

Apart from Anthony Bright Boadi-Mensah, the incumbent MP none of the candidates that had competed in the 1996 parliamentary elections for the Obuasi constituency did so again in 2000. Boadi-Mensah, the NPP candidate, is a 64 year old Associate Member of the Chartered Institute of Insurance and hails from Adansi Apagya. The first of the new entrants into the race for the constituency was the NDC's Yaw Nsiah-Pepprah a 50-year old university don of the Kwame Nkrumah University of Science and Technology. A graduate of the University of Wales in Cardiff, Dr Nsiah-Pepprah hails from Odumasi in the constituency. The second is Sarfo Kantanka, the CPP candidate, who is a 40-year old self-employed industrial designing consultant and who obtained a Teacher's Certificate "A" in 1983.

He hails from Bedomasi in the constituency. In addition, there were Mohammed Nurudeen, Abdulai Issaku, an Akan but not Asante and Douglas Freduah-Agyeman as the candidates for the PNC, the United Ghana Movement (UGM) and the National Reform Party (NRP) respectively. These three candidates represented the "new revolutionary order" of the entry of the lowly placed into the inner circles of national power. Mohammed Nuradeen hails from Tamale in the Northern Region but was born in Obuasi and was educated at the New Edubiase Secondary School. He has a General Certificate of Education Ordinary (GCE "O") Level, which was obtained in 1990 only two years before the return to constitutional rule. He is a self-employed butcher. Abdulai Issaku, the UGM candidate, was born in 1970 in Obuasi and hails from Dunkwa-on-Offin in the Central Region. He is a mechanic and holds a GCE "O" Level which was obtained in 1997, three years before his candidature for parliament. The NRP candidate, Douglas Freduah-Agyemang, was born in 1952 and holds GCE "O" Level. He is a professional driver.

By far, it was only Dr Nsiah-Pepprah and Mr Boadi-Mensah both of who are Asante who were in serious contention for the seat. The rest were mere token candidates. This was reflected in the rivalry between the NDC and the NPP in the constituency[2]. Every part of the constituency was reached by the overt propaganda of these contestants and their parties. There was therefore an active expression of partisanship in favour of both NDC and NPP. In 1996, Boadi-Mensah received 58.7% of the votes in the constituency and the NDC candidate, Peter Kenneth Owusu, took 34%. In our survey, 47.1% of the respondents in the constituency said they voted for NPP in 1996 but only 27.5% of those captured in the study declared that they would vote for the NPP. In contrast, 22.5% of the respondents said they voted for the NDC in 1996 and only 5.9% said they would vote for the NDC in 2000. Even though the NPP candidate won the constituency seat with 64.9% of the votes, the results reflected the ethnic diversity of Obuasi. The final results for the constituency were Dr Yaw Nsiah Pepprah (NDC) 18,011; Sarfo Kantanka (CPP) 4,198; Mohammend Nurudeen (PNC) 1,636; Abdulai Y. Issaka (UGM) 806; Douglas Freduah-Agyemang, (NRP), 623; Anthony Boadi-Mensah, (NPP), 46,787.

In comparative terms the NPP candidate for Obuasi did better in 2000 than in 1996. In 1996 he polled 44,721 votes, representing 58.5% of the votes of the constituency. In contrast, the NDC candidate did not fare as well. In 1996, the NDC candidate, Peter Kenneth Owusu, polled an impressive 25,984 votes representing 34% of the votes.

The results of the presidential elections showed a similar pattern. Manhyia was heavily weighed in favour of the NPP and Obuasi reflected a spread across the board for all parties. Again the constituents tended to vote for the same party in both the parliamentary and presidential elections. Thus, out of 74,558 valid votes cast in Manhyia constituency, J. A. Kufuor's nearest competitor, John Atta Mills of the NDC, polled less than 9,000 votes. The constituency results were Daniel A. Lartey of the Great Consolidated Popular Party (GCPP) 190; John Evans Atta Mills, (NDC) 8,935; George Panyin Hagan (CPP), 269; Edward N. Mahama (PNC) 1,120; Charles Wereko-Brobby (UGM) 49; Gossie O. Tanoh (NRP), 129 and John Agyekum Kufuor, 63,866. The Obuasi results were Daniel Lartey, 333; Atta Mills, 18,434; George Hagan, 567; Edward Mahama, 1,234; Charles Wereko-Brobby 108; Goosie Tanoh, 289; John Kufuor, 47,821.

Again, as in the parliamentary election in the Obuasi constituency, Atta Mills, the presidential candidate for the NDC, fared less well than his predecessor, Jerry Rawlings who had polled a respectable 28,780 in 1996. In contrast, John Kufuor's votes appreciated marginally.

Factors that Influenced the Outcome of the Elections in the Constituencies

Even though 22.5% of respondents in Manhyia and 18.6% in Obuasi indicated a strong attachment to their ethnic group, it would be stating the obvious to say that the success of the NPP candidates in the Manhyia and Obuasi constituencies was assisted by the general popularity of the NPP in the Ashanti Region where the tendency of all was to rally behind the NPP. Not surprisingly, a member of the NDC in Manhyia who responded to the questionnaire confided to us that it was thought un-Asante for him not to belong to the NPP. Further, in 2000, the Obuasi constituents had passed an unfavourable judgement on the NDC rule. The factors that we alluded to in our discussion of the pre-election situation in Obuasi must have influenced this judgement.

Secondly, we must consider the issues. The foremost issue that agitated respondents was the national economy. Several respondents be moaned the general poverty throughout the country and indicated that "life was difficult", for which reason there ought to be a change in the political leadership. In Manhyia a significant 88% of respondents ranked the economy as the leading issue in the 2000 elections over concerns about "continuity and stability"; "change and development"; and "Ghana's future in the 21st century". Similarly, in Obuasi, 64% of respondents ranked the economy over all others as the main issue in the election. Again, in Manhyia as many as 78% of respondents and 50% in Obuasi said that the economy was very bad. Not surprisingly, none of the respondents in Manhyia and only 5.9% in Obuasi thought that the economy was "good" or "very good". Further, as many as two-thirds of the respondents (76%) in Manhyia and 41.2% in Obuasi said that they had suffered a reduced standard of living since the last elections. Finally, a whopping 91% of the respondents in Manhyia and 54.9% in Obuasi said that their household income was hardly adequate to meet their needs. There was, therefore, clearly an overwhelming condemnation of the economic policies of the NDC government and this influenced the decision of the electors in December 2000.

Additionally in Obuasi, concern was expressed about the exploitation of the gold resources of the town without corresponding development of its infrastructure. As many as 32.4% of respondents placed the development of "a good road network" the top development issue over "employment" and the supply of potable water.

Even though the members of the NDC pointed to the mobilisation of machinery on site by a reputable construction firm as a demonstration of the desire of the government to rehabilitate Obuasi town roads, all the opposition parties naturally exploited the lack of road and social infrastructure in their campaign. The NPP went further than the others. The party indicated that the loyalty of the constituency would be handsomely rewarded. There were thus copious promises in the campaign messages of the NPP of jobs in Obuasi and of the repair of the town roads.

The third issue that was articulated, even if more evidently in Manhyia than in Obuasi, was the longevity of the incumbent government. For many the NDC, taken to be the same as its predecessor, the PNDC, had ruled long enough and must yield to others. More than half of the respondents in Manhyia and Obuasi believed that NPP's Kufuor "represented a change" and he was the "right person for the job" of the president. In this regard, the dominant theme was the repudiation of the ills of the NDC. There were loud denunciations of corruption, abuse of human rights, ethnicity and political arrogance even though none of these was substantiated to us. The inevitable verdict was that the NDC's umbrella has lost its ability to shield Ghanaians from the vagaries of the economy and the elephant was ready to step out. Thus for many, purely for reasons of the appropriation of power for nearly two decades, Jerry Rawlings and his NDC must be shown the exit.

Thirdly, we must consider the participation of the respondents in the political process and their views on the conduct of the elections. Nearly all respondents in the two constituencies exhibited a remarkable degree of political awareness. There was however, a touch of irony to their perception of the electoral process and their participation in it. Most respondents mistrusted the electoral process. As many as 68% of respondents in Manhyia and 30.4 % in Obuasi believed that the 1996 elections had not been free and fair. Again 62% of respondents in Manhyia and 42.2% in Obuasi believed that the Electoral Commission was not independent but was subject to government control. In spite of this, as many as 97% of respondents in Manhyia voted in the 1996 election and 84.3% voted in Obuasi. Again, similar large numbers, 98% (Manhyia) and 99% (Obuasi) evinced their intention to vote in the 2000 election. Further, 98% of respondents in both constituencies followed the activities of political parties in the media, particularly on radio even though much smaller numbers, 31% in Manhyia and 26.5% in Obuasi attended political rallies.

The greater press freedom enjoyed nationally since the last elections seems to have accounted for the high level of political consciousness and the unprecedented high level of interest shown in the activities of the political parties by the respondents in the two constituencies. FM stations, in particular, were in the forefront of bringing political issues and the activities of the political parties to the attention of the general populace. Kumasi has the second largest number of FM stations, (eight in all) second only to Accra which has 14 stations. Significantly, the stations in Kumasi followed the example of those in Accra and mounted several discussion and phone-in programmes on politics, political parties and the elections. These programmes were remarkably engaging, particularly so, as the stations permitted the use of Ghanaian languages by all participants. They also invited political dignitaries who were passing through Kumasi or the Ashanti Region to participate in their programmes. During the period of the fieldwork, Vice President Atta Mills, the UGM leader, Dr Wereko-Brobby and the NRP's Gossie Tanoh were all campaigning in the Ashanti Region and were hosted variously by *Garden City FM* and other stations.

Even though broadcasts from the stations in Kumasi were received clearly in Obuasi, the town also had its own station: *Shaft FM,* donated to the town by AGC as part of its social responsibility programme. *Shaft FM*, like all other FM stations, also hosted several discussion and phone-in programmes and it is to its credit that it graciously announced the presence of our research team in Obuasi and explained our mission to the listening public.

The Presidential Run-off

Before we conclude, we must turn our attention to the presidential run-off. The 1979 Constitution, for the first time, introduced the American style executive presidency into Ghanaian politics. The first and only elections held under that Constitution led to a presidential run-off, incidentally, between PNP's Dr Hilla Limann and NPP's forebear, the PFP, which was led by Victor Owusu. The run-off led to an interesting alliance of political parties. The 2000 presidential elections repeated the experience of 1979. It also led to a presidential run-off and occasioned the birth a big coalition of all minority parties against the dominant NDC. The undeclared marriage of the minority parties alluded to earlier on was finally celebrated when the presidential run-off was announced. All the parties that stood opposed to the NDC declared an alliance, the sole purpose of which was to complete the defeat of the NDC, which lost its majority in parliament on 7 December, by voting the NPP candidate, John Kufour into the presidency.

For the NPP, victory has finally come, the first since the victory of their predecessor, the PP, in 1969. The presidential run-off was only to confirm this victory. Bolstered by the support of all the minority parties, the NPP started celebrating victory before it finally occurred. Not only did the voter turnout increase significantly in both Manhyia and Obuasi, but also the NPP mopped up all the votes of all the parties opposed to the NDC and even took some of the NDC's first round votes away from it. In Manhyia 8% of respondents and 13.9% in Obuasi said that even though they had not voted for the NPP on 7 December they had done so in the presidential run-off. Thus, Professor John Evans Atta Mills of the NDC came out of the run-off with reduced votes. The results for the Manhyia constituency were J.E.A. Mills, 8,282 and J.A. Kufuor, 67,778, a respective net loss and gain of 653 and 3,912. For Obuasi, J. E. A. Mills polled 17,106 and J.A. Kufuor, 53,673 again a respective loss and gain of 1,328 and 5,852.

Conclusion

In conclusion, we must address the question of the effect of the elections on the general direction of politics in Ghana. The results of the successful 2000 elections were pregnant with several lessons[3]. Firstly, the people of Ghana demonstrated that government can be changed through the ballot box. Indeed, for the first time in the history of Ghana, Ghanaians have voted an incumbent government out of power. This is quite significant, particularly so, since the incumbent government was in full control of all state apparatuses and was determined to remain in power. Secondly, the experiment in democratic governance recommenced in 1992/3 has begun to take root because Ghana has gone through the third successive successful elections. Finally, it is clear that Ghanaians are beginning to appreciate and enjoy the true tenets of democratic pluralism, that is, to express their political views in all manners possible without fear or favour. For the effect of the election on the general direction of politics in Ghana therefore, we can, at least, be cautiously optimistic. In 1975 John Dunn, (Austin & Luckham, 1975), who observed the 1969 elections in Ghana reflected sadly, when the successful PP government was literally shot down by the military only 27 months later, that on that showing Ghanaians would be doing well if they were free once in every fifteen years. There was a basis for that belief in 1975. Twenty-five years on in 2000, Ghanaians have shown unequivocally that, with goodwill by all, they will be free once in every four years.

NOTES

1. Asante, in keeping with current orthography, is used in reference to the peoples of Asante as distinguished from the region, which is denoted Ashanti in official records.
2. The author of this chapter and his research assistant, Mr K. Adum Kyeremeh, were treated with scant respect when they visited the NDC constituency headquarters in Obuasi to introduce themselves and to administer questionnaires. We were told that nobody in the office would entertain us unless we sought permission from the District Chief Executive. Subsequently, in the streets of Obuasi, the members of the NDC who accused us of collecting data on non-NPP members threatened us with assault. They declined to respond to our questionnaire. Ironically, not long thereafter, we were arrested by members of the NPP who charged that we were agents of the NDC and were collecting the voter identity cards of non-NDC members and were destroying them. Our research materials were confiscated and we were reported to the police after the sitting MP, Anthony Boadi-Mensah, could not persuade his supporters that our cause was genuine. It took the intervention of the District Electoral Officer, Mr. Gabriel Manu, for our materials to be restored to us two days later.
3. Nearly every chapter in this book refers to some of the lessons of the 2000 general elections and presidential run-off. Only a few of these lessons will, therefore, be mentioned here.

REFERENCES

Allman, J. M. (1993) *The Quills of the Porcupine: Asante Nationalism in an Emergent Ghana* (Madison: University of Wisconsin Press).
Austin, D. (1970) *Politics in Ghana, 1946–1960* (London: Oxford University Press).
Austin, D. and Luckham, R. (eds) (1975) *Politicians and Soldiers in Ghana, 1966–1972* (London: Frank Cass).

CHAPTER 17

Election 2000 and the Presidential Run-off in Birim North and Yilo Krobo Constituencies

EMMANUEL DEBRAH

Introduction

The 2000 elections produced a number of significant outcomes for the third wave of Ghana's democratization process (Huntington 1991). First, they represented a crucial test for the country's fragile and prolonged transition to multiparty democracy initiated in 1992 with the birth of the Fourth Republic on 3 January 1993. Second, they marked the end of long reign of J. J Rawlings and his pseudo-democratic regime (Diamond 1996) and the opening of a new chapter in Ghana's democratization process. And third, the successful conduct of the elections and subsequent peaceful transfer of power from the incumbent to the victorious New Patriotic Party (NPP) have show-cased Ghana as an example of peaceful political change through the ballot box in the continent of African. By this electoral turnover and power transfer, Ghana's democratization process is firmly consolidated (Gyimah-Boadi 2001; Bratton 1995; Huntington 1991). The survey analyses respondents' views on several critical elections, democratic as well as development and governance issues prior to and after the 2000 elections.

Profile of Constituencies

With a population of 87,000 and registered voters of 49,834, Yilo Krobo is the home of the Krobos. Sharing boundaries to the north with Fanteakwa and East Akim, the south with Lower Manya, north-west with Koforidua and south-west with Akuapim, Yilo Krobo is popular for its rich Kloyosikplemi and Dipo cultures. Farming and petty trading are the main occupation of the people and it has the Boti Falls and Krobo Mountains as two major tourist destinations. Historically the voting pattern of Yilo people reveals a higher preference for the Nkrumah political tradition (Twumasi 1975) before 1992 and Rawlings's National Democratic Congress (NDC) after 1992 (see Table 17.1).

Table 17.1: Voting Pattern in Yilo Krobo Constituency
(Presidential Elections)

Candidates	1992	1996	2000-run-off
A. A Boahen	3225 (14.5%)		
Hila Limann	410 (1.8%)		
K. Darko	569 (2.6%)		
J. J Rawlings	17840 (80.3%)		
E. Erskine	173 (0.8%)		
J. A Kufuor		8539 (18.4%)	11494 (45.7%)
E. Mahama		388 (1.1%)	
J. J Rawlings		28622 (80.5%)	
J. E. A Mills			13673 (54.3%)

Consequently, many Ghanaian political commentators often refer to the constituency as the NDC "second World Bank". Admired for being handsome, Rawlings more than the NDC party is the popular choice in the constituency. His exit from power and not being a candidate for the presidential race was therefore a crucial test for the party in the constituency.

Also located between latitude 1.25 west and 0.50 east and longitude 6.30 north and 5.55 south is the Birim North constituency. Adjoining East Akim and Kwaebibirem to the east, Kwahu South to the north, Ashanti Region to the west and Birim South to the south, the Birim North Constituency covers a land area of 1,250 square kilometers with a total population of 123,579 and a voting population of 63,787. Birim North is home to majority Akyems and minority settler farmers including Ewes, Krobos, Guans as well as northern migrants.

Election results before 1992 in the constituency show the overwhelming support of the people for Danquah/Busia tradition (Twumasi 1975). The trend has however, changed since 1992. With total valid votes of 15,943 (56%), J. J Rawlings beat Adu Boahen who obtained 11,422 (40.6%) in the 1992 presidential poll even though J. A Kufuor 22,192 (49.8%) was slightly ahead of Rawlings 21,882 (49.15%) in the 1996 polls. Inteestingly, however, it was the NDC candidate who won the 1996 parliamentary poll.

Methodology

Pre- and post-election 2000 surveys were conducted in the Yilo Krobo and Birim North constituencies. In each survey, 100 questionnaires were administered in each constituency over a period of 14 days. The sampling criteria used were based on each constituency's percentage of registered voters. Constituency capitals were allowed 40% of the sample questionnaire for the constituency, peri-urban areas 20% and rural areas 40%. The selection of the urban, peri-urban and rural areas was based on the profile of the districts prepared by the District Assemblies. Selection of respondents followed a simple random sampling method. Contrary to the earlier determination to ensure gender balance, it could not be achieved because the women showed apathy towards the exercise particularly in the rural areas. Hence male respondents outnumbered females in a 65% to 35% ratio.

Demographic Data of Respondents

Gender

In Ghana, far fewer women than men participate in key political issues and activities. The traditional belief that the man is the head of the family and therefore responds to all questions posed by visitors has had a debilitating effect on attitude of women to survey interviews. Scenarios from both the pre- and post-elections surveys data in Table 17.2 confirm the dominance of Ghanaian men in national political life.

Table 17.2: Sample Questionnaire Distribution Among Genders

Gender	Pre-election		Post-election	
	Yilo Krobo	Birim North	Yilo Krobo	Birim North
Male	69	66	64	68
Female	31	34	36	32
TOTAL	100	100	100	100

Age distribution

Over 80% of respondents fall in the 18-50 age group, an indication of ever growing awareness and show of interest among the youth and active working group in Ghanaian politics and democratization processes. Since the success of democracy in Ghana largely depends on their commitment to upholding free and fair elections, their participation in electoral activities gives hope for the future of Ghana's democracy.

Educational Background of Respondents

The level of education of respondents was well above the national average with over 45.5% having received some form of secondary or teacher training education. Very few, about 0.5% had tertiary education and as many as 33% had education up to Primary/Middle/JSS levels. Only a little below 21% had not received any formal education.

Occupation of Respondents

An overwhelming majority of respondents were farmers, representing 53%. Significant figure of 20% were petty traders, 7% teachers, 8% artisans and 6% were either professionals or public servants. Less than 6% indicated that they were unemployed.

Religious Background

As many as 67.3% in both surveys declared that they were Christians. Those in the Islamic faith constituted 21.2%. An insignificant 3.5% identified with Traditional African beliefs with 8% belonging to other unclassified faiths.

Income of Respondents

The sample was skewed towards the low income groups with 72.3% reporting a monthly income of ¢100,000–¢400,000. As few as 18.3% received monthly income of ¢401,000–¢1m. Only 9.4% did not receive any income at all.

Political Participation

Responses from the two constituencies support the claim that Ghanaian citizens are alive to their civic responsibilities as evident in their active involvement in activities of political parties and exercising their franchise. As many as 97% and 98% of respondents registered and voted in the 2000 elections in Birim North and Yilo Krobo respectively. Sadly, however, only 36.3% in Birim North were registered members of a political party and 18.7% expressed interest in contesting future elections to party executive positions in the constituency. On the contrary, a significant 63% in Yilo Krobo were card-bearing members of parties and more than half were eager to become executive members of their parties.

Survey evidence further shows that participation of citizens in politics transcends voting and registration with political parties to encompass activists canvassing support for their preferred candidates, posting and distributing party posters and paraphernalia, shouting party slogans, attending rallies and contributing financially to the up-keep of their parties in the constituency. Asked to indicate the extent of their participation in party activities, over 64% and 71% respondents in Birim North and Yilo Krobo respectively were regular attenders of rallies and participated in "Keep Fit" and 'jama' forms of activity.

The high interest in party activities was attributed to the competitive nature of the 2000 elections. Early mobilization drives pursued by the parties before the poll had contributed significantly to the high electorate interest in politics. The researcher learnt that parties, particularly the NPP and NDC embarked on intensive revitalization of their party's structures in the constituencies as early as January 1998 and also trained party volunteers who engaged in house-to-house campaigns to whip up popular support for their parties. A reasonable voter turnout of 51% and 59.5% for Yilo Krobo and Birim North constituencies respectively in the polls amply demonstrates the extent of popular participation in political activities in the constituencies.

Voter Perception of Political Parties

It is inconceivable to have a democracy without political parties. The extent of their performance therefore has a direct implication for democratic governance. In their assessment of political parties since 1992, an overwhelming 70% and 16% of respondents in Birim North perceived political parties as doing a good job and a very good job respectively. As a result, 74% thought that party politics had improved the quality of life of the ordinary Ghanaian. Only 10% believed that political parties had divided the nation and an insignificant 4% regarded party politics as a dirty game. Survey evidence from Yilo Krobo, however, presents different scenarios. As few as 13% of respondents thought that political parties were doing a good job. In the opinion of 24% of respondents, parties were doing neither a good nor a bad job. Similarly, 30% and 32% respectively responded that party politics had brought division among the people and had enriched the life of few even though 25% in the constituency still perceived political parties as doing a very good job. The general view was that political parties were capable of turning the nation around for the better. Hence overwhelmingly respondents disagreed with the view that irrespective of the party in power, there would be no difference in what happened at national level. The majority of people thought that a change of government could greatly alter the management of the country at national level because every political party has its own style and ways of doing things (see Table 17.3).

Table 17:3 Do you agree with the view that Irrespective of the Party in Power there is no Difference in what Happens at National Level?

Responses	Birim North Frequency	%	Yilo Krobo Frequency	%
Yes	3	3	20	20
No	94	94	67	67
Don't Know	3	3	13	13

The Ghanaian Economy

The vote for positive change was a vote on the Ghanaian economy. Survey evidence shows that the majority of respondents were conversant with the state of the economy of Ghana and the responses are indicative of their total rejection of the economic management pursued under the NDC government. Not only did the people see the economy as very bad but they also registered their displeasure about the worse state of the economy (see Table 17.4). Respondents identified inflation 46.5%, depreciation of the *Cedi* 26%, unemployment 20% and high interest rates 17.5% as major economic problems confronting the nation especially over the past four years. The harsh economic conditions had worsened 42% and 38.6% living standards of respondents in Birim North and Yilo Krobo respectively. As many as 58.7% household's standards of living had become a little worse and more than 68% had witnessed a sharp deterioration in their living standards. Only a little less than 4% have improved their standard of living over the past four years.

Table 17.4: Voters Perception about the State of the Economy

Responses	Birim North Frequency	%	Yilo Krobo Frequency	%
Very good	5	5	3	3
Good	6	6	9	9
Bad	29	29	19	19
Very Bad	58	58	69	69
Neither good or bad	2	2	11	11
Don't Know	–	–	–	–
TOTAL	100	100	100	100

Respondents' perceptions about the economy were informed by their monthly incomes. One notices a strong relationship between income and those who regarded the economy as being bad. Of those who said the economy was very bad in Yilo Krobo, 86.3% receive ¢ zero–¢ 400,000 a month. As many as 91% of the same group in Birim North receive a monthly income of ¢ 201,000–¢500,000.

Evaluating the Democratic Process

Consensus exists among different political groups in Ghana that democracy is the most preferred system of government. Not only does democracy enhance free expression of divergent and dissenting views but also citizens exercise their franchise to endorse or reject political office holders. The majority of Ghanaians in the National Survey 67.2% agreed that Ghana had come a long way in the democratization process began in 1992. Attesting to this, 70% and 71% of respondents in Birim North and Yilo Krobo respectively described Ghana as a democratic country. 63% and 54.5% in Birim North and Yilo Krobo respectively also conceded that democracy had remarkably improved over the past four years. They thought that the press, political parties and civic associations enjoyed more freedom than before 1996 (see Tables 17:5 and 17:6). Only a minority 22.6% in both constituencies responded in the negative to any suggestion of improvement in democratic governance in Ghana over the past four years.

Table 17.5: Do you think that the Press has more Freedom now than Four Years Ago?

Responses	Birim North Frequency	%	Yilo Krobo Frequency	%
Yes	82	82	67	67
No	14	14	28	28
Don't Know	4	4	5	5
TOTAL	100	100	100	100

Table 17.6: Do you think that Political Parties and other Associations have more Freedom now than Four Years Ago?

Responses	Birim North Frequency	%	Yilo Krobo Frequency	%
Yes	79	79	71	71
No	14	14	26	26
Don't Know	7	7	3	3
TOTAL	100	100	100	100

Constant interaction between Members of Parliament (MP) and the electorate is a crucial ingredient in a democracy but survey evidence from the two constituencies reveals that 72% and 65.8% in Birim North and Yilo krobo respectively have had no contact with their MPs over the past 12 months. In spite of this 28% and 34.2 % in Birim North and Yilo Krobo respectively have interacted with their MPs at party meetings 15% and during commissioning of development projects 5%. Consequently as many as 73% and 68% in Birim North and Yilo Krobo respectively thought that their MPs had not represented them they way they expected. Only 16% said that they had been well represented by their MPs because they had brought development to their constituencies.

Election Issues

Why do people choose one candidate over the other? This question is not easy to determine but generally individual voting choices may be analyzed as products of long-term and short-term forces. These may arise from a candidate's attributes, party identification and issues of the time. In the two constituencies party affiliation was a crucial determining factor in the choice of a candidate. When asked whether they would vote for a candidate, party or both, nearly half (49.3%) in both constituencies said they would vote for a candidate of their preferred parties. Only 32.7% said they would vote on account of the candidates' own attributes and 18% responded making their choice on the basis of both.

In the post-election survey respondents in both constituencies identified education 52.9%, unemployment 63% and the economy 73.4% as national issues that informed them of their choice of candidates or parties. They were hopeful that their parties would be capable of addressing these socio-economic problems. Similarly, good roads 60%, water 51% and unemployment 67% were the main local issues that determined the choice of candidates in the two constituencies. Consequently, candidates in the two constituencies focused their campaign messages on policy concerns of their respective parties. The campaign of positive change of the NPP appeared to have gone down well with many voters. Sixty six per cent and 62% in Birim North and Yilo Krobo admitted voting for the NPP and its candidates because they best articulated the development concerns of people in the constituencies.

Anatomy of Constituency Campaigns

Modern election campaigns and party organization stress the need to achieve several interrelated objectives in a competitive elections including formulating strategies and designing instruments to canvass support. While in parties such as the CPP, NRP GCPP and PNC organization was often little more than a loyal following within the parties both the NPP and NDC recruited and trained "foot soldiers" who adopted a house-to-house campaign mobilization strategy. Brass band procession, keep-fit and "jama" became the new style of mobilizing voters. Interviewers were told of the potency of the strategy and how it influenced floating voters and even members of opponent parties.

No political party or candidate had been denied access to free campaigning and throughout the period, campaigns were smooth. Seventy four per cent of respondents alluded to the fact that all candidates enjoyed free campaigning and the campaigns were also devoid of any intimidation (68.7%). Only less than 18.3% believe that there had been some forms of intimidation. Admittedly, the message delivered by a candidate gives substance to a campaign and helps tremendously to shape the political agenda, mobilize "backers" and win more votes. The researcher learnt during the pre-election survey that G. Omaboe, the NDC parliamentary candidate for Birim North Constituency, and Christian Tettey, NPP parliamentary candidate for Yilo Krobo had campaign messages that were more captivating than those of their rivals. They weaved their personal and policy stances into thematic messages, which depicted what they wished to do for the people. The messages were clear and conveyed a sense of emotional urgency that reflected the voters' perception of political realities. Unfortunately, they lost because the majority of voters identified their arch-rivals in the opposite parties in the two constituencies with decency, loyalty, honesty, hard work and other traditional cherished values.

The Media

Since the opening of the media waves in 1996 both the print and electronic media have constantly engaged political parties and candidates in the discussion of several election issues, helped parties to send campaign messages to their teeming supporters, and covered political events from party campaigns to announcing polling station results.

In the rural areas in the two constituencies, most people (63.2%) reported getting more of their news about the elections and national political issues from the private radio stations than from any other source. A little over sixty two per cent also cited private newspapers as their news source compared with less than 18.7% who mentioned the state-owned television and less than

10% who relied on state-owned newspapers. Not only are the private radio and newspapers the respondents' most important source of news but they are also rated as trustworthy because they are truthful about their news reportage.

News "anchor persons" in the village communities were identified as useful and reliable source of elections information. About 66% of respondents said that they had also heard the news about the elections and campaign activities of their parties at both constituency and national levels through their friends and ward/constituency executives.

Another revelation from the survey was that small groups of news sophisticates such as teachers assemblymen/women and some health workers (40.6%) in the villages read newspapers and listened to news programmes about the elections on radio. The much larger group of other serious news consumers (59.4%) in the urban and peri-urban areas listen to radio broadcasts, read both state and private newspapers and watched television. The survey further shows that the level of education was strongly related to news attentiveness and nearly 93% of news sophisticates had formal education. Among other factors age bears no relationship to news attentiveness but sex/gender had a decided effect with news sophisticates being more males 63% and 37% females.

Evaluating the Electoral Process

An overwhelming number of respondents 97% and 86% in the post-elections survey in Birim North and Yilo Krobo respectively thought that the elections had been generally free and fair because media coverage of parties and elections activities was adequate (80%) and also fair (64%) to all parties. The smooth and orderly polling process gave voters satisfaction about the elections. The presence of the police at the poll (70%) to maintain law and order and assistance provided by elections officials (88%) obviated any intimidation (90%) at the polls. Far fewer people voted with thumb-print ID cards (less than 1%) than photo ID cards (99%).

Running Mates

The choice of a presidential running mate became a critical issue in the 2000 elections. Ninety-two per cent and 96% of respondents in the pre-election survey in Birim North and Yilo Krobo respectively responded that who became running mate to their parties' presidential candidate was very important for their votes for their party. While 51% and 31% in both constituencies preferred gender and ethnic balance respectively only 13% thought that regional balance should be the most important factor to be considered in the choice of a running mate. An insignificant 5% believe that experience and party loyalty should be the yardstick for the selection of a running mate.

The Presidential Run-off

As many as 97% and 95% of respondents in Birim North and Yilo Krobo respectively voted in the presidential run-off elections on 28 December 2000. Of these, 58% and 43% in Birim North and Yilo Krobo respectively said that they voted for J. A. Kufuor. Only 39% and a little above half (52%) in Birim North and Yilo Krobo respectively said they cast their ballots for J. E. A Mills. Ninety per cent and 80% in Birim North and Yilo Krobo respectively admitted having voted for the same candidate in the first round elections. While the campaign of continuity 18% and honesty 10% decided the votes for Mills, Kufuor's message of positive change for a better Ghana (46%) was powerful enough to defeat Mills. Also Kufuor's campaign policies were perceived to be more realistic (22%) than Mills (4%).

Conclusion

The weight of evidence from the survey shows that the vast majority of voters in the two constituencies made informed choices when voting in the elections. They had knowledge about the candidates and elections issues and also took time to discern and chose the one that best presented their views and what was in the nation's interests. It further shows that party campaigns were rigorous, intensive and free from violence and intimidation. Campaign messages of candidates focused on policy concerns of their respective parties such as a strong economy, job creation, domestic tranquility, quality education, and wealth creation among other issues. NPP won in Birim North because the party articulated the local aspirations of the people. In Yilo Krobo, the NDC's victory was in response to the peoples' love for J.J Rawlings's party.

REFERENCES

Bratton, M (1995) 'Are Competitive Elections Enough'? Richards Joseph (ed.) *Africa Demos*, Vol. 3, No. 4 (March).

Diamond, L (1996) 'Is the Third Wave Over?' *Journal of Democracy*, Vol. 7, 3.
Gyimah-Boadi E (2001) *Report on the December 2000 Elections in Ghana*, March, Center for Democratic Development.
Huntington, S. P. (1991) *The Third Wave: Democratization in the Late Twentieth Century* London, University of Oklahoma Press.
Twumasi Y. (1975) 'The 1969 Elections', in D. Austin and R. Luckham (eds.) *Politicians and Soldiers in Ghana 1966–1972*, London, Frank Cass.

CHAPTER 18

Ghana's Election 2000: A Study of Political Behaviour in the Mampong and Effiduase Asokore Constituencies

MIKE OQUAYE

Introduction

This is an empirical study of political behaviour in Ghana with reference to electoral choice through the ballot box in a multi-party setting. Focusing on two constituencies in the heart of Ashanti, the stronghold of the then opposition New Patriotic Party (NPP), this chapter analyses some of the factors which influenced electoral choice in Election 2000 as captured in the pre- and post-election surveys conducted in October 2000 and January 2001 respectively.

Political behaviour makes interesting study. The factors involved are varied and complex. Barker (1987) has observed, however, that people have set predictable patterns of political behaviour. It is only in extraordinary circumstances that they break out of the normal structure of political and social life to create new political settings. Most of the time however, political life is contained within standardized and repetitive social settings and sustained by structures of economic, social and bureaucratic power (Baker 1987: 1).

For two constituencies which have traditionally supported the Danquah-Busia tradition and have proved hostile to both the military and constitutional regimes of Rawlings, were there any reasons for them in the 2000 Elections to change their voting behaviour?

Profile of the Constituencies

Mampong constituency is one of the two in the Sekyere-West District. It consists of Mampong township, the district headquarters, and its immediate environs. Thus compared to the other constituency in the district, Nsuta-Kwamang, Mampong is the more urban. Situated at the heart of Ashanti region, on a plateau surrounded by hills, it shares borders with the Ejura-

Sekyedumase, Nsuta Kwamang, Effiduase-Asokore constituencies among others. The people of Asante Mampong have traditionally played a dominant role in the history of the Asante Kingdom and the Mamponghene is second-in-command to the Asantehene. They are also noted for their bravery; a recent example was General Afrifa whose execution by the AFRC in 1979 dictated the constituency's attitude towards Rawlings and the NDC (Oquaye 1998: 399).

In the 1996 presidential elections, the constituency had voted 3:1 in favour of J. A. Kufuor against Rawlings (Oquaye 1998: 408). For the 2000 elections Mampong had a voter population size of 44,040.

To the East of Mampong Constituency lies the Effiduase-Asokore Constituency whose capital, Effiduase, doubles as the district headquarters of the Sekyere-East District. In 1996, the constituency had also supported the NPP against the NDC. For the 2000 election, the registered voters were 27,443.

The two constituencies belong to the same traditional council and had historically been part of the same district. The populations in both constituencies are largely homogenous, predominantly Ashantis, with a few Guans, Ewes, Gas and Mole Dagbani (Manu, 1998:482).

This researcher had in previous elections conducted research in Mampong and it was chosen to upgrade existing knowledge. The choice of neighbouring Effiduase-Asokore was to see if there were any similarities or differences in the voting patterns.

Profiles of Respondents

Gender

Of the 100 respondents interviewed in the pre-election survey from each of the two constituencies, 60% were males and 40% were females in Mampong Constituency and 62% and 38% respectively in Effiduase-Asokore. For the post-election survey, the figures were 63% and 37% respectively for Mampong and 58% and 42% for Effiduase-Asokore. Even though the surveys had intended to give equal opportunity to both sexes the females were not as forthcoming and normally preferred to defer to their male counterparts. The figures in both constituencies interestingly, compared favourably with the national figures for these surveys.

Age Distribution

Most respondents in both constituencies were young. In Mampong 74% were between 18 and 40 years, 20% in the 41–60 years bracket and 6% of 61 years and more. In Effiduase-Asokore, the respective percentages were 80%, 15% and 5%.

Educational Background

Eleven percent of interviewees in Mampong and 14% in Effiduase-Asokore indicated that they had had no formal education. Of those who had attended school, 30% in Mampong had had only elementary school education while 59% had a secondary or post secondary education. In comparison, Effiduase-Asokore had 43% elementary education and 43% for secondary or post-secondary education. The relatively larger proportion of better educated respondents in Mampong is a reflection of the fact that the Asante Mampong township is the citadel of education in Asante. Currently Mampong boasts one of the campuses of the University College of Education, Winneba (UCEW), a teacher training college, a technical teachers college and a number of secondary schools.

Occupation

It is significant that about 20% of the respondents particularly the youth (between 18 and 30 years) in both constituencies were unemployed. Of those gainfully employed, the majority in Mampong were teachers and in Effiduase-Asokore, farmers.

Religion

Most respondents interviewed in both constituencies identified themselves as Christians. In Mampong 88% were Christians, 9% Muslims and 3% of traditional religions. In Effiduase-Asokore the respective percentages were 85%, 11% and 4%.

Income

A significant proportion of respondents (30% in Mampong and 40% in Effiduase-Asokore) did not indicate their annual income either because they were unemployed or lived from hand-to-mouth. Of those who indicated most of them (63% in Mampong and 60% in Effiduase-Asokore) earned less than five million cedis; in the latter constituency, nobody earned five million or more.

Pre-election Political Participation

While virtually all respondents (99% in Mampong and 100% in Effiduase-Asokore) were registered voters a large proportion (68% and 77% respectively) were not registered members of any political party on the excuse that they did not like partisan politics for personal reasons. This antipathy to party politics however did not prevent a good number of them being sympathizers of the major parties, NPP (52% in Mampong and 66% in Effiduase-Asokore) followed by the NDC (15% and 11% respectively).

The willingness of respondents to vote was not in doubt. Eighty seven per cent in Mampong and 90% in Effiduase-Asokore had voted in 1996 and an even higher proportion (93% and 100% respectively) were prepared to vote in 2000. However, their participation in political rallies in connection with the 2000 Elections remained low in both constituencies about 45% in each instance. Part of the reason was that the various parties had not organized any major rallies at the time of the survey; while the NPP laid emphasis on mini rallies and house-to-house campaign, the NDC seemed to adopt a low profile approach in a rather hostile terrain. Many respondents, nevertheless, had been following the activities of the various political parties through the news media.

Voter Perception of the Economy

Most respondents, according to the survey data (see Tables 18.1–18.3), were not happy with the economy. Eighty five per cent in both constituencies felt the economy was in bad shape (see Table 18.1); 83% in Mampong and 77% in Effiduase-Asokore felt the economy had either become worse or sharply deteriorated over the last four years (see Table 18.2); 83% and 73% respectively felt their standard of living had become worse since the previous election (see Table 18.3). In the view of respondents in both constituencies the three most important economic problems in Ghana were unemployment, inflation and the depreciation of the *Cedi*.

Table 18.1: Respondents' Perception of the Ghanaian Economy

	Percentage % Mampong	Percentage % Effiduase-Asokore
Very good	–	–
Good	4	4
Bad	19	13
Very bad	66	72
Neither good or bad	9	8
Don't know	2	3
TOTAL	100	100

Table 18.2: Trend of the Ghanaian Economy over last Four Years

	Percentage % Mampong	Percentage % Effiduase-Asokore
Considerably improved	6	14
Just improved	7	3
Become worse	73	21
Sharply deteriorated	10	56
Don't know	4	6
TOTAL	100	100

Table 18.3: Respondents' Household Standard of Living since last Elections

	Percentage % Mampong	Percentage % Effiduase-Asokore
Much better	–	4
A little better	13	18
A little worse	23	13
Much worse	60	60
Don't know	4	5
TOTAL	100	100

Evaluation of the Democratic Process

In their response to whether or not Ghana could be characterised as a democratic country respondents in Mampong were more affirmative than in Effiduase-Asokore where opinions were evenly split. In Mampong 62% were positive; 29%, negative; and 9% were undecided. For Effiduase-Asokore 44% said yes, 35% said no and 21% did not know. A similar pattern prevailed when respondents were asked whether democracy in Ghana had improved over the previous four years. In Mampong 65% compared to 4% in Effiduase-Asokore affirmative; 30% and 38% respectively, negative; and 5% and 21% respectively were undecided.

Respondents were of the view that the press in Ghana had had more freedom than four years before (see Table 18:4).

Table 18.4: Press Freedom

	Percentage %	
	Mampong	Effiduase-Asokore
Yes	75	38
No	13	33
Don't know	12	29
TOTAL	100	100

When respondents were asked whether political parties and other associations had more freedom than the previous four years, their reaction is contained in Table 18.5.

Table 18.5: Associational Freedom

	Percentage %	
	Mampong	Effiduase-Asokore
Yes	70	40
No	19	39
Don't know	11	21
TOTAL	100	100

On both issues above, most respondents (about 70%) in Mampong were certain of improvement but in Effiduase-Asokore a significant proportion over 20% were undecided. Thus on the whole, Mampong was more positive in its evaluation of the democratic process than Effiduase-Asokore.

Evaluation of the Electoral Process

While respondents in Mampong were evenly split as to the freedom and fairness of the 1996 Elections, those in Effiduase-Asokore were more definite that they had not been, even though a third were undecided (see Table 18:6). The major reason cited was rigging in certain polling stations.

Table 18.6: Free and Fair Elections — 1996

	Percentage % Mampong	Effiduase-Asokore
Yes	40	24
No	40	46
Don't know	20	30
TOTAL	100	100

For the 2000 elections 57% in Mampong felt conditions existed in Ghana for free and fair elections but in Effiduase-Asokore only 43% were so convinced, and as many as 39% were undecided.

Respondents in both constituencies had negative perception of the Electoral Commission. Less than a third in both cases (30% in Mampong and 27% in Effiduase-Asokore) thought the Commission was independent of control. Sixty two per cent (62%) in Mampong said it was not while 43% in Effiduase-Asokore were undecided (see Table 18:7).

Evaluation of the Party System

Respondents were asked to examine the possibility of an opposition party winning the presidential election as compared to the ruling party. As one would expect in an opposition stronghold, the response was positive in both

Table 18.7: Independence of the Electoral Commission

	Percentage % Mampong	Effiduase-Asokore
Yes	30	27
No	62	30
Don't know	8	43
TOTAL	100	100

constituencies but more definite in Effiduase-Asokore (74%) than in Mampong (66%). On the reverse, 26% in Effiduase-Asokore compared to 34% felt the ruling party had a better chance of winning the presidential election. Similarly, respondents in Effiduase-Asokore were more confident (67%) than those in Mampong (57%) that there would be no second round presidential run-off.

On the issue whether parties in Ghana projected personalities more than their policies, a majority in both constituencies, 62% in Mampong and 61% in Effiduase-Asokore, disagreed. This also was not surprising since the NPP towards which most respondents had sympathies did not have domineering leaders to the same extent as Rawlings in the NDC. But on whether respondents would vote for the party, the candidate or both in the 2000 elections, the two constituencies expressed divergent views. In Mampong 14% declared their intention to vote for the party, 22% for the candidate and 53% for both party and candidate compared to 35%, 30% and 35% respectively in Effiduase-Asokore.

State financing of political parties became a major issue in Election 2000 following the introduction of the new political parties bill in parliament by the NDC government which ruled it out completely. One would therefore have expected that in both constituencies an overwhelming majority would support state funding of parties. But about 40% in both constituencies either said no or were undecided.

Evaluation of Running Mates

Apparently, one of the most highly contested issues in Election 2000 was the choice of running mates, particularly in the case of the NDC and the NPP.

The major consideration, according to media reports, were ethnic, regional and gender balance. Interestingly, these factors ranked far below party loyalty and experience as the most important in the choice of the presidential running mate in both constituencies. More than 75% in each constituencies favoured either party loyalty or experience. No respondent considered gender balance important. 95% in Mampong and 75% in Effiduase-Asokore were of the view that the choice of running mate would not affect their vote.

Election Issues

Respondents were asked to identify 3 main issues at national level in the 2000 Elections. In both constituencies the economy was overwhelmingly the most important (87% in Mampong and 95% in Effiduase-Asokore) with continuity and stability and change and development as very minor issues. This is a bit surprising for an election which was being fought by the two major parties on change whether progressive or positive. But the identification of the economy as the most important issue meant that those who had managed it over the years would suffer for it.

On the local front, respondents in Mampong identified education, employment and water as the three most important developmental needs while for Effiduase-Asokore theirs were water, education and markets.

The 7 December Election Results

Respondents in Mampong constituency had predicted 62% victory for the NPP in the presidential election with 21% for the NDC. For Effiduase-Asokore the predictions were 76% for the NPP and 13% for the NDC. Each constituency also expected the NPP parliamentary candidate to win: 65% in Mampong and 70% in Effiduase-Asokore. To what extent were these predictions reflected in the 7 December election results? J. A. Kufuor (NPP) won in both constituencies in the first round — 80.3% in Mampong and 76.8% in Effiduase-Asokore while for J. E. A. Mills (NDC), the respective percentage were 17.6% and 21.8% (Electoral Commission, 2000). For the parliamentary elections the results were as follows (see Tables 18.8 and 18.9). It is clear from the above that in each case the election had gone as predicted with victory for the NPP, but in Mampong the actual margin of victory had been higher in both the presidential and parliamentary elections than predicted. Thus the pre-election survey was more reflective in Effiduase-Asokore than in Mampong.

Table 18.8: Parliamentary Results 7 December 2000 — Mampong

Candidate	Party	Votes	Percentage %
Solomon K. Sarfoh	NPP	23,352	74.3
Elizabeth Nicol	NDC	6,286	20.0
Agyei A. Boasiako E. Y.	IND	618	2.0
Patrick K. A. Bonsu	CPP	594	1.9
Tahiru A. Kubi	NRP	264	0.8
Mohammed Issahaku	PNC	221	0.7
Owusu Sekyere	UGM	85	0.3

Source: EC: Parliamentary Results Data Sheet, 2000

Table 18:9: Parliamentary Election Results 7 December 2000— Effiduase-Asokore

Candidate	Party	Votes	Percentage %
Grace Coleman	NPP	13,954	71.2
Kwasi Amakye-Boateng	NDC	4,408	22.5
Osei Kwabena	CPP	729	3.7
Osei Addiya	NRP	246	1.3
Lovia Yeboah	PNC	235	1.2
Alfred O. Baah	UGM	35	0.2

Source: EC: Parliamentary Election Results, 2000

Presidential Run-off

The 28 December 2000 presidential run-off followed the pattern of the first round (see Table 18.10) except that J. A. Kufuor had only a 2% increase in Mampong compared to the 5% increase in Effiduase-Asokore.

Post Election Survey: Assessment of the Elections

It must be noted that the post-election survey was conducted in obviously changed circumstances. Respondents had already cast their votes and the election results had also been declared and they were therefore not as enthusiastic as in the pre-election survey.

Table 18.10: Results of December 2000 Presidential Run-off

	Mampong Vote	Percentage %	Effiduase-Asokore Vote	Percentage %
J. E. A. Mills (NDC)	5,064	16.1	3,677	18.6
J. A. Kufuor (NPP)	26,320	83.9	16,103	81.4

Source: EC: Presidential Run-off Results Data Sheet, 2000

Among other things, respondents were asked to express their views on whether or not the 2000 Elections had been free and fair and to show how long they had voted.

Freedom and Fairness of Election 2000

It is interesting to note that 99% in both constituencies said the 2000 elections had been generally free and fair and the only respondent, in each case, who was not positive was undecided. Respondents' reactions to the various ingredients of free and fair elections — media coverage, logistics, freedom to campaign, lack of intimidation etc. — were also equally interesting. 90% in Mampong and 95% in Effiduase-Asokore believed that all the parties had been given the chance to campaign freely but only 25% and 32% respectively agreed that all the parties had had adequate logistics to campaign. In a similar vein almost all respondents agreed that the coverage of the elections by the state print and electronic media was adequate, but a lower proportion believed that the coverage had been fair to all parties and candidates.

Party Preference in Election 2000

In the first round presidential election 92% in Mampong and 89% in Effiduase-Asokore claimed they had voted for the NPP and 5% and 6% respectively for the NDC. For the presidential run-off there were slight increases for the NPP. In the case of the parliamentary election 91% in Mampong and 82% in Effiduase-Asokore indicated they had voted NPP. The percentages are generally higher than the votes cast for the NPP but this should not be surprising given than success has many fathers while failure is an orphan.

Conclusion

It should be clear from the discussion so far that for the constituents in Mampong and Effiduase-Asokore nothing drastic had happened to force them to change their support for the Danquah-Busia tradition represented by the NPP. If anything, the deplorable economic situation in the country for which they blamed the ruling NDC strengthened their resolve to vote for change.

REFERENCES

Barker, J. S. "Political Space and the Quality of Participation in Rural Africa: A Case from Senegal", *Canadian Journal of African Studies*, Vol. 21, No. 1, 1987.

Manu, Yaw, "The 1996 Elections: Survey in the Sekyere West and Sekyere East District", in J. R. A. Ayee (ed.), *The 1996 General Elections and Democratic Consolidation in Ghana*, Department of Political Science, Accra, 1998: 479–485.

Oquaye, Mike, "Politics in Asante Mampong: A Study of the 1996 Elections", in J. R. A. Ayee (ed.), *The 1996 General Elections and Democratic Consolidation in Ghana*, Department of Political Science, Accra, 1998: 395–425.

Electoral Commission of Ghana Parliamentary Results — Election 2000, December, 2000.

Electoral Commission of Ghana — Presidential Run-off Results Data Sheet, December, 2000.

CHAPTER 19

A Comparative Analysis of Electoral Survey of Nkawkaw and Afram Plains South Constituencies in Ghana's Election 2000

A. KAAKYIRE DUKU FREMPONG

Introduction

Election 2000 occupied an important milestone in Ghana's political history. For the very first time, an elected head of state had completed his two terms and a new leader was to be elected to replace him, together with (also for the first time) the third parliament for the Fourth Republic. Added to this the outgoing President, J. J. Rawlings, had been on the political scene for almost two decades and for the most part as a military ruler. This raised speculation as to how Ghanaian voters would react to the situation and how the political fortunes of the various political parties would look like in the post-Rawlings era.

This gave an added impetus to the Department of Political Science, University of Ghana, supported by DANIDA, to continue its research project begun during the 1996 Elections aimed at identifying and explaining specific variables that impact on the Ghanaian voter's behaviour and how they enhance or inhibit democratic consolidation. The Department also expanded the scope of the research survey to cover 40 constituencies spread throughout the ten regions of the country, (compared to 27 constituencies in 1996).

This paper, an analysis of the findings of the research survey in the Nkawkaw and the Afram Plains-South Constituencies in the Eastern Region, then, is part of the wider research effort undertaken by the Department on Ghana's Election 2000.

The Election 2000 Project involved pre- and post-election surveys conducted in October 2000 and January 2001 respectively. In each constituency, a hundred questionnaires were administered for each of the pre- and post-election surveys, spread through both urban and rural parts of the constituency.

The Choice and Profiles of Constituencies

The choice of Nkawkaw and Afram Plains-South was deliberate if not strategic. Before 1988 both constituencies formed part of the former Kwahu District Council in the northern part of the Eastern Region. Today the former is in the Kwahu South District and the latter in the Afram Plains District. The very name of the latter district has been a major source of controversy and has to some extent influenced voting patterns in the two constituencies. In the two previous elections (1992 and 1996), the two constituencies had voted differently; while Afram Plains South was very supportive of the National Democratic Congress (NDC), Nkawkaw had pitched camp with the New Patriotic Party (NPP). For instance, in the 1996 presidential election the former had voted 84.7% for Rawlings (NDC) while for the latter it was 63.4% for J. A. Kufuor (NPP). In addition, Nkawkaw constituency had defied the Great Alliance's allocation of that constituency to the People's Convention Party (PCP) and voted the NPP candidate to parliament in 1996. Did either constituency have any cause to change its mind in 2000? Interestingly, the two constituencies are each close to the regional stronghold of the party it had supported — the Volta Region in the case of Afram Plains South and the Ashanti Region in the case of Nkawkaw. Again, the two constituencies had not featured in the previous election survey of the Political Science Department and therefore fulfilled the need to break new ground.

The profiles of the two constituencies also reveal further differences which justify a comparative study. The Nkawkaw Constituency, unlike the other two in the Kwahu South District (Abetifi and Mpraeso), which are largely on the Kwahu Mountains, lies in the low-lying areas of the district. It obtained its name from the constituency capital, Nkawkaw township, which is the only urban centre in the constituency and covers nine of the eighteen electoral areas. In addition, the villages making up five of the remaining nine electoral areas lie along or close to the main Accra-Kumasi highway making the constituency one of the most accessible in the Eastern Region.[1] The Nkawkaw Constituency shares borders with the Mpraeso, Abetifi, Atiwa and Birim North Constituencies, all in the Eastern Region, and Asante-Akim South in Ashanti Region.

The population is made up of largely native Kwahus who form about 66% (Nkansa-Kyeremateng, 2000: 28). This fact was amply demonstrated in the backgrounds of the five Election 2000 parliamentary candidates, four of whom were native Kwahus.[2] The main occupation is trading in the constituency capital and farming in the rural areas. Nkawkaw had 50,057 registered voters for the 2000 Elections (Electoral Commission, 2000).

For its part, Afram Plains South and its northern counterpart form the two constituencies in the Afram Plains District. Located in the northernmost part of the Eastern Region, the Afram Plains South Constituency is not as accessible as Nkawkaw. The main entrance to the constituency is by a very rough road from the Kwahu South District through Kwaku Tafo to Kwahu Adawso where the three-kilometre-wide Afram River is crossed by ferry to Ekye-Amanfrom, the only other rural-urban settlement, in addition to Tease, the constituency capital.[3] The electoral areas are broad with scattered villages and hamlets and largely inaccessible roads.[4] Some of the settlements are 'overseas' and are accessible only by motor-boats (crucial in the elections). Afram Plains South shares borders with constituencies, which are in Eastern, Ashanti, Brong Ahafo and Volta Regions.

The constituency, (in fact the whole district), traditionally belongs to Kwahus but it is also an important migrant destination for people from the Volta, Ashanti, Brong Ahafo, Northern and Upper Regions. The background of the parliamentary candidates for Election 2000 reflected the settler nature of the area. Among the four candidates was a Kwahu, an Anum, a Krachi and a Northerner from Navrongo.[5] The population is also male dominant with 53% males and 47% females (Profile of Afram Plains). Being one of the major breadbaskets of the country, most of the people are engaged in farming. For Election 2000, the Afram Plains South Constituency had a voter population of 29,786 (Electoral Commission, 2000).

Profile of Respondents

Gender

Of the 100 respondents interviewed in the pre-election survey from each of the two constituencies, 58% were males and 42% females in the Nkawkaw Constituency while 64% were males and 36% females in the Afram Plain South Constituency. For the post-election survey the corresponding figures were 59% and 41% respectively for Nkawkaw and 67% and 33% for Afram Plains South. This is clear evidence of a dominance of male respondents even though the surveys had given equal opportunities to both sexes. This was

---

* Except otherwise indicated, the data provided in this book are taken from the Department of Political Science 2000 Elections survey.

because in both constituencies many women preferred to defer to their husbands or male relations. The relatively higher number of female respondents in the Nkawkaw constituency was because of the cosmopolitan nature of the constituency capital — the Nkawkaw township. In Afram Plains South, there was the added factor that the population is male-dominated.

Age Distribution

The age distribution for the two surveys indicated 56% between 18 and 40 years; 34% in the 41–60 years bracket and 10% of 61 years and more, in Nkawkaw. In Afram Plains, the respective percentages were 62%, 35% and 3%. Though there was no significant difference between the two constituencies, the relatively lower percentage of those over 61 years in Afram Plains South was indicative of the fact that it was the abled-bodied who migrated to the area in search of work.

Educational Qualification

On the educational qualification of respondents 11% and 5% reported that they had not had any schooling in the Nkawkaw and the Afram Plains South constituencies respectively. This would seem strange given the background of the two constituencies. The fact however is that, in the latter constituency, many of those who had not been formally educated were very suspicious of the survey exercise and declined to be interviewed. Of those who had attended school over 30% had had primary education, over 20% secondary level and less than 10% a higher or post secondary education, in both constituencies.

Occupation

According to the survey data only a small number of interviewees in both constituencies, reported they were unemployed, while the rest were in gainful employment of various kinds. More revealing was the fact that 38% of respondents in Nkawkaw were traders and 39% in Afram Plain South were teachers (see Table 19.1). The situation in Nkawkaw confirms Kwahus' traditional flair for trading and Nkawkaw as the main marketing centre in the District. On the other hand, the situation in Afram Plains South was indicative that in a more rural setting, teachers still hold prominence as opinion leaders.

Table 19.1: Occupation of Respondents

	Percentage % Nkawkaw	Afram Plains South
Unemployment	4	6
Teacher	17	39
Businessman	6	4
Manager	–	–
Professional	12	6
Farmer	11	13
Trader	38	11
Artisan	10	11
Public Servant	1	6
Other (Specify)	1	4
TOTAL	100	100

Income

Most respondents particularly in Nkawkaw were not willing to declare their annual incomes. As many as 58% of respondents in Nkawkaw did not declare their income claiming they did not know. But given that a majority of them were traders, their reluctance had to do with the bitter experiences they had during the revolutionary era when some of them had been harassed for 'kalabule'. Of those who indicated their incomes 31% earned less than five million *cedis*, 11% between five and ten million and none beyond 10 million *cedis*. In the case of Afram Plains South, 76% were below five million *cedis* per annum, 6% between five and ten million *cedis* and 18 percent did not declare their incomes.

Religion

Of the respondents who indicated their religion, more than 85% in both cases were Christians. 12% and 9% respectively in Nkawkaw and Afram Plains South were Muslims and 3% in each case belonged to African traditional religions.

Pre-election Political Participation

All respondents in both constituencies were registered voters but a large proportion of them, 81% in Nkawkaw and 69% in Afram Plains South were not registered members of any political party. The major reason for this phenomenon was that for personal reasons they did not like partisan politics (50% and 53% respectively for Nkawkaw and Afram Plains South). However respondents showed their inclination towards the various parties (see Table 19.2).

Table 19.2: Respondents Inclination towards various Political Parties

	Percentage % Nkawkaw	Afram Plains South
CPP	8	1
NDC	10	19
PNC	1	4
UGM	–	–
GCPP	–	2
NPP	57	47
EGLE	–	–
NRP	2	7
DPP	2	–
Don't know	20	20
TOTAL	100	100

While the 57% inclination in Nkwakaw towards the NPP was in line with the party's performance in the 1996 Elections, there seemed to be a drastic shift from the NDC (19%) towards the NPP (47%) in Afram Plains South. Whether or not this would reflect in the actual election will be discussed later.

It is also worth noting that 64% and 65% of respondents in Nkawkaw and Afram Plains South had predicted victory for the NPP as compared to 14% and 15% respectively in the presidential election. For the parliamentary elections it was 63% for NPP and 13% for the NDC in Nkawkaw and 69% and 11% for the NDC in Afram Plains South.

The apparent apathy towards membership of political parties did not so much affect their desire to vote. Most respondents (95% in Nkawkaw and 83% in Afram Plains South) had voted in the 1996 parliamentary and presidential elections and for those who didn't vote, the major reason was that they had not attained the voting age. Most of them also indicated their willingness to vote in the 2000 Elections (see Table 19.3).

Table 19.3: Frequency Distribution of Respondents Willing to Vote in the 2000 Elections

	Percentage % Nkawkaw	Afram Plains South
Yes	99	97
No	1	1
Don't know	–	2
TOTAL	100	100

Their participation in political rallies in connection with the 2000 Elections however remained low in both cases: 34% in Nkawkaw and 23% in Afram Plains South. In both cases the major reason was that most of the parties had not held rallies in their area at the time of the survey. However 95% in Nkawkaw and 84% in Afram Plains South admitted they followed the activities of the various parties through the news media.

Voter Perception of the Economy

According to the survey data most respondents were not happy with the economy. 66% in Nkawkaw and 79% in Afram Plains South felt the state of the Ghanaian economy was in very bad shape (see Table 19.4); 82% and 89% respectively felt the economy had either become worse or sharply deteriorated over the last four years (see Table 19.5); and 78% and 80% respectively felt their standard of living had become worse since the previous election (see Table 19.6). The three most important economic problems in Ghana according to respondents in Nkawkaw were unemployment, inflation and depreciation of the *cedi*. For Afram Plains South the order was depreciation of the *cedi*, inflation and unemployment (see Table 19.7).

Table 19.4: Respondents' Perception of the State of the Ghanaian Economy

	Percentage % Nkawkaw	Afram Plains South
Very good	3	–
Good	5	3
Bad	15	12
Very bad	66	79
Neither good or bad	18	6
Don't know	3	–
TOTAL	100	100

Table 19.5: Trend of the Ghanaian Economy over the last Four Years

	Percentage % Nkawkaw	Afram Plains South
Considerably improved	4	2
Just improved	11	6
Become worse	50	68
Sharply deteriorated	32	21
Don't know	3	3
TOTAL	100	100

Table 19.6: Respondent's Household Standard of Living since last Elections

	Percentage % Nkawkaw	Afram Plains South
Much better	5	7
A little better	14	13
A little worse	19	23
Much worse	59	57
Don't know	3	–
TOTAL	100	100

Table 19.7: Major Economic Problem in Ghana

	Percentage %	
	Nkawkaw	Afram Plains South
Inflation	25	34
Competition from cheap imports	2	–
High interest rates	5	–
Unemployment	28	23
Lack of private investments	3	5
Depreciation of the cedi	24	36
Other	9	–
Don't know	4	2
TOTAL	100	100

Evaluation of the Democratic Process

Respondents were called upon to opine whether or not Ghana could be characterized as a democratic country. In Nkawkaw opinion was evenly split. 48% were positive, 45% negative and 7% were undecided. But in Afram Plains South 68% said Yes, 25%, No and 7% did not know. As to whether or not democracy had improved in Ghana during the previous four years 51% in Nkawkaw and 44% in Afram Plains South were positive as against 39% and 54% respectively in the two constituencies. While 10% were undecided in Nkawkaw it was only 2% in Afram Plains South. It is clear from the above that on the two-fold issue of democracy, opinions in Nkawkaw were more evenly split than in Afram Plains South.

Respondents were further asked to state their views on some of the factors that either facilitate or hinder democratization in Ghana. A larger proportion in Nkawkaw were not in doubt that the media, political parties and other associations were freer to operate and express their opinion than there had been in the past four years compared to Afram Plains South where opinions were more evenly split (see Tables 19.8a & b).

Evaluation of Electoral Process

Only a quarter and a third of respondents in Nkawkaw and Afram Plains South respectively felt the 1996 General Elections had been free and fair;

more than half in both cases felt they had not been; while 20% and 14% respectively could not give an opinion (see Table 19.9).

Among the major reasons given for the unfairness of the elections were vote rigging in certain polling stations, multiple voting, intimidation, threats voting by minors, the demand by the Electoral Commission for security before

Table 19.8a: More Media Freedom

	Percentage % Nkawkaw	Afram Plains South
Yes	65	48
No	24	50
Don't know	11	2
TOTAL	100	100

Table 19.8b: More Associational Freedom

	Percentage % Nkawkaw	Afram Plains South
Yes	75	49
No	16	48
Don't know	9	3
TOTAL	100	100

Table 19.9: Freedom and Fairness of 1996 Elections

	Percentage % Nkawkaw	Afram Plains South
Yes	23	34
No	57	52
Don't know	20	14
TOTAL	100	100

announcing results and non-collation of votes. On the other hand, those who said the elections had been free said nothing untoward happened in their areas.

Asked whether conditions existed for free and fair elections for the 7 December 2000 elections respondents in Nkawkaw were almost equally divided on the issue: 39% were positive, 29% negative and 32% were undecided. For Afram Plains South the corresponding percentages were 45%, 39% and 16%. This means that in both constituencies there was more confidence in the possible freedom and fairness of the 2000 elections than those of 1996. The 26% in Nkawkaw and 39% in Afram Plains South who responded negatively, indicated among other things that the voters' register was bloated, the NDC had more resources than the other parties, the Electoral Commission was not cooperative or trustworthy and the NDC was noted for its tricks and riggings.

The negative perception of the Electoral Commission was confirmed in both constituencies when respondent were asked if they thought the Commission was independent of government control. Fifty-eight per cent and 64% in Nkawkaw and Afram Plains South respectively said it was not; 16% and 18% answered yes but 26% and 18% respectively were undecided (see Table 19.10). On the other hand, the two constituencies had divergent perception of their respective district electoral offices. About two thirds of the respondents in Nkawkaw were not decided whether the district office had been fair to all parties or not. But in Afram Plains South 44% were positive that the district office had been fair (see Table 19.11).

A fairly significant proportion of respondents (25% and 35% in Nkawkaw and Afram Plains South) believed that apart from the Electoral

Table 19.10: Independence of Electoral Commission from Governmental Control

	Percentage % Nkawkaw	Afram Plains South
Yes	16	18
No	58	64
Don't know	26	18
TOTAL	100	100

Table 19.11: Perception of fairness of District Electoral Office

	Percentage % Nkawkaw	Afram Plains South
Yes	23	44
No	13	24
Don't know	64	32
TOTAL	100	100

Commission there were other ways of manipulating elections. These included incumbency advantage, use of ghost names, buying of voter identity cards and bribing party agents. While these respondents supported the opposition parties' fears of possible election rigging, there was an even more significant proportion, 38% in both constituencies who did not believe in the above rigging tools and another 37% and 26% in Nkawkaw and Afram Plains South respectively who had no opinion.

Evaluation of the Party System

Respondents were asked to assess the chances of an opposition party winning the presidential election against the ruling party (see Tables 19.12 and 19.13).

Table 19.12: Chances of an Opposition Party Winning the Presidential Election

	Percentage % Nkawkaw	Afram Plains South
Very Good	53	69
Good	12	8
Not so good	17	22
Don't know	18	1
TOTAL	100	100

Table 19.13: Chances of the Ruling Party Retaining the Presidency

	Percentage % Nkawkaw	Afram Plains South
Very Good	12	20
Good	10	9
Not so good	56	62
Don't know	22	9
TOTAL	100	100

The response from Afram Plains South to the twofold issue above was particularly interesting for a constituency which in 1996 had given 84.7% of its votes to the ruling party (Electoral Commission, 1997). According to the survey an overwhelming 77% felt an opposition party had at least a good chance of winning the presidential election (see Table 19.12). On the other hand, the corresponding response for the ruling party was only 29% (see Table 19.13). Was the ruling party going to lose one of its strongholds in the Eastern Region? For Nkawkaw, a constituency which gave 63.4% of its votes to the leading opposition candidate in 1996 (Electoral Commission, 1997), its response of 65% for the opposition (see Table 19:12) and 22% for the ruling party (see Table 19.13) was very normal.

In response to whether it was more likely to have a second round presidential run-off in the 2000 Elections than in 1996, almost half in each constituency said no, while about a fifth were undecided (see Table 19.14).

Table 19.14: Possibility of a Presidential Run-off

	Percentage % Nkawkaw	Afram Plains South
Yes	33	34
No	49	49
Don't know	18	17
TOTAL	100	100

Of the third in both constituencies who felt a run-off was more likely, their major reason was that the number of parties contesting the election had increased.[6] As it turned out, it was the minority which predicted correctly.

Scholars have noted that political parties in post-independence Ghana, when allowed to operate, have as a whole, revolved around personalities more than policies (Chazan, 1983: 95–105, Chazan *et. al.*, 1992: 161–182 and Drah, 1998: 499). But in the survey for Nkawkaw and Afram Plains South the two constituencies had divergent views. 33% in Nkawkaw felt parties in Ghana projected personalities more than their policies, with 50% against and 17% undecided (see Table 19.15). In Afram Plains South, a significant 58% agreed to the assertion, 33% opposed it and only 9% were undecided (see Table 19.15).

Table 19.15: Political Parties: Personalities over Policies?

	Percentage % Nkawkaw	Afram Plains South
Yes	33	58
No	50	33
Don't know	17	9
TOTAL	100	100

The divergence of views should not be surprising since Nkawkaw in the previous elections had supported the New Patriotic Party (NPP) in which there was no dominant father-figure as Rawlings was in the National Democratic Congress (NDC), which had controlled Afram Plains South in 1992 and 1996.

Interestingly, however, the majority in each constituency declared their intention to vote for both the party and the candidate in both the presidential and parliamentary elections in 2000. In both instances, Nkawkaw was more insistent than Afram Plains South on this middle road (see Tables 19.16 and 19.17).

One major issue of debate since the 1996 elections has been state funding of political parties. In 1992 the Interim National Electoral Commission (INEC) had shared a number of Niva vans among the contesting parties, but this assistance had been withdrawn in 1996. More significant of the 1996

Table 19.16: Voter Preference for Party or Candidate: Presidential

	Percentage % Nkawkaw	Afram Plains South
The party	8	22
Both party and candidate	73	52
The candidate	16	20
Don't know	3	6
TOTAL	100	100

Table 19.17: Voter Preference for Party or Candidate: Parliamentary

	Percentage % Nkawkaw	Afram Plains South
The party	6	12
Both party and candidate	71	51
The candidate	19	28
Don't know	4	9
TOTAL	100	100

Elections were the "gravy-train" of the ruling NDC and the penury of the opposition parties.

Against this background, it was interesting that more than sixty percent of respondents in both constituencies agreed that most parties in Ghana were not financially sound (see Table 19.18). Quite surprising however was that more respondents in the NDC stronghold of the Afram Plains South (70%) supported state financing of political parties than the NPP controlled Nkawkaw constituency (56%) (see Table 19.19).

Respondents were invited to express opinions on their party's choice of parliamentary candidate and the mode of his/her selection. Tables 19.20 and 19.21 indicate the responses to the two issues in the two constituencies.

It is clear from the above data that most respondents in both constituencies liked their parties' parliamentary candidates, but on the mode of selec-

Table 19.18: The Financial Soundness of most Political Parties

	Percentage % Nkawkaw	Afram Plains South
Yes	17	27
No	68	64
Don't know	15	9
TOTAL	100	100

Table 19.19: State Financing of Political Parties

	Percentage % Nkawkaw	Afram Plains South
Yes	56	70
No	39	30
Don't know	5	–
TOTAL	100	100

Table 19.20: Likeability of Party's Parliamentary Candidate

	Percentage % Nkawkaw	Afram Plains South
Yes	72	77
No	4	14
Don't know	24	9
TOTAL	100	100

tion they were not so sure. Of respondents from Afram Plains South Fifty one per cent said the process had been democratic but 48% did not know because they were not privy to the process of selection. Most of those who saw the process as democratic indicated that their candidate was declared unopposed at primaries. This researcher has the feeling that candidate selection has not been made open enough to the rank and file of the various parties.

Table 19.21: Mode of Selection of Party's Parliamentary Candidate

	Percentage %	
	Nkawkaw	Afram Plains South
Democratic	51	68
Not democratic	1	14
Don't know	48	18
TOTAL	100	100

Election Issues

National

Respondents were asked to identify 3 main issues at national level in the 2000 elections and in both constituencies the economy overwhelmingly topped the list with change and development and change and stability almost non-issues (see Table 19.22). This might seem surprising in an election in which change (whether progressive or positive) was the main slogan of the leading political parties. It was clear, however, that the group which had supervised the economy was going to pay for the economic downturn. While improving democracy did not feature in Nkawkaw it was the second major issue in Afram Plains South.

In the course of the survey, the research team discovered a number of issues which though apparently local had somewhat national dimensions and sought the views of various groups on them. These included:

- the refusal of the Kwahu chiefs to hold a durbar as requested by their DCE to welcome the Vice President on the excuse that he was an NDC presidential candidate and that the 1992 Constitution debars chiefs from involving themselves in partisan politics.
- The call of the Kwahu chiefs for the government to rename the Afram Plains District, the Kwahu North District. This was itself a manifestation of the conflict between the Kwahu landowners and the settlers in the Afram Plains.
- The deplorable state of the Afram Plains District even though the government adopted the Afram Plains name ostensibly to attract development.

Table 19.22: Main National Issues

	Percentage % Nkawkaw	Afram Plains South
The Economy	93	86
Continuity and stability	2	2
Change and development	5	3
Ghana's future in the 21st Century	-	3
Improving democracy	-	6
TOTAL	100	100

Responses to the "non partisanship" issue were varied in the Nkawkaw Constituency. The NDC constituency executive at a focus group discussion with this researcher reserved its comment on the issue. But to the chairperson of the National Reform Party (NRP) who had defected from the NDC, the chiefs' attitude was confrontational and it was not good for anybody or group to be seen to be at daggers drawn with the government of the day. On the other hand, the NPP parliamentary candidate was full of praise for the Kwahu chiefs for the singular act of departing from the sycophancy of other chiefs elsewhere in the country. For his part, the CPP candidate, an Accra newspaper editor whose paper had earlier commended the Kwahu chiefs (*The Ghanaian Chronicle*, 21–22 August 2000, p.5), said it was the right of a people to stand up and defend the Constitution. Other respondents offered a historical dimension — how in the AFRC days, Chairman Rawlings at a durbar of chiefs held in his honour, at Nkawkaw, reportedly insulted the chiefs for their alleged involvement in "Kalabule".

Opinion was also divided in Nkawkaw over the issue of renaming Afram Plains. The NPP and the CPP saw the demand of the Kwahu chiefs, the traditional owners of the area, as a legitimate one to help them assert their authority in response the various attempts to take over their lands by settlers. But the NDC and NRP felt the renaming was not necessary and that the current name was strategic enough to attract development from foreign source.

Respondents in Afram Plains South claimed that the most important thing to them was long-awaited development and that they did not care about names. However there were tell-tale signs among the Ewe settlers particularly, who have given Ewe names to their villages, that the demand by the Kwahu chiefs was meant to drive them out.

Local

The data on local needs reveal a number of surprises. Nkawkaw, a very accessible constituency, had a good road network on top of its list while the very inaccessible Afram Plains South recorded only 6% for a good road network, even lower than KVIPs. In the case of Nkawkaw, the road net work within the township was in very deplorable state particularly the one linking the main lorry station to the Holy Family Hospital. Similarly, the feeder roads linking those settlements which are not along the main Accra-Kumasi main roads are also not good. But admittedly they were not as bad as those of Afram Plains. To the latter, it seemed they had waited for far too long for good roads. It is interesting also that though very close to the Volta Lake and also surrounded by the Afram and Oti rivers potable water was still a more serious problem in the Afram Plains South constituency.

The greatest local need in the Afram Plains South constituency was education (see Table 19.23). Not only are schools few and far apart but they are also dilapidated and ill-equipped. School children, sometimes encouraged by the poverty of their parents, found farming, trading and fishing more profitable than schooling. Post-harvest losses and lack of security were also some local problems. The only police station which is at Tease, the constituency capital, was without a vehicle.

Focus group discussion in Nkawkaw also revealed other interesting local issues. There was a general demand for the creation of a new district out of Kwahu South with Nkawkaw as the district capital. Among the reasons given were that:

- The Kwahu South District was among the largest in the country and as a result its share of the District Assembly Common Fund was inadequate for the development of the area.
- The low-lying condition of Nkawkaw with its environs makes it geographically distinct from the areas on the Kwahu Mountains.
- The constituency is larger in size than the nearby New Abirem District which also doubles as the Birim North constituency.

Table 19.23: Main Development Issues in the Constituency

	Percentage % Nkawkaw	Afram Plains South
Market	2	5
Water	6	21
Toilet (KVIP)	3	12
Good road network	34	6
Education	18	34
Hospital bills/Hospital/Clinic/ Health center	3	6
Low salary/poverty	3	3
Electricity	6	5
Street/security lights	5	–
Telecom/Post office/ Radio stations	1	–
Sanitation	5	3
Employment	14	5
TOTAL	100	100

Another strand in this issue was that at least the district capital should be moved from Mpraeso to Nkawkaw which is the most cosmopolitan in the district.

In addition, there was a demand for the establishment of more second cycle institutions in the constituency. Nkawkaw Secondary School remains the only one in the constituency whereas the two other constituencies in the District — Abetifi and Mpraeso share between them about ten.

Furthermore the allocation of stores and stalls in the Nkawkaw market had been a source of conflict between the DCE and the president of the Market Men's and Women's Association who happened to be the NPP constituency Vice-Chairman.

Evaluation of Running Mates

In the 2000 Election, the choice of running mates particularly for the NDC and the NPP became a major electoral issue perhaps far more contested than the choice of the presidential candidates. Among the major considerations were ethnic, regional or gender balance. Respondents were asked to comment on some of these. Table 19.24 indicates what respondents considered the most important factor in the choice of a presidential running mate.

Table 19.24: Most Important Factor in Choice of Running Mate

	Percentage %	
	Nkawkaw	*Afram Plains South*
Ethnic background	12	3
Regional balance	14	6
Gender balance	–	–
Experience	43	69
Party loyalty	28	19
Other	3	3
TOTAL	100	100

It is significant that in both constituencies, experience and party loyalty (71% in Nkawkaw and 88% in Afram Plains South) emerged stronger than ethnic and regional balance (26% in Nkawkaw and 9% in Afram Plains South) which seemed to be the dominant issues on the media landscape. Was it that those issues were media hype or the respondents were cautious enough not to be associated with them? It is also clear that respondents in both constituencies were not ready for a female veep.

On the more specific question whether or not it was important to have a regional balance on the presidential ticket, opinion was far more evenly balanced in Nkawkaw than in Afram Plains South. 42% and 37% respectively said yes; 35% and 12% felt it did not matter; 21% and 33% said no;

while 2% and 18% were undecided. A similar pattern also existed for ethnic balance (see Table 19.25).

Table 19.25: Need for Ethnic Balance of Presidential Ticket

	Percentage % Nkawkaw	Afram Plains South
Yes	34	28
Doesn't matter	30	19
No	31	43
Don't know	5	10
TOTAL	100	100

On the whole 91% in Nkawkaw and 85% in Afram Plains South felt that the choice of the presidential running mate would not affect the party they would vote for.

Media

Asked from which source they received most of their information about issues and candidates in the election, most (46% in Nkawkaw and 40% in Afram Plains South) indicated television, followed by radio (24% and 35% respectively). On the other hand, most respondents found radio (44% in Nkawkaw and 45% in Afram Plains South) most useful in deciding whom to vote for in the constituency as compared to 12% and 31% respectively for television. However, most of them found the private radio and private newspapers (56% in Nkawkaw and 51% in Afram Plains South) as most likely to tell the truth.

In the Nkawkaw Constituency a local FM station, Life FM, was educating the populace through its programme "PLATFORM" which allowed aspirants to present their visions and responded to phone-ins from the electorate. The constituency also benefitted from electoral programmes conducted by FM stations in both Kumasi and Accra. A popular one was the "HARD BALL" programme by FOX FM in Kumasi on Saturday evenings.

On the other hand, there was no local FM station in the Afram Plains South constituency but the electorate had access to Volta FM in Ho and FOX FM in Kumasi.

The 7 December 2000 Presidential and Parliamentary Results

It is necessary to examine the presidential and parliamentary results of 7 December 2000 to see the extent to which they matched with or deviated from the views expressed in the pre-election survey. Tables 19.26–19.28 show that the two dominant parties, NDC and NPP retained their control of the Afram Plains South and Nkawkaw respectively in both the parliamentary and presidential elections. It would seem nothing had changed since the previous elections; a few points are however worth noting:

- The parliamentary results in Nkawkaw returned the incumbent NPP candidate with a higher percentage (64.9%) over 1996 (52.1%) and in line with the pre-election survey prediction of 64%.
- The NPP presidential candidate obtained a higher percentage in Nkawkaw (71.1%) in 2000 than in 1996 (63.4%). The pre-election survey had predicted a 64% victory for the NPP.
- The parliamentary results in Afram Plains South returned the incumbent NDC candidate but with a smaller percentage (46.1%) compared to (53.2%) in 1996. This deviates from the pre-election survey which had predicted victory for the NPP.
- In Afram Plains South, the Independent parliamentary candidate, a defector from the NDC, performed better (30.6%) than the NPP candidate (13.7%).
- The NDC presidential candidate won in Afram Plains South with a smaller percentage (69.4%) than in 1996 (84.7%). This deviated from the pre-election survey which had predicted a 65% victory for the NPP.

It can thus be inferred that in both parliamentary and presidential elections, the pre-election survey was confirmed in Nkawkaw but not in Afram Plains South. This might be because the survey in Nkawkaw covered most of the 18 electoral areas while in Afram Plains South the 'overseas' areas could not be reached. In fact among the political parties the NDC was the only one with a motor boat to campaign in those areas.

However, the reduced percentages in the NDC's victory in both cases in the Afram Plains South is indicative of the general yearning for change. In fact, the 15% reduction in the NDC's presidential vote in Afram Plains South compares favourably with the 12% national average. The fear of the settler chiefs of losing the lands they occupied also remained a major issue in the voting pattern in the Afram Plains.

Table 19.26: Presidential Results 7 December 2000

		Percentage % Nkawkaw	Afram Plains South
Dan Lartey	GCPP	0.7	1.9
J. E. A. Mills	NDC	25.5	69.4
George Hagan	CPP	1.0	0.7
E. N. Mahama	PNC	0.9	1.8
C. Wereko-Brobbey	UGM	0.1	0.5
Goosie Tanoh	NRP	0.7	2.3
J. A. Kufuor	NPP	71.1	23.3

Source: EC: Presidential Results Data Sheet, 2000

Table 19.27: Parliamentary Results — Nkawkaw 7 December 2000

		Votes	Percentage %
K. A. Okerchiri	NPP	20,481	64.9
W. K. Agyare	NDC	8,574	27.2
E. K. Antwi	CPP	1,716	5.4
E. O. Aboagye	NRP	456	1.4
T. S. Basuri	PNC	314	0.1

Source: EC: Parliamentary Results Data Sheet, 2000

Table 19.28: Parliamentary Results — Afram Plains South 7 December 2000

		Votes	Percentage %
Kwakye Addo	NDC	7,011	46.1
Anthony Adongo	IND	4,660	30.6
John A. Amponsah	NPP	2,079	13.7
Anthony Mensah	NRP	1,459	9.6

Source: EC: Parliamentary Results Data Sheet, 2000

Presidential Run-off

A second presidential ballot between the two leading contestants became necessary three weeks from the 7 December 2000 elections when none of the presidential candidates could gain more than 50% of the votes cast nationwide. The front runner, J. A. Kufuor of the NPP had 47.3% and the runner up, J. E. A. Mills of the NDC had 44.8%. Table 19.29 presents the results of the presidential run-off in Nkawkaw and Afram Plains South.

Table 19.29: Results of 28 December 2000 Presidential Run-off

	Nkawkaw Vote	Percentage %	Afram Plains South Vote	Percentage %
J. E. A. Mills (NDC)	6,452	21.2	10,328	68.3
J. A. Kufuor (NPP)	23,925	78.8	4,800	31.7

Source: EC: Presidential Run-off Results Data Sheet, 2000

The presidential run-off results in the two constituencies followed closely the 7 December presidential results except that there was a 7.7% and 7.4% increase in Kufuor votes in Nkawkaw and Afram Plains South respectively. On the other hand, Mills lost 4.3% and 1.1% respectively in both constituencies. This reflected the national trend and was due in part to the support the other political parties give to the NPP.

Post Election Survey: Assessment of the Elections

In the second survey, respondents were given an opportunity to express their views on whether or not the 2000 general elections had been free and fair and to show how they had voted.

Free and Fair Elections

When asked whether they thought the 2000 elections had been generally free and fair, a large proportion (88% in Nkawkaw and 85% in Afram Plains South) were positive. But on the specific ingredients of free and fair elections — media coverage, logistics, freedom to campaign, lack of intimidation, etc.

— respondents were not always so sure. While 76% in Nkawkaw and 86% in Afram Plains South believed all parties had been given the chance to campaign freely in 2000, only 21% and 33% respectively agreed that all the parties had adequate logistics for campaigning.

Similarly, 80% and 77% in Nkawkaw and Afram Plains South agreed that the coverage of the elections by the state print and electronic media had been adequate; a smaller proportion 52% and 59% respectively believed the coverage had been fair to all the parties and candidates. Again, while 29% in Nkawkaw and 49% in Afram Plains South said some party members and supporters had been intimidated by others during the election campaigns only 6% and 8% respectively had felt intimidated at the polling stations. While 21% and 24% in Nkawkaw found the NPP and NDC respectively guilty of intimidation in the Afram Plains South it was higher for the NDC (43%) than for the NPP (12%). A particular incident of electoral violation is worth considering in some details because of its implications for future elections in Ghana. In the 28 December run-off, a group of people reportedly thugs of the NDC disrupted voting in one of the polling stations in the rural area of the Nkawkaw constituency when they took a ballot box containing thumb-printed ballot papers and made away with it in a Nissan Pickup. Six people including the NDC parliamentary candidate were tried recently and two of them — the driver of the vehicle and the ward chairman — have been jailed for two years each and the vehicle confiscated to the state and handed over to the Kwahu South District Assembly for use. The others, including the parliamentary candidate were, however, acquitted and discharged for lack of evidence (Ghanaian Chronicle, 5 July 2001, p.5).

Party preference in the 2000 Elections

In the 7 December vote in Nkawkaw, 54%, claimed to have voted for the NPP in the presidential election, 41% for NDC, 2% for CPP and 0% for the PNC. In Afram Plains South, surprisingly 71% indicated supporting the NPP, 25% for NDC, 3% for PNC and 0% for CPP. For the parliamentary election 54% voted NPP and 43% NDC in Nkawkaw while 62% and 27% respectively said they had voted NPP and NDC.

A similar pattern emerged from the response to the presidential run-off. 41% and 56% in both Nkawkaw and Afram Plains South indicated they had voted for Mills and Kufuor respectively. The situation on the ground (as earlier shown) however differed markedly in the case of Afram Plains South.

There seemed to be reluctance on the part of some respondents in Afram Plains South to reveal how they truly voted. The NPP had been declared winners before the post-election survey, it had therefore become more fashionable and/or safer to be seen to be part of the winning side.

It is interesting to note that in both constituencies, almost all of those who voted Kufuor claimed it was because he represented change. For those who voted Mills it was either they thought he was a better candidate or it was for the sake of continuity.

Conclusion

A few conclusions emerge from the foregoing discussions. First, the results in the parliamentary, presidential and the presidential run-off elections were consistent in Nkawkaw with the pre-election prediction in the election survey. The study had predicted a victory for the NPP in each case but its share of the votes was far higher than predicted. Second, though the results from Afram Plains South seemed to contradict the survey prediction, these were in line with the national trend which gave the NDC a smaller percentage vote even when it won. Third, the 2000 elections in both constituencies were considered generally free and fair.

NOTES

1. This accessibility allowed the research survey to be conducted in sixteen out of the eighteen electoral areas in the constituency.
2. The four native parliamentary candidates were William Kwasi Agyare (NDC), Kwabena Adusa Okerchiri (NPP), Eben Kesse Antwi (CPP), and Eugene Osei Aboagye (NRP) only Tatiga Samspson Basuri (PNC) was a Northerner.
3. Both settlements have a population of less than 5000.
4. Because of inaccessibility, the survey was restricted to only six electoral areas out of the 22.
5. The candidates were Kwakye Addo (NDC) — Kwahu; Anthony Adongo (IND) — Northerner; John Addo Amponsah — Anum and Anthony Mensah — Krachi.
6. Compared to 1996 when there were only three presidential candidates in 2000 there were seven.

REFERENCES

Chazan, N. (1983) *An Anatomy of Ghanaian Politics: 1969–1982*, Westview Press, Boulder.

Chazan, *et. al.*, eds. (1992) *Politics and Society in Contemporary Africa*, Lynne Rienner Publishers, Boulder.

Drah, Francis K. (1998), "The 1996 Elections and Democratisation: A Case Study of Okaikoi", in J. R. A. Ayee (ed.), *The 1996 General Elections and Democratic Consolidation in Ghana*, Department of Political Science, Accra.

Nkansah-Kyeremateng, K., (2000) *Kwahu Handbook*, Trade Power Agency, Accra.

CHAPTER 20

Ghana 2000 Elections — A Survey of Asunafo North and Tano North Constituencies

PAUL AGBEDOR

Introduction

The 2000 General Elections in Ghana were very remarkable in the history of Ghana. In the first place, it was the first time in the history of Ghana that a civilian government had ruled for a two-year term and there was going to be a change of leadership through the ballot box. Secondly, the economic situation at the time was so explosive that people were agitating for a change. It was therefore necessary to find out what the majority of the people thought about the situation at the time, and to find out their expectations in the 2000 elections. According to Shiveley (1997: 183), elections are not meant only to bolster support for a regime; they are also the means by which leaders and policies are chosen by the people. The pre-election survey was designed to find out what the people had to say about the existing regime and its policies. The post-election survey sought to find out whether or not the expectations and reactions of the people during the pre-election survey had been met.

The two constituencies, Asunafo North and Tano North were selected because of their strategic positions in the Brong-Ahafo Region. The region is made up of Ahafo and Brong groups. The Ahafos are believed to be Ashantis, and most of them regard themselves as Ashantis. The Ashantis are believed to be predominantly NPP, while Brong-Ahafo was mixed. The two constituencies are on the boundary with the Brong side of the region. It was therefore deemed necessary to find out the party allegiance of the Ahafo side and compare that with the Brong side.

A total of one hundred respondents were randomly selected from five electoral areas in each constituency. The results of the survey are discussed below.

Demographic Data

What follows is the demographic information about the respondents in the two constituencies covered. The information covers gender, age and educational distribution, occupation, religion and income.

Gender Distribution

In the pre-election survey, gender distribution was almost even in both constituencies. In the Asunafo constituency, there were 47 male respondents, representing 56.4%, and 44 females representing 43.6 %. In Tano North we had 52 male and 48 female representing 52 and 48 percent respectively. In the post-election survey, the balance tilted slightly towards males. We had 58 males as against 42 females, out of 100 in Asunafo. This represents 58% and 42 % respectively. In Tano North, the trend was similar; there were 55 male and 45 female out of 100. That translates to 55% and 45% respectively (see Table 20.1).

Table 20.1: Gender Distribution

Gender	Asunafo North Pre-election %	Asunafo North Post-election %	Tano North Pre-election %	Tano North Post-election %
Male	47 56.4	58 58	52 52	55 55
Female	44 43.6	42 42	48 48	45 45
TOTAL	101	100	100	100

Age Distribution

The ages of the respondents in the two surveys ranged from 18 years to 71 and above. In Asunafo, about 80% of respondents ranged between 18 and 50 in the pre-election survey, while in Tano North, 90% of the respondents fell within the range of 18 to 50. In the post-election, Asunafo recorded 82% within the same age range of 18–50, while Tano North recorded 95% in the same age range. The age range 31–40 recorded the highest number of respondents in both constituencies (26.7% in Asunafo and 33 % in Tano.

While there were seven respondents above 71 in Asunafo, Tano North did not record any respondent above 71.

In the post-election survey, the age distribution pattern differed a little. In Asunafo a slightly higher percentage (82%) of respondents fell within the 18-50 range. Tano North however, recorded a lower figure for the same age range than it did in the pre-election. This time it had 74% as opposed to 90% in the pre-election. Also, the age range with the highest percentage of respondents remained range 31–40 for Tano North, but shifted to 26–30 in Asunafo (see Table 20.2).

Table 20.2: Age Distribution in the Pre- and Post-Election Surveys

Age	Asunafo North Pre-election		Post-election		Tano North Pre-election		Post-election	
18–25	24	23.8	23	23	16	16	20	20
26–30	13	12.9	26	26	31	31	17	17
31–40	27	26.7	23	23	33	33	22	22
41–50	16	15.8	10	10	15	15	15	15
51–60	9	8.9	15	15	2	2	9	9
61–70	3	3	1	1	3	3	7	7
71 and above	6	6.9	–	–	–	–	6	6
TOTAL	100	100	100	100	100	100	100	100

The age distribution in these two constituencies compares closely with the national figure. The age range 31–40 recorded the highest percentage at national level in both the pre- and post-election surveys. The percentages for that age range (31–40) for the two surveys were 26.7% and 23.4% respectively. These figures are very close to the Asunafo North figures, which were 26.7% and 23% respectively.

Educational Distribution

As far as the educational background of the respondents in the pre-election survey was concerned, those with primary education topped the list in Asunafo North (57.8%), while in Tano North, those with secondary education topped the list with 33%. The next in ranking in Asunafo North were those with no education at all, with 15.8%. Tano North had those with primary education as the second highest, with 29%. In the post-election survey, both Asunafo North and Tano North recorded different categories in the top two positions. In Asunafo North, the list was topped by primary and secondary, with 37% and 34% respectively. Tano North had the same categories at the top, with primary and secondary scoring 66% and 13% respectively. The percentage difference in the two top categories is very high in Tano North (i.e. 53%), while the figure was only 3% in Asunafo North (see Table 20.3).

Table 20.3: Educational Background of Respondents

Type of Education	Asunafo North Pre-election %	Asunafo North Post-election %	Tano North Pre-election %	Tano North Post-election %
None	15.8	4	11	12
Primary	57.8	37	29	66
Secondary	14.9	34	33	13
Teacher Training	8.9	7	17	1
Polytechnic	2	5	8	1
University	1	3	1	–
Technical	–	–	–	4
Vocational	–	4	–	–

Occupational Distribution

There was high unemployment among the population surveyed in the Asunafo North constituency in the pre-election survey. The percentage of respondents that claimed to be unemployed in this constituency was 39.6%. The next three top percentages were farmers (15.8%), professionals (14.9%) and traders (11.9%). In Tano North, the largest occupational group surveyed was made up of farmers, with 18%. The unemployed, traders and artisans followed in that order with 16%, 15% and 12% respectively.

In the post-election survey, farmers topped the list in Tano North, with 25%. They were followed by traders, teachers and the unemployed in that order, with 18%, 13% and 12% respectively. In Asunafo North, the unemployed topped the list with 30% followed closely by the farmers with 29%. The next two groups were traders (11%) and public servants with 7% (see Table 20.4).

Table 20.4: Occupational Distribution of Respondents

Occupation	Asunafo North Pre-election %	Asunafo North Post-election %	Tano North Pre-election %	Tano North Post-election %
Unemployed	39.6	30	16	12
Teacher	3	3	16	13
Businessman	3	5	9	9
Manager	–	–	–	–
Professional	14.9	1	–	–
Farmer	15.8	29	18	25
Trader	11.9	18	15	11
Artisan	–	9	12	4
Public Servant	4	2	5	7

One can see from the figures above that the percentage differences in the categories of occupation do not differ very much for the two surveys. For example, Asunafo had 39% and 30% of unemployed, while Tano North had 16% and 12% in the same category for the two surveys.

Religion

Three main religious groups were represented by the respondents. These are Christian, African Traditional and Muslim religions. The Christians topped the list in both constituencies in both surveys. In the pre-election survey, Asunafo North had 83.2% Christian, 7.9% African Traditional Religion (ATR), and Muslims had 6.9%. Tano North recorded 81% for Christians, 16% for ATR and nothing for Muslims. In the post-election survey, Asunafo North had 84% Christians, 2% ATR and 7% Muslims. This time, the Muslim population exceeded the ATR population. In Tano North, the Christians recorded 89%, ATR 6% and Muslims 4%.

Income

Poverty seems to be very deep in these two constituencies. While as many as 53.5% did not declare their incomes in Asunafo North during the pre-election survey, about 37.6 % reported incomes below 5 million *cedis* per annum. This constituency also recorded 8.9% with incomes between 5 and 10 million *cedis* per annum. Nobody earned above 10 million *cedis*. In Tano North, 79 % earned below 5 million, and 17% between 5 and 10 million. Nobody earned above 10 million here either. In the post-election, where the figures are more elaborate, about 92% earned below one million *cedis* per annum in Tano North, and 95% in Asunafo North. These figures reflect the rate of unemployment recorded in Table 20.4.

Political Participation

As far as participation in party politics is concerned, we can identify two types of participation:

a. participation in the political process — i.e. voting or exercising one's right to vote.
b. being an active member of a political party.

The first type of participation was quite high in the two constituencies. In other words, the greater majority of the people in the two constituencies exercised their voting rights. In the first place, all respondents in the two constituencies were registered voters. Secondly, about 87.1% and 90% of respondents had voted in the 1996 elections in Asunafo North and Tano North respectively. In the 2000 Elections, the figures were 98% and 99% for the respective constituencies. This is a good indication of the high degree of involvement in one aspect of political participation, i.e. exercising the franchise.

As far as the second type of participation is concerned, the story is different. The respondents did not participate as actively in this type as in the first type. The first indication of low participation in this respect is found in the number of respondents who were registered members of political parties. In Asunafo North, only 36.1% of respondents in the pre-election survey had registered with a political party, while the figure for the post-election survey was 49%. Even though the figure for the post-election was a little higher, both figures show a rather low rate of direct participation in the activities of political parties. For Tano North, the figures were 19% and 17% for the pre- and post-election surveys respectively. The parties that rated high among the registered respondents were NDC and NPP, with NPP on the edge in both Asunafo North, where 30.7% of registered respondents belonged to NPP and 5.9% belonged to NDC. CPP had only 1%. In Tano North, the equation was balanced, with NDC and NPP having 10% each. For the majority who were not registered members of any political party, their inclination towards a political party showed clearly that the NPP and the NDC were the two major parties they favoured. Asunafo North recorded a 46.5% inclination towards NPP and 12.8% towards NDC. Tano North had 52% for NPP and 22% for NDC. The figures for CPP and NRP were quite negligible, an indication that the major parties in the area are NPP and NDC.

One other indicator of low participation in political party activity is attendance at political rallies. Attendance at political rallies was quite low in both constituencies. In Asunafo North, only 29.7% of respondents attended political rallies in connection with the 2000 elections. Tano North recorded 24% attendance. All these figures show that even though respondents had shown a lot of awareness of the need to exercise their franchise, they did not care very much about participation in political party activities. The main reason given for low registration in political parties was personal (i.e., that they did not like party politics). It was also found that a majority of the respondents who belonged to a political party had become members by their own decision (51.5% for Asunafo North and 84% for Tano North). A few of them had become members through their parents (9.9% for Asunafo North and 9% for Tano North).

On the issue of the trend in voting in both parliamentary and presidential, it was discovered that most respondents voted for the same party in the 1996 Presidential and parliamentary elections (71.2% for Asunafo North and 81% for Tano North). It was also discovered that even though the two major parties in the two constituencies are NPP and NDC, the two parties that emerged as the traditional party group supported by parents of the respondents were CPP (30.7%) and UP/NPP (45.5%) in Asunafo North. In Tano North, however, the two major traditions were UP/NPP (54%) and NDC (31%). The lack of a strong CPP tradition in Tano North may seem strange, considering the fact that NDC is a recently formed party. But this may be explained by the claim of NDC to be a Nkrumahist party.

On the issue of past political participation, high participation was recorded for the 1996 presidential and parliamentary elections. About 81.1%

of the respondents in Asunafo North voted in the 1996 Presidential elections, while 83.2% voted in the parliamentary. For Tano North, we had 88% and 86% for the presidential and parliamentary respectively. This corroborates the assertion earlier that respondents were highly aware of the need to exercise their franchise. As for the parties they voted for in 1996, NPP and NDC emerged as the two traditionally most important parties in the area. NPP topped the list. The Table 20.5 explains the rate of voting in 1996 elections.

Table 20.5: Voting in 1996 Elections

	Asunafo North Presidential %	Asunafo North Parliamentary %	Tano North Presidential %	Tano North Parliamentary %
NPP	52.5	50.5	54	55
PNC	–	–	5	–
DPP	–	–	–	2
NDC	35.6	32.7	30	30

It is obvious from Table 20.5 that NPP and NDC are the two great traditions in these two constituencies. At national level, more respondents voted for NDC in the presidential elections (44.7%) than the NPP (36.4%). The parliamentary elections followed the same trend: NDC had 44% and NPP 36%.

During the pre-election survey all respondents in the two constituencies said they would vote in the 2000 elections, and as expected two parties emerged as the major parties they would vote for: NPP and NDC. In Asunafo North, 76.2% said they would vote for NPP and 17.8 % opted for NDC. In Tano North the figures for NPP and NDC were 56% and 23% respectively. CPP had only 1% in both constituencies. The National Reform Party (NRP) had only 1% in Asunafo North but 11% in Tano North.

In the 2000 presidential elections, 87% of Asunafo North respondents reported that they had voted for NPP, and 10% for the NDC. The figure for NPP was a little higher than the percentage that said they would vote for NPP during the pre-election survey. The NDC had a lower percentage than in the pre-election survey. In Tano North, the percentage that had voted for NPP was much higher than the percentage in the pre-election survey (77%

and 56% respectively). For reasons why people voted for the parties they voted for, the answers varied between the constituencies. In Asunafo North, the main reasons were that there was the need for change of national leadership (64%), and also that that was the trend of voting in the family (15%). In Tano North, the main reasons given were that the party they voted for had good policies to ensure the development of the nation (57%) and also that the candidates were good and honest (29%).

The voting trend in the 2000 parliamentary elections was not different from the Presidential one. In Asunafo North 76% of respondents reported that they voted for NPP, while 9% voted for NDC. In Tano North NPP had 78% and NDC 20%. The reasons given for the voting trend in the parliamentary elections were the same as those given for the presidential elections.

Voter Perception of the Economy

As far as the economy is concerned, the respondents believed that it was bad. While about 12.9% of respondents in Asunafo North thought that the economy was bad, as many as 72.3% thought it was very bad. In Tano North, only 2% thought it was bad and 72 % went for very bad. Surprisingly, 11% of respondents in Tano North thought the economy was good, compared to 5% in Asunafo North. A majority of respondents were also of the view that the economy of Ghana over the past four years had become worse (85.2% in Asunafo North and 74% in Tano North). The trend was not different with regard to the standard of living. A majority thought that standards of living had worsened since the last elections in 1996 (86.1% in Asunafo North and 74% in Tano North). About 5.9% and 13% of the respondents thought the standard of living had improved in Asunafo North and Tano North respectively. For the major economic problems of Ghana, respondents were varied in their responses. But the majority of them thought the major problem was unemployment. This was followed by inflation and the depreciation of the *cedi* (see Table 20.6).

To sum up, a majority of respondents perceived the Ghanaian economy to be bad, and standards of living to have become worse.

Evaluation of the Democratic Process

That Ghana is a democratic country was in doubt after so many years of military rule and about eight years of civilian rule which was tainted with

Table 20.6: Perception of Respondents on the Economy

	Asunafo North%	Tano North%
Inflation	24.8	30
High Interest Rates	1	1
Unemployment	50.5	37
Lack of private Investment	2	–
Depreciation of cedi	10.9	14
Don't know	1	13

military characteristics. The party in government was the brainchild of the former military ruler turned civilian. He therefore tried to incorporate some military mannerisms into his civilian administration. This made a lot of people wonder whether Ghana was a truly democratic country at the time. Most respondents in the two constituencies were of the view that Ghana could be described as a democratic country. However, the figures differ very sharply between the two constituencies. While only about 57.4% of respondents in Asunafo North thought that Ghana was a democratic country, as many as 88% of respondents in Tano North had that view. Quite an appreciable percentage of respondents in Asunafo North did not think that Ghana was a democratic country (27.7%). This is quite significant, and Tano North's figure of 10% is also fairly significant. About the same number of respondents thought that democracy had improved in Ghana over the past four years. With regard to the freedom of the press in Ghana, respondents in both constituencies were varied in their responses. Only 35.5 % of Asunafo respondents thought that the press in Ghana had more freedom now than four years ago. This contrasts sharply with an overwhelming 89% for Tano North respondents. One striking result from Asunafo North is that a majority of respondents could not determine whether or not there was more press freedom in Ghana now than four years ago. As many as 47.5% of them answered "Don't know". An appreciable percentage of respondents in the same constituency (27.7%) did not know whether political parties and other associations had more freedom now than they had four years ago. Most of the Tano North respondents, however, thought that there was more freedom for political parties and other associations now than four years ago. At national level, a majority of respondents thought Ghana could be described as democratic (67.2%). Furthermore, 60.7% thought that democracy had improved over the past four years. As far as freedom of the press is concerned, 62.6% of respondents nationwide thought that the press had more freedom now than before. On the freedom of political parties and other associations, 67.5% were also positive.

Evaluation of the Electoral Process

The evaluation of the electoral process by respondents varied with the various constituencies and with each type of question. One question sought to find out whether or not conditions existed in the country for free and fair elections on 7 December 2000. Of Asunafo North respondents 58.4% thought such conditions existed and Tano North recorded 76% for the same question. The figure for Asunafo North is on the low side because as many as 27.7% did not know. At national level 62.4% thought that the conditions existed for free and fair elections in December. To the question whether the 1996 elections had been free and fair, the responses were varied as well. But it is clear that a majority of respondents thought they had not been free and fair (73.3% in Asunafo North and 55% in Tano North). For those who thought the 1996 elections had been free and fair, Asunafo North (AN) had 18.8% and Tano North (TN) had 29%. The main reason given by those who thought the elections had not been free and fair was that there had been a lot of intimidation and threats[1]. With regard to the independence of the Electoral Commission from governmental control, the reactions were mixed. There was not a great percentage difference between the positive and the negative responses, even though the negative responses were higher. For example, in AN, 41.6% thought that the Electoral Commission was not free from governmental control and manipulation, while 25.7% thought it was independent. In TN, 35% thought the EC was still under some form of government control, and 30% thought it was independent of such control. In both constituencies, a large proportion of respondents could not draw any conclusion; they opted for "Don't Know" (28.7% for AN and 31% for TN).

Apart from the general assertion that the EC was not independent, some respondents also identified other ways to influence the elections. Over twenty five per cent (25.7%) in AN claimed there were other ways, and 41% made similar claims in TN. Among the other ways suggested by these respondents were:

(a) foreigners voting;
(b) printing of ballot papers for rigging;
(c) the press can influence elections;
(d) bribing party agents;
(e) buying of votes/voter ID cards;
(f) intimidation of voters;
(g) use of ghost names/multiple voting.

Despite the general castigation of the EC, the district offices of the EC seemed to enjoy some goodwill among some respondents. Many respondents thought that the district office of EC had been fair to all parties (38.6% in AN and 31% for TN). However, a majority of respondents could not draw any conclusions regarding the fairness of the district offices of the EC (48.5% in AN and 61% in TN). Among the reasons given for EC's unfairness to all parties were:

(a) election date was changed in favour of NDC;
(b) EC is government apparatus and is therefore not independent;
(c) EC cannot be trusted.

A majority of respondents were also of the view that the party in power had an undue advantage over the parties in opposition. In AN 68.3% shared this view and 66% in TN. Those who did not share this view were 20.8% in AN and 25% in TN.

At national level, the percentage of uncertainty as to the fairness of the district offices of the EC was 40.2%, which is quite high, though 46.1% thought the district office of the EC had been fair to all parties. With regard to the advantage of incumbency, 55% of respondents at national level supported the assertion that the party in power had an undue advantage over opposition parties, and 22.5% rejected the assertion.

Despite all these negative assertions from some sections of the public, the 2000 elections were seen to be generally free and fair by both constituencies (95% in AN and 98% in TN). There was also unanimous approval of the media coverage, which almost all respondents thought had been fair to all the parties and candidates. The elections were virtually incident free in the two constituencies. This time security was provided by police and fire service personnel. There had been no report of the presence of the military as we had in 1996.

Evaluation of the Party System

It was very clear from the survey that the people of Ghana needed a change of government. This view was clearly demonstrated in the responses of respondents to the question regarding the chances of an opposition party winning the presidential elections. Of AN respondents 63.4% thought that the chances were very good. TN recorded 62% in this regard. As far as the chances of the Progressive Alliance (comprising NDC, EGLE and DPP) were concerned, 56.4% of AN respondents thought their chances were not so good. As many as 28.7% could not draw any conclusions. In TN only 44% had similar sentiments, while 35% thought the chances of the Progressive Alliance winning the elections were very good. TN respondents were also not unanimous in deciding on a likely run-off in the presidential elections. While 46% thought there would be no run-off, a close 44% predicted a run-off. In AN, it was a clear 69.3% for no run-off, and 21.8% could not decide. This implies that a majority of the AN respondents wanted a first round win for an opposition party. Those who predicted a run-off gave the increased number of political parties as a reason. They were proven right when the run-off had to be called because no presidential candidate obtained the required fifty per cent of votes plus one.

It has been the view of most Ghanaians that political parties projected personalities rather than policies. This assertion was rejected by a majority of respondents in the two constituencies (90.1% in AN and 71% in TN).

At national level, a small majority predicted that an opposition party would win the presidential election (38.3%), and 37.9% thought that the chances of the Progressive Alliance in winning were not very good. Most respondents at national level (52.7%) also forecast a first round win for a party, and 28.9% forecast a run-off on the grounds of:

(a) increase number of parties;
(b) lack of charismatic presidential candidate;
(c) similarity of party manifestos.

A small majority at national level (47.6%) rejected the assertion that parties in Ghana projected personalities rather than policies.

On the financial status of the parties, most respondents thought that most parties were not financially sound (57.4% in AN; 68% in TN). The majority also thought that the government should finance the political parties (56.4% in AN and 73% in TN). Nationally, 59% thought that the parties were not financially sound; 26% thought they were. As to whether the parties should be financed by the government, the "Yes" and "No" responses were virtually the same (44.3% Yes; 44.4% No).

A majority of respondents in both constituencies approved of the candidates nominated by their parties (86.1% for AN; 91% for TN). The selection process was also approved as democratic by a majority of respondents, though the percentage in AN was a little lower (50.5%), compared to TN's 76%. While 40.6% of AN respondents could not decide only 1% in each constituency thought the process had been undemocratic. At national level, the story is not different. The candidates nominated by their parties were approved of by 78.5% and 60.5% thought that the process had been democratic.

Evaluation of Running Mates

As far as the choice of presidential running mates was concerned, most respondents in AN consider experience as the most important factor (67.3%), even before party loyalty (11.9%). In TN, however, a small majority of 23% consider party loyalty as the most important factor. This was followed by experience (16%) and regional balance (14%). It was also discovered that the choice of running mate would not affect respondents' votes (85.1% in AN; 88% in TN).

One other issue that was hotly debated in the Ghanaian media in election year was the consideration of regional and ethnic balance in the presidential election. This view was held by most respondents of AN where 61.4% thought that regional balance was important, and ethnic balance attracted 66.3% as important. For the majority of respondents in TN, however, regional or ethnic balance did not matter (75% and 81% respectively).

At national level, experience emerged as the most important factor for the choice of a running mate. For 84.8% of those respondents, the choice of running mate would not affect their votes. This is quite close to the constituency figures of 85.1% (AN) and 88% (TN). On the issue of regional balance, only 38% of the national figure thought that it was important, and for ethnic balance a small majority of 38.5% thought it did not matter; 28.5 % thought it was important, while 26.9% thought it was not important.

Election Issues

The most important issue at national level for the AN respondents was the economy (89.1%). Change and development took second spot with only 7%. Improving democracy came next with only 2.5%. In TN, the economy emerged as the most important with 68%, followed by continuity and stability with 30%. Change and development had only 1%. The economy and stability thus emerged as the two most important issues in the two constituencies. The development issues in the constituencies are in Table 20.7.

Table 20.7: Development Issues in the Two Constituencies

Issue	AN%	TN%
Water	22.8	6
Good road network	18.8	5
Toilet	9.9	13
Education	12.9	6
Health	9.9	7
Employment	2.0	61

The responses in Table 20.7 show that the focus in AN was water, a good road network and education in that order, while in TN, the focus was on employment and toilets. Education did not seem to be a priority in TN (only 6%), and it ranked third in AN. This shows how varied respondents' perceptions are as to what is important.

One other election issue that came up during the survey was the target for the respondents' votes. For the presidential election 42.6% of AN respondents said they would vote for the party, while 45.5% decided to vote for both party and candidate. For the former, the party was paramount, and for the latter, both party and candidate mattered very much. Only 5% would vote for the candidate. In TN, both party and candidate took the centre stage (84%). Thirteen percent would vote for the candidate, and only 1% would vote for the party. In TN therefore, the party alone did not matter; neither did the candidate alone. The candidate was as important as the party.

For the parliamentary election, the story was not different. Of AN respondents, 39.6% would vote for the party, 43.6% for both party and candidate, and 15% for the candidate. In TN, the figures were the same as we had for the Presidential, i.e., 84% for party and candidate, 13% for candidate and 1% for the party.

At national level, the major national issues for the 2000 elections were:

(a) the economy   31%
(b) change and development   34%
(c) improving democracy   15%
(d) Ghana's future (21st century)   14.7%
(e) continuity and stability   12.6%

For development issues in the constituencies, a good road network, education and employment came in that order. In both presidential and parliamentary elections, the voting target was both party and candidate (61.8% and 60.1% respectively, just as we had for the constituencies.

During the 2000 election itself, it was discovered from the survey that the three most important issues at national level were education, employment and hospitals in AN, and employment, education and agriculture in TN. At constituency level, the most important issues were good roads, water and education in that order in AN. In TN, we had good roads, education and employment in that order. In the view of most respondents, it was the NPP that best articulated the most important national and constituency development issues.

At national level, education, employment and the economy emerged as the three most important issues, while good roads, water and employment were the most important needs of the constituencies.

The Media

The major sources of information on issues and candidates, according to the results of the survey were TV and radio. In AN, TV scored 68.3% and radio 16.8%. In TN, TV scored 54% and radio 41%. The percentage gap between TV and radio is greater in AN than in TN. AN has a third significant source of information — friends and family (11%), which was not prominent in TN. As to the question which of the media played the greatest role of influencing respondents' votes, the TV and radio were on top gain. The radio was on top in AN with 50.5%, while TV topped in TN with 79%. TV took third spot in AN, behind friends and family. This underscores the significance of family and friends as a source of information and influence in AN. Radio took second spot in TN with 15%. Private radio enjoyed high patronage in AN as the most trusted medium (57.4%), while state-owned TV took first spot in TN (52%). State-owned TV came second in AN with 11.1%, while private radio took second spot in TN with 28%. Private TV had a more favourable rating in TN (14%) than in AN (only 1%).

At national level, radio and TV emerged as the most important sources of information on issues and candidates, just as we had in the constituencies (43.1% for radio and 29.6% for TV). The two again emerged as the most influential media (46.6% and 19.3% respectively). The most trusted media at national level were private radio (27.8%) and state-owned TV (19.8%). State-owned radio followed with 14.3%.

Identities and Social Capital Issues

A lot of respondents in AN grew up in the rural area (53.5%), while a close 44.6% grew up in the urban area. In TN, the number that grew up in the urban area was much higher (61%) than those who grew up in a rural setting (32%).

As far as identities are concerned, AN respondents had a very strong attachment to their religion (67.3% at level 5). Apart from religion which enjoyed such a high degree of attachment, ethnic group attachment was also high in AN (62.4% at level 4). Regional attachment was also quite high on the borderline between weak and strong attachment (42.6% at level 3). Attachment to an association was also significant on the borderline (34.7% at level 3). TN respondents did not show any appreciable attachments. The highest attachment was to an association on the borderline (67% at level 3). Apart from this all other attachments were weak.

The question what respondents felt most strongly attached to revealed very interesting results. In AN, the family came out strongest with 52.5% followed by the region where they lived (21.8%). In TN however Ghana as a whole came up tops with 45%, with region coming second with 32% and family third with 19%. The interesting thing was the high premium the respondents in TN put on national identity. In other words, most of them would regard themselves first as Ghanaians before anything else. This is the kind of patriotism Ghana needs for national stability.

On the issue of standard of living, most respondents said their household incomes were not enough to survive on (87.1% in AN and 77% in TN).

One hopes that the air of democracy blowing over Ghana will continue to blow, and that the seed of national identity that is being sown in TN will be dispersed to other parts of the country so that Ghanaians will always identify themselves first with Ghana before anything else. By so doing Ghana can have the peace that is required for national development.

NOTES

1. This assertion was given concrete expression in Tano North, where many respondents were initially reluctant to answer questions posed by the researchers. We had to do a lot of talking to convince them that the exercise was purely academic. The story that was told to explain their reluctance was that in the 1996 elections, a lot of people had been beaten up by soldiers who were brought into the area a day prior to the election. During the elections soldiers were patrolling the area, and this frightened many people away from the polling stations. After the elections, according to the sources, the soldiers went "wild" and indiscriminately beat up people. It was therefore the view of many people that the research had been organised by a particular political party to identify those who were opposed to them so that they would targeted for intimidation as happened in 1996.

REFERENCE

Shiveley, Phillips. W. (1997) *Power and Choice: An Introduction to Political Science*. The McGraw-Hill Companies, New York and London.

It was also a popular view of respondents that their households' stand[ard of] living over the past five years had got worse (82% in AN and 74% in [TN]). Despite this negative situation however, most respondents in AN th[ought] their households' standard of living would get much better in the nex[t five] years. This is an indication of the confidence they had in the new govern[ment] they were expecting to take over from the NDC.

Conclusion

The results of the election surveys outlined above revealed a few essen[tial] points. In the first place, it was noted that political awareness was high amo[ng] the people. As noted earlier, the people were much more aware of the need [to] exercise their franchise. On the other hand, participation in the affairs [of] political parties was on the very low side. Very few people are actively involv[ed] in or registered with the various political parties. The high awareness migh[t] have come about as a result of improvements in information dissemination through the proliferation of private media. Second is the people's need for a change, which really did come. Third, the emerging importance of radio as a means of information dissemination also came out clearly. It was observed that radio and TV were the major media. Private radio was rated much higher than state-owned radio. This low rating for state-owned radio was probably due to the perception that the state-owned mass media were government-controlled, and therefore were manipulated to "sing their master's voice". Fourth, the economy also came up as having got worse. Many people were living below the poverty line. It was however hoped that the next five years would see an improvement in the economy and their standard of living. Fifth, in the case of identities, we found out that most people were strongly attached to their families. There was however one interesting observation in TN, where a majority of people were more attached to the nation rather than the family or region. This, I think, is a very healthy development worthy of emulation. Sixth, the elections, according to reports from the two constituencies, were virtually incident free despite the high tension in the country prior to the elections. Maybe the press helped to deflect any plans that certain groups might have been hatching to cause confusion. There had been very few instances of intimidation and the absence of the military at the polling stations was also a positive development. On the whole the elections were believed to have been free and fair, and the results were thus accepted without any serious problems.

CHAPTER 21

A Survey of the 2000 Elections in the Asante Akim North and South Constituencies

E. OFORI-SARPONG

Introduction

During the past quarter-century, the "third wave" of global democratization has brought more than 60 countries around the world from authoritarian rule toward some kind of democratic regime. This is no small achievement, of course, but it has also become apparent that sustaining democracy is often a task as difficult as establishing it. In the immediate aftermath of all these democratic transitions, pressing concerns have quickly arisen about how to strengthen and stabilize these new regimes.

Democracy is define here as a type of political regime in which (a) meaningful and extensive competition exists between individuals and organised groups for all effective positions of government, at regular intervals and excluding the use of force; (b) a highly inclusive degree of political participation exists in the selection of leaders and policies, such that no major (adult) social group is excluded; and (c) sufficient civil and political liberties exist to ensure the integrity of political competition and participation.

In practice, these conditions can only be met through the regular conduct of free, fair, transparent and universal elections. A democratic transition is the process through which a democratic regime of this sort replaces a non-democratic regime. Democratic transitions almost always culminate at distinct moments such as on the inauguration of a freely elected government that marks the beginning of the new regime (O'Donnel & Schmitter, 1986: 6).

Even in very poor countries with under-developed infrastructure, widespread illiteracy, limited experience of multiparty competition and ethnic/regional tensions, a fairly free and open national election can be arranged. Of course, a government and opposition must acquiesce in financing and providing sophisticated electoral technology and international monitoring teams. Advocates of democratisation, both domestic and external, hope that elections will build the legitimacy, effectiveness, responsiveness and legality of governments. While free elections help achieve these goals, they are only the first step towards effective democratic governance. Some combination of four factors accounts for democratic openings: strong domestic protest, splits among the top government leaders, contagion induced by democratic experiments elsewhere, and pressure from donor countries. It is against this backdrop that this chapter analyses the Pre-Elections and Post-Elections Surveys of the attitudes to and the opinions on a variety of issues of respondents in the Asante Akim North and South constituencies.

Pre-election Analysis

Demographic Profile

The survey covered the two constituencies of Asante Akim District of Ashanti Region. The Asante Akim District is predominantly a rural district. Consequently, priority was given to the rural settlements. One hundred and thirty respondents were selected from twenty-three rural settlements in the two constituencies while 70 respondents were also selected from seven urban centres. This gives a rural/urban ratio of 130:70 respectively or 65% and 35% respectively. The constituency capitals Konongo and Juaso for Asante Akim North and South respectively, recorded the largest administered questionnaires because of their status as both district/constituency capitals.

Gender Distribution

The sample covered 50 males and 50 females in Asante Akim North and 58 males and 42 females in the south. There were systematic efforts by the research team to acquire fair distribution of both sexes as well as the need to overcome the situation in which men represent the entire society in research. Also in Asante Akim the degree of feminism in the political landscape has changed the impression about women due to their firm grasp of current affairs and national issues.

The survey clearly demonstrates that the interviewees in the South were more youthful than those in the North. The respondents between the ages of 18 and 50 represented 81% in the South whereas within the same age brackets the North recorded 66% of respondents. However, the North had a fair representation of all the age groups. It may also be noted that, the 71 and above age group recorded the least number of respondents in both constituencies which could be interpreted as the apolitical attitude of the aged for several reasons.

Table 21.1: Age Distribution of Respondents

Age	North	South
18 – 25	9	15
26 – 30	17	22
31 – 40	22	24
41 – 50	18	20
51 – 60	15	9
61 – 70	16	4
71 and above	3	6

Educational Background

Ashanti Region is considered the third region in Ghana after Central and Greater Accra Region endowed with educational institutions and facilities. This however has not been reflected in either Asante Akim North or South Districts. They have not therefore had their fair share of this distribution. In spite of the low level of education in Asante Akim, respondents in the North were more educated as 91% of the respondents had up to secondary education with 81% with no education or primary education. In the Asante Akim South Constituency, about 87% of the respondents also had up to the tertiary education level (polytechnic) while 68% also had no education or primary education.

Table 21.2: Educational Background of Respondents

Level	North	South
None	18	22
Primary	63	46
Secondary	10	15
Polytechnic	–	4
Teacher Training / Technical College	9	10
University	–	2

Religion

The sample covered 93%, 3% and 4% Christians, African Traditional Religion and others respectively in the North. Whereas, the south also covered 87% Christians, 3% African Traditional Religion, 5% Moslems and 4% others. The glaringly uneven religious distribution, particularly in the North is due to the general uneven religious distribution in the Ashanti Region. The Ashanti Region is predominantly a Christian Region as far as National Religious distribution is concerned. Christian missionaries succeeded in planting several churches in the Region and also established several educational and health institutions.

Occupation

The results of the survey indicate that a high percentage of respondents were farmers. As rural communities located in the forest belt of the country, their main sources of livelihood are various forms of farming (see Figure 21.1).

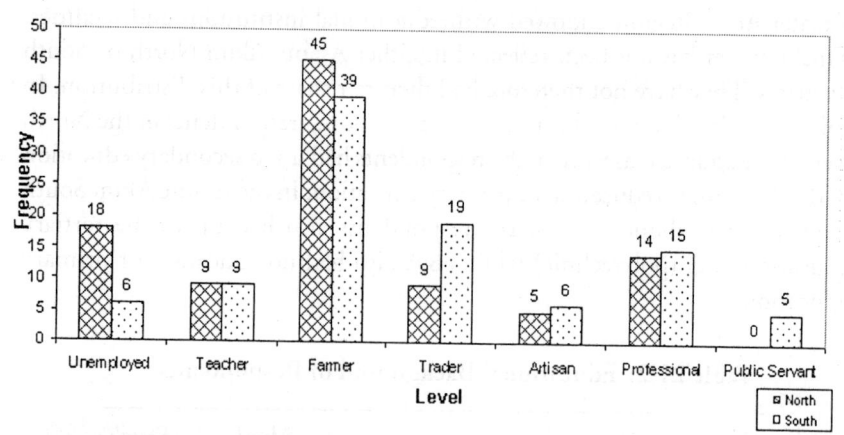

Fig. 21.1: Main Sources of Livelihood.

The employment patterns of the North and South are similar with the exception of public servants and unemployed respondents. Whereas 18% were unemployed in the North, only 6% were unemployed in the South. 5% of respondents in the South were public servants whereas none of the respondents was a public servant in the North. Trading activities were however, higher in the South than in the North, and this was the only employment area where the South exceeded the North in a significant way.

Income

The studies lay bare, the low incomes of the two constituencies. In the North 94% earned less than 5 million *cedis* per year while 6% could not describe their incomes. In the South the situation was very different. 80% of respondents were receiving less than 5 million *cedis* per year. 10% earned between 5 million and 10 million *cedis* per year. One respondent earned above 10 million cedis while 9 % could not describe their incomes. The seemingly better incomes of the South could be attributed to higher number of professional as well as higher levels of education of the respondents.

Political Participation

In principle, political parties constitute the central intermediary structure in a democracy. Strong parties may augment both governmental responsiveness and the resolution of conflict by articulating and aggregating the demands of diverse constituencies in the form of public policies. For new democracies to survive in the current context of extreme deprivation, party systems must be able to mediate the many tensions that inevitably arise. In addition, parties may broaden political participation, at a minimum by disseminating political information and opinions and by mobilising voters in elections. Finally, parties are valuable to the extent that they enhance government accountability via their role as a "loyal opposition." Opposition parties contribute to better governance when they expose counter-productive policies and abuse of power.

In Asante Akim North, all respondents were registered voters who were very active in the political situation and development in their constituency. In the South, as many as 97% were registered voters, a paltry three percent were not registered. Surprisingly, more than two-thirds were not registered members of any political party. In the North, only 26% were registered members. NDC had four registered members whereas NPP had registered 21 members out of the 100 respondents. Asante Akim South had registered 34 members of the major political parties, NPP had 5%, CPP and PNC had 2% each. Overall, the NPP obtained the highest percentage of registered party members in Asante Akim constituencies. In the North and South 71% of the respondents who were not registered with any political party, claimed, it was their personal decision not to register with any political party.

In spite of low membership in terms of registration with political parties, respondents demonstrated high inclination towards NPP even though, they were not registered with NPP: 90% in the North and 70% in the South. Seventy six per cent of registered members of political parties took a personal decision to register with a political party.

Participation in Elections

The 1996 election was a very significant election for the two constituencies, because it was recognized as the most opportune moment to determine the political inclination of Ghanaians. The 1992 elections, which broke the rod of the Provisional National Defence Council (PNDC) dictatorship, had a series of controversies, which eventually led the opposition parties to boycott the parliamentary election. By 1996 all the conditions which were acceptable to all the major actors in the electioneering process, were fully met with a significant amount of support from the international donor community. Hence 98% and 78% of respondents in the South and North respectively voted.

Political Parties and 2000 Elections

The election notices in both constituencies depicted seven political parties and candidates contesting the presidential seat. The seven parties were the NPP, NDC, PNC, NRP, UGM, GCPP and CPP. In the Asante Akim North constituency, six out of the seven political parties contested the parliamentary seat. The only party which did not contest the seat is the GCPP. On the other hand, five political parties also contested the Asante Akim South parliamentary seat. UGM and GCPP did not contest a parliamentary seat in the constituency.

Apparently, it was observed that, the seven parties in both constituencies in effect reduced to barely two (the NPP and NDC) with the others almost non-existent. Apart from the fact that, few of their party posters and flags that were found affixed on walls or mounted on bamboo poles, no other political campaign activities were seen among the remaining five political parties.

Of the two prominent political parties (NPP and NDC) the NPP was seemingly the stronger and perhaps better organized in both constituencies. The party's offices remained open throughout the survey period, whilst the

NDC Constituency Head Office at Konongo in the Asante Akim North constituency remained closed throughout the survey period. This is not to say that the NDC was defunct in that constituency, perhaps it might be due to a predominance of sympathizers of the NPP in the constituency and traditional seat of Danquah-Busia tradition. However, the activities of the NDC were concentrated relatively more in the rural settlements in comparison with the urban towns.

In terms of political rallies, it was the NPP that held two political rallies in each of the two constituencies during the survey period. According to some respondents, the other political parties especially the NDC and PNC also held rallies before the survey had been carried out. Though the two prominent political parties (NPP and NDC) were always seen using campaigning vans as their method of campaigning, house-to-house campaign strategies were also intensified particularly in the Asante Akim South constituency. Interestingly, it was realized that almost all the political parties in both constituencies sometimes gave gifts or incentives to electors just to win their votes. This was however, actively done by the NDC activists who normally gave out cash to the electorates. There were reported cases of NPP activists also giving 'T' shirts to the electorates.

Voter Attitude and Perception of the Economy

The constituents of Asante Akim also suffered from the deteriorating economic woes, which bedeviled the entire country in the year 2000. Salaries were extremely low, the prices of consumer goods were very high, whereas incomes continued to shrink or remained stagnant. On the state of the Ghanaian economy, an insignificant proportion of 3% agreed that it was very good while 97% asserted it was very bad in the North. Respondents in the South however, were not clustered into very good and very bad. Thirteen per cent agreed, the economy was good, 34% responded it was bad. Thirty-nane per cent also claimed it was very bad while 14% argued it was neither good nor bad. Respondents had different perceptions about improvement of the economy especially in the South. Five per cent and 35% agreed that it had improved considerably and just improved respectively. Whereas 35% and 25% argued it had worsened and sharply deteriorated respectively. The North responses were 97% in favour of sharp deterioration and 3% for just improved. Respondents considered unemployment, inflation and depreciation of the Ghanaian *Cedi* the major economic problem of the country.

Evaluation of the Democratic Process

With regard to democracy in the country on the eve of 2000 elections, a very large proportion of respondents considered it to be a democratic country. Only a small proportion felt it was undemocratic, or could not decide (see Figure 21.2).

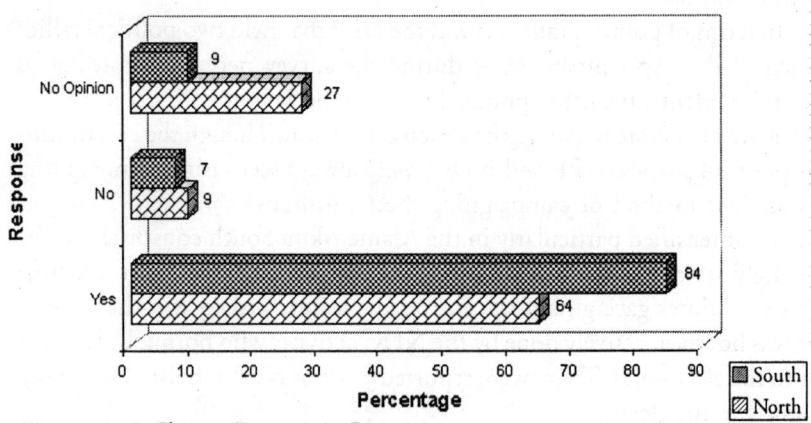

Fig. 21.2: Is Ghana a Democratic Country?

Perception of Respondents on the Democratic Process

There was however, a huge disparity between the two constituencies as to whether democracy ha improved over the last four years. Respondents in the South agreed that democracy ha improved over the period, whereas respondents in the North considered otherwise (see Figure 21.3).

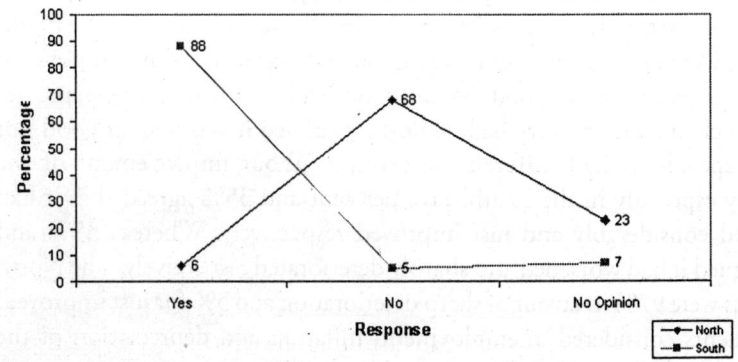

Fig. 21.3: Has Democracy in Ghana Improved Over the lastFour Years?

Evaluation of the Electoral Process

An almost equal number of respondents in both constituencies opined that existing conditions in Ghana could guarantee free and fair election in December 2000 (see Figure 21.4).

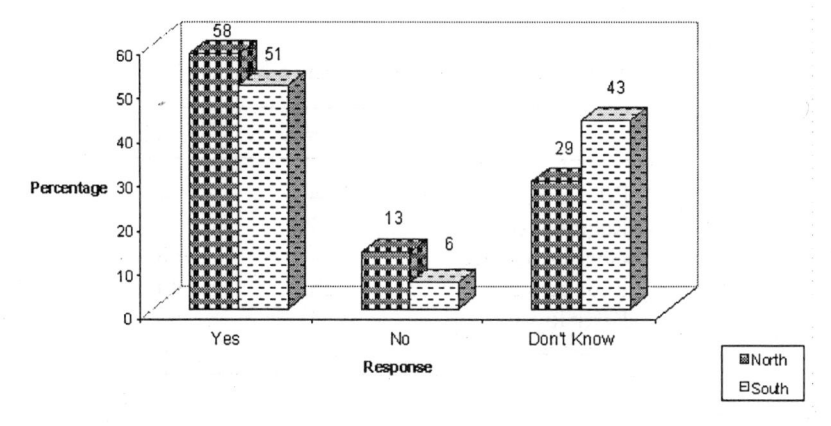

Fig. 21.4: Do Conditions for Free and Fair Elections Exist?

Paradoxically, respondents had mixed responses about the freedom and fairness of the 1996 election. Forty-two per cent and 40% agreed to free and fair election in 1996 in North and South respectively, and equal percentages of 29% did not have any opinion as to whether there was free and fair election in 1996.

The conduct of free and fair election in any country depends on existing conditions as well as the political institutions that are responsible for the electoral process. The independence and impartiality of these organizations are a sine qua non of free and fair elections. In Ghana, the Electoral Commission is charged with the arduous task of conducting all public elections. Even though a sizeable percentage of respondents in Asante Akim constituencies agreed that conditions existed for free and fair elections, they were however sceptical about the independence of the Electoral Commission from government control. They however contended that the district electoral officer had been fair to all the political parties and candidates in the district.

Evaluation of Running Mates

The running mate of any political party must be qualified as a candidate for the presidency. In the event of the incapacity of the elected president, the choice of running mate was a very important political issue in the 2000 elections. Several factors emerged, which included religion, region and ethic background. Respondents in Asante Akim considered ethnic background as unnecessary in choosing presidential running mates (see Table 21.3).

Table 21.3: Choice of Running Mate

	North	South
Ethnic background	–	–
Regional balance	43	5
Gender balance	–	8
Experience	28	44
Party loyalty	3	35
Other factors	26	8

However attitudes of respondents in North and South on the impact of running mate on their voting pattern differed. The North considered a running mate very important in influencing their choice of presidential candidate while the South viewed it as unnecessary (see Figure 21.5).

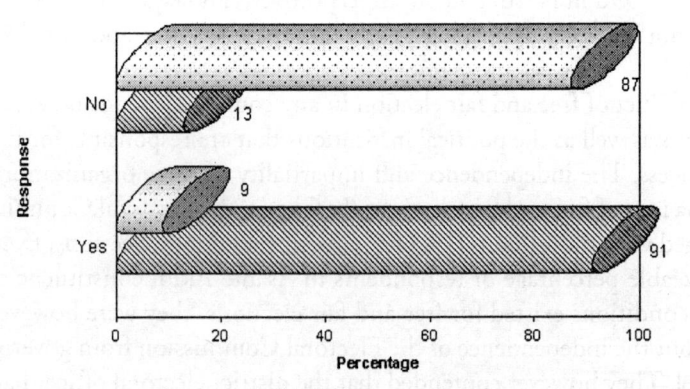

Fig. 21.5: Is a Presidential Running Mate Important?

Media

In principle, the privately- owned media play important roles in democratic life. They inform citizens on matters of public policy by presenting and debating alternatives. Where parties remain too weak to fill this policy role, newspapers, radio and television may fill the gap in forging a more informed electorate. In practice, Africa's independent media must overcome crippling weaknesses in order to fulfil this democratic mandate. First, governments in new democracies regard the independent media with suspicion — perceiving them as partisan in political struggles rather than unbiased chronicles — hence seek to tame or bypass them. Asante Akim District has no radio station located in the district. Inhabitants however receive programmes from Accra based local FM Stations and Kumasi local FM Stations. They also have access to all television stations available to Kumasi inhabitants. The proliferation of private FM Stations in the country serves as the main source of information for most people in the rural areas, who cannot read or afford a newspaper, or where television is not accessible to them. The main sources of information available to voters in the Districts to help their analysis are in Table 21.4.

Table 21.4: Main Sources of Information Available to Voters

Source	*North*	*South*
Television	5	20
Newspaper	3	3
Friends and Family (word of mouth)	11	7
Candidate Rallies	4	5
Radio	66	57
Poster/Fliers	2	4
Others	9	4

In assessing the sources of media information available, respondents in the North considered private radio stations as the main source, and the most trusted to tell the truth. Respondents in South however considered the state-owned television — Ghana Television as the most credible source of media information since pictures were always shown to substantiate their facts (see Table 21.5).

Table 21.5: Most Trusted and Credible Media

Source	North	South
State-owned Television (TV)	6	44
Foreign radio	–	2
State-owned newspaper	3	3
Don't know	12	5
Private television	2	2
State-owned Radio	2	17
Private radio	65	21
Private newspaper	7	4
Other	3	2

Post-election Analysis

The circumstances under which the pre-election survey was conducted had changed at the time of the post election survey. Voters had cast their vote in the 7 December and 28 December 2000 in parliamentary and presidential, and the presidential run-off respectively. These two constituencies are traditional seats of the Danquah-Busia tradition, now New Patriotic Party. The political atmosphere had obviously changed because the strongest party in the constituency had come to power. The youth, who constituted 40% of registered voters, had never witnessed a change in political leadership in the country through the ballot box after voting in 1992 and 1996 general elections. The respondents interviewed were selected from twenty-eight towns/urban centres and villages/rural areas in the constituencies. In the post-election survey prominence in terms of numbers was given to rural settlements rather than urban centres because, the responses from the urban centres were skewed towards the NPP. Forty per cent of respondents were interviewed from eight urban towns with populations of 5000 and above, while 60% were selected from 20 villages. The survey covered 200 respondents who voted in the 2000 general elections.

The sex distribution was more balanced in the two constituencies than in the survey sample. A systematic sampling procedure was adopted which included the opinion of women (see Figure 21.6).

Demographic Profile

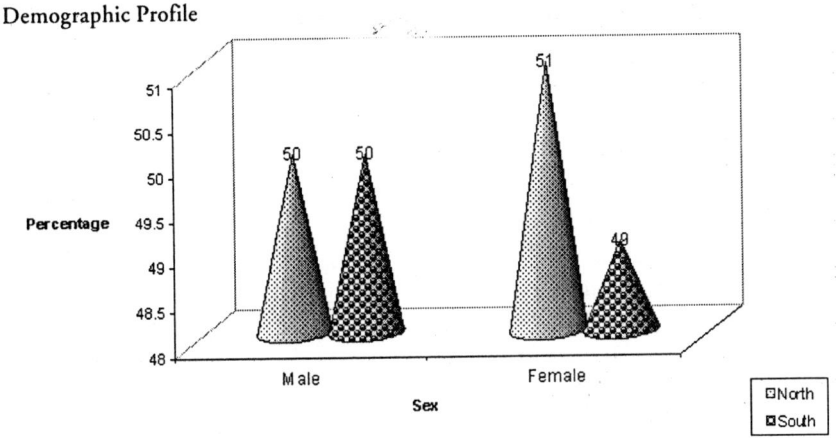

Fig. 21.6: Sex Distribution within Samples.

The figures show that, compared with the pre-election survey, the age distribution of post-election reflects a more youthful sample in the South (74% in the 18–40 age group) than in the North (51% in the same age range). In each constituency, those aged 50 and over, were rather less represented (23% in the North and (11%) in the South than in the previous sample (see Table 21.6).

Table 21.6: Age Distribution

Age	North	South
18–25	4	17
26–30	20	30
31–40	31	27
41–50	17	15
51–60	17	7
61–70	6	1
71 and above	5	3

As in survey 1, the vast majority in both constituencies had only primary education. The educational level of the respondents in the North had improved over the first survey. However, in respect of secondary/higher school backgrounds, the South with 29% still had the edge over the North with 17% (see Table 21.7).

Table 21.7: Educational Background

Level	North	South
None	7	24
Primary	74	42
Secondary	7	14
Polytechnic	1	3
Teacher Training / Technical College	9	10
University	1	2

Religious Affiliation

The findings for this variable post-election are the same as in pre-election survey. The vast majority of respondents were Christians (see Figure 21.7).

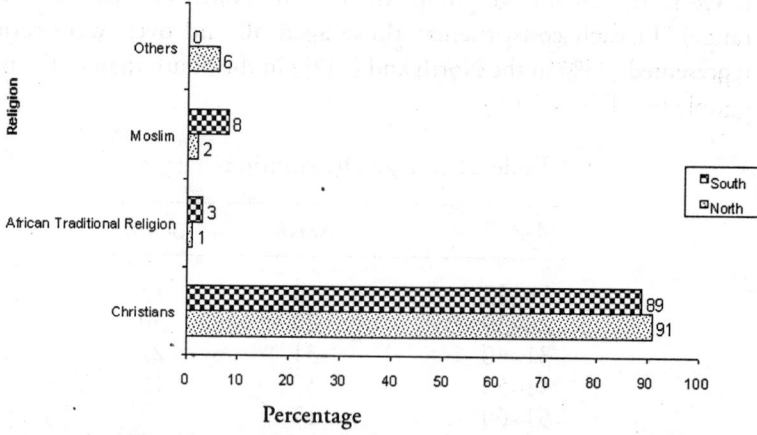

Fig. 21.7: Religious Affiliations.

Political Participation in Previous Elections

Respondents were not only active in the 2000 election but had a creditable history of political participation. Ninety-two per cent voted in 1996 general elections in the North, and 77% voted in the South in the same election. Of the 92% who voted in 1996, 79% voted for NPP, whereas 13% voted for NDC in the North. In the South, 49% of respondents voted for NPP whereas 25% voted for NDC. In the 1998 District Assembly election 82% and 70% voted in the North and South respectively. Eighteen per cent and 30% respectively did not vote in the 1998 District Assembly election due to non-availability of ballot papers at the registered polling stations, or not being qualified due to age.

Voter Perception and Involvement in Political Parties

Asante Akim District is like most political units in Ghana, a paltry number of respondents register with political parties. Even those who register with political parties, do so in anticipation of a political contest within and outside the political party. In the 2000 elections, 25% in the North and 15% in the South had registered with their political parties. Seventeen of the 25% and 11 of 15% were registered with NPP in the North and South respectively. The respondents did not hesitate in declaring their party inclinations even though, they were not registered with their party. In the North 71% had inclinations towards the NPP and 61% in the South. Three per cent had inclinations towards NDC in the North and 16% in the South. In the North 1% were for PNC and 4% in the South. The respondents also follow with keen interest the activities of various political parties in their constituencies even though there was no keep fit/jama at either village or constituency level. Due to low registration at party level, most respondents could not share an opinion whether their party was financially sound or lacked the necessary resources to win or maintain power. Also interest in the result of the elections for the leadership of political parties was negligible both at the constituency and village/town level because they had not registered with their party. Only paltry numbers of 8% in the North and 6% in the South have ever attended their party congress. No respondent had ever contested for parliamentary candidacy of his or her parties.

Evaluation of the Electoral Process

Respondents in the two constituencies generally regarded the 2000 elections as free and fair; 97% in the North and 80% in the South considered them free and fair. Two per cent in both constituencies did not see it as being free and fair. One per cent in North, and 18% in South did not know whether the elections were free and fair. On polling day, 11% in South had some problems ranging from difficulty in locating their names and shortage of ballot papers and had to wait, but they were finally allowed to vote. None of the respondents in the North had any problem on polling day. Security personnel ranged from police, soldiers and fire service to warders who assisted in the two constituencies to ensure orderliness and smooth conduct of the election. The respondents were happy about the security in the polling station. 100% in North and 95% in the South regarded the elections as orderly.

Media

The respondents also assessed the media as channels of communication from the contesting candidates to the electorate. Sixty-two per cent in the North and 73% in the South considered the electronic media adequate in covering the election. Thirty-five per cent in the North and 23% in the South did not share their opinion. Three per cent and 4% in the North and the South respectively expressed no opinion.

The disparity between the two constituencies depended on the idiosyncrasies of the individual respondents because the two constituencies receive the same Radio and Television programmes from the same source.

Presidential Run-off Election — Reflections

In comparison, most respondents were of the view that the 28 December 2000 presidential run-off in the constituency was more peaceful than in the previous elections. Though tension was very high prior to the election, voting went on smoothly and satisfactorily. According to some respondents, prior to the election, it was only the NPP that held rallies namely at Juaso and Asankare on two different occasions. The NDC was relegated to the background in terms of presidential run-off campaigns. Though the NDC had just moved to the newly built party office at Juaso, it was opened once prior to the presidential run-off. This created the impression that the NPP was unopposed in the constituency as far as the presidential run-off was concerned. Respondents argued that the NDC accepted defeat in the constituency before the voting took place, because they failed to campaign. Nothing really showed that the party was contesting the presidential run-off elections. Meanwhile, the NPP organized "fun" football matches, "jama" and held rallies particularly in the villages.

A few polling stations in the constituency recorded some form of election violence or intimidation.

At Juaso, the voting at the Juaso Day Senior Secondary School (SSS) polling station at Asikafoamatem electoral area nearly ended abruptly. It was alleged that at about 9:45 am on polling day, the NDC party agents at the polling station tried to intimidate and disenfranchise three students on the ground that they were below the age of 18. The students and the NPP party agents on the other hand insisted that, once they had voted during the 7 December 2000 elections, under no circumstances should they be disenfranchised or intimidated. Again, they insisted that once they were duly registered to exercise their franchise, they should be allowed to vote. This brought voting, which was hitherto orderly and peaceful to a halt for over 30 minutes. Furthermore, two of the students' parents brought their birth certificates to testify to their age. This coupled with the assistance of the NDC parliamentary candidate in the constituency, Mr Kwaku Kyeremanteng, and the policeman on duty at the polling station, enabled the misunderstanding to be settled amicably.

Again at Obogu, an NDC member who attempted to use his late brother's thumb printed ID card to vote was nearly lynched by NPP supporters who were standing about 120 metres away from the polling station.

The story was that a man went to the polling station to use his late brother's ID card to cast his vote, probably because they had the same surname. Unfortunately, luck eluded him. One of the NPP party agents knew this man as a registered voter at a different polling station. So when he was questioned, he initially insisted that the ID card belonged to him. Upon further interrogation, he admitted telling lies and pleaded for forgiveness, and was later released to go away. However on his way home he was confronted violently by the NPP supporters who were curiously monitoring the voting and observing what was happening. But for the timely intervention of the NPP party Chairman at Obogu, who incidentally happened to appear on the scene, he would have been lynched.

It was also ascertained that, at Asankare, an NDC activist who went about boasting that he had voted four times was severely beaten by NPP supporters. At the time of the survey, the victim was on admission at Juaso Government Hospital. All efforts to interview the victim proved futile.

Why the NPP Won the 2000 Elections in the Two Constituencies

A number of reasons were given by respondents for voting the NDC government out of power. It should be noted that the NPP won in both the parliamentary and presidential election in the constituencies. The reasons for the NPP's victory were seen in both the weaknesses of the NDC and the advantages of the NPP.

The Weaknesses of the NDC

(a) most respondents alleged that the NDC government had stayed in power for over 19 years, and that they had become corrupt members. They therefore wanted to change the government.
(b) It was also alleged that, the NDC government was very arrogant in its unwillingness to relinquish power to any other party. Respondents complained of the former president of Ghana and leader of the NDC party's comments such as "to hand over power to who?" as a sort of pride and arrogance.
(c) The youth who had not witnessed any other rule apart from the PNDC/NDC wanted a change of government.
(d) The economic crisis that Ghana went through just before the 2000 elections also contributed to the defeat of the NDC. Respondents were in the view that, the NDC could no longer liberate Ghanaians from their economic woes.

The Advantages of the NPP

(a) Traditionally, the electorates in the constituencies belong to the Danquah-Busia tradition, and they decided to vote for the NPP which also emerged from this tradition.
(b) The "Positive Change" campaign message of the NPP was also embraced by the constituents. They were really bent on changing the then incumbent government.
(c) The promise made by the NPP to provide the youth with jobs was another factor, which contributed to their victory in the two constituencies.

Conclusion and Recommendations

Although there were some cases of political violence and intimidation in the Asante Akim South and North constituencies, the political atmosphere at the time of the interviews was very peaceful and congenial. It was also observed during the interviews that, the 7 and 28 December 2000 elections were seen by majority of the respondents as free and fair. According to the respondents, the peaceful transition that the country went through was a great achievement, which every Ghanaian should be proud of. Some of them were of the view that it was a recipe for the achievement of Ghana's multi-party democracy.

Although the electorate was happy about NPP's victory, it was also observed that, their expectations from the Government were high. Some of them urged the government to expedite action and implement some of the policies, which needed urgent attention. Some of the frequently mentioned development issues in the constituency in order of importance were:

- Creation of employment or job opportunities;
- Improvement in the educational sector, particularly the establishment of scholarship schemes;
- Eradication of bribery and corruption as well as favouritism associated with high government officials;
- Reduction in prices of goods and stability of the currency;
- Strict supervision and monitoring of the DCEs;
- An increase in the minimum wage and commensurate increases in the salaries of government employees; and finally
- Development of infrastructural facilities and social amenities, especially rehabilitation of the bad roads in the constituencies.

Another interesting observation, made during the interviews was that the electorate in the constituency was more politically awakened than before, and had embraced "Positive Change" as a principle in their political life. Even though quite a number of them voted purely on tribal and family relations grounds, the youth in particular were prepared to change the government in subsequent election through the ballot box should it fail to deliver the goods set out the party's manifesto and campaign promises.

On the basis of these developments it is recommended that, in order to curtail election violence in the near future, political parties and all stakeholders should intensify their education on the need to tolerate each other's views during electioneering campaigns. Political parties should therefore concentrate more on "tolerance" during campaigns.

Again, it is recommended that law enforcement agents should also investigate cases brought to them thoroughly and bring the perpetrators to book. This should be done without fear or favour and without delay as well.

Finally since the expectations of the electorate in the constituencies were high, it is recommended that the NPP government should make every effort to set its priorities right and tackle the most important development needs of the people in order of preference. It is suggested that the creation of jobs, improvement in the educational sector particularly establishment of scholarship schemes, and the removal of the "cash and carry" system from the hospitals should be the NPP government's top priority. This, it is expected will stimulate positive thoughts among the electorate and provide grounds for sober reflection as far as subsequent elections are concerned.

REFERENCES

O'Donnell, G. and Schmitter, C. (1986) *Transitions from Authoritarian Rule: Tentative Conclusions about Uncertain Democracies* (Baltimore: The Johns Hopkins University Press).

CHAPTER 22

The 2000 Presidential and Parliamentary Elections in Ghana: Wa Central and Sissala Constituencies

GEORGE AKANLIG-PARE

Introduction

The 2000 Presidential and parliamentary elections were historic in the political annals of Ghana for several reasons. First of all, they marked the successful completion of two terms of one constitutionally elected president who had been head of state in three different phases of the political history of Ghana. Secondly, several members of parliament were seeking a second or third term in parliament. Coupled with these novelties in the political history of the country, was the continuous ill-feeling generated in the country as a result of the rising cost of living. In fact it was clear during the electioneering period, that there was deep-seated dissatisfaction among both rural and urban communities. Yet all political parties contesting the elections did not relent in their pursuit of the mandate of the population. Big and small in both size and popularity all the parties, in exercising their political rights, thought they stood as front runners.

The Profile of the Two Constituencies

To gauge the political momentum and also to find out the various variables that shape the behaviour of the voters within the period, the pre- and post-election surveys were conducted in 40 constituencies, with a minimum of two from each administrative region.

Wa Central and Sissala constituencies were selected for the Upper West Region. Wa is the home of the Wala. It is also the administrative capital of the region. As an urban centre therefore, it was expected that it would provide viewpoints that were representative of cross sections of different people of various educational, social, ethnic and religious backgrounds. In fact the selection of Wa was deliberate, being an identified stronghold for a long time of the then ruling NDC government. And as it is a commercial town, it was hoped that the views expressed would throw light on the attitudes of the various people, in the face of the economic decline of at particular region.

Sissala was chosen not only to provide variety since it has a different ethnic inhabitants, but also because it is a Rural area. Besides Gwollu, which is the home village of late President Hilla Limann who was sworn in and overthrown later by ex-president Rawlings, is in this constituency and not too far away from constituency headquarters. It was expected that the Limann factor would impact on the behaviour of voters in this constituency, given the dissatisfaction at the time with the policies of the then government. Following is the analysis of the data gathered for the pre-and-post-election surveys conducted in these two constituencies in October, 2000 and January, 2001.

Demographic Profile

The survey sampled people of various ages, genders, occupations, educational background and religious backgrounds. This sampling was done randomly. It was meant to find out how age, gender, educational background and religious affiliations of the respondents impacted on their choice of political parties and perception of the political and economic state of the country. As it was being said, the younger generation, who experienced the outburst of Rawlings onto the political stage were expected to be swayed to his party. How much this hypothesis could be substantiated would be determined for example, by the age distribution in the demographic data. In all, 350 people were interviewed in the Wa and Sissala constituencies during the pre and post-election surveys.

Gender Distribution

The gender make-up of the sample surveyed in both pre-and post-elections shows the greater number of respondents to be males. Of the valid instruments analysed for Wa central, an average of 63% were male while 34% were female. The picture is not different for Sissala 58% male; 38% female. This proportion does not look skewed in relation to the national figure where males outnumber females. Nationwide, an average 57% was recorded for males in both pre-and post election surveys, while for females, an average 40% was recorded (see Table 22.1).

Table 22.1: Gender Distribution

Gender	Wa	Sissala	National
Male	63%	58%	57%
Female	34%	38%	40%

Age distribution

In both pre-and post-election surveys, respondents to the questionnaires were preponderantly within the youthful 18-40 years bracket in both Urban Wa-Central and Rural Sissala constituencies. In Wa for example, 67% was recorded during the pre-election survey and 86% during the post-election for the 18-40 years.

For Sissala, the percentage is similar: 71% for the pre-election and a whopping 94% in the post-election survey were aged 18–40 years.

For these elections, the significance of these percentages should not be lost. This age group, constituting the bulk of the productive section of the economy, is also one that has lived for most of their life time under one form of governance or influence led by a PNDC/NDC government which was the government of the day (see Table 22.2).

Table 22.2: Age Distribution

Age	Wa Central % Pre	Post	Sissala % Pre	Post
18–25	11.2	56.3	8.9	9.8
26–30	16.3	28.8	28.9	58.5
31–40	39.8	1.3	33.3	25.9
41–50	18.4	1.3	18.9	2.4
51–60	12.2	3.0	5.6	2.4

Education

One of the key factors that impact on voter behaviour and democratic consolidation is the education of a population. The better educated a community, the more rational the voter pattern and the greater the degree of participation of the people in decision making and implementation of policies.

Historically, the Northern part of Ghana was systematically neglected by the colonial government in this area for reasons that we will not discuss here. But the effect of this neglect is the low levels of education recorded even today.

Urban centres are usually privileged in having not only better access to education, but access to quality education as well. However, this privilege is not so characteristic of the Rural-Urban dichotomy in the North. So for example, of the sampled participants, in Wa Central during both pre- and post-election surveys, an average 13% had some form of tertiary education whilst Rural Sissala recorded 10.89%. The bulk of the sample had had mostly secondary and teaching training education (see Table 22.3).

Table 22.3: Educational Background

Background	Wa Central % Pre	Post	Sissala % Pre	Post
None	15.4	5	7.8	17.1
Primary	6.1	26.3	5.6	2.4
Secondary	36.7	31.3	38.9	41.5
Teacher Training	25.5	11.3	23.3	30.5
Technical Training	–	–	–	–
Vocational	–	3.0	–	1.2
Polytechnic	6.1	8.8	7.8	–
University	5.1	5.0	8.9	4.9
Other	–	–	–	–

Occupation

The occupations of respondents show teachers and traders to be in the majority in both constituencies during the both pre- and post- election surveys. In Wa Central, 20.4% were teachers and 22.4% traders in the pre-election survey. In the post election survey, 20% were teachers and 10% traders. In Sissala,

28.9% and 20% were teachers and traders respectively during the pre-election survey while they were 28% and 18.8% respectively in the post-election survey. In the National distribution, teachers and traders, featured equally prominently during the survey.

Personal Incomes

The personal incomes of respondents sampled, in the two constituencies show that nobody was above the ¢5m per annum threshold. A link can therefore be drawn between education, occupations and income levels. Most of the sampled respondents had only secondary or teacher training education and subsequently went into teaching or petty trading. It is not strange therefore, that the incomes they quoted fall within this range. On the whole, it can be conjectured that people in these two constituencies are generally poor.

Religious Affiliation

The two major religions practised by people in these constituencies are Islam and Christianity. An average of 60% of respondents in Wa Central are Moslems and 40% Christians. In Sissala, the difference between the two is not so great: 53% were Moslems and 45% Christians; about 1% represented African Traditional Religion.

Compared with the National figures, the statistics for these constituencies are skewed. While the National figure shows a predominantly Christian outlook, that is, an average of 76%, the two constituencies show a strong Moslem presence: an average of 57%.

Regional Affiliation

The percentages show most respondents were born in the constituencies. The percentages also show that a majority of them have continued to live in where they were born. For the pre-election survey, 74.5% of respondents said they were born in the Upper West Region whilst 99% of the respondents said they live there. In Sissala, 73.3% said they were born in the Upper West while 97.8% of respondents also said they lived there. Given the gap between place of birth and place of residence, it is quite possible, that the majority of those who were born there, still live there.

Political Participation

One of the major objectives of the surveys was to find out how much voters were involved in general as well as party politics and then draw from their reactions their perceptions of the entire political system of Ghana.

Voter Involvement and Perception of Political Parties

In the pre-election survey, 100% of respondents in Wa Central and 99% in Sissala were registered voters. In the post-election survey, 99% each of the respondents from both constituencies registered to vote. This gives an average of 99% for the two constituencies for both surveys. This figure is about equal to the National average of 98.6%.

Though a near perfect number were registered to vote in the 2000 elections not all of them were registered members of the contending political parties. In Wa Central for example, during the pre-election survey, 91.8 were registered party members whilst only 74% wielded party cards in Sissala. Of the 91.8 in Wa, a significant 38.8% were NDC while UGM had only 1%. In the Sissala constituency PNC was top with 38.9 (see Table 22.4).

Table 22.4: Respondents' Registration in Parties

Party	Wa %	Sissala %
CPP	3.1	1.1
NDC	38.8	30.0
PNC	15.3	38.9
UGM	1	–
GCPP	–	–
NPP	26.5	3.3
DPP	–	–
EGLE	2	–
NRP	6.1	4.4

Three parties stood out clearly as strong contenders. These were the NDC, NPP and PNC in that order in Wa Central and PNC, NDC and NRP in that order in Sissala.

Table 22.5 shows how the voters intended to vote in both presidential and parliamentary elections.

Table 22.5: Presidential and Parliamentary Elections

Party	Wa % Presidential	Wa % Parliamentary	Sissala % Presidential	Sissala % Parliamentary
NPP	8.6	27.6	5.6	4.4
CPP	4.1	4.1	–	–
UGM	1	1	1.1	1.1
NDC	40.8	39.8	35.6	35.6
PNC	17.3	18	44.4	45.6
NRP	6.1	8.2	4.4	6.7

The picture is not radically different for the parliamentary elections; but for a slight upward change in figures, for PNC and the NRP, they look the same as for the presidential elections. In these two constituencies therefore, people voted basically along party lines and not for personalities.

Party financing is a critical issue given that the constitution of Ghana regulates how this should be done. Party financing should come significantly, from party membership. This restriction however, puts a huge strain on some of the parties as membership contributions do not seem forthcoming, as the data show in the Wa Central and Sissala constituencies.

When asked in the post-election survey whether they contributed financially towards party activities, 29, representing 36.3% of registered voters in Wa Central and 9, representing 11% in Sissala said they did. But the majority of them, constituting 46, that is 57.3% in Wa Central, and 73, representing 89% in Sissala, said they did not. They preferred financing the party be the duty of others (see Table 22.6).

No wonder then, that in reaction to the question what they thought was lacking in their parties at constituency, regional and national levels, a majority of respondents mentioned adequate financing.

Yet a large majority of respondents again, think that the state should not come in at all to fund political parties (see Table 22.7).

When asked how actively involved they were in the activities of their parties in the pre-election survey, 74 representing 75.5% in Wa Central, and 59 representing 65.6% in Sissala said they attended party rallies.

Table 22.6: Party Financing

	Wa %	Sissala %
Party Chairman	15	2.4
Party Treasure	–	–
Contractors in Part	6.3	9.8
Businessmen in Party	20	40.2
Don't know	26	15.9

Table 22.7: State Financing

	Wa %	Sissala %
Yes	9.2	16.7
No	89.9	76.7

In the post-election survey however, 35% and 57% respectively in Wa Central and Sissala said they attended rallies. Apart from rallies, parties devised other strategies for meeting in small groups. One such medium was the keep fit concept. In Wa Central and Sissala, 4 representing 5% and 11 representing 13.4% respectively said they went to keep fit because of party politics.

Apart from party rallies and the keep fit concept, the media were another way by which the voters kept track of the (parties) activities. Forty-seven respondents, representing 58.8% and 66, representing 80.5% in Wa Central and Sissala respectively followed the activities of their parties in the news media.

Evaluation of the Party System

The survey asked what respondents thought about the political party system in Ghana today (see Table 22.8).

Table 22.8: Evaluation of Party System

	Wa %	Sissala %
A dirty game	28.8	32.9
Improved quality of living of Ghanaians	32.5	4.9
Brought division among Ghanaians	20	50
Enriched few people	17.5	11

When asked to comment on the performance of the political party system, the responses were at variance with what they thought about the nature of party politics (see Table 22.9).

Table 22.9: Performance of Political Parties

	Wa %	Sissala %
Doing a very good job	23.8	62.2
Doing a good job	55	24.4
Doing neither good nor bad	11.3	1.2
Doing a bad job	5	3.7
Doing a very bad job	–	1.2

With regard to the nominees for the parliamentary elections, 93.9% in Wa Central, and 84.4% in Sissala said they accepted them; 5.1% and 4.4% in Wa Central and Sissala respectively however dissented. Again in response to how they saw the nomination process of the candidates, 78.6% in Wa Central and 80% in Sissala thought it had been democratic while 11.2% and 5.6% respectively thought otherwise, citing among other reasons, that the candidates had been either imposed on them by National Executives or that there had been simply no alternatives.

In the pre-election survey, respondents assessed the chances of the opposition on one hand and the Progressive Alliance on the other of winning the elections (see Table 22.10).

Table 22.10: Chances of Parties

	Wa Central %	Sissala %
Opposition		
Very good	41.8	46.7
Good	25.5	26.7
Not so good	27.6	16.7
Progressive Alliance		
Very good	38.8	34.4
Good	40.8	42.2
Not so good	16.3	17.8

Respondents in both constituencies also predicted that there would be a presidential run-off. An average of 48% in both Wa Central and Sissala predicted for, whilst 45.7% predicted against the possibility of the run-off.

In the post-election survey respondents agreed by an average 94.5% in both constituencies that the campaigns to the 2000 elections had been free. However, in terms of logistics for the campaign some parties had been more endowed. By the estimation of an average 71% of respondents, not all parties had had adequate logistics; but 7% thought all parties had been equally endowed.

Even though some party followers were intimidated during this period, intimidation was minimal. Seventy-three per cent of respondents were not intimidated whilst 14% said they witnessed it citing the NDC as the main culprits, followed by the NPP in Wa Central, and the NDC alone as the culprit in Sissala. In most cases, they were purportedly aided by the military.

Evaluation of Electoral Process

A good percentage of respondents in the pre-election survey thought conditions in Ghana existed for free and fair elections — 76.5% in Wa Central and 57.8% in Sissala. 8.2% and 12.2% in Wa and Sissala respectively, however thought otherwise (see Table 22.11).

With regard to the 1996 elections, 46.9% and 53.3% in Wa and Sissala respectively, thought they had been free and fair; 35.7% and 31.1% in Wa and Sissala respectively however said they had not been free and fair. The predominant reason why they thought it had not been free and fair was that there had been vote rigging.

Table 22.11: Electoral Process

	Wa %	Sissala %
EC is controlled by government	4	–
Voter register was bloated	2	1.1
NDC is noted for rigging votes	2	4.4
Opposition lacks enough logistics	–	1.1
Vote buying	–	1.1
Intimidation / threats	–	4.4

A good number also thought the Electoral Commission was not independent of government. In fact 46.99% and 34.4% in Wa and Sissala respectively thought so. To buttress this claim, 55% in Wa and 56% in Sissala insisted the incumbent party had been using its position to gain undue advantage over the opposition. Reactions of respondents on the electoral system during the post-election survey were not as gloomy as those in the pre-election survey.

Overall, the electoral process in the 2000 elections was seen to be fair by respondents. An average 97% of them responded so. They also thought the coverage of the election by the state print and electronic media was good enough.

At the polling stations, arrangements and procedure for voting were rated very highly by respondents. 87.5% and 94% in Wa Central and Sissala respectively, said they did not encounter any problems on polling day. They cited election officials as very helpful. The security presence was also very well appreciated. In Wa Central for example, 96.3% of respondents were happy to see them, and in Sissala, 98% were delighted.

Just before the elections, there was so much hue and cry about what type of identification was to be accepted before one could cast a vote. In the end, the controversial thumb-print ID card was accepted for use used along side the voter ID card. Of the respondents, 96% in Wa Central and 93% in Sissala used the photo ID card. The rest who used the thumb-print ID card said they did not have any problem voting.

Evaluation of Democratic Institutions and Processes

By the estimation of 91.8% of respondents in Wa Central and 72% of those in Sissala, Ghana could be described then, as a democratic country. They also thought the democratic dispensation prevalent in the country had been growing for the previous four years. For example they thought that the press, political parties and other associations now enjoyed more freedom than they had four years then.

Members of Parliament are at a strategic level of the democratic process. As conduits and representatives of their electoral constituencies, they should interact with their constituents more often. When respondents were asked whether they had contacts with their MP during the last 12 months in Wa Central, only 18.8% said yes, and 77.5% said No. In Sissala, 26.8% had met the MP whilst 72% had not. Those who had contact with their respective MPs did so when they were at party rallies or as in the case of Sissala when a project was being commissioned for them. A majority of those who had not had contact stated that there was just not anything to bring them into contact. Other reasons given included the fact that their MPs were not approachable and that they belonged to opposing parties.

It is not surprising, then that 61.3% in Wa Central, and 74.4% in Sissala claim their MPs did not represent their interest the way they would have liked in the second parliament of the Fourth Republic.

Voter Perception of the Economy

Just as it is country-wide, respondents perceived the economy of Ghana in general to be in a mess, with 64.3% in the Wa Central constituency, and 69% in Sissala ranking it from bad to very bad. The ailing economy naturally did not better their lot. So 75% in Wa Central and 64.4% in Sissala stressed that the standard of living of their households declined miserably over the previous four years. They diagnosed the major economic problems in Ghana to be the depreciation of the *cedi*, unemployment, inflation and lack of private investment in the country.

Evaluation of Running Mates

The most important factor in selecting a running mate according to respondents in Wa and Sissala was experience. To 90% of respondents in Wa and 92.2% in Sissala, the choice of a presidential running mate would not affect the party they would vote for in the 2000 elections. On the issue of whether regional balance should be considered in the choice of the running mate, 23.5% in Wa and 17.8% in Sissala were positive; 29.6% in Wa and 60% in Sissala said it didn't matter while 42.9% in Wa and 21.1% in Sissala responded negatively. Ethnicity as a factor to consider in choice of running mate was rejected by 87.8% of respondents in Wa Central; in Sissala, 36.7% thought it was an insignificant factor while 54.4% rejected it outright.

Election Issues

The ailing economy was top on the agenda of national issues during the period leading to the elections. There was no doubt it was the main national issue of concern to respondents. Two other issues were identified along with it (see Table 22.12).

Table 22.12: National Issues

	Wa %	Sissala %
The Economy	81.6	86.7
Cont. and stability	5.1	4.4
Change and Development	9.2	8.9

At constituency level, respondents in Wa Central showed that a market place, water and sanitation, a good road network and education were top of their priorities. The market place I presume was mentioned due to the fact that trading is one of the main occupations of the people living there. The list of priorities of respondents in Sissala was not radically different, except that employment was the top of their priorities but not so prominent in Wa Central.

In the pre-election survey, an overwhelming number of respondents said they would vote for both party and the candidate presented by the party. In Wa Central, 89.8% voted this way in the presidential and 87.6% in the parliamentary. In Sissala, it was 87.8% for both presidential and parliamentary elections.

In the post-election survey, 63.8% of respondents in Wa Central and 81% in Sissala said their votes were influenced by both national and constituency issues. Parties that articulated these issues to their satisfaction, got their votes (see Table 22.13).

Table 22.13: Articulation of Election Issues

	Wa % National	Wa % Constituency	Sissala % National	Sissala % Constituency
NPP	52.5	52.5	43.9	36.6
NDC	25	25	9.8	7.3
PNC	7.8	8.8	42.7	45.1
CPP	–	–	–	–
NRP	5	5	2.4	1.2
GCPP	–	–	–	–
UGM	–	–	–	–

Evaluation of the Media

The media provided information about political activities at constituency and national levels. In this respect, the TV was given the highest rating with 51% in Wa Central and 50% in Sissala. The radio came second. But it was the political party rallies that ranked highest as the main source that influenced them most in casting their votes; Wa Central scored 44.2% and Sissala 41.1 for it. The TV came second with 31.6% in Wa Central and 27.8% in Sissala. Of all the media, the TV was adjudged the most credible by respondents in both constituencies. It scored 64.3% in Wa Central; and 57.8% in Sissala.

Identities

It is a normal social phenomenon for people to belong to groups. Such groups play very crucial roles in determining voting patterns. For instance the philosophy of a group could, with the ambitions of their leadership, lead members of a group to vote in one way or the other.

In Wa Central, 42.9% of respondents felt strongly attached to their religious groups which in the main is Islam; 25.5% on the other hand were also strongly attached to their ethnic groups. In Sissala too, a large majority felt strongly attached to their religious groups. This is made up of 57.8% of respondents Ethnicity, scored only 14.4%.

Social Capital

In the main a majority of respondents could not make ends meet considering their income in relation to the size of their households. On this a total of 95% respondents in Wa Central said they could barely survive on their income. In Sissala 86.6% could barely survive on their income. An average 66% in both constituencies also said that the standard of living of their households had deteriorated over the previous five years.

If they were to seek help elsewhere to help alleviate their dire situations, a majority of respondents in both Wa Central and Sissala constituencies — 84.7% and 77.8% respectively — felt they could most probably get it from neighbours. Family members came second in both constituencies, scoring 12.2% and 15.6% respectively.

The District Assembly is at the heart of decision making and policy implementation. If a problem required the attention of the Assembly, 60.2% of respondents in Wa Central would contact officials of the District Assembly; 37.8% would contact their representatives on the Assembly. In Sissala too, 52.2% would contact officials of the District Assembly, while 46.7% would contact their representatives on the Assembly.

With regard to effectiveness in resolving problems in the constituencies, 46.5% of respondents in Wa Central thought their representatives on the District Assembly were the most effective. This is followed by the actions of concerned citizens of the communities, which scored 23.5%. In Sissala too, representatives on the District Assembly were rated by 46.7% of respondents as most effective, followed by concerned citizens with 34.4%.

Presidential Run-off

From the responses in Wa Central and Sissala, respondents were prepared for the run-off and when it happened, 67.5% in Wa Central, and 87.8% in Sissala voted for Mr J. A. Kufuor. He got the vote mainly because, according to them, he was the right person to bring about the change they wanted. Significantly nobody voted for him on tribal grounds. Interesting too, 60% in Wa Central and 50% in Sissala voted for the same candidate in the first round of presidential elections as in the run-off.

It is quite significant too that an overwhelming majority of respondents did not encounter any problems during the run-off. Rather, they were appreciative of the election officials as well as the security. The voting procedure was orderly according to 96.8% and 96.3% respondents from Wa and Sissala, respectively.

Conclusion

These surveys have revealed very important features in the two constituencies in the North that can be used as yardsticks to measuring the pace and direction of the democratisation process in Ghana. With a sample of respondents who fell largely within the most productive age bracket of 18–40 years, the responses given to the questions should not be taken lightly.

One major milestone in the democratisation process in nations is that voters vote on issues and not ethnicity. This has been amply demonstrated in the responses provided here. That people voted the incumbent government out of power largely as a result of their failure to manage the economy well, cannot be disputed. As the aggregate national responses in the surveys indicate 65.4% of respondents thought ethnicity was not a major factor in determining the outcome of the election of a president and a vice. Rather, the indicators were the state of the economy and its manifestations were the determining factors.

The reactions of respondents also show that the media and the democratic institutions such as the parliamentary system, the Electoral Commission, and the political parties as well as the security services, all have a crucial role to play in ensuring that democracy is nurtured to grow in Ghana.

If there are any lessons for politicians to learn from the results of these surveys, then it surely should be that rural Ghana is fast growing in terms of imbibing the processes of democratisation and that people voted for parties that articulated well issues that are close to them. To get their votes therefore, it is imperative to sell yourselves very well to them.

REFERENCES

Bening, R. B. (1990) *A History of Education in Northern Ghana, 1907–1976*. Ghana Universities Press, Accra.

Ghana, Republic of (1988 and 2000) *Ghana Living Standards Survey: 1988 and 2000* Ghana Statistical Services. Accra.

CHAPTER 23

The Future of Democratic Consolidation in Ghana

JOSEPH R. A. AYEE

Introduction

The findings from these two volumes (thematic and constituency studies) have shown that the 2000 general elections and presidential run-off in Ghana held on 7 December and 28 December 2000 respectively will certainly go down in history as ones that have played an important role in the complex and often difficult process of consolidating a new democracy like that of Ghana. In a country without a history of competitive elections, it can take several elections before all political actors understand, accept and effectively participate in the electoral process. The success of the 2000 general elections and the presidential run-off and especially their relatively high quality have significantly contributed to the process of consolidation by institutionalizing the electoral process and enhancing the legitimacy of the democratic process. In other words, the elections were not divisive, violent or disputed so as to seriously undermine democratic consolidation.

The purpose of this chapter is to summarize the findings and consider their significance for democratic consolidation.

Summary of Findings

A number of useful findings from the two volumes (the thematic and constituency studies) are worth highlighting. They are:

- Incumbency has advantages and sometimes disadvantages;
- Political parties in Ghana lack internal democracy;
- Two key functions need to be strengthened if political parties are to successfully play a significant role in support of democratic governance: (i) representation — increasing capacities to communicate regularly and effectively between both the citizenry and elected

representatives; and (ii) policy pluralism — improving the capacities of elected officials and representative institutions to identify, formulate and evaluate policy options and to present constructive alternatives;
- The quality of elections and the EC's contribution to democratic consolidation appear to have been influenced by the democratic intent and seriousness of the political and administrative elites;
- There was a muddled perception of the lack of independence of the EC, in spite of its efforts to fine-tune the electoral process and thereby make it more acceptable to all key players;
- The media are not only an important source of information but also key players in the democratization process;
- The non-partisan election-monitoring efforts of CODEO and the Forum of Religious Bodies (all CSOs) have been critical in deterring fraud, enhance voter confidence and affirm the legitimacy of the result. This shows that CSOs have explicit democracy-building purposes that go beyond leadership training (Diamond, 1994);
- Although international observers are likened to "democracy police" because their presence at elections were expected to deter blatant fraud and expose irregularities, questions have been raised about their variable standards and procedures and more seriously their allegiance;
- The high level of inclusiveness, involvement and participation of stakeholders in the electoral process promotes trust, consensus and credibility, essential in legitimising the outcome of the elections;
- What goes before polling is the main key to both success and failure. In other words, election quality is not achieved by concentrating on election day activities only, far from it, even though they are still important — but only if the course of events during the pre-polling phase is acceptable by the stakeholders (Elklit, 1999);
- Voting motivations are based on the economic issues such as employment and living conditions;
- There is a relatively low response concerning issues like law and order, qualities of candidates, ethnicity, group protection and moral standards;
- Majority of Ghanaians see Ghana as a country on the right path of democracy and have faith in it;
- As a result of three elections in succession, the Ghanaian voter is becoming more and more sophisticated regarding electoral choice and issues;
- Majority of respondents even though conceded that political parties

lack financial resources and logistics, they do not support state funding of political parties;

Conclusion: Implication of the Findings for Democratic Consolidation

The concept of democratic consolidation defies clear-cut definition. Indeed as rightly pointed by Schedler (1998), there are so many different definitions of democratic consolidation that the concept has expanded beyond all recognition. It has become to include such divergent items as follows:

- Popular legitimation;
- The diffusion of democratic values;
- The neutralization of anti-system actors;
- Civilian supremacy over the military, elimination of authoritarian enclaves;
- Party building;
- The organization of functional interests;
- The stabilization of electoral rules;
- The routinization of politics;
- The decentralization of state power;
- The introduction of mechanisms of direct democracy;
- Judicial reform;
- The alleviation of poverty; and
- Economic stabilization (Schedler, 1998).

Nonetheless, there appears to be some consensus on two features of democratic consolidation:

(i) The widespread acceptance of the general principle of democratic competition. For instance, according to Burton *et. al.* (1995) consolidation denotes the condition of a political system in which all major political actors and social groups expect that government leaders will be chosen through competitive elections and regard representative institutions and procedures as their main channel for pressing claims on the state. For Gunther *et. al.* (1986) a democratic regime is consolidated when all politically significant groups regard its key political institutions as the only legitimate framework for political contestation, and adhere to the democratic rules of the game.

(ii) Mass acceptance of democracy, in particular the degree to which the population is satisfied with democracy. Many believe that satisfaction with the democratic experience promotes a greater commitment to democracy and hence signifies an important tend towards democratic consolidation. In the words of Diamond (1994: 15) consolidation is the "process by which democracy becomes so broadly and profoundly legitimate among its citizens that it is very unlikely to break down. It involves behavioural and institutional changes that normalize democratic politics and narrows its uncertainty. This normalization requires the expansion of citizen access, development of democratic citizenship and culture, broadening of leadership recruitment and training, and other functions that civil society performs. But most of all, and most urgently, it requires political institutionalisation". Indeed, Gunther et. al. (1986) acknowledge that widespread support for and satisfaction with democracy may be an important and necessary condition, particularly insofar as they increase the chances that whatever new governmental system or regime may come into existence will be democratic. However, by itself, widespread support for democracy undervalues or ignores the importance of the absence of fundamental disputes among politically significant groups over the acceptability of the basic framework for political contestation, and what this implies for democratic stability, predictability and ultimately sustainability (Przeworski et. al., 1996). Therefore, it is not a sufficient condition for the onset of democratic consolidation. This notwithstanding, although widespread support of democracy may not by itself be a sufficient condition for democratic consolidation, it certainly is recognized as a contributory factor.(Burnell and Calvert, 1999).

The findings show that most, if not all, stakeholders in the electoral process are interested in, and committed to competitive elections while Ghanaians are satisfied with the democratic experiment so far. This, no doubt, augurs well for the future of democratic consolidation in Ghana. It seems, however, that this is not enough to promote democratic consolidation. Consequently, the following strategies and issues need to be considered in Ghana's efforts for democratic consolidation:

- Effective state institutions, which do not guarantee wise and effective policies but at least ensure that the government formulates and implements programmes aimed at a reduction in the appalling poverty, inequality and social injustice.

- The international community might be able counteract democratic setbacks and de-democratization, but further democratization should normally come within Ghana. The present arrangement whereby Ghana's democratisation process is largely funded by foreign donors is not in the best interest of democratic consolidation because as the saying goes "He who pays the piper calls the tune". While not suggesting unbridled and unrestrained interference in the process, the role of foreign donors influencing electoral programmes cannot be easily dismissed.

- It is possible for a country to establish a façade that has all the outward appearance of a democratic system without developing the "participatory, democratic political culture" necessary to sustain it. Ghana needs sufficient time to nurture this set of orientations. Of course, it would certainly be naïve to assume that democratic institutions could be established in Ghana in a few years after decades of authoritarian rule, government mismanagement, and economic conditions which are, at least, extremely difficult. The democratic advances made by the country seem to be largely structural and/or constitutional. Vis-à-vis the era of PNDC authoritarian rule and NDC rule, the outcome of the 2000 elections is certainly a strong breath of fresh air. One should however, be cautious that it does not end up as only cosmetic and/or temporary.

- External expressions of support for democracy in Ghana will sound convincing to political parties and voters only if it is acknowledged that democracy is more than just another election, and that it cannot "be brewed like a cup of instant coffee" (Nyong'o, 1988). In the words of Geisler (1993: 637):

  > We all need to come to terms with the contradiction that democracy is about self-determination and that political and economic conditionalities are externally imposed.

REFERENCES

Burnell P. and Calvert, P. (1999) "The Resilience of Democracy: An Introduction", *Democratization*, Vol. 6, No. 1: 1–32.

Burton, M., Gunther, R. and Higley, J. (1995) "Introduction: Elite Transformations and Democratic Regimes", in Higley, J. and Gunther, R. (eds) *Elites and Democratic Consolidation in Latin America* (Cambridge: Cambridge University Press).

Diamond, L. (1994) "Rethinking Civil Society: Toward Democratic Consolidation", *Journal of Democracy*, Vol. 5, No. 3: 4–17.

Elklit, J. (1999) "Electoral Institutional Change and Democratization: You Can Lead a Horse to Water, but You Can't Make it Drink", *Democratization*, Vol. 6, No. 4 (Winter): 28–51.

Geisler, G. (1993) "Fair? What Has Fairness Got to Do with It? Vagaries of Election Observations and Democratic Standards", *The Journal of Modern African Studies*, Vol. 31, No. 4: 613–637.

Nyong'o, P.A. (1988) "Political Instability and the Prospects for Democracy in Africa", *African Development*, Vol. 13, No. 1: 34–47.

Przeworski, A., Alvarez, M., Cheibub, J. A. and Limongi, F. (1996) "What Makes Democracies Endure?", *Journal of Democracy*, Vol. 7, No. 1 (January): 39–55.

Schedler, A. (1998) "What is Democratic Consolidation?" *Journal of Democracy*, Vol. 9, No. 2 (April): 91–107.

APPENDIX 1

Pre-2000 Elections Survey Questionnaire

Introduction

The Department of Political Science, University of Ghana, is conducting a research into the 2000 Parliamentary and Presidential Elections. This questionnaire is a major part of this study.

The research is necessary to establish the facts of the elections for present and future generations of Ghanaians and to deepen general understanding of elections in Ghana and Africa.

The research is not intended to probe into people's private lives, neither is it intended to collect personal information for the government or any of its agencies.

It is an independent academic research, initiated designed and executed by the Department of Political Science. It is our hope that you will co-operate with our field staff and answer the questions without looking over your shoulders.

This research is supported and funded by DANIDA.

Thank you for your co-operation.

BACKGROUND DATA

Name of Interviewer ....

Questionnaire I.D ....

Region ....

Name of Constituency ....

Electoral Area ....

This Electoral Area is in: 1. Urban Area   2. Rural Area

House No. ....

Time of Interview ....

Date of Interview ....

Language of Interview ....

QUESTIONNAIRE

1. PRESENT POLITICAL PARTICIPATION

1.1 Are you a registered voter?

    1. Yes 2. No

1.2 If no, why not?

1. Voting does not bring any improvement in my life or to my community; it benefits only the politicians.
2. I had more important personal commitments and could not spare time to register.
3. I had travelled outside the country.
4. I could not change my thumb-printed ID card for a photo ID card.
5. Other (specify)..................................

1.3 Are you a registered member of a political party?

    1. Yes   2. No

1.4 If yes, which party? [If yes go to Q1.7]

1. CPP   6. NPP
2. NDC   7. DPP
3. PNC   8. Egle
4. UGM   9. NRP
5. GCPP

1.5 If no, give reasons.

1. For personal reasons I don't like party politics.
2. None of the existing parties is good enough for me.
3. Political parties in Ghana do not concern themselves with policies; they are based on personalities.
4. Party politics in Ghana has lost its meaning and purpose and turned into a money game.
5. Other (specify)..................................

1.6 If you are not a registered member of any political party, which one of the following parties do you have an inclination towards?

  1. CPP   6. NPP
  2. NDC   7. DPP
  3. PNC   8. Egle
  4. UGM   9. NRP
  5. GCPP

1.7 Do you follow the activities of the political parties in the news media?

  1. Yes   2. No

1.8 Have you been attending political rallies in connection with the 2000 elections?

  1. Yes   2. No

1.9 Did you vote in the 1996 Presidential elections and Parliamentary elections?

  1. Yes   2. No

1.10 If No, give reasons.

  1. I know that whoever comes to power it would not make any difference in my life.
  2. My kind of presidential/parliamentary candidate was not in the race.
  3. I don't believe in party political contests.
  4. Politicians are all the same; they seek their own welfare and not that of the people.
  5. I had more important personal commitments.
  6. Other (specify)....................................

1.11 Did you vote for the same party in the 1996 Presidential/Parliamentary elections?

  1. Yes 2. No

1.12 If no, give reasons.

   1. My party did not field a presidential candidate because of the alliance.
   2. I liked the presidential candidate of my party but not its parliamentary candidate.
   3. I liked the parliamentary candidate of my party but not its presidential candidate.
   4. Politicians are all the same; they seek their own welfare and not that of the people.
   5. I had more important personal commitments.
   6. Other (specify)..

1.13 Did you vote in the 1998 District Assembly elections?

   1. Yes   2. No

1.14 If no, give reasons.

   1. District Assemblies have little or no power; they are under the control of central government.
   2. Absence of parties makes district assembly elections uninteresting to me.
   3. I consider district assembly elections to be farce because the DCE is not elected by the people.
   4. The election coincided with more important personal commitments.
   5. Other (specify)..

1.15 Indicate the traditional political party group that your parents support.

   1. CPP Group   4. UP/NPP Group
   2. NDC Group   5. I don't know
   3. No Group   6. Other (Specify) ....

2. VOTER PERCEPTION AND IDENTIFICATION

2.1 If you belong to any political party, how did you become a member or sympathizer?

   1. Through my parents.
   2. My personal decision
   3. I was a member of the party's youth wing
   4. Through peer group
   5. Though professional association
   6. Other (Specify)..

3. **PAST POLITICAL PARTICIPATION (1996 ELECTIONS)**

3.1 Did you vote in the 1996 Presidential elections?

   1. Yes 2. No

3.2 If yes, which party did you vote for?

   1. NPP   4. NDC
   2. PNC   5. PCP
   3. Independent 6. DPP

3.3 Did you vote in the 1996 Parliamentary elections?

   1. Yes   2. No

3.4 If yes which party did you vote for?

   1. NPP   4. NDC
   2. PNC   5. PCP
   3. Independent 6. DPP

4. **THE 2000 ELECTIONS**

4.1 Will you vote in the 2000 elections?

   1. Yes   2. No   3. Don't know

4.2 If yes, which party will you vote for in the Presidential election?

   1. NPP   6. NDC
   2. CPP   7. PNC
   3. UGM   8. NRP
   4. GCPP   9. Independent
   5. Don't know   10. Other (Specify) ....

4.3 If no, why not?

   1. It does not matter who comes to power, it will not make any difference in my life.
   2. My kind of party and political leader has not yet come on to the scene.

3. I don't believe in party politics.
4. Politicians are all the same, they seek their own welfare and not that of the people.
5. Other (Specify)...

4.4 If you vote in the 2000 parliamentary elections which party will you vote for?

1. NPP   6. PNC
2. CPP   7. NRP
3. UGM   8. Don't Know
4. GCPP   9. Other (Specify) ....
5. NDC

5. VOTER ATTITUDE AND PERCEPTION: THE ECONOMY

5.1 What do you think about the state of the Ghanaian economy today?

1. Very good
2. Good
3. Bad
4. Very bad
5. Neither good nor bad
6. Don't Know

5.2 Would you say that over the past four years the Ghanaian economy has improved or become worse?

1. Considerably improved   3. Become worse   5. Don't know
2. Just improved   4. Sharply deteriorated

6. EVALUATION OF THE DEMOCRATIC PROCESS

6.1 Do you think Ghana today could be described as a democratic country?

1. Yes   2. No   3. Don't Know

6.2 Over the past four years has democracy improved in Ghana?

1. Yes   2. No   3. Don't know

6.3 Do you think the Press in Ghana has more freedom now than four years ago?

1. Yes   2. No   3. Don't know

6.4 Do you think political parties and other associations have more freedom now than four years ago?

    1. Yes   2. No   3. Don't know

7. EVALUATION OF THE ELECTORAL PROCESS

7.1 Do you think conditions exist in Ghana for free and fair elections for the December 7 2000 elections?

    1. Yes   2. No   3. Don't know

7.2 If no, give reasons.

....

....

....

7.3 In your view do you think the last (1996) general elections was free and fair?

    1. Yes   2. No   3. Don't know

7.4 Give a reason for your answer in Q7.3

....

7.5 Do you think the Electoral Commission is independent of government control?

    1. Yes   2. No   3. Don't know

7.6 Apart from the Electoral Commission do you think there are any other ways to influence the elections?

    1. Yes   2. No   3. Don't know

7.7 If yes, please specify the way(s)

....

....

7.8 Do you think that the district office of the Electoral Commission is fair to all the parties?

　　1. Yes   2. No
　　3. Don't Know   4. Other (Specify).......................................

7.9 If no, in what way(s) has the Electoral Commission not been fair to the parties?

....

....

....

7.10 Do you think the party in power gets undue advantage over the parties in the opposition when it comes to elections?

　　1. Yes   2. No   3. Don't know

7.11 If yes give a reason(s).

....

....

....

8. EVALUATION OF THE PARTY SYSTEM

8.1 What are the chances of an opposition party winning the presidential elections?

　　1. Very good   2. Good
　　3. Not so good   4. Don't know

8.2 What are the chances of the Progressive Alliance (NDC, Egle, DPP) winning the presidential elections?

　　1. Very good   2. Good
　　3. Not so good   4. Don't know

8.3 Do you think a second round presidential run-off is more likely in the 2000 elections than in the 1996 one?

    1. Yes   2. No   3. Don't know

8.4 If yes, give reasons.

    1. The number of parties contesting the presidential elections has increased.
    2. Lack of a charismatic presidential candidate
    3. Similarity in party manifestoes
    4. Other (Specify) ....

8.5 Do parties in Ghana project personalities more than their policies?

    1. Yes   2. No   3. Don't know

8.6 Do you think most of the parties in Ghana are financially sound?

    1. Yes   2. No   3. Don't know

8.7 Do you think parties should be financed by the state?

    1. Yes   2. No   3. Don't know

8.8 Do you like the candidate who has been nominated by your party to stand for election in your constituency?

    1. Yes   2. No   3. Don't know
    4. Other (Specify)...

8.9 What do you think of the process for the selection of the candidate to stand for your party in your constituency?

    1. Democratic   2. Not democratic
    3. Don't know   4. Other (Specify) ....

8.10 Give reasons for your answer.

....

....

....

9. EVALUATION OF RUNNING MATES

9.1 What do you consider as the most important factor in the choice of a Presidential running mate?

    1. Ethnic background   2. Regional balance
    3. Gender balance   4. Experience
    5. Party loyalty   6. Other (Specify).................................

9.2 Will the presidential running mate chosen affect the party you will vote for?

    1. Yes   2. No

9.3 If yes, how will it affect your vote?

....

....

....

9.4 For the Presidential election, do you think it is important to have a *regional* balance (President and Vice President) on the ticket?

    1. Yes   3. No
    2. Doesn't matter   4. Don't know

9.5 For the Presidential election, do you think it is important to have an *ethnic* balance (President and Vice President) on the ticket?

    1. Yes   3. No
    2. Doesn't matter   4. Don't know

10. ELECTION ISSUES

10.1 What do you consider to be the 3 main issues at the national level in the 2000 elections?

    1. The Economy   4. Improving democracy
    2. Continuity and Stability   5. Ghana's future in the 21st century
    3. Change and development   6. Other (Specify)............................

10.2 What do you consider to be the 3 most important development issues in your constituency in the December 2000 elections?

1. ....

2. ....

3. ....

10.3 In the December 7, 2000 Presidential election would you vote for the political party, the candidate or for both?

1. The party 3. The candidate
2. Both party and candidate 4. Don't know

10.4 In the 2000 Parliamentary election, would you vote for the political party, the candidate or for both?

1. The party 3. The candidate
2. Both party and candidate 4. Don't know

11. MEDIA

11.1 From what sources have you received most of your information about the issues and candidates in the election?

1. Television 5. Radio
2. Newspaper 6. Magazine
3. Friends and family (word of mouth) 7. Posters/fliers
4. Don't know 8. Other (Specify).....................

11.2 Which source have you found to be the most useful in deciding who to vote for in your constituency?

1. Television 6. Magazines
2. Newspaper 7. Posters/fliers
3. Friends and family (word of mouth) 8. Don't know
4. Candidate rallies 9. Other (Specify) ....
5. Radio

11.3 In general, which source of media information do you trust most to tell the truth?

1. State-owned (public) television
2. Foreign television
3. Foreign radio
4. State-owned (public) newspapers
5. Don't know
6. Private television
7. State-owned (public) radio
8. Private radio
9. Private newspapers
10. Other (Specify)...............

12. **IDENTITIES AND SOCIAL CAPITAL ISSUES**

12.1 What Ghanaian language can you:

1. Speak............................ 2. Write................................

3. Read............................. 4. Understand.........................

12.2 What is your mother tongue? ....

12.3 Which of these is a better description of the place where you lived when you were growing up?

1. Urban Area   2. Rural area

12.4 How strongly or otherwise do you feel towards the following? (Rank from 5 = strongly attached to 1 = weakly attached).
Rank
1. A Region   ( )
2. A religion   ( )
3. An ethnic group   ( )
4. An association   ( )
5. Other (Specify)....................... ( )

12.6 To which of the following do you feel most strongly attached? [Choose any 3]

1. The region where you now live
2. The region where you grew up
3. Ghana as a whole
4. Your family
6. The people that work with you
7. Your friends

8. People of your own ethnic group
9. People of your own religion
9. People who speak your language
10. People whose income is about the same as your own
11. Your trade union
12. The political party that you would vote for in national elections
13. Your local District Assembly
14. Don't know

12.7 Taking account of the number of people in your household, how adequate is your household income?

1. Not really enough to survive on.
2. Only just enough to survive on
3. Enough for a fair standard of living
4. Enough for a good standard of living
5. Don't know

12.8 Over the last five years, has your household's standard of living got:

1. Much better
2. A little worse
3. Don't know
4. A little better
5. Much worse

12.9 Looking ahead to the next five years, do you expect your household's standard of living to get:

1. Much better
2. A little worse
3. Don't know
4. A little better
5. Much worse

12.10 If your household really could not survive on our own household income, where do you do you think you might get help from? (Choose the 3 most important to you)

1. Neighbours
2. Family members
3. Friends
4. Trade Union
5. Your own church or religious organization
6. Another religious or charitable organization
7. A party or political organization

8. Officials of the your District Assembly
9. Officials in some government office
10. Your Member of Parliament
11. Other (Specify) ....

12.11 And of all these, which one would be likely to provide the <u>most</u> help? (Choose only one)

1. Neighbours
2. Family members
3. Friends
4. Trade Union
5. Your own church or religious organization
6. Another religious or charitable organization
7. A party or political organization
8. Officials of the your District Assembly
9. Officials in some government office
10. Your Member of Parliament
11. Other (Specify) ....

12.12 If you are concerned about a problem that could be solved by the District Assembly, which of the following would be the most effective way of getting the District Assembly to take the necessary action: [Choose the 3 most effective]

1. Contacting officials of the District Assembly itself
2. Contacting your own representative on the District Assembly
3. Writing to the newspapers about the problem
4. Signing a petition
5. Taking part in a protest of some kind
6. Going through your trade union
7. Going through your church or religious organization
8. Going through a party or political organization
9. Going through your Member of Parliament
10. Contacting your friends and neighbours about the problem
11. Contacting other members of your ethnic group about the problem
12. Joining together with others who were specially concerned about the problem

12.13 Which one do you think would be *most* effective? [Rank the 3 chosen in Q 12.12 from 3 = most effective to 1 = least effective]

1. Contacting officials of the District Assembly itself ( )
2. Contacting your own representative on the District Assembly ( )
3. Writing to the newspapers about the problem ( )
4. Signing a petition ( )
5. Taking part in a protest of some kind ( )
6. Going through your trade union ( )
7. Going through your church or religious organization ( )
8. Going through a party or political organization ( )
9. Going through your Member of Parliament ( )
10. Contacting your friends and neighbours about the problem ( )
11. Contacting other members of your ethnic group about the problem ( )
12. Joining together with others who were specially concerned about the problem. ( )

12.14 In the last five years have you been concerned about any particular problems that could be solved by your own District Assembly?

1. Yes   2. No   3. Don't know

12.15. If yes what were the three most important problems?

1. ....

2. ....

3. ....

12.16 If you tried to get your District Assembly to take action on any problem, what result did you get?

1. Successful
2. Unsuccessful
3. Did not try
4. Don't know

12.17 If you were unsuccessful, what were the reasons?

....

....

....

DEMOGRAPHIC DATA

D.1 Gender

    1. Male   2. Female

D.2 Age

1. 18–25
2. 26–30
3. 31–40
4. 41–50
5. 51–60
6. 61–70
7. 71 and over

D.3 Educational Background

1. None
2. Secondary
3. Polytechnic
4. Primary
5. Teacher Training/Technical college
6. University

D.4 Occupation

1. Unemployed
2. Teacher
3. Businessman
4. Manager
5. Professional
6. Farmer
7. Trader
8. Artisan
9. Public Servant
10. Other (Specify).......................

D.5 Religion

1. Christian
2. African Traditional
3. Muslim
4. Other (Specify).............................

D.6 Personal/Individual Income Level (p.a.) ....

D.7 Region in which you were born

1. Ashanti
2. Central
3. Greater Accra
4. Upper East
5. Volta
6. Brong Ahafo
7. Eastern
8. Northern
9. Upper West
10. Western

D. 8. Region in which you are now living

1. Ashanti
2. Central
3. Greater Accra
4. Upper East
5. Volta
6. Brong Ahafo
7. Eastern
8. Northern
9. Upper West
10. Western

APPENDIX 2

Post-2000 Elections Survey Questionnaire

Introduction

The Department of Political Science, University of Ghana, is conducting a research into the 2000 Parliamentary and Presidential Elections. This questionnaire is a major part of this study.

The research is necessary to establish the facts of the elections for present and future generations of Ghanaians and to deepen general understanding of elections in Ghana and Africa.

The research is not intended to probe into people's private lives, neither is it intended to collect personal information for the government or any of its agencies.

It is an independent academic research, initiated designed and executed by the Department of Political Science. It is our hope that you will co-operate with our field staff and answer the questions without looking over your shoulders.

This research is supported and funded by DANIDA.

Thank you for your co-operation.

BACKGROUND DATA

Name of Interviewer ....

Questionnaire I.D ....

Region ....

Name of constituency ....

Electoral Area ....

House No. ....

Is this constituency in   1. Urban Area   2. Rural Area

Time of Interview ....

Date of Interview ....

Language of interview ....

POST-ELECTION SURVEY QUESTIONNAIRE

1. GENERAL POLITICAL PARTICIPATION

1.1 Are you a registered voter?

    1. Yes   2. No

1.2 Did you vote in the 1996 Presidential elections?

    1. Yes   2. No

1.3 If yes, which presidential candidate did you vote for?

    1. J. A. Kuffour   2. J. J. Rawlings   3. Dr Edward Mahama

1.4 If no, give reasons.

....

1.5 Did you vote in the 1996 Parliamentary elections?

    1. Yes   2. No

1.6 If yes, which party's candidate did you vote for?

    1. PCP   2. NDC   3. NPP   4. PNC
    5. Other..................

1.7 If you did not vote in the 1996 parliamentary elections, give reasons.

....

1.8 Did you vote in the 1998 District Assembly elections?

    1. Yes   2. No

1.9 If no, give reasons.

....

1.10 Did you vote in the 2000 Presidential and Parliamentary elections?

   1. Yes   2. No

2. **VOTER PERCEPTION OF, AND INVOLVEMENT WITH, POLITICAL PARTIES**

2.1 Are you a registered member of a political party?

   1. Yes   2. No

2.2 If yes, which party are you registered with?

   1. NPP   2. NDC   3. PNC   4. CPP   5. NRP   6. GCPP
   7. UGM

2.3 If you are not a registered member of a political party, give reasons.

   1. I don't know the registration procedure.
   2. I was not encouraged by the party to register.
   3. I don't like party politics.
   4. None of the existing parties is good enough for me.
   5. Other (specify) ....

2.4 If you are not a registered member of any political party, which of the following parties do you have an inclination towards?

   1. NPP   2. NDC   3. PNC   4. CPP   5. NRP   6. GCPP
   7. UGM

2.5 Do you follow the activities of the political parties in the news media?

   1. Yes   2. No

2.6 Did you attend political rallies for the just ended December 7, 2000 elections?

   1. Yes   2. No

2.7 Did you attend keep fit/Jama for the just ended December 7, 2000 elections?

   1. Yes   2. No

Appendix

2.8 If you belong to a political party, how often do you hold meetings?

    1. Weekly   2. Fortnightly
    3. Monthly   4. Other (Specify) ....

2.9 Do you participate when your party holds a rally/keep fit/Jama in your town or village?

    1. Yes   2. No

2.10 Do you participate when your party holds a keep fit/Jama in your town/village?

    1. Yes   2. No

2.11 Do you contribute financially towards your party's activities?

    1. Yes   2. No

2.12 If you don't contribute financially, who do you think provides the money to run your party's activities?

1. The party Chairman
2. The party Treasurer
3. Contractors in the party
4. Business people in the party
5. Don't know
6. Other (Specify) ....

2.13 What do you think is lacking in your party's organization in your constituency?

1. Adequate finance
2. Lack of logistics (cars, loudspeakers etc.)
3. Campaign materials (posters, banners and pamphlets)
4. Active honest and dedicated leadership
5. Loyal and committed members
6. Clearly articulated policies
7. Other (Specify)......................................

2.14 What do you think is lacking in your party's organization in your region?

1. Adequate finance
2. Lack of logistics (cars, loudspeakers etc.)
3. Campaign materials (posters, banners and pamphlets)

4. Active honest and dedicated leadership
5. Loyal and committed members
6. Clearly articulated policies
7. Other (Specify).................................

2.15 What do you think is lacking in your party's organization at the national level?

1. Adequate finance
2. Lack of logistics (cars, loudspeakers etc.)
3. Campaign materials (posters, banners and pamphlets)
4. Active honest and dedicated leadership
5. Loyal and committed members
6. Clearly articulated policies
7. Other (Specify).................................

2.16 What do you think about party politics in Ghana today?

1. It is a dirty game.
2. It has improved the quality of living of Ghanaians.
3. It has brought division among Ghanaians.
4. It has enriched a few people
5. Don't Know

2.17 What do you think of the performance of political parties in Ghana?

1. They are doing a very good job.
2. They are doing a good job.
3. They are neither doing a good nor a bad job.
4. They are doing a bad job.
5. They are doing a very bad job.
6. Don't Know

2.18 Do you agree with the view that irrespective of the party in power, there is no difference to what happens at the national level (Obiaa ba saa)?

1. Yes   2. No   3. Don't know

2.19 If yes, why do you think so?
....
....
....

2.20 If no, why do you think so?

   ....
   ....
   ....

2.21 If you are a registered member of a political party, do you belong to the party executive?

   1. Yes   2. No

2.22 Are you interested in holding a leadership position in your party?

   1. Yes   2. No

2.23 If yes, why?

   ....
   ....
   ....

2.24 If no, why?

   ....
   ....
   ....

2.25 If you belong to your party's executive, do you hold any position in the party?

   1. Yes   2. No

2.26 If yes, what position do you hold?

   1. Chairman
   2. Vice Chairman
   3. Secretary
   4. Assistant Secretary
   5. Treasurer
   6. Vice Treasurer
   7. Organizing secretary
   8. Deputy organizing secretary
   9. Youth organizer
   10. Women's organizer
   11. Other (Specify)........................

2.27 At what level do you hold this position?

 1. Ward
 2. Village/Town
 3. Constituency
 4. Regional
 5. National

2.28 Have you ever attended a regional/national congress of your party?

 1. Yes   2. No

2.29 Have you ever contested for a party position?

 1. Yes   2. No

2.30 Have you ever contested for the parliamentary candidacy of your party?

 1. Yes   2. No

2.31 Have you ever contested for any party executive position in your constituency?

 1. Yes   2. No

2.32 If yes, what position?

 1. Chairman
 2. Vice Chairman
 3. Secretary
 4. Assistant Secretary
 5. Treasurer
 6. Vice Treasurer
 7. Organizing secretary
 8. Deputy organizing secretary
 9. Youth organizer
 10. Women's organizer
 11. Other (specify).........................

2.33 Did all parties have the chance to campaign freely in the 2000 elections?

 1. Yes   2. No   3. Don't know

2.34 Did all parties have adequate logistics (cars, loudspeakers) for their campaign in the 2000 elections?

 1. Yes   2. No   3. Don't know

2.35 Was there intimidation of some party members and supporters by others in the 2000 elections?

    1. Yes   2. No   3. Don't know

2.36 Which parties were guilty of such intimidation in the 2000 elections?

    1. NPP   2. NDC   3. CPP   4. PNC
    5. NRP   6. GCPP   7. UGM

2.37 What were some of the election violations?

....

....

2.38 Which of the parties did you vote for in the 2000 Presidential elections?

    1. NPP   2. NDC   3. CPP   4. PNC
    5. NRP   6. GCPP   7. UGM

2.39 Why did you vote for this party?

1. They have good and honest candidate.
2. They have good policies to ensure the development of the country.
3. Traditionally this is how my family and I have voted.
4. There is the need for change of national leadership.
5. There is need for continuity and stability.
6. Other (Specify)..

2.40 Which of the parties did you vote for in the 2000 Parliamentary elections?

    1. NPP   2. NDC   3. CPP   4. PNC
    5. NRP   6. GCPP   7. UGM

2.41 Why did you vote for this party?

1. They have a good and honest candidate.
2. They have good policies to ensure the development of our constituency.
3. Traditionally this is how my family and I have voted.
4. There is the need for change of the M.P. for my constituency.
5. There is need for continuity and stability.
6. Other (Specify)..

3. EVALUATION OF DEMOCRATIC INSTITUTIONS AND PROCESS

3.1 Have you had any contacts with your member of parliament (MP) during the past 12 months?

    1. Yes   2. No   3. Don't Remember

3.2 If yes, why did you contact the MP?

....

....

3.3 If no why have you not had contacts with your MP?

....

....

3.4 Do you think your MP has represented you the way you expected him/her over the past four years?

    1. Yes   2 No   3. Don't Know

3.5 If yes, what kind of representation did you get from your MP?

....

....

4. EVALUATION OF THE ELECTORAL PROCESS

4.1 Do you think the 2000 elections were generally free and fair?

    1. Yes   2. No   3. Don't know

4.2 Was the coverage of the elections by the state print and electronic media adequate?

    1. Yes   2. No   3. Don't know

4.3 Was the coverage of the elections fair to all the parties and candidates?

    1. Yes   2. No   3. Don't know

4.4 When you went to vote, did you face any problems at the polling station?

    1. Yes   2. No

4.5 If yes, what was the nature of the problem?

    1. I did not find my name.
    2. I was not allowed to vote because of photo ID
    3. There was shortage of ballot paper and I had to wait.
    4. Other (specify) ....

4.6 Were election officials helpful when you went to vote?

    1. Yes   2. No

4.7 Did anybody try to intimidate you at the polling station?

    1. Yes   2. No

4.8 What kind of security personnel were at the polling station?

    1. The Police   4. Warders
    2. Soldiers   5. Other (specify).........................
    3. Fire service

4.9 Were you happy to see the security personnel at the polling station?

    1. Yes   2. No   3. Don't know

4.10 How would you describe the voting at the place you voted?

    1. Orderly   3. Chaotic
    2. Not orderly   4. Don't know

4.11 Did you vote with a photo ID card?

    1. Yes   2. No

4.12 If no, did you use a thumbprint ID card?

    1. Yes   2. No

4.13 If yes, did you have problems using the thumbprint ID card to vote?

    1. Yes   2. No

4.14 If yes, what was the nature of the problem?

....

....

4.15 Was this problem resolved to your satisfaction?

    1. Yes   2. No

5. **ELECTION ISSUES**

5.1 Name **THREE** of the most important development issues at the national level?

    1. ....

    2. ....

    3. ....

5.2 Name **THREE** of the most important development needs of your constituency?

    1. ....

    2. ....

    3. ....

5.3 Which issues influenced your vote the most on December 7, 2000?

    1. National issues.   3. Both issues
    2. Constituency issues   4. Don't know

5.4 In your view, which of the political parties best articulated the most important national development issues?

    1. NPP   2. NDC   3. CPP   4. PNC
    5. NRP   6. GCPP   7. UGM

5.5 In your view, which of the political parties best articulated the most important development need in your constituency?

    1. NPP   2. NDC   3. CPP   4. PNC
    5. NRP   6. GCPP   7. UGM

6. **PRESIDENTIAL RUN-OFF**

6.1 Did you vote in the presidential run-off elections on December 28?

    1. Yes   2. No

6.2 If yes, which candidate did you vote for?

    1. Prof. J. E. Atta-Mills   2. Mr J. A. Kufuor

6.3 If no, why not?

....

....

6.4 If you voted for Prof. Mills give reasons for your answer.

....

....

6.5 If you voted for Mr Kufuor give reasons for your answer.

....

....

6.6 Did you vote for the same presidential candidate in the first round?

    1. Yes   2. No

6.7 When you went to vote in the run-off, did you face any problems at the polling station?

    1. Yes   2. No

6.8 If yes, what was the nature of the problem?

    1. I did not find my name.
    2. I was not allowed to vote because of photo ID
    3. There was shortage of ballot paper and I had to wait.
    4. Other (specify) ....

6.9 Were election officials helpful when you went to vote?

    1. Yes   2. No

6.10 Did anybody try to intimidate you at the polling station?

    1. Yes   2. No

6.11 What kind of security personnel were at the polling station?

    1. The Police   4. Fire service
    2. Soldiers   5. Other (specify)...........................
    3. Warders

6.12 Were you happy to see the security personnel at the polling station?

    1. Yes   2. No   3. Don't know

6.13 How would you describe the voting at the place you voted?

    1. Orderly   3. Chaotic
    2. Not orderly   4. Don't know

D.0 DEMOGRAPHIC DATA

D.1 Gender

1. Male   2. Female

D.2 Age

1. 18–25
2. 26–30
3. 31–40
4. 41–50
5. 51–60
6. 61–70
7. 71 and over

D.3 Educational Background

1. None
2. Primary/Middle
3. Secondary
4. Teacher Training
5. Technical college
6. Vocational
7. Polytechnic
8. University
9. Other (specify) ....

D.4 Occupation

1. Unemployed
2. Teacher
3. Businessman
4. Manager
5. Professional (Lawyer, Doctor etc.)
6. Farmer
7. Trader
8. Artisan
9. Public Servant
10. Other (Specify)...............

D5. Personal/Individual Income Level (per month) in Cedis.

1. Zero
2. 1–100,000
3. 101,000–200,000
4. 201,000–300,000
5. 301,000–400,000
6. 401,000–500,000
7. 501,000–600,000
8. 601,000–700,000
9. 401,000–500,000
10. 501,000–600,000
11. 601,000–700,000
12. 701,000–800,000
13. 801,000–900,000
14. 901,000–1,000,000
15. Over 1,000,000

D.6 Religion

    1. Christian   3. African Traditional
    2. Muslim   4. Other (Specify) ....

D.7 Region in which you were born

    1. Ashanti   6. Brong Ahafo
    2. Central   7. Eastern
    3. Greater Accra   8. Northern
    4. Upper East   9. Upper West
    5. Volta   10. Western

D.8 Region in which you are now living

    1. Ashanti   6. Brong Ahafo
    2. Central   7. Eastern
    3. Greater Accra   8. Northern
    4. Upper East   9. Upper West
    5. Volta   10. Western

Bibliography

Abramson, P. R., J. H. Aldrich and D. W. Rohde (1994) *Change and Continuity in the 1992 Elections* (Washington, DC: Congressional Quarterly Press).

Adejumobi, S. (1998) "Elections In Africa: A Fading Shadow of Democracy", *Africa Development*, Vol. 23 No. 1.

Afari-Gyan, K. (1991) *Understanding Politics* (Accra: Asempa).

Ake, Claude (1996), *Democracy and Development in Africa*, (The Brookings Institution, Washington D.C)

Allah-Mensah, B. (1998) "Politics, The Economy and Voting Behaviour in the 1996 Elections", in J. R. A. Ayee (ed.) *The 1996 General Elections and Democratic Consolidation in Ghana* (Accra: Department of Political Science).

Allman, Jean Marie, (1993): *The Quills of the Porcupine, Asante Nationalism in an Emergent Ghana* (Madison: University of Wisconsin Press).

Alt, James E. and K. Alec Chrystal (1983) *Political Economics* (Berkeley and Los Angeles: University of California Press).

Annan, K. (2000) "Africa's Thirst For Democracy," *Evening News*, December 6: 7.

Anebo, F. K. G. (2000), "Voting Patterns and Electoral Alliance in Ghana", in Okwadiba Nnoli (ed.) *Government and Politics in Africa — A Reader*, (Harare: AAPS Books).

Apter, David E., (1991), " Institutionalism Reconsidered", in *International Social Science Journal: Rethinking Democracy*, August, No. 129.

Asher, Herbert B (1992) *Presidential Elections and American Politics: Voters, Candidates and Campaigns Since 1952, 5th Edition* (Pacific Grove, CA: Brooks/Cole, 1992).

Austin, D. (1970) *Politics in Ghana, 1948–1960*, London, Oxford University Press.

Austin, D. & Luckham, R. (eds) (1975) *Politicians and Soldiers in Ghana 1966 – 1972*, (London: Frank Cass).

Ayee, J. R. A. (1996) "The Measurement of Decentralization: the Ghanaian Experience", *African Affairs*, vol. 95, no. 378 (January): 31–50.

Ayee, J. R. A. (1997) "The December 1996 General Elections in Ghana", *Electoral Studies* Vol. 16, No. 3 (September): 416–27.

Ayee, J. R. A. (ed.) (1998), *The 1996 General Elections and Democratic Consolidation in Ghana* (Accra: Department of Political Science).

Ayee, J. R. A. (1998) "Measuring Public Opinion on Key and Economic Issues: A Survey of the December 1996 General Elections in the Keta and Anlo Constituencies", in Ayee, J. R. A. (ed.). *The 1996 General Elections and Democratic Consolidation in Ghana* (Accra: Department of Political Science).

Ayee, J. R. A. (1999) "Decentralization and the Provision of Local Public Services in Ghana" in Karl Wohlmuth *et. al.* (eds.) *Good Governance and Economic Development*, African Development Perspective Yearbook 1997/98, Vol. 6: 459–78.

Ayee, J. R. A. (2000a) "Decentralization and Civil Society in Ghana: Lessons for the African Continent" in Thomas Scheidtweiler (ed) *Human and Economic Development: The Importance of Civil Society and Subsidiarity.* Africa Publications Vol. III (KAAD, Bonn): 27–45.

Ayee, J. R. A. (2000b) "The State of Decentralization in Ghana", Consultancy report to the Canadian International Development Agency for its Governance Strategy Programme in Ghana, August-October 2000.

Barker, J. S. (1987) "Political Space and the Quality of Participation in Rural Africa: A Case from Senegal", *Canadian Journal of African Studies*, Vol. 21, No. 1.

Bell, David V. J., Deutsch, Karl W., Lipset, Segmour, M. (1970) *Issues in Politics and Government* (Boston: Mutton).

Bening, R. (1975) "Foundations of the Modern Native States of Northern Ghana," *Universitas* 5: 116–38.

Bening, R. B. (1990) *A History of Education in Northern Ghana, 1907–1976* (Accra: Ghana Universities Press).

Bibby, J. (1995) *Governing by Consent: An Introduction to American Politics, Second Edition* (Washington, DC: Congressional Quarterly Press).

Bluwey, G. K. (1993) *Political Science: An Introduction* (Accra: Anansesem Publishers, 1993).

Bluwey, G. K. (1993) "The Opposition in Democratic Government", in K. A. Ninsin and F. K. Drah (eds) *Political Parties and Democracy in Ghana's Fourth Republic* (Accra: Woeli Publishers): 207–23.

Bluwey, G. K. (1998) "Determinants of Political Choice in the Agona-West and Effutu Constituencies", in J. R. A. Ayee (ed.) *The 1996 General Elections And Democratic Consolidation in Ghana* (Accra: Department of Political Science): 341–54.

Borroumand, Ladan with Borroumand, Roya (2000) "Once Again Reformist Victory Has Been Followed by Political Setback", *Journal of Democracy* Vol. II No. 4 (October): 114–28.

Bratton, M (1995) 'Are Competitive Elections Enough'? Richards Joseph (ed) *Africa Demos*, Vol. 3, No. 4 (March).

Bratton, M, P. Lewis and E. Gyimah-Boadi (1999) *Attitudes to Democracy and Markets in Ghana*, Afobarometer Paper No. 2, (Michigan: Department of Political Science, Michigan State University).

Breton, A. and Galeott, G. (1985) "Is Proportional Representation Always the Best Electoral Rule?" *Public Finance*.

Burnell P. and Calvert, P. (1999) "The Resilience of Democracy: An Introduction", *Democratization*, Vol. 6, No. 1: 1–32.

Burton, M., Gunther, R. and Higley, J. (1995) "Introduction: Elite Transformations and Democratic Regimes", in Higley, J. and Gunther, R. (eds) *Elites and Democratic Consolidation in Latin America* (Cambridge: Cambridge University Press).

Campbell, A., P. E. Converse, W. E. Miller and D. E. Stokes (1960) *The American Voter* (New York: Wiley).

Centre for Democracy and Development, Ghana (December 200) *Democracy Watch*, Accra, Vol. 1, No. 4.

Chalfin, B. (1996) "Market Reforms and the State: The Case of Shea in Ghana," *Journal of Modern African Studies*, Vol. 34: 421–40.

Chalfin, B. (2000) "Risky Business: Economic Uncertainty, Market Reforms and Female Livelihoods in Northeast Ghana," *Development and Change*, Vol. 31: 987–1008.

Chalfin, B. (2001) "Border Zone Trade and the Economic Boundaries of the State," *Africa*, Vol. 71: 7–32.

Chambas, M. (1980) "The Politics of Agricultural and Rural Development in the Upper Region of Ghana: Implications of Technocratic Ideology and Non-participatory Development." Unpublished Ph.D. Dissertation in Political Science, Cornell University.

Chazan, et. al., eds (1992) *Politics and Society in Contemporary Africa* (Boulder: Lynne Rienner).

Chilcote, R. H. (1981) *Theories of Comparative Politics: The Search for a Paradigm* (Boulder, CO: Westview).

Clausen, T. (1998) "State-Civil Society Relations in Ghana's Fourth Republic," in J. R. A. Ayee (ed.) *The 1996 General Elections and Democratic Consolidation in Ghana* (Accra: Department of Political Science): 183–210.

Cohen, D. L. (1985) "Elections and Election Studies in Africa" in Yolamu Barongo (ed) *Political Science in Africa* (London: Zed Books).

Commonwealth Secretariat (1997) *The Presidential and Parliamentary Elections in Ghana, 7 December 1996: the Report of the Commonwealth Observer Group* (London: Creative Base Europe).

Crook, R. C. and Manor, J. (1998) *Democracy and Decentralization in South Asia and West Africa: Participation, Accountability and Performance* (Cambridge: Cambridge University Press).

Dahl, R. A. (1971) *Polyarchy: Participation and Opposition* (New Haven, CT: Yale University Press).

Davis, D. 1987. "Then the White Man Came with his Whitish Ideas," *International Journal of African Historical Studies*, 20: 628–46.

Dennis, C. M. (1989) *Public Choice II* (London: Cambridge University Press).

Diamond, L. (1994) "Rethinking Civil Society: Toward Democratic Consolidation", *Journal of Democracy*, Vol. 5, No. 3: 4–17.

Diamond, Larry (1996) "Introduction: Roots of Failure, Seed of Hope" in Diamond, Larry; Linz, Juan J.; and Lipset, Seymour M.; *Democracy in Developing Countries: Africa*, (Lynne Rienner Publishers, Boulder, Colorado).

Diamond, L (1996) 'Is the Third Wave Over? *Journal of Democracy*, Vol. 7, No. 3.

Diamond, L. (2000) "Is Pakistan the (Reverse) Wave of The Future?", *Journal of Democracy* Vol. II No. 3: 91–120.

Drah, F. K. (1996) "The Concept of Civil Society in Africa: A Viewpoint" in F. K. Drah and M. Oquaye (eds.) *Civil Society in Ghana* (Accra: Friedrich Ebert Foundation).

Drah, F. K. (1998), "The 1996 Elections and Democratisation: A Case Study of Okaikoi", in J. R. A. Ayee (ed.) *The 1996 General Elections and Democratic Consolidation in Ghana* (Accra: Department of Political Science).

Drucker-Brown, S. (1975) *Ritual Aspects of the Mamprusi Kingship* (Cambridge: African Studies Centre)

Dumor, E. (1998) "Keynote Address: The 1996 Elections Democratic Consolidation", in Ayee, J. R. A. (ed.) *The 1996 General Elections and Democratic Consolidation in Ghana.* (Accra: Department of Political Science).

Dunn, J. and A. F. Robertson (1973) *Dependence and Opportunity: Political Change in Ahafo*, (Cambridge: Cambridge University Press).

Dye, T. R., and Zeigler, H. L. (1978) *The Irony of Democracy: An Uncommon Introduction to Politics* (North Duxbury Press).

Ehrmann, H. W. (ed.) (1963) *Democracy in a Changing Society* (Bombay: Vakils, Feffer & Simons).

Elklit, J. (1999) "Electoral Institutional Change and Democratization: You Can Lead a Horse to Water, but You Can't Make it Drink", *Democratization*, Vol. 6, No. 4 (Winter): 28–51.

Eng, Peter (1998) "The Democracy Boom", *Development Dialogue*: 23–36.

Estandiari, H. (2000) "Is Iran Democratizing?: Observations on Election Day", *Journal of Democracy* Vol. II No. 4 (October): 108–113.

E. A Fieldhouse, C. J. Pattie R. J. J. Johnston (1996) "Tactical Voting And Party Constituency Campaigning At the 1992 General Election In England", *British Journal of Political Science* Vol. 26 Part 3 (July): 403–39.

Flanigan, W. H. and N. H. Zingale (1994) *Political Behavior of the American Electorate, 8th Edition* (Washington, DC: Congressional Quarterly Press).

Fortes, M. (1945) *The Dynamics of Clanship Among the Tallensi* (London: Oxford University Press).

Frazer, J. (1994) "Electoral Success: Harbingers of Hope?" *Africa Today* Vol. 41 No. 3.

Geisler, G. (1993) "Fair? What Has Fairness Got to Do with It? Vagaries of Election Observations and Democratic Standards", *The Journal of Modern African Studies*, Vol. 31, No. 4: 613–37.

Ghana, Republic of (1992) *Constitution of the Republic of Ghana, 1992* (Tema: Ghana Publishing Corporation).

Ghana Statistical Service (GSS) (1998) "Quarterly Digest of Statistics." Accra: Ghana Statistical Service. March.

Ghana Statistical Service (GSS) (2000a) "Poverty Trends in Ghana in the 1990s." Accra: Ghana Statistical Service. October.

Ghana Statistical Service (GSS) (2000b) "Ghana Living Standards Survey: Report of the Fourth Round (GLSS 4)." Accra: Ghana Statistical Service. October.

Ghana, Republic of (2000) *2000 Population & Housing Census (Provisional Results)* Accra: Ghana Statistical Service).

Gills, B. et. al; (eds) (1993) *Low Intensity Democracy: Political Power in the New World Order* (London: Pluto).

Goody, J. (1967) *The Social Organization of the Lowiili* (London: Oxford University Press for the International African Institute).

Grant, D. (1998) "Searching For The Downsian Voter With a Simple Structural Model", *Economics And Politics*, Vol. 10, No. 2 (July).

Gyimah-Boadi, E. (1994) "Ghana's Uncertain Political Opening", *Journal of Democracy* No. 5: 75–86.

Gyimah-Boadi, E. (1999) "Ghana: The Challenges of Consolidating Democracy" in Richard Joseph (ed.) *State, Conflict, and Democracy in Africa* (Boulder: Lynne Rienner): 409–27;

Gyimah-Boadi E. (2001) *Report on the December 2000 Elections in Ghana*, March, (Accra: Centre for Democratic Development).

Gyimah-Boadi, E. (2001) "A Peaceful Political Turnover in Ghana" *Journal of Democracy* Vol. 12, No. 2 (April): 103–17.

Hart E. and E. Gyimah-Boadi (January 2000) *Business Associations in Ghana's Transition* (Critical Perspectives No. 3), (Accra: Centre for Democracy and Development).

Hess, H. (1994) *Party Work in Social Democratic Parties: A Practical Handbook* (Bonn: Friedrich Ebert Foundation).

Huntington, S. P (1991) *The Third Wave: Democratization in the Late Twentieth Century* (London: University of Oklahoma Press).

Hyden, G. and Bratton, M. (1995), "Introduction", in Hyden, G. and Bratton, M. (eds) *Governance and Politics in Africa*, (Lynne Rienner Publishers, Boulder, Colorado).

Ibrahim, J. (1994) "Political Exclusion, Democratization and Dynamics of Ethnicity in Niger" in *Africa Today* Vol. 41 No. 3.

IBRD (1997) *World Development Report: The State in a Changing World* (New York: Oxford University Press).

Iliasu, A. A. 1971. "The Origins of the Mossi-Dagomba States," *Research Review* (University of Ghana), Vol. 7: 95–113.

Jeffries, R. and Clare Thomas (1993) "The Ghanaian Elections of 1992" *African Affairs*, Vol. 92, No. 368 (July).

Jeffries, R. (1996) "He Who Cares Wins: Electoral Politics in Ghana" SOAS, London (mimeo).

Johnston, A. M. and R. W. Johnson (1997) "The Local Elections in Kwazulu Natal" *African Affairs* Vol. 96 No. 384.

Jonah, K. (1998) "Agency and Structure in Ghana's 1992 and 1996 Presidential Elections" in Ayee, J. R. A. (ed). *The 1996 General Elections and Democratic Consolidation in Ghana* (Accra: Department of Political Science).

Jonah, K. (1998). "The 1996 Elections and Politics in the Ahanta West and Shama Constituencies", in Ayee, J. R. A. (ed.) *The 1996 General Elections And Democratic Consolidation in Ghana* (Accra: Department of Political Science).

Joseph, Richard (1999) (ed.), *State, Conflict and Democracy*, (Lynne Rienner Boulder, Colorado).

Key, Jr. V. O. (1966) *The Responsible Electorate* (Cambridge, MA: Harvard University Press).

Kieh, G. K. (1999), "Democratization in Africa: A balance Sheet" in Mbaku, John Mukum; *Preparing Africa for the Twenty-First Century: Peaceful Co-existence and Sustainable Development*, (Aldershot: Ashgate).

Kontoh Emmanuel (1998) "The Impact of Ethnic Politics on the 1996 General Elections: The Case of the Kumasi District", A B.A. (Hons) Dissertation presented to the Department of Political Science, University of Ghana, Legon, (Unpublished).

Kousoulas, G. D. (1978) *On Government and Politics* (North: Duxbury Press).

Kramer, G. H. (1971) "Short-Term Fluctuations in U.S. Voting Behavior, 1896–1964," *American Political Science Review*, Vol. 65 (March): 131–43.

Ladouceur, P. (1979) *Chiefs and Politicians: The Politics of Regionalism in Northern Ghana* (London: Longmans).

Lamb, K. A. (1978) *The People, May Be* (North Duxbury Press).

La Palombara, J. (1974) *Politics Within Nations* (Englewood Cliffs, N.J.: Prentice-Hall).

Lindeke, W. A. and Winnie Wanzala (1994) "Regional Elections in Namibia: Deepening Democracy and Gender Inclusion", *Africa Today* Vol. 41, No. 3.

Luckham, R. and Gordon White (1996) *Democratization in the South: The Jagged Wave* (Manchester: Manchester University Press).

Manoukian, M. 1951. *Tribes of the Northern Territories*. London: International African Institute.

Manu, Yaw, (1998) "The 1996 Elections: Survey in the Sekyere West and Sekyere East District", in J. R. A. Ayee (ed.), *The 1996 General Elections and Democratic Consolidation in Ghana* (Accra: Department of Political Science).

Mcfaul, M. (2000) "One Step Forward Two Steps Back", *Journal of Democracy*, Vol. II No. 3: 9–32.

Mouffe, C. (1989) *The Return of the Political* (London: Verso).

National Commission for Civic Education (NCCE) (1997) *An Assessment of the Performance of District Assemblies*, A study conducted by the Research Department of the National Commission for Civic Education (October).

Nelson, Michael (1993) *The Elections of 1992* (Washington, DC: Congressional Quarterly Press).

Nkansah-Kyeremateng, K., (2000) *Kwahu Handbook* (Accra: Trade Power Agency).

Nohlen, Dieter (1996), *Elections and Electoral Systems*, 2nd edn (New Delhi: Macmillan).

Nyong'o, P. A. (1988) "Political Instability and the Prospects for Democracy in Africa", *African Development*, Vol. 13, No. 1: 34–47.

Oquaye, M. (1995) "The Ghanaian Elections of 1992: A Dissenting View" *African Affairs*, Vol. 94: 259–75.

Oquaye, Mike (1998) "Politics in Asante Mampong: A Study of the 1996 Elections", in Ayee, J. R. A. (ed.), *The 1996 General Elections and Democratic Consolidation in Ghana* (Accra: Department of Political Science).

Owusu, M. (1970) *Uses and Abuses of Political Power: A Case Study of Continuity and Change in the Politics of Ghana* (Chicago: Chicago University Press).

Peverill Squire and Eric R. A. N. Smith (1996) "A Further Examination of Challenger Quality In Senate Elections", *Legislative Studies Quarterly*, Vol. XXI No.2 (May): 235–48.

Polsby, N. W. and A. Wildavsky (1991) *Presidential Elections: Contemporary Strategies of American Electoral Politics*, 8th Edition (New York: Free Press).

Pomper, G. (ed.) (1993) *The Elections of 1992: Reports and Interpretations* (Chatham, NJ: Chatham House).

Przeworski, A., Alvarez, M., Cheibub, J. A. and Limongi, F. (1996) "What Makes Democracies Endure?", *Journal of Democracy*, Vol. 7, No. 1 (January): 39–55.

RePass, David E. (1971) "Issue Salience and Party Choice," *American Political Science Review*, Vol. 65 (June): 389–400.

Riker, W. H. (1988) *Liberalism Against Populism: A Confrontation Between the Theory of Democracy and the Theory of Social Choice* (Prospect Heights, IL: Waveland Press, Inc.).

Roncoli, M. C. (1994) "Managing on the Margins: Agricultural Production and Household Reproduction in Northeastern Ghana." Ph.D. Dissertation in Anthropology, State University of New York and Binghamton.

Schedler, A. (1998) "What is Democratic Consolidation?" *Journal of Democracy*, Vol. 9, No. 2 (April): 91–107.

Scholottner, M. (2000) "We Stay, Others Come and Go: Identity Among the Mamprusi in Northern Ghana", in Carola Lentz and Paul Nugent (eds) *Ethnicity in Ghana: The Limits of Invention* (New York: St. Martin's Press): 49–67.

Sherrill, K. S., and Vogler, D. I. (1977) *Power, Policy and Participation* (New York: Harper & Row).

Shevtsova, Lilian (2000) "Can Electoral Autocracy Survive?", *Journal of Democracy* Vol. II No. 3.
Sivan, E. (2000) "Arabs and Democracy: Illusions of Change", *Journal of Democracy*, Vol. II, No. 3: 69–82.
Smith, D. (2001a) "Ghana's 2000 Elections. *Electoral Studies*. (forthcoming).
Smith D. (2001b) *The Structural Underpinnings of Ghana's December 2000 Elections: A Critical Perspectives*, No. 6 February (Accra: The Centre for Democratic Development).
Syme, J. K. G. (1932) *The Kusasis: A Short History*. Mimeograph.
Talbi, M. (2000) "Arabs and Democracy: A record of Failure", *Journal of Democracy*, Vol. II No. 3: 58–67.
Tufte, Edward R. (1980) *Political Control of the Economy* (Princeton, NJ: Princeton University Press).
Twumasi Y. (1975) "The 1969 Elections", in D. Austin *et. al.* (eds) *Politicians and Soldiers: in Ghana 1966–1972* (London: Frank Cass).
Wattenberg, M. P. (1991) *The Rise of Candidate-Centered Politics* (Cambridge, MA: Harvard University Press).
Wittman, Daniel A. (1969) "Parties As Utility Maximizers" *American Political Science Review* (June).

Newspapers

Free Press (2000) 26 April
Accra Mail (2000) 21 December
Daily Graphic (2000) September–December
Daily Graphic (2000) 11 October
Daily Graphic (2000) 19 October
Daily Graphic (2001) 8 January
Daily Graphic (2001) 10 January
Daily Graphic (2001) 26 June
Free Press (2001) 25 April–1 May
Ghana Palaver (2000) September–November
The Chronicle (2000–2001) October–January
The Evening News (2000) January–December
The Guide (2000–2001) 19 December–2 January
The Crusading Guide (2000) 21–27 December
The Dispatch (2000) 29 November–5 December

The Ghanaian Chronicle (2001) 23–24 April
The Ghanaian Chronicle (2001) 2 July
The Guide (2001) 17–23 January
The Guide (2001) 28 February–5 March
The Independent (2000) November–December
The Independent (2001) 11 January
The Weekend Statesman (2000) November–December
Public Agenda (2000) 11–17 September
Public Agenda (2000) 20–6 November